ALSO BY MICHAEL PATERNITI

The Telling Room
Driving Mr. Albert

LOVE AND OTHER WAYS OF DYING

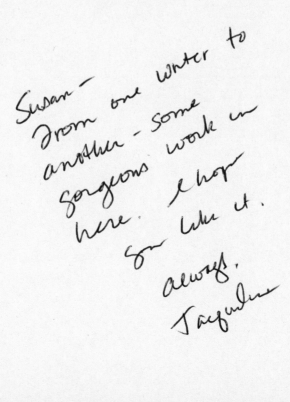

Susan —
From one writer to
another — some
gorgeous work in
here. I hope
you like it.
always,
Jacqueline

LOVE AND OTHER WAYS OF DYING

essays

MICHAEL PATERNITI

DIAL PRESS
NEW YORK

2016 Dial Press Trade Paperback Edition

Copyright © 2015 by Michael Paterniti

All rights reserved.

Published in the United States by The Dial Press, an imprint of
Random House, a division of Penguin Random House LLC, New York.

THE DIAL PRESS and the HOUSE colophon are registered
trademarks of Random House LLC.

Originally published in hardcover in the United States by
The Dial Press, an imprint of Random House, a division of
Penguin Random House LLC, in 2015.

The following essays have been previously published:
"The Long Fall of Flight One-Eleven Heavy," "He Might Just Be a Prophet,"
"Eating Jack Hooker's Cow," "The American Hero (in Four Acts)," "11:20,"
"The House That Thurman Munson Built," and "The Last Meal" in *Esquire;*
"The Giant," "The Accident," "The Fifteen-Year Layover," "The Most Dangerous
Beauty," "The Suicide Catcher," "Mr. Nobody," "Never Forget," and
"The Man Who Sailed His House" in *GQ;* "Driving Mr. Albert"
in *Harper's;* "City of Dust" in *The New York Times Magazine.*

Library of Congress Cataloging-in-Publication Data
Paterniti, Michael.
[Essays, Selections]
Love and other ways of dying : essays / Michael Paterniti.
pages cm
ISBN 978-0-385-33703-8
eBook ISBN 978-0-8129-9751-4
I. Title.
PS3616.A8668A6 2015
814'.6—dc23   2014033162

Printed in the United States of America on acid-free paper

randomhousebooks.com

246897531

Book design by Elizabeth A. D. Eno

For Sara,
every page of it:
wonder, thanks, ridiculous love.

Well, here's your box. Nearly everything I have is in it, and it is not full. Pain and excitement are in it, and feeling good or bad and evil thoughts and good thoughts—the pleasure of design and some despair and the indescribable joy of creation. . . . And still the box is not full.

John Steinbeck

CONTENTS

INTRODUCTION

DOWN HERE IN THE BASEMENT WE'VE built a city out of blocks, divvied up the Matchbox cars, the toy soldiers and model planes, and begun yet again what we call The Game. We've been playing it for years now, my brother and I, on the cool tile floor in humid summer, on the warm shag come frigid winter. In our city anything can happen—and does. We've fought back alien incursions, faced down an armed opposition, lost citizens and mighty warriors to various calamities. We're a widowed, wounded race, living moments of beauty and hardship. Allies have been found out to be spies—and have thus been eliminated. Strange creatures have appeared (one of our AWOL gerbils among them), muttering in gruff tones, here to crush or help us, we don't know which. Cars collide; planes crash. Everything's going great in our city, and then, a split second later—blam!—it all unravels. A giant kicks down a building in the north sector, and police and fire come screaming in to repair the damage, check the crime scene.

What gets televised in our house through the evening news filters into The Game, too. An evil group known as Black September takes hostages. A bad guy named Brezhnev is hell-bent on destroying us. There's a Matchbox that can fly, driven by a great man named Muhammad Ali. Every moment waits expectantly for a hero, and usually we oblige. Ours is a Manichean universe, in which light must eventually triumph over darkness, angels over devils.

Of course, our parents are forbidden from entering when we play, in part because we don't want their explanations or lessons. Stuff happens in The Game, heavy, unknowable stuff, that baffles even us. Sometimes when we arrive at a pause in the action, one of us wonders aloud about what should happen next. Then, in the western sector, the giant drops a block bomb, or karate-kicks a building—and it all bullies into action again.

The Game is our supersaturated, hypermediated reflection of a world we don't understand—and the opposite of our peaceful suburban town. Upstairs our mom is drinking Tab, getting dinner ready as she watches a jowly man on TV preside over the Watergate hearings. Where we live, there seems to be little sentiment about this, or about the war in Vietnam. Meanwhile, in the basement, among the massacres and raids, we channel all of our emotion and drama into The Game. We spend hours down here, making a stand, waiting for deus ex machina to arrive.

There must come a day when we play for the last time, but I don't remember it. After all those hours, days, *years,* there's no goodbye. No final triumph, no clinking glasses of grape juice. Perhaps we've come to the realization that the world isn't quite so Manichean, or that the stakes here will never be high enough to make it real, that this indeed is *a game*—and we want to be lifted by some huge hurricane, or swept away by a powerful ocean wave. We want to stand on some distant shore where the answers

are written in a strange new language of whale bones and scattered mussel shells.

In revisiting the pieces in this essay collection—both old
and up-to-the-minute, seventeen in all, spanning almost two
decades—I've been reminded of The Game, because what I've
chosen to do with my life ends up being similar in some ways to
what transpired in our childhood playroom all those years ago.
For better or worse, I've continued building block cities, only
out of words, and as reflections of events shaped by the fist of a
more cosmic hand. If The Game was fantasy and The Work has
been cold reality, in both cases they've come to represent, at least
for me, the same underlying need to make sense of the way that
love and loss, justice and devastation, and beauty and pain can
fuse to make some bearable, or at least fathomable, whole.

It can be unsettling for any writer to go back and reread his
or her work. It's like watching yourself age right before your
eyes. Or like seeing a batch of photographs, some in which the
fashions and automobiles seem retro. It's like unearthing so many
time capsules, and wondering why you buried them in the first
place. You begin to see your obsessions laid bare, certain themes
repeating. At the beginning, none of this is clear. You don't set out
saying, It's time again to go on that quest for the ecstatic! Or:
Hey, let's memorialize the underdog! Or: Anyone for an elevator
ride down into darkness? These themes crop up later, when you
sit down to write an introduction like this one.

There's something else that comes up, a couple of questions
that keep nagging. What are these stories trying to say, anyway?
Or better: What have I been trying to say *through* them?

Well, here's a stab: Perhaps no matter how bad it gets—or
good—we're beholden not to look away from the things we fear
or revere. The more we examine the grooves and scars of life, the
deeper we go in our forensic investigations by trying to name the

thing that appears before us, the more free and complete we become, the more capable of identification and compassion and opposition. But it's not just that. The more willing we are to suffer pain and loss and even great throes of happiness, to live fully inside these big emotions, the closer we come to—what?

The folded hands of the universe?

Our humanity?

Infinity?

It must be something.

We each have our way of finding meaning: work, faith, family, sport, avocation, etc. I guess mine has been this everyday ritual of reporting and writing, these trips into other worlds. I know I ate François Mitterrand's last meal including its famous birdie, or visited the Sudan during a vicious famine, or that I found true happiness one night in Catalonia, Spain, after consuming the food of Ferran Adrià, because I've written it down here. I know that nearly two million people vanished in a country called Cambodia, and that I picked apples with a real giant, named Leonid Stadnik, one autumn afternoon in Ukraine. I know I once stood on a suicide bridge in Nanjing, China, wrestling with a hopeless man who had come to jump, just as I know that one winter, feeling particularly lost in the world, I drove cross-country with Einstein's brain in the trunk of my rental car, all because these stories now tell me so.

For me, writing is a vital act of memory, and every once in a while, with a lot of hard labor, it can also be means for transcendence. Like a runner's high, you keep running to get it. And sometimes, with the help of great editors, assiduous fact-checkers, and trusted readers—sometimes you can feel the words lift ever so slightly, and something you never thought before, some Ouija messsage, briefly reveals itself.

When I left that basement for good all those years ago, little did I know all the wondrous and horrible things that lurked in those other worlds beyond, all of them real. On those faraway shores, armies clashed, planes fell from the sky, giants stomped their feet.

I was lucky to be there.

And the greatest gift, for me at least, was that I got to write about it.

LOVE AND OTHER WAYS OF DYING

THE LONG FALL OF FLIGHT ONE-ELEVEN HEAVY

IT WAS SUMMER; IT WAS WINTER. The village disappeared behind skeins of fog. Fishermen came and went in boats named *Reverence, Granite Prince, Souwester*. The ocean, which was green and wild, carried the vessels out past Jackrock Bank toward Pearl Island and the open sea. In the village, on the shelf of rock, stood a lighthouse, whitewashed and octagonal with a red turret. Its green light beamed over the green sea, and sometimes, in the thickest fog or heaviest storm, that was all the fishermen had of land, this green eye dimly flashing in the night, all they had of home and how to get there—that was the question. There were nights when that was the only question.

This northerly village, this place here of sixty people, the houses and fences and clotheslines, was set among solid rocks breaching from the earth. It was as if a pod of whales had surfaced just as the ocean turned to land and then a village was built on their granite backs. By the weathered fishing shacks were rusted anchors like claws and broken traps and hills of coiled line. Come spring, wildflowers appeared by the clapboard church. The priest said mass. A woman drew back a curtain. A man hanged himself by the bridge. Travelers passing through agreed it was the prettiest earthly spot, snapping pictures as if gripped by palsy, nearly slipping off the rocks into the frigid waves.

Late summer, a man and woman were making love under the eaves of a garishly painted house that looked out on the lighthouse—green light flashing—when a feeling suddenly passed into them, a feeling unrelated to their lovemaking, in direct physical opposition to it: an electrical charge so strong they could taste it, feel it, the hair standing up on their arms, just as it does before lightning strikes. And the fishermen felt it, too, as they went to sea and returned, long ago resigned to the fact that you can do nothing to stop the ocean or the sky from what it will do. Now they, too, felt the shove and lock of some invisible metallic bit in their mouths. The feeling of being surrounded by towering waves.

Yes, something terrible was moving this way. There was a low ceiling of clouds, an intense, creeping darkness, that electrical taste. By the lighthouse, if you had been standing beneath the flashing green light on that early-September night, in that plague of clouds, you would have heard the horrible grinding sound of some wounded winged creature, listened to it trail out to sea as it came screeching down from the heavens, down through molecule and current, until everything went silent.

That is, the waves still crashed up against the granite rock, the lighthouse groaned, a cat yowled somewhere near the church, but beyond, out at sea, there was silence. Seconds passed, disintegrating time . . . and then, suddenly, an explosion of seismic strength rocked the houses of Peggy's Cove. One fisherman thought it was a bomb; another was certain the End had arrived. The lovers clasped tightly—their bodies turning as frigid as the ocean.

That's how it began.

It began before that, too, in other cities of the world, with plans hatched at dinner tables or during long-distance calls, plans for time together and saving the world, for corralling AIDS and feeding the famine-stricken and family reunions. What these people held in common at first—these diplomats and scientists and students, these spouses and parents and children—was an elemental feeling, that buzz of excitement derived from holding a ticket to some foreign place. And what distinguished that ticket from billions of other tickets was the simple designation of a number: SR111. New York to Geneva, following the Atlantic coast up along Nova Scotia, then out over Greenland and Iceland and England, and then down finally into Switzerland, on the best airline in the world. Seven hours if the tailwinds were brisk. There in time for breakfast on the lake.

In one row would be a family with two grown kids, a computer-genius son and an attorney daughter, setting out on their hiking holiday to the Bernese Oberland. In another would be a woman whose boyfriend was planning to propose to her when she arrived in Geneva. Sitting here would be a world-famous scientist, with his world-famous scientist wife. And there would be the boxer's son, a man who had grown to look like his legendary father, the same thick brow and hard chin, the same mournful eyes, on a business trip to promote his father's tomato sauce.

Like lovers who haven't yet met or one-day neighbors living now in different countries, tracing their route to one another, each of them moved toward the others without knowing it, in these cities and towns, grasping airline tickets. Some, like the Swiss tennis pro, would miss the flight, and others, without tickets, would be bumped from other flights onto this one at the last minute, feeling lucky to have made it, feeling chosen.

In the hours before the flight, a young blond woman with blue, almost Persian eyes said goodbye to her boyfriend in the streets of Manhattan and slipped into a cab. A fifty-six-year-old man had just paid a surprise visit to see his brother's boat, a refurbished sloop, on the Sound, just as his two brothers and his elderly mother came in from a glorious day on the water, all that glitter and wind, and now he was headed back to Africa, to the parched veldts and skeletal victims, to the disease and hunger, back to all this worrying for the world.

Somewhere else, a man packed—his passport, his socks—then went to the refrigerator to pour himself a glass of milk. His three kids roughhoused in the other room. His wife complained that she didn't want him to fly, didn't want him to leave on this business trip. On the refrigerator was a postcard, once sent by friends, of a faraway fishing village—the houses and fences and clotheslines, the ocean and the lighthouse and the green light flashing. He had looked at that postcard every day since it had been taped there. A beautiful spot. Something about it. Could a place like that really exist?

All of these people, it was as if they were all turning to gold, all marked with an invisible X on their foreheads, as of course we are, too, the place and time yet to be determined. Yes, we are burning down; time is disintegrating. There were 229 people who owned cars and houses, slept in beds, had bought clothes and gifts for this trip, some with price tags still on them—and then they were gone.

Do you remember the last time you felt the wind? Or touched your lips to the head of your child? Can you remember the words she said as she last went, a ticket in hand?

Every two minutes an airliner moves up the Atlantic coast, tracing ribboned contrails, moving through kingdoms in the air demarcated by boundaries, what are called corridors and highways by the people who control the sky. In these corridors travel all the planes of the world, jetliners pushing the speed of sound at the highest altitudes, prop planes puttering at the lowest, and a phylum in between of Cessnas and commuters and corporate jets—all of them passing over the crooked-armed peninsulas and jagged coastlines and, somewhere, too, this northern village as it appears and disappears behind skeins of fog.

The pilot—a thin-faced, handsome Swiss man with penetrating brown eyes and a thick mustache—was known among his colleagues as a consummate pilot. He'd recently completed a promotional video for his airline. In it, he—the energetic man named Urs—kisses his beautiful wife goodbye at their home before driving off, then he is standing on the tarmac, smiling, gazing up at his plane, and then in the cockpit, in full command, flipping toggles, running checks, in command, toggles, lights, check, command.

So now here they were, in their corridor, talking, Urs and his copilot, Stephan. About their kids; both had three. About the evening's onboard dinner. It was an hour into the flight, the plane soaring on autopilot, the engine a quiet drone beneath the noise in the main cabin, the last lights of New England shimmering out the west side of the aircraft, and suddenly there was a tickling smell, rising from somewhere into the cockpit, an ominous wreathing of—really, how could it be?—smoke. Toggles, lights, check, but the smoke kept coming. The pilot ran through his emergency checklists, switching various electrical systems on and off to isolate the problem. But the smoke kept coming. He was breathing rapidly, and the copilot, who wasn't, said, We have a problem.

Back in the cabin, the passengers were sipping wine and soda, penning postcards at thirty-three thousand feet. In first class, some donned airline slippers and supped on hors d'oeuvres while gambling on the computer screens in front of them. Slots, blackjack, keno. Others reclined and felt the air move beneath them—a Saudi prince, the world-famous scientist, the UN field director, the boxer's son, the woman with Persian eyes—an awesome feeling of power, here among the stars, plowing for Europe, halfway between the polar cap and the moon, gambling and guzzling and gourmandizing, oblivious as even now, the pilot was on the radio, using the secret language of the sky to declare an emergency:

Pan, pan, pan, said Urs. We have smoke in the cockpit, request deviate, immediate return to a convenient place. I guess Boston. (Toggles, lights, check, breathe.)

Would you prefer to go in to Halifax? said air traffic control, a calm voice from a northern place called Moncton, a man watching a green hexagon crawl across a large round screen, this very flight moving across the screen, a single clean green light.

Affirmative for one-eleven heavy, said the pilot. We have the oxygen mask on. Go ahead with the weather—

Could I have the number of souls on board . . . for emergency services? chimed in Halifax control.

Roger, said the pilot, but then he never answered the question, working frantically down his checklist, circling back over the ocean to release tons of fuel to lighten the craft for an emergency landing, the plane dropping to nineteen thousand feet, then twelve thousand, and ten thousand. An alarm sounded, the autopilot shut down. Lights fritzed on and off in both the cockpit and the cabin, flight attendants rushed through the aisles, one of the three engines quit in what was now becoming a huge electrical meltdown.

Urs radioed something in German, emergency checklist air conditioning smoke. Then in English, Sorry . . . Maintaining at ten thousand feet, his voice urgent, the words blurring. The smoke was thick, the heat increasing, the checklists, the bloody checklists . . . leading nowhere, leading—We are declaring emergency now at, ah, time, ah, zero-one-two-four . . . We have to land immediate—

The instrument panel—bright digital displays—went black. Both pilot and copilot were now breathing frantically.

Then nothing.

Radio contact ceased. Temperatures in the cockpit were rising precipitously; aluminum fixtures began to melt. It's possible that one of the pilots, or both, simply caught fire. At air traffic control in Moncton, the green hexagon flickered off the screen. There was silence. One controller began trembling, another wept.

It was falling.

Six minutes later, SR111 plunged into the dark sea.

The medical examiner woke to a ringing phone, the worst way to wake. Ten-something on the clock, or was it eleven? The phone ringing, in the house where he lived alone, or rather with his two retrievers, but alone, too, without wife or woman. He lived near the village with the lighthouse, had moved here less than three years ago from out west, had spent much of his life rolling around, weird things following him, demons and disasters. Had a train wreck once, in Great Britain, early in his career, a Sunday night, university students coming back to London after a weekend at home. Train left the tracks at speed. He'd never seen anything like that in his life—sixty dead, decapitations, severed arms and legs. These kids, hours before whole and happy, now disassembled. Time disintegrating in the small fires of the wreckage. After the second night, while everyone kept their stiff upper lips, he sobbed uncontrollably. He scared himself—not so much because he was sobbing, but because he couldn't stop.

There'd been a tornado in Edmonton—twenty-three dead. And then another train wreck in western Canada, in the hinterlands fifty miles east of Jasper. Twenty-five dead in a ravine. He'd nearly been drummed out of the job for his handling of that one. The media swarmed to photograph mangled bodies, and the medical examiner, heady from all the attention and a bit offended by it, knowing he shouldn't, stuffed some towels and linens on a litter, draped them with a sheet, and rolled the whole thing out for the cameras. Your dead body, gentlemen.

Later, when they found out—oh, they hated him for that. Called for his head.

This had been a frustrating day, though, driving up to New Glasgow, waiting to take the stand to testify in the case of a teen-age killer, waiting, waiting, four, five, six hours, time passing, nothing to do in that town except pitter here and there, waiting. Got off the stand around six, home by nine, deeply annoyed, too late to cook, got into the frozen food, then to bed, reading the paper, drifting, reading, drifting. And now the phone was ringing, a woman from the office: A jet was down. Without thinking, he said, It's a mistake. Call me back if anything comes of it. Set the phone in its cradle, and a minute later it rang again.

There's a problem here, she said.

I'll get on my way, he said, and hung up. He automatically put a suitcase on the bed, an overnight bag, and then it dawned on him: There'd been no talk about numbers yet, the possible dead. There could be hundreds, he knew that, yes, he did know that now, didn't he? He walked back and forth between his cupboard and his bed, flustered, disbelieving, maybe hundreds, and then the adrenaline released, with hypodermic efficiency. Hundreds of bodies—and each one of them would touch his hands. And he would have to touch them, identify them, confer what remained of them to some resting place. He would have to bear witness to the horrible thing up close, what it did up close, examine it, notate, dissect, and, all the while, feel what it did, feel it in each jagged bone.

Flustered, disbelieving, it took him forty minutes to pack his bag with a couple of pairs of khakis, some underwear, shirts, a pair of comfortable shoes, some shaving gear, should have taken five minutes.

He was a sensitive, empathetic man—at least he thought so (did his ex-wife? did his two faraway daughters?)—with a sharp if morbid sense of humor, a kind of loner in this northern place, Nova Scotia, where clans had carved out their lives over centuries and generations, where someone's great-great-grandfather had once fished someone else's great-great-grandfather from a storm at sea. He was an outsider, had always been, which qualified him for what was now coming, lurching toward him at the speed it would take him to drive in that thick night, in the warm rain that now fell like pieces of sky, from his home to his office.

No, he didn't know then, as he left his retrievers, Dan and Deputy, behind, as he closed the door on his house, everything freezing in time as he did, magazines fanned on a table, milk in the refrigerator, didn't know that summer would pass and fall would arrive, that the leaves would vanish from the trees before he returned.

But now all he did was drive, doing the math: There were twelve in the office and six in the morgue. The local hospitals might be able to cough up thirty more, but that didn't even begin to cover it. Where the hell were they going to find enough body bags?

More phones rang, more people woke. The coast guard, the Mounties, ministers, presidents. The navy, the airline, the media, everyone scrambling to figure out what was going on; without realizing it, everyone was now caught in the spreading fire. In the village, boats left for sea. The fishermen rolled from their beds, threw on rain gear, buddied up, and started out, unquestioning, reflexively. (You couldn't keep the sea and sky from what it would do.) Many of the fishermen thought they were going in search of survivors, were convinced of it, owing to the legacy of ship-wrecks in these parts, which often meant someone was out there somewhere in all that inky black, in a yellow raft, waiting for help, cold, shivering, alive, waiting for someone, waiting for them.

The television reporter stood on the shore, with a growing cabal of other reporters, fellow parasites. He stood apart, shifting from foot to foot, antsy, squinting out at the ocean. Shit, where? Others worked their cell phones, frantically scrounging for the story, but still nobody knew anything. Someone living in a trailer home nearby claimed to have seen a huge fireball on the horizon; another said the plane had come so close to the village that you could see inside, cabin lights flickering on and off, people lit, then black, see those last moments playing out from the ground.

These waters were his, that's what the reporter thought. He'd sailed these coves and inlets all summer long, sailed past the lighthouse so many times it seemed a natural outcropping of the landscape. He was a solid, good-looking man who spoke quickly, moved at a clip, all of forty-two, with just-thinning hair. He'd worked twenty years on the nautical beat, covering the navy and ship sinkings and whatever else came along. He never forgot to register a name, and then never forgot it, kept a card catalog in his head that connected everyone to everyone else. One of his great strengths. And when he saw what looked like falling stars in the distance, parachute flares, he knew that was where the plane was. He turned to the cameraman.

We need to be under those, he said, pointing to the falling stars.

Before he left the office, he'd stashed extra cell-phone batteries in his pocket. You never knew, or maybe you already did. And now, in this night, in the seamless dark (there was no marking land but for the lighthouse, green light flashing), he was on his way in a hired boat with a cameraman. The wind blew, heavy swells, ten-foot waves, on his way, to see what? And why? He was as bad as the others, wasn't he? A fucking parasite. There were a lot of people on that plane, he knew that. At the UN, they called it the diplomatic shuttle: dinner meeting in Manhattan, breakfast meeting in Geneva. And now here they were, lost off the coast of this forgotten place.

It took an hour in those seas. The parachute flares and spotlights were blinding at first, the smell of diesel overwhelming. Sea King helicopters whirred overhead, aiming white beams; boats drifted through the wreckage aimlessly, the water a bottomless black. They couldn't see anything, just heard it on the VHF radio, fishermen talking to one another: I got something over here. I think she's alive. Then thirty seconds passed. I need a body bag. And then other voices, this morbid call and response:

We got another one.

Over here, too.

Need a body bag, now!

Jesus, we got a foot in the water.

We have an arm.

We need a body bag! Who's got body bags?

Then the reporter saw a half-inflated life raft. Alive— someone was alive! But when they came upon it, it was empty, had inflated on impact. There were shoes fanning everywhere around them, hundreds and hundreds of shoes, in procession, riding the water's windrows—some with the laces still tied up. And underwear and ripped shirts, Bibles and stuffed animals.

Money floating on the surface of the ocean now. Dollars and marks, rupees and francs and drachmas. You'd haul up a purse and expect to find a wallet, a driver's license, lipstick, anything, and it would be empty.

The plane had hit the water at more than four hundred miles per hour, nose first, two engines still firing, very unusual, extremely rare; the jet was two hundred feet long, and the tail rammed straight into the nose, everything exploding into more than a million pieces. Later, someone would be in charge of counting pieces at the military base, in a hangar where bits of the plane would fill thousands of crates and cardboard boxes. At impact, the bodies on board had been what the medical examiner would call degloved, simply shorn from the bones. You couldn't pick them up in your hands. You had to scoop them in nets.

No one has survived this crash, the television reporter told the world. From what we are seeing, there are no survivors.

But, said an anchorperson, the coast guard is calling this a search and rescue.

There are no survivors.

Until dawn, he was the only reporter under the parachute flares, a bizarre, surreal time, no believer in God, but you could feel something, 229 of them in this place. There were body parts and shoes—he'd dream about them for a long time. He was beamed into television sets around the world. No survivors. He told the pilot's wife that her husband was dead. He told the famous boxer that his son was dead. He told the father of the woman with Persian eyes that his daughter was dead.

When he finally came to shore the next day, when he stood near the lighthouse, under the green light, doing more live feeds, carefully choosing his words for the world, running on adrenaline, he noticed a large man glaring at him. The man was a very big man, with a pockmarked face and greased-back hair, scary-looking, glaring. And the reporter, exhausted and paranoid, thought, He's going to kick my ass for being a parasite, for feeding off all these bodies.

When the reporter finished, the oversized man started for him and the reporter could do nothing but ready himself for the blow. But it never came. Something else did.

I want to thank you, he said. You told me my fiancée was dead. I got a phone call last night, in New York, and I was told there might be survivors, and I thought, Well, if anybody survived this it was her, because we're gonna get married—and everyone was saying there are survivors, and you told me she was dead. You told me the truth. I needed to hear that.

Needed to hear that? This man needed to hear that? Yesterday the reporter had been covering some minor promotion ceremony at the military base; today he had told the world they could say goodbye to these 229 human beings, the ones with X's on their foreheads, the ones turning to gold, once wearing shoes, ghosts now, goodbye. And then the big man was gone, too, before the reporter could offer thanks back, or rather condolences, before he could think to ask the living man's name.

It was early morning in Geneva, and the father of the woman with the blue Persian eyes—a slight, erudite man with fine hair turning from orange to gray, turning at that very moment even—sat before a television, watching the reporter, in disbelief. He woke his wife and asked, Did she phone last night? And his wife said, She'll be phoning soon to have you fetch her in Zurich. And he said, She won't; the plane has crashed.

His wife roused herself, still half tangled in sleep, and stared at the reporter, listening, trying to grasp words that made no sense. It's all right, she said. There's nothing to worry about. We'll wait for her call.

The phone rang. It was her boyfriend in New York. What plane did she take? he asked. And the father said, But you tell me. No, he said, because we parted company at four in the afternoon, and she didn't know which plane she was on. And can you please tell me that she was on the Zurich flight?

No, the father said. And then he called the airline and insisted they tell him whether his daughter had been on the Zurich flight or the crashed Geneva flight. We cannot, a voice said. But you must. You must . . . There was silence, then a rustling of papers. We have to tell you, the voice said, she is not on the Zurich list.

Thank you, said the father.

Then he told his wife, and she said, Until they phone us with the news, we have to believe. And the man said, But darling, they're not going to phone with news like that. They'd come to the door—

And before he'd finished his sentence, the doorbell rang.

Grief is schizophrenic. You find yourself of two minds, the one that governs your days up until the moment of grief—the one that opens easily to memories of the girl at six, twelve, eighteen—and the one that seeks to destroy everything afterward. The man was fifty-eight and he'd given his daughter every advantage he could afford; the circumstances of his life—his work for a luxury-car company and then a fine-watch company— had provided the riding lessons and top-notch education and summer home in France. But then she'd given so much of herself, too. She'd been a championship swimmer and show jumper. She had a great knack for simplifying things, for having fun, for enjoying the moment so fully that those around her wanted to live inside those moments with her. She was contagious and beautiful and twenty-four, with those amazing eyes. She was about to come home and take a job.

After she was gone, the husband and wife made a promise to each other: They would stop their imaginations at that place where their daughter had boarded the plane, their minds would not wander past that particular rope. As usual, he broke the promise, unable to divert his mind from picturing his daughter at the end—it's possible she, like all of them, was unconscious at impact from the crushing g-forces inside the aircraft. Or that she suffered horribly, screaming, her entire life playing before her eyes. Whom did she sit next to in those moments? What was said?

The man couldn't help but imagine the pilots, too, their fate connected to a recurring dream he'd had for many years of himself as a pilot, trying to land a jet on a motor launch and not knowing what the hell he was doing. Though his wife stopped her mind on the gangway as her daughter stepped into the jet, he followed his girl into the sea.

Nothing made sense, time was disintegrating, everything was a confusion, chaos. Walking through town, he'd see the river and have to keep himself from slipping into it. He'd go to the station and hold back from throwing himself before a train: how good it would feel, a matter of time now, not whether but *when*— Today? Tomorrow? What would it feel like?

Since he couldn't sleep, he drank a bottle of Scotch daily, then couldn't remember anything. He followed the news accounts, halfheartedly reading words like *investigation, black box, recovery effort, debris field*. There had been a Picasso on board the plane and millions in rubies and diamonds. One day a postcard arrived from his daughter, detailing her stay in New York. Authorities called, wanting to send some of her effects (others now slept with ripped shirts and favorite sweaters, passports and stuffed animals), but the thought horrified him. What was worse, what the man could never have foreseen after thirty years of marriage, after having done so much to put a life together, was how quickly it became undone. He'd spent those decades stitching up a beautiful life—the watch on his wrist, a mysterious blue, cost the same as a small house. Now he didn't want to be with anybody, just alone, and his wife, his best friend—his wife had stopped at the gangway. How could she? How could she not follow their beloved daughter into the ocean? Silly words comforted her while they enraged him; having family nearby was a source of strength for her, torment for him. This response or that response of hers seemed so . . . *wrong*. In his mind he was asking: What's the point of this life? And she said, We must forget.

There was one thing that made him feel better. He flew alone to the northern village a few days after the crash, thinking he'd have to identify his daughter, drove down along the coast road to the lighthouse. (The media was now encamped here, among the houses and rocks and clotheslines, long-range lenses trained on anybody shedding a tear, beaming the image to the world.) He came to this village, and he felt something, some part of him rising, too. He knew he was going mad—and yet he could feel these waves churning inside him, his daughter there, too. When he returned to Geneva, he simply went back to devising ways to kill himself.

The full severity of the crash dawned on the medical examiner only the morning after, when he rode a Sea King out to the debris field. The fishermen and others in Zodiacs kept shuttling body parts to a huge command ship, the captain on the radio to these men talking in calm tones. (Many would later say it was that voice, that reassuring voice, that pulled them through the night.) The media had already begun a body count, based on the bags

coming ashore, and yet there were no bodies out here whatsoever, not one intact body in those bags, which were running out
fast. But for one, they couldn't identify a single soul visually.

Back at the military base, the medical examiner set up in
Hangar B, refrigerated trucks called reefers parked outside to
hold the remains. There were huge fans and scented candles to
mask the smell, the whole place lit and guttering like a church.
Like the strangest church. On one wall hung a huge diagram of
the plane, a seating chart, and as the remains of a passenger were
identified by dental records or DNA, by a distinctive tattoo or a
wedding ring, a blue dot was placed on the passenger's seat. The
medical examiner would eventually be in charge of four hundred
people here—a cadre of pathologists and DNA experts, morti-
cians, media liaisons, and staff. But when he came back to the
hangar after having been at sea that first time, he thought, What if
I go now, bugger off right now? But where? Back to his dogs? No,
what he realized as the parts began to fill the hangar and the reefers, as the stench became overpowering, was that he was too
afraid to leave. With each passing day inside the hangar, there was
nowhere to vanish but inside these people, these bodies.

One day he was waiting to go on the stand in dead-end New
Glasgow, killing time, and the next this complete Armageddon.
There were three hundred family members gathered now at a
hotel, and the medical examiner was asked to address them. Others spoke first—officials, the president of the airline, offering
their deepest sorrow to these people—and then he stood up nervously, cleared his throat, perhaps recalling that day years before
when he'd made a body out of rolled-up towels for the media,
how simple and, well, hilarious that had been. At least to him.
But how do you tell grieving family members the average body is
now in one hundred pieces, one hundred little stars? (A fisherman saw a human heart on the surface of the water.) You will

never see your loved ones again, he said. Those were the first words out of his mouth, and the crowd let out a massive exhalation, as if hit in the stomach. One man began sobbing uncontrollably and was led from the room. Not only are they dead, you will never see them again.

He'd said it. However painful, he knew this much: If you look away, if you self-justify or obfuscate, then you're stuck with the lie. You may make it through the moment, but in a day, a week, a year, it will bring you down, like cheetahs on a gazelle. Yes, he told them. If anything, they could see their own fear in his eyes, feel their quaver in his voice, their tears welling in his eyes. No stiff upper lip here. Fuck the macho and whatever it was that made you a man. (There was a heart on the surface of the water.) He vowed he would not betray these people, there'd be no fake body under a sheet. He'd try to talk to each of them, answer their concerns and desires, treat each body as if he himself were the next of kin: the father, the son, the lover, the brother.

Inside the hangar, days and nights of horrific work, checking dental records, X-rays, fingerprints. And on several occasions the medical examiner took fingers from which they could not get accurate prints, decomposed fingers, made an incision, and stuck his own finger inside, went inside these bodies, became them, so that he could lay an accurate mark of them on paper, return them to their rightful place. He knew each passenger by name and blood type. He found himself intensely identifying with one in particular, a newspaper executive named John Mortimer—couldn't shake him and his wife from his mind. He put himself in that seat next to John Mortimer's wife, tried to imagine the dreadful plummet, the smash of atoms. He tried to do the math: A loving couple falls through the sky at four hundred miles per hour, with maybe six minutes until impact. What did they say? What could be done?

Day after day, more blue dots came to fill the seats of the imaginary plane. He was not a believer in God, but a priest had come to the hangar, and the medical examiner said, Do you feel it? And the priest said, The souls are hovering. And the medical examiner looked up and said, Yes. Yes they are.

Then that November day came when they were done. There would be more dredging, hundreds of pounds of remains to come, jagged bones in piles (the plane hitting so hard some were embedded with quarters and nickels), clean as a whistle from the currents of the sea, but they were basically done. There were only a few technicians left in the hangar and they were going to shut it down, and the medical examiner came in early, when no one was there.

He knew it was perverse, but he didn't want it to end. He was convinced that his entire life, one full of mistakes and masterstrokes, had been leading to this moment. He was exhausted, flirting with a breakdown. He knew that, could feel it, but he knew, too, that if he'd run, the cheetahs would have caught him, somewhere out there on the veldt they would have dragged him down. It was fall, the leaves off the trees. A season had passed. How many seasons had passed? Nothing made sense. He was going back to his life (his dogs, the daughter who thought he was grandstanding now, saw his public empathy as something he'd never once offered her), his best self traded back for his flawed self, and he stood for a long while in silence, time disintegrating. When he turned to walk away—even later when he retired and packed up and moved back west—most of him stayed right here.

The passengers were blue dots now, and yet they were still alive. After that first night, even as time passed and the story fell from the news, the television reporter had been driven deeper into it;

he learned the names, who connected to whom. He tracked the possible causes of the crash: a spark thrown from the wiring of the elaborate entertainment system, the flammability of the Mylar insulation. He was haunted by the prospect that if the pilot had landed immediately, hadn't gone by the book, dallying with checklists, just put the jet down, everyone might be alive.

But then he met the pilot's wife. He went to Zurich, flew in the cockpit of the same kind of jet that had crashed, with one of the dead pilot's best friends, an awesome feeling of power up in that kingdom of sky, plowing for Europe. He met the pilot's wife at her expensive home in a ritzy neighborhood with a lap pool and lots of sunlight inside. The woman was startlingly attractive, especially when she smiled, which wasn't often these days. In her former life, when she wanted to go to Manhattan or Hong Kong or Tokyo, she didn't go first class, she went in the cockpit. And when her husband spoke, a dozen people jumped. They'd met when she was a flight attendant, and now here she was describing how she and her three children were trying to carry on without their father, her husband, Urs.

She told a story about going to the crash site, on board a boat that took the families there, about how hard it had been for everyone, how the kids were down, very down, and coming back, over the side, in the water, there were suddenly dolphins running in the ocean, an amazing vision, like electrical currents, these dolphins up from the deep and slipping alongside them. Not too long after, she decided that she was going back to work as a flight attendant, for the same airline. Her first flight was the New York–Geneva route, on the same type of aircraft as the one her husband had ridden into the sea.

There were others, too, people so moved by the graciousness of those in this northern place that they returned or even bought property to be closer. One man sailed his sloop here, in

honor of the brother who'd taught him to sail in the first place, the brother trying to save the world. The boxer, now an old man of seventy-eight but once a world champion, came despite himself and said he felt lighter when he left, after looking out from the lighthouse at the spot where his son's life ended. It somehow made him feel lighter. Others came and saw the hangar where the remains had been, the hangar where the million pieces of plane were still boxed and numbered, seats over here, armrests over there. The three jet engines were there, too, big, hulking things with mangled rotors.

How did these people do it? How did they go on? How could they? One woman whom the reporter had interviewed in New York had a box of stuff that had once been her daughter's: a French-English dictionary, a cup, a pair of binoculars, some glasses, a locket that she, the mother, had given her. She spent hours touching these things. And then another woman, who lost her husband, heard that they had found parts of his hand, had tested its DNA, and she asked that the remains be sent directly to her, though usually the remains were sent to funeral homes or hospitals. The reporter knew a counselor who spent four hours on the phone with the wife who had her husband's hand, and she finally sent the police because the woman was trying to put it back together. I can get the thumb, she said, but I can't get the next part.

The reporter didn't have the luxury of a breakdown, what with three kids. He still had the nightmares—shoes and body parts. He saw a therapist a few times, and she told the reporter to put the dream in a box, take the image of that black, bottomless sea and the debris field with its body parts and shoes, the smell of fuel drenching everything, and place it all in a box, take the box and put it high on a shelf. He did that, and he got past it. Yes, in an imaginary closet somewhere in his head, in an imaginary box, was everything that had actually, really, horrifically happened, and now sometimes, on a very good day, after some beers, maybe watching the news or roughhousing with the kids, he could imagine for a moment that it hadn't.

One day, the man from Geneva boarded a plane and came back to the village, left his wife behind, riffled through his closet of finely tailored suits and ridiculous leather dress shoes and packed some jerseys and books and left, for good, the only remnant of his former life that wristwatch with the stunning blue face, the same color as the sea here on certain windswept days, the color of his daughter's eyes.

The man left his wife, yes, but to save her from him. It sounded odd, but it was true. They'd made a promise and he'd broken it. He kept following his daughter into the ocean.

On his last visit to the village in this northern place, he'd seen a roadside restaurant and convenience store for sale nearby, and now, knowing nothing about restaurants or convenience stores, he bought it. It was a barnlike building with living quarters on the second floor, in some disrepair, but if grief was schizophrenic, then maybe here he could find a balancing point for his life before he lost his daughter and his life after. He had never conceived of the possibility that anything he did could be undone, let alone that he himself would become undone. But he'd become undone.

So he set to work, seven days a week, up at five thirty, readying the coffee, cleaning the grill, playing opera on the stereo, checking the weather in the cove that let onto the ocean, a stunning place, and his daughter in this place. He'd open the doors at seven, and at seven thirty a man named Leroy came to clean. They said he'd been half a man, a backward boy, before he'd been given this job, mopping floors and cleaning toilets at the restaurant. Now he was coming into his own. When the man asked him to do something, he smiled and saluted and said, Okay, copy ya!

The man redid the walls, opened up the dining space, began to build a large deck. He'd once traveled to the Middle East to sell hundreds of thousands of dollars' worth of watches at a time, and now he cooked Surf 'n' Turf burgers ($5.52) and Bacon & Egg Double Deckers ($2.99) just to hear someone, anyone, say, I think I've been sufficiently sufficed. Thank you kindly. He joked and laughed with the fishermen and the construction crews and the older men, too, who came just to sit and drink coffee. He stood in the middle of his restaurant in a rugby jersey, wearing a white apron, near a photograph of his daughter, and told a story about her.

She was sent to convent school when she was six years old, her hair cut incredibly short, not like it was at the end, long and streaked blond. There was an open school day, a parents' day, and they organized games for the kids. In one of the games you could fish for goldfish with a net, and his daughter came to him and said, Oh, can you imagine! All my life, my whole life, I've wanted a goldfish! I can't remember when I haven't wanted a goldfish! And the man looked at his daughter, who was beaming at him, her eyes lit all the blues of the world, and he laughed, her whole life and she was just six years old, sweet and precocious and it really was too funny. Well, a quarter of her life was over by then, doesn't seem—but it was, it was funny.

No, he hadn't left his wife. He talked to her every day, his best friend. But Geneva was her home and this was his now, this village. His beard had gone more gray over the winter here. Who could ever imagine where life might carry you, humbled and hopeful, lost and found and lost again as a storm blew in from

sea? There would be a day when he and his wife would be together again. They would reach an understanding, and they would
perhaps travel down to Morocco, to Marrakech, a place they'd
loved for its colors and light, for its people, together again, released, absolved, together.

It would be a strange, wonderful resolution, thought the
man, imagining it. They would make themselves clean. But now
there were hungry men at a table, and so this man with the spectacular wristwatch tied on his apron, went to the grill. This man,
though he was hungry, too, he fed the others first.

It was summer; it was winter. The village disappeared behind
skeins of fog. Fishermen came and went in their boats, boats
that had been at the crash site all those seasons ago, under that
dark ceiling of night clouds, in those swells of black, bottomless
water. One of the men fished a baby from the sea, kneeling on
deck, lit by the parachute tracers, holding fast to what was left
of the child, time disintegrating. Those who braved the night
said that something happened out there, something horrible,
and then—and this is the odd part—something beautiful. In the
strange, eerie silence, everything drenched in fuel, you could
feel it, almost taste it, something rising up from this spot, up
through the ocean, through the men who stood out there in
boats, among the shoes, something rose through them, like
electricity.

At the edge of the rocks stood the lighthouse, green light
flashing, flashing. Sometimes, in the heaviest storm, that was all
the fishermen had of land, this green eye dimly flashing in the
night, all they had of home, and how to get there, that was the
question. And there were other questions that lingered, too,
when they dared to consider them. Even at noon on the brightest

days of the year, especially on the brightest days of the year, when the wind whipped the laundry on the line, the questions lingered. Yes, what had happened here? And why did the clothes on the line look as if they were filled by bodies, though there were no bodies in sight anymore?

HE MIGHT JUST BE A PROPHET

I. [ON THE NATURE OF HAPPINESS]

ONE NIGHT LAST SUMMER I went to dinner at El Bulli, a Michelin three-star restaurant famous for serving some of the world's most curious food. It's a long distance from where I live, so I had to fly to Paris, then south to Barcelona. From there, I drove another three hours north to a busy beach town near the French border called Roses, then turned onto a neglected, potholed road that led up a mountain—houses falling away, the stunted Johannesburg trees bent like old, shadowy men. On the other side was a forgotten inlet with a few boats bobbing at anchor, lights starring the water—reds and greens and whites blurring on the surface of the Mediterranean.

If getting to El Bulli for dinner required crossing six time zones and a certain pilgrim's leap of faith, actually getting in was even harder, as the restaurant rarely has an available table. I followed some stone steps from a dead man's curve in the road down to the restaurant, a low-slung, whitewashed villa, where I was met by the smell of consommé and chocolate, rosemary and bacon, licorice and seawater. I passed the great lit window through which El Bulli's kitchen appears as a gleaming space-age chamber. On the other side, forty white-coated chefs moved in a silent, surreal symphony, chopping and sautéing and mumbling to themselves, a ghostly machine. Black-coated waiters poured in and out with trays of strange, brightly colored concoctions: glowing lollipops and wobbly gelatin cubes and a plate simply dusted with colored spices.

Amid the hurly-burly was a short, commanding man with dark, springy hair who wore old black shoes and a beaten red wristwatch. I watched him prowl the length of one silver counter, then turn on a heel and dive in among his pastry chefs, who were streaking what looked to be green paint over transparencies. He corrected the brushwork, then nosed his way to a bank of burners, took up a strainer, and inspected a yellow orb of yolk that he removed from boiling water. He slipped it into his mouth, nodded his approval, then spun to a station at the head of the kitchen to point out some deficiency in what appeared to be a dollop of bright red foam.

The year was 2000, and the man's name was Ferran Adrià. I instantly recognized him from photographs I'd seen in cooking magazines, but he was still more rumor than legend. It was said that he was opening a new culinary path, finding a new sea route, searching for India. And he was brash. He'd brazenly declared that it was over for the French chefs (in cuisine, that's a little like announcing that it's over for Jesus Christ) and that he and his food were the future. From him, it wasn't so much a boast as a truth he held to be self-evident.

It was also said that despite having money, he possessed no home, no car, no television, no mailbox, no stove of his own. During the six months that his restaurant was open, he supposedly slept nearby in a tiny, furnitureless room. The rest of the year, he lived out of hotels or at his parents' small house in the Barcelona barrio of his childhood, in the very room in which he grew up. And like a child, he could be whimsical. Once, he flew to Brazil in response to an invitation from a very rich man who'd faxed a page with only three words: *I am hungry*.

I'd come a long way for dinner. But my intentions were pure. Aside from the growing hype about Ferran Adrià——when asked, five of the world's greatest chefs had picked him as the greatest of all——I'd heard that his food could accomplish one simple thing: It could make you happy. So how far was too far to travel for that? And, I wondered, what in the world does happiness taste like?

I entered El Bulli and sat. No silverware on the table, no menu. I didn't ask for a thing, nor was I asked if I wanted anything. A welcome drink suddenly appeared, brimming in a small martini glass, a pomegranate-colored liquid that was announced as a whiskey sour, though who knew what it was. Around me were others like me, bound by hunger, expectant. Everyone had traveled some distance to be here; everyone was about to travel farther. I saw dishes jet by but couldn't name a single one of them. There were white spoons filled with a green jelly and topped with what seemed to be caviar, there were foams of green and yellow and pink, and there was a plate that, by my best estimation, was covered with orange worms.

The warm sea lapped just beyond the patio, and a kind of reverent hush was disturbed by the occasional tinkling of silverware and wineglasses. I noticed a woman sitting at a nearby table. She had put something into her mouth, and now her whole body shook slightly, as if she was having a fit of hiccups. She sat with her head bowed, her shoulders moving up and down, until she looked up at the man she was with. She had tears in her eyes, and when she met his gaze, she started laughing—unafraid laughter that made him laugh, too.

I noticed another man who I'd later learn was an American molecular biologist and a devotee of El Bulli for years, who considered Ferran Adrià a prophet. With each new course, he stood up and somewhat awkwardly switched seats, claiming later that the only way the meal made sense to him was by changing his spatial relationship to the food.

Was this madness or heaven? What kind of food makes people weep or sets them moving around a table like the hands of a clock?

When my first plate arrived, I was a bit frightened. I'd never been to a restaurant where a chef completely decides what you're going to eat and drink. At El Bulli, choices were left to Ferran Adrià, *el jefe máximo,* and the food was delivered in bits and combinations that didn't look like food at all, accompanied by instructions from the waiter: "This is a childhood memory. Take in one bite." Or: "This is trout-egg tempura. Two bites, quickly."

It came down to a question of faith. And I suddenly felt the presence of this man, Ferran Adrià, somewhere in the shadows, holding the fork in my hand, guiding it to the plate, impaling a mound of caramel-covered, sweet-smelling tenderness that had been introduced as "rabbit apple," and lifting it to my mouth, which, despite my misgivings, had been watering in anticipation of this very moment and watered still, now that the moment was here.

2. [ON HUNGER]

To discover what happiness tastes like, I'd persuaded my wife, Sara, to join me in Spain with our baby boy and a couple of friends, Melissa and her husband, Carlos, who would help translate. In the months leading up to the trip, Sara and I had lived in the first flush and ridiculous urgency of new parenthood. We'd passed each other in the middle of the night, as if underwater, handing off Baby. We'd changed Baby's diaper twenty times a day. We'd gauged every second of our ticking lives by the general well-being of Baby, by every hilarious burp and pleasing snore. I can't say I'd tasted a thing I ate during that time, nor do I remember a single dream, as meals and sleep came in desperate spasms. So we'd arrived slightly zombified, our former lives figments of our former imaginations.

It was August, high season on the Costa Brava, and we stayed in the last two rooms available in Roses, at a German-run hotel, rooms that might have made a good alternate setting for the next celebrity sex video du jour—shiny pillows and mirrors everywhere, and a shower with glass sides that could be viewed from the bed. Out on the beach in front of the hotel was a whole galaxy of overripe, topless bathers and lingam-hugging Speedos that made us feel that much more pale and alien.

The arrangement was simple: Carlos, who was the portrait of *gallego* smooth in a goatee and ponytail, would join me, who was Spanishless, each day with Ferran, who was Englishless, in hopes that we would make it back to toast the sunset with wine and cheese and our wives.

One twilight early on, while we sat drinking red wine on the balcony off our room as the sun skittered across the Mediterranean in goldfish-orange to the horizon, a man in the adjoining room came out on his balcony, too, in white briefs and a tank top, with his own bottle of wine, just to breathe the warm air. He told us he'd driven sixteen hours to get here from Italy, that his brother, who owned a restaurant in Naples, was apprenticing at a famous restaurant, and that he and his own family had arrived to taste the delicacies of the great head chef who worked there.

Of course—El Bulli. The man smiled.

"You've heard of it, too," he said. "My brother tells me that Ferran Adrià does the impossible."

"And your brother likes working in the kitchen?" I asked.

"He's exhausted," the man said. "Fifteen-hour days, seven days a week. If it weren't for Ferran Adrià, he'd probably go home right now. But in twenty, thirty, forty years, they're going to say Ferran Adrià was the best that ever was, and it's going to be an honor for my brother to say he chopped his vegetables."

He paused and offered us some of his wine, which we accepted. "It's a good wine," he said, poking his nose into the goblet and inhaling. "Not so overpowering. It's a bit of a secret." He admired the label, then said, "If you'll excuse me, I'm finally eating there tonight." Then he disappeared into his room of shiny pillows to prepare for his own trip up the mountain and down the other side to El Bulli.

We stood with our glasses full of wine, our faces lit a most otherworldly orange, and—we couldn't help it—we stared at the place where he'd just been standing, our envy framing the void, our hunger filling it.

3. [ON THE END OF THE WORLD]

Ferran Adrià often speaks of moments that mark a before and an after. For most, a dozen of these eurekas in a life is a lot. For Ferran, not a day passes that he doesn't assume he is on the verge of yet another one, that the world he's made for himself will simply explode under the weight of the new one rising from it.

His very first before-and-after came in 1985, when he was twenty-three. He was not yet the kind of strange celebrity he's becoming today, recognized on the street or in restaurants or at parties as a modern Willy Wonka, as the supposed savior or destroyer of cuisine. It was this young and unknown Ferran Adrià who was standing in his kitchen, staring at yet another order for partridge. How many times had he made this dish? Hundreds? Thousands?

There was nothing haute or nouvelle about the partridge dish. It was a *plato típico,* a common plate, *escabeche de perdiz,* made by every chef at every restaurant in Spain. It was simply an obligation to have it on the menu. The finished product looked as if it had been electrocuted at altitude, in midflight, and then had fallen two miles to the plate, battered and charred. But on this one particular evening, Ferran Adrià found himself suddenly incapable, frozen by some internal pause button.

How to deal with this sad bird? With the sameness of every day, of making every plate again that he'd already made before, by copying, copying, copying the recipes of dead or dying French and Spanish chefs? Wasn't there something greater, some secret waiting for release in this food? Perhaps Ferran Adrià had no right to see the partridge for what it wasn't, or for the multiplicity of what it could be, but if eating is as necessary as laughter or a sob, then where was the emotion in having charred partridge delivered to your table?

So he began to play with the bird. He plucked the wings and pinched some meat from the bones, which gave tenderly between his fingers. He removed the partridge from the partridge, as it were, and peppered the meat and swirled it with vegetables, some asparagus shoots and zucchini and finely shaved carrots, some leeks and onions at their most succulent. Then, on a whim, he tossed in some local *langosta,* lobster. Because it pleased him. And without another thought he sent it out to the dining room. A deconstructed partridge. No, a deconstructed, Mediterraneanized partridge. *Vaya!*

But the greatest surprise came when it wasn't sent back, as the faceless diner put fork to bird and bird to mouth, participated in the deconstruction, and actually liked it. And with that began the revolution, the alchemy, the culinary miracles. He experimented with gazpacho, vacuuming it into a liquidless, cold dish. When people ordered gazpacho expecting gazpacho, they suddenly did a double take at what appeared before them in a bowl: a sculpture garden of beheaded tomatoes, slivers of cucumber set like juju sticks, peeled whole onions . . . but where was the soup? And while other chefs certainly improvise from time to time, or as a last resort, Ferran Adrià couldn't help himself. It was jazz, abstract painting. Dervishly, pathologically, he began changing everything.

One day he got to thinking about ice cream, why it's always sweet, why, when confronted with it, your entire body prepares for that great blast of sugar and cool cream—not an unpleasant sensation, especially on the hot Costa Brava, but nonetheless the same sensation triggered by the same food—and so he set out to obliterate the sameness of ice cream. And he did, mixing a batch, cream and milk and ice, but then, at the last moment, substituting salt for sugar. *Vaya!* What he tasted in his mouth felt like something cool and mineral, as if it had been scooped from the dark side of the moon.

Now he saw the whole world in his kitchen: the autonomous march of history repeating history, the tyranny of that repetition. Chocolate: Why not add another texture, another taste to the tongue? He made some rich dark chocolate and smeared it with Japan—streaks of green wasabi that suddenly gave it a kick, a delicious burn that transformed the idea of chocolate into chocolate of some higher power. Bread: Why not make it explode? After baking bite-sized spheres of bread, he took a syringe and infiltrated the spongy interior with warm olive oil. He saw a simple croquette and injected it with seawater. People put them in their mouths expecting the expected—a little crunch, some chew, air—and were suddenly dealing with a burst and flood, victual chaos, palatal dyslexia, a tilting universe.

The new big bang.

Once, when Ferran Adrià was back in Barcelona for the winter, he bought a truckload of perfectly ripe tomatoes. He had no idea what he was doing. He and his brother, Albert, took the tomatoes back to their workshop, where Ferran dumped them on the floor and impulsively grabbed a bicycle pump. He stuck a tomato with it and furiously began pumping. For a moment, Albert regarded his brother quizzically, and the tomato itself seemed impervious until . . . it exploded everywhere! Covered in red gook, Ferran fell upon the wreckage, sifting through it, and triumphantly lifted one shard aloft. A fine, pinkish spume bubbled along the line where air had forced a fissure. He tasted it, a tomato without body—earth salt and juice, which suddenly disappeared like sparklers. After that, the brothers spent the afternoon blowing up tomatoes to see what more there was to discover.

It was air that created this tomato foam, but then how could you make it in the kitchen? You couldn't very well have someone in a back room blowing up tomatoes with a bicycle pump, could you? And also, the foam bubbled for a moment, but then flattened and quickly vanished. The brothers were stymied. Ferran felt that finding the key to making this foam would be like discovering a new planet.

After some experimentation with an old whipped-cream canister, and with the addition of the perfect proportion of gelatin, they finally happened upon it: a tomato foam, straight from a metal canister, that could stand on its own! A fine, floating, airy thing that tasted like . . . like . . . some new mesospheric formation they called cloud. And the tomato was just the beginning. Soon there were curry and beet clouds, strawberry and apple clouds. Once in your mouth, they bubbled, effervesced, and evaporated, leaving a tingle of taste.

His foam was soon being copied by nearly every innovative

young chef in Paris and Milan and New York, and made Ferran
Adrià famous in foodie circles, as much for striking out a new
course in cuisine as for the whimsy of how he'd done it. But today
at his restaurant, less than five years later, Ferran is almost dis-
missive of those foams, using them sparingly. "It's not so conscious," he told me in his kitchen, the first time we met. "It's just
that we opened a path and now that path is open. We may not
serve any foams next year. Most restaurants are museums, but
not El Bulli." I asked him what El Bulli was all about, then. He
considered for a moment, then gestured at the white-coated
chefs chopping like sped-up metronomes. "El Bulli is crazy," he
said. "It's the drunkenness of all the new things that can be."

4. [APHORISMS FROM THE PROFESSOR]

"Painting, music, movies, sculpture, theater, everything—we can
survive without it," Ferran said. "You have to eat, or else you die.
Food is the only obligatory emotion."

"The taste of a lemon is incredible!"

"There are eight degrees between warm and cold."

"You must always eat with two hands."

"I prefer to spend my money on a bottle of champagne at
the Ritz in Paris than on a pair of shoes. I'll always remember the
champagne. I'll never remember the shoes."

"The tomato is American."

"The prawn head is Spanish."

"In the end everything already exists; we're not inventors of
anything. But this is the definition of creativity. It's seeing what
other people don't see."

"Laughing brings out the good in food. It's good to laugh. If
you don't laugh, you're going to magnify. And if you magnify,
you're going to die."

"The important thing is the miniskirt, not what color it is."

5. [CONCERNING THE EFFECT OF TOMATO HEARTS ON WEDDED DISCOURSE]

One afternoon Carlos and I took the long drive into the mountains along the Mediterranean toward El Bulli. Up there everyone vanished, the sky came closer, the sea sparkled. If it was treacherous to drive the hairpins and potholes, it was suddenly much easier to breathe. Later, when I asked Ferran to describe the perfect meal, he stressed that there had to be magic in arrival. That it had to be a place hard to get to or somehow earned. That the journey, more than any appetizer or cocktail, would remind you of your hunger.

Now it was time to eat. Carlos and I had been invited to have lunch in the kitchen so we could taste and watch at the same time. It felt like an exploratory mission, a warm-up to the main event, which would come a few nights later. We were seated at a wide wooden table with two place settings and a couple of wine goblets full of light. We were asked if we had any allergies (none) and then came the welcome cocktail, what the waiter called a "hot-cold margarita." When I picked it up, the glass was partly warm and partly cool to the touch, since by some process the drink had been both heated and chilled at once. The margarita was tangy and airy, and the temperature difference, the movement from hot to cold, created a tumbling sensation, a tequila wave with a triple sec undertow, ending on one arctic, sweet note. We were startled into smiles.

And though whimsy has made Ferran Adrià famous, one soon realizes that a meal at El Bulli is driven by calculation and logic, coordinated through the phalanx of chefs at their various stations. Each guest eats roughly two dozen dishes, and if the diner simply rises to go to the bathroom, she can break an almost sacred rhythm that Ferran feels is crucial to the meal, to the variations in temperature and texture that help give his food its character. "The plate is a song," he says. "If the harmony is too slow, the person who receives the plate isn't receiving what the chef intended. There's a rhythm that's hard to explain, but it changes everything." Ferran's sense of time, then, guides the journey of every morsel from kitchen to mouth, and once it's there, he wants you to taste it as he does. And that occasionally requires spoken instruction. "The feeling of cold and hot is very different in one bite than in two bites," he says. "Sometimes, two bites makes all the difference."

Because much of what's eaten here seems without context, the meal itself, the rush of these dishes, builds a new context in which tastes emerge with shot-glass intensity from a nebula of cool mists and jellies. The idea is that a new dish will be launched every five minutes, no more than ten seconds after it's ready, and in those intervals between dishes, a guest will experience both sensual and psychic liftoff, to be repeated five minutes later. In theory, this makes the meal two hours long, though often people will linger a couple of hours longer at the table.

"We are inviting fifty people into our home every night," says Ferran. "It should be the greatest event of their lives."

The trick, of course, is to translate the ideas of Ferran's fertile mind into living dishes, up to two hundred different ones in a night. Further, each dish must be prepared en masse, then delivered to the table according to a nearly-impossible-to-achieve Ferran standard. And the fear of not reaching that standard is what drives the dizzying, obsessive pace in the kitchen.

From our vantage point, it was all just an endless rush of plates passing to and fro. Suddenly, a tray crowded with goodies appeared before us, and another, and another—what Ferran calls first and second and third "snacks," which are meant to be fun and lighten the mood before the main courses. None were recognizable.

There was dried quinoa in a paper cone, and, when I tilted it back into my mouth, the quinoa lightly pelted my tongue and echoed in my ears like a fine rain turning crunchy. There were also seaweed nougat (salty and sublime), deep-fried bits of prawn (so light they disintegrated before they could be rightly chewed), and strawberries filled with Campari (every cell cloying, the strawberries more strawberry because of the liqueur). No sooner would one marvel cease, one of us sputtering, What was *that*?, than the next bit of Martian food would arrive. It all ended in a strange, caramelized cube that I lifted with my thumb and forefinger and gently slid onto my tongue. Only after shattering it between my teeth did the object reveal itself: yogurt bursting from its candied shell in a warm, smooth flood.

Ferran shuttled between our table and his capos—the white-shirted generals running the kitchen—as an unceasing drift of guests came back to meet him. There was a famous wine critic who produced a rare Japanese spice. Some fabulously rich people shook Ferran's hand and gushed, "You don't see this every day," and Ferran said, "No, this is every day." A photographer from a Danish magazine, a tanned woman with very blond hair and long legs, wearing a sheer pinafore and a light-blue bikini underneath, climbed onto a table and started taking photographs. And for a second, everything stopped, sighed . . . then resumed in double time.

"Where the hell are the tapiocas?" a capo yelled at the hunched-over chefs on the line. "We're going to get punished here. Let's go!"

It was hard not to feel ridiculous, supping on delicacies while people worked at breakneck speed to get them to us. But we didn't overanalyze this because the main dishes, fourteen in all, began to arrive. And each dish was . . . was . . . how to explain it?

In Ferran Adrià's restaurant, nothing is for certain once his food crosses the Maginot Line of your mouth. He feeds you things you never thought existed, let alone things you'd think to eat: a gelatin with rare mollusks trapped inside (it was so odd, the cool, sweet jelly parting for salty pieces of the sea, that it tasted primordial and transcendent at once), tagliatelle carbonara (chicken consommé solidified and cut into thin, coppery, pasta-like strands that, once glistening on the tongue, dissolved back into consommé that poured down the throat), cuttlefish ravioli (the cuttlefish sliced with a microtome, then injected with coconut milk, another sweet explosion that seemed to wrap the fish in a new sea), rosemary lamb (we were told to raise sprigs of rosemary to our noses as we munched on the lamb, both of us now with rosemary mustaches, the smell of rosemary becoming the lamb as if the two were the same) . . . and it went on like this.

I will tell you: We were happy. We were served an eighty-year-old vinegar pooled in an apple gelatin with ginger, and vinegar has never tasted so gentle, so perfectly between sweet and sour, with a trace of gin, so unlike vinegar that it redefined vinegar. I would drink that vinegar every day, if I could, to start every day with a little pucker and smile. There was dessert, too . . . a first dessert and a second dessert and then more snacks. At the end, when we went to him, Ferran waved us off, saying, "Today you eat, tomorrow we'll think."

And so Carlos and I drove back down to Roses and the hotel. The clouds appeared as purple-lit dirigibles, and more light beamed across the sea. When we returned to the hotel and took a swim (the sea tasting like something made by Ferran Adrià) and sat down for some sangria on the terrace, when I tried later to describe the meal to Sara, I couldn't find any words. There were no words that came to mind. But I tried.

I tried to describe one dish in particular, an amazing, complicated thing, really. It was monkfish liver served as a pâté and, floating on top of it, a froth of soy foam. On the plate, in orbit around this foie-soy structure, were quasars of orange, lemon, grapefruit, and, finally, what stopped me, what I startled at, tomato hearts. They were just the guts of the tomato, really, its oozing seeds and essence.

What I meant to tell my wife, but couldn't, was that when I ate the substance of liver and foam with some grapefruit and then scooped the heart, naked and dripping, into my mouth, I'd felt, in all my happiness and weird heady lightness, something else, too: an undercurrent of impermanence, some creeping feeling of danger and fear. All of it in this single bite that slid down my throat. I might have grimaced as I swallowed it; I might not have. But when I looked up, I met the gaze of Ferran Adrià, who stood across the kitchen, watching, and I wondered whether he thought I didn't like what I was eating. Or whether he knew exactly what I felt, had searched for that expression on my face, because he knew what it was to eat a heart, and he'd felt it, too.

6. [ON THE AHISTORICAL CONUNDRUM OF THE GREAT FERRAN ADRIÀ]

It's as likely that he'd have ended up a car mechanic as a chef, if not for the pleasure of beer. After quitting high school and moving to Ibiza with the full intention of living the party life, Ferran took a job washing dishes to pay for his cervezas. Up until that moment, he had subsisted on beefsteak and french fries. That's all he ate—and that's all he wanted to eat.

But working in restaurants, he slowly indoctrinated himself into a multifarious world of taste, its bombast and truths. And by the time Ferran left Ibiza at twenty, he had decided: He would learn everything he could about cuisine, and through cuisine he would know everything about the world. He read Escoffier and

Larousse. He made the recipes of dead chefs with zealous devotion. He had a friend who was working up the coast from Barcelona at El Bulli, a two-star restaurant with a loyal if somewhat limited clientele, and in 1983, he hitched three hours north with the thought of picking up some quick money. Eighteen years later, he's still here.

Ferran is thirty-nine now and no more than five foot five in black-stockinged feet. He has a hairless chest with no muscles, exactly, and a bulging belly. (This vision appeared to me one day when he changed into his chef's whites without thought of anyone else in the room.) He does, in fact, possess almost nothing of his own. He never cooks for himself or friends and always eats out, usually traveling the world two or three times a year to eat, except for Christmas Day, when he cooks with his brother for their parents at home. Though he could buy them a Mercedes, and would, they don't want one. It would change the context of their lives, he says, and they're happy with their lives.

In the kitchen, Ferran Adrià is demanding, withering, Napoleonic. His dissatisfaction may manifest itself like an unexpected thunderstorm. But he's almost preternatural to watch, like Picasso captured on film, changing a strawberry to a rooster to a woman in a few brushstrokes.

Even now he dreams of a day when a restaurant will be less a museum (serving the same, same, same) than an experiment (serving the new), when a computer screen will bring the revolution into all of our homes, Ferran greeting us after work with a fifteen-minute recipe for his chicken curry, a succulent, deconstructed confusion of solid curry and liquid chicken that turns chicken curry on its head.

And yet, it's odd: For being one of the most self-actualized men I've met, he is also one of the most ahistorical. When I ask him to describe the best meal he's ever eaten, he says he erases his memories so he doesn't live for a moment he can never bring back. When I ask about his grandparents, he can recall nothing about them. "I think my grandfather died in the Spanish Civil War," he said. "Ten times—ten times I've been told, and ten times I've forgotten. Since I didn't know him, it's as if he never existed." When I suggest that it's a bit strange not to know the first thing about your grandfather but then to be able to quote a recipe by Escoffier from 1907, he says, "Not at all. My life is kitchen, kitchen, kitchen. History doesn't interest me, the kitchen does."

Politics? "I'm in the center. It doesn't play into my life."

Religion? "Do I pray when someone's sick? Yes. Otherwise, no."

Hobbies? "Hobbies?"

Mentors? "I came as a virgin to the kitchen."

When I ask if it troubles him when people don't understand the invention and game of his cuisine, he says, "Some people come here and see God; a few come and see the devil. The truth is relative."

The truth is relative? "I mean that only the tongue tells the truth. History doesn't tell it, religion doesn't. All that concerns me really is what the food tastes like. I am the chef, so I have to ask: Does it amaze me? Is there a before and after? If there is, then good. Let's eat."

7. [ON TASTE]

"The difference between a grand chef and a magical chef," Ferran said as we whizzed down the mountain, "is that a magical chef knows not just what he's eating, but how to eat."

"And how does a magical chef eat?" Carlos asked. Ferran's eyebrows rose at that, and an "Ahh" passed his lips. Then he grinned and said, "You are about to see."

We had asked Ferran to pick his favorite place for lunch in

Roses. He had us park and led us down an alley that spilled into another alley that opened onto a walking street outside a place called Rafa's. The restaurant, named after its owner, was a simple, traditional, open-air seafood grill with wooden tables. And Rafa himself seemed plainly hungover. While we sat, he disappeared into the back, then reappeared with a red bandanna that he wrapped deliberately around his head, ears jutting out. And once he'd knotted it, he was suddenly transformed. "Okay," he said in a gruff voice. "Okay." Samurai Rafa.

"There's nothing like this place," said Ferran, pleased. When the waitress read the day's menu, when she was through reciting twenty or so items, Ferran looked at her and simply said, "Yes," and then clarified, "Yes, all of it. A little bit of all of it. And whatever else the chef has." She looked over her shoulder at Rafa, who nodded slightly and winked. And then the dishes came, each *plato* reflecting the way food has been served in Catalonia for hundreds of years. Tomatoes slathered on peasant bread. Sliced prosciutto on a plate. Succulent anchovies, lightly peppered, in olive oil. A small mountain of *tallarines,* tiny, buttery clams that we pried from their shells with our tongues, the empty shells piling like fantastic, ancient currency.

With each dish, Ferran distinguished himself, for the act of eating was a full-on, full-contact orgy. His mouth, with its thin, quick lips and athletic tongue, worked frenetically. And at times, he didn't just eat the food, he wore it. He took the fresh prosciutto, fine, bright prosciutto that smelled like . . . well, like sex . . . and rubbed it on his upper lip (the same as sniffing wine, he said, or eating lamb with a sprig of rosemary beneath your nose). His fingers were soon bathed in olive oil and flecked with pepper, dancing quickly from plate to plate, so quickly, in fact, that our own fingers began to dance for fear that the food would vanish.

Platos came and went. Crustaceans arrived, various shades of orange, pink, and purple, just scooped from boiling water, with waggling antennae. Ferran picked up a prawn, one about the length of his hand, that looked like a shrunk-down lobster. Its shell was covered on the outside with small white eggs (a prawn that I would have studiously avoided altogether), and he began to lick the eggs with such ferocity that I decided I must have been missing something important and went digging for an eggs-on-shell prawn myself.

While I don't consider myself a delicate eater, next to Ferran I felt effete as hell. Particle by particle, cell by cell, he imbibed and inhaled and ingested until particle by particle and cell by cell he seemed changed by the food itself. Even when he sipped his cold beer, it was as if he were gulping from a chalice, washing everything clean. Now he held his prawn before me, its creepy black eyes staring into mine, and asked what it looked like. Face-to-face with the prawn, I was speechless. "It's intimidating, it's scary, it's prehistoric," Ferran said for me. "But in this context, it's normal. For generations, we've been eating prawns. If tomorrow someone puts a spider on the plate, then everyone's going to say it's crazy. But I don't see the difference. For you to understand what the ocean is, you have to understand something that Americans would think is crazy. You have to suck this . . ."

He suddenly tore the head of the prawn from its carapace and held it in the space between us. "You mean the head?" I said, stating the obvious, stalling for time, processing a simple thought: I don't think I want to eat the head. It doesn't seem like something I want to eat.

"Yes, the head," said Ferran. "If I can describe in one word the taste of the sea, it's sucking the head of this prawn. At home, my parents sucked the head. I tasted it and comprehended it. Just suck it."

He took the head, put the open end to his lips, and crushed

the shell until everything in it (brain and viscera, bits of meat and shell) had been expelled into his mouth, caramel-colored liquid dribbling down his chin. He savored it for a long moment, his eyes closed, and he seemed to have reached some kind of ecstasy. When he opened his eyes, it was my turn. I started tentatively, but there was no tentative way to crush a prawn head and suck it dry, so I just began crushing and slurping, juice running down my chin now. It was a profound and powerful taste, oddly sublime; the essence of this thing was, yes, salty, but also deeply evolved. It was cognac and candy, bitter and sweet, plankton and fruit. It seemed like the whole chemical history of the world in one bite.

"This is taste," said Ferran. "Not *the* taste, it *is* taste. You can't explain this."

He went on. "In a restaurant like this, we can eat the head. Spanish people find it provocative. They have an affection for it," he said. "At El Bulli, no, people are not prepared to eat the head. Ninety-nine percent of the people won't eat the head. It's not permitted in high cuisine." He took another prawn in his hand, pulled off the head, and crushed it. This time the caramel-colored liquid pooled on the plate before him.

"But if I pour this over food in my kitchen, I've changed the context. I can do this and people will eat it. People will eat it and taste the Mediterranean. This is what I look for. This is what I search for. This potency. Double the potency. The depths of the sea . . ." He sat back for a moment, considered. Then he reflexively leaned forward, swiped a finger through the puddle of prawn nectar, brought it to his mouth, and licked it.

"*Mágico,*" he said.

8. [APHORISMS FROM THE PROFESSOR, SEQUEL]

In the kitchen, scribbling in a notebook marked SISTEMA CREATIVO: "Anarchy is fine but only after logic."

Before we said goodbye one night: "There's more emotion,

more feeling, in a piece of ruby-red grapefruit with a little sprinkle of salt on it than in a big piece of fish."

To me, spoken conspiratorially: "The perfect meal: Have a reservation so that you can look forward to being there. In a secluded place, where there's a certain magic in arriving. Four people, everyone on a level playing field gastronomically. There shouldn't be a leader. Equals. When the food starts coming, concentrate on the dish, then speak about the dish. You have to laugh a lot. For me, it would be better to go with my partner because I like to have a woman by my side."

At the end: "Until I can serve an empty white plate on a white tablecloth, there's a lot to be done."

9. [ON MEXICO]

During my August sojourn at El Bulli, Ferran invited me to return to Barcelona in the winter to watch him, his brother, and a third young chef, Oriol, at the workshop, where during their off months they like to experiment wildly. The workshop is located in a very old building in the Gothic quarter of Barcelona just off the Ramblas, which, when I arrived, was brightly lit with Christmas lights. I climbed a worn stone staircase that led through an enormous set of carved wooden doors, and then the workshop appeared like a modernist's dream: a cool, high-ceilinged space with pine floorboards and white walls and Omani rugs. Upstairs, a library houses hundreds of cookbooks, as well as everything—shelf after shelf—that's been written by or about Ferran Adrià.

From a balcony on the second floor, it's possible to look down on the kitchen as if from a luxury box, witnessing the consternations and elations of Albert, Oriol, and Ferran. Albert is a fairer, younger version of his brother, and Oriol, at twenty-seven, is simply a madman, according to Ferran. On this morning, Oriol had just returned from the market while Albert was in hand-to-hand combat with a food processor known as the Pacojet.

It was this device that broke one day in the kitchen at El Bulli, prompting Ferran to see what would happen if they ran frozen chocolate in it, broken. From that came something called "chocolate dust," very fine dust devils of chocolate—a kind of vanishing chocolate, something between solid and air—that Ferran seized upon as a wholly new substance.

Now the group was working on about thirty things at once, among them "basil cylinders" (flavored ice frozen in the shape of a perfect emerald cylinder, to be filled with a yet-undetermined ice cream, perhaps Parmesan), something called "sponge ham" (a complete mystery to everyone), and a bowl of foie gras and apple foam, into which the diner would pour a broth, disintegrating everything to a soup for which they were also seeking a third and fourth ingredient.

"We're going to be much more interactive this year," said Ferran. He showed me a morsel of grilled chicken on a white plate and then seven spice holders (marked MEXICO, INDIA, JAPAN, MOROCCO, et cetera). "With this dish, you decide the end of the film," he said. "We give you the chicken, and you decide the spice." Oriol and Albert had already spent much time trying to refine each of the spice mixtures, making sure that a full octave of taste was present in each, the best curry from India or wasabi from Japan, and that each complemented the rest.

Now it was time for Ferran to try. Oriol and Albert crowded around him as he approached the plate, staring solemnly at the nugget of chicken. He picked up the container marked MEXICO and shook a bit on his finger, then sampled it. He said nothing. Then he shook it over the chicken, the specks raining down in a red shower, and then he grabbed another shaker and shook it, too.

"Look out, uncle, that's salt!" said Albert, appearing stricken.

"Don't get dizzy here, I know," said Ferran, concentrating. He popped the chicken into his mouth and chewed. He stared

into the middle distance. His eyebrows rose and fell as if registering a series of gustatory sensations. He considered it for a long
time, then after a while longer, he shook his head emphatically . . . No. "It's not Mexico," he said.

Albert looked flabbergasted. "For me, it is!"

"It's not. You taste tomato, cilantro, but it's not Mexico."

"It's my Mexico," said his brother.

"It needs more, but I won't call that Mexico."

Both brothers glared at the plate, at the specks of red spice
left on the white porcelain. Disappointment lingered for a moment, then suddenly it was converted to forward motion again.
Ferran cocked his head, then Albert did, too, noticing his brother's shifting mood.

"That would taste good on clouds," Ferran said. "You'd taste
the spices individually, eating it off a cloud. Try India on that.
Let's try it!"

Albert pushed Oriol toward the refrigerator, Oriol produced a bowl of apple foam that he'd made for the foie soup and
dolloped some into a bowl, Albert shook India onto the highest
peaks of the lather, and Ferran spooned it up. Though there was
nothing solid in that spoonful, his mouth moved as if he were
chewing. His eyes began to light, but still he didn't speak. His
eyebrows followed the taste and texture up and down, and when
it was over, he looked up. "That's beautiful," he said reverently.
"That's really beautiful."

Albert took a spoonful, and then Oriol. And each had the
same reaction, the same facade of skepticism giving way to some
new quizzical appreciation for the taste in his mouth, and then a
grin. "Uncle, that's good," said Albert. Oriol just nodded his approval vigorously. Now Ferran handed me a spoon, and I tried,
too. Each spice of India (the cocoa and lemongrass, the lime and
curry) seemed to burn down individually, while the cool apple

spread out beneath it, lifting it from the tongue. It felt like the Fourth of July in your mouth.

Before I could say anything, though, we'd moved on. To a quail egg. And now we were crowded around a pot of boiling water. The quail egg, which was the size of a small Superball, had been Oriol's obsession throughout the morning. I'd watched him crack egg after egg, strain them between brown-speckled shells until he was left with only the miniature yolks, and then boil them for five, ten, twenty, thirty, sixty seconds, removing the golden globe of yolk with a metal catcher, cooling it for a moment, and then tasting it—just to see what he got each time. After some consultation, it was agreed that the ten-second yolk was the best, sublime even, somewhere between raw and cooked but tasting like neither, the liquid inside warm and already swarming down the back of the throat by the time it touched the tongue. In fact, Ferran was afraid to do more to it. Oriol suggested covering the yolk in baked Parmesan, and he crumbled some over it. Ferran let a drop of olive oil fall on it, then spooned it up.

And this time there was no doubt; his response was immediate. "It's a natural ravioli!" he said, nodding, Yes, yes, yes. "We can serve it just like that." He turned and walked away, turned back again. He could hardly contain himself. Again, everyone tried one. "That's it," he said, on the verge of levitation. "We can try other things with it, but that's it!" He turned to me. "This is when I'm happiest. Finding the egg."

And here's what it tasted like: It tasted like a first—the first time you dove into an ocean wave or made something good or touched her lips. The first time you jumped from fifty feet, that feeling in the air when you forgot the gorge was beneath you, air and sun rushing, and you kept falling, and you opened your eyes and you were in the bright, underwater lights of a kitchen in Barcelona before an elfin man with hair springing from his head, quail yolk in your belly, and you could think of only two words to say, but you said them at least two times before you stopped yourself.

"Thank you," you said, laughing. "Thank you."

10. [ON THE PLEASURES OF THE TABLE]

On the last of our August days in Spain, Ferran said simply: Bring your wife and arrive by nine. Of course, I did as told. Being here had done our family good. We had swum. We were tan. Back home, phones were ringing, bills were piling, office workers were shooting each other dead, but the higher we climbed the mountain, the easier we could breathe again. It was the simplest thing.

Ferran had reserved us a table on the patio, beneath a stone arch and a nearly full moon. Even before the meal began, we experienced the odd sensation of being alone for the first time in many months, without Baby. The calm was almost exotic.

I had no doubt that somewhere back in the kitchen, Ferran knew everything that transpired at our table. While I at least had some vague sense of what might be coming, Sara was a neophyte. We barely got past "a childhood memory" (the dried quinoa) before she was smiling. By the time we spooned up our "cloud of smoke," we were both simply untethered from any concerns but those of the table. Taste became our cynosure, night a thing to be eaten with stars and moon. Ferran Adrià revealed himself in every bite now.

"It's as if he's climbed inside my mouth," Sara said, laughing, taking a second nibble of trout-egg tempura, caviar grazing her lip and disappearing on her tongue.

"Is that good or bad?" I asked.

"It's . . . disorienting, but fine by me because, really, it's"— her face brightened—"so fantastic."

Next, in a rush, came corn ravioli with vanilla, wasabi lobster, sea urchin with flowers of Jamaica—each one of these dishes weaving the unexpected with the vague outline of something we recognized. At some point, I'll be honest, I ceased to actually taste the food so much as feel it through Sara, who for the first time in months was no longer someone I passed at 3:00 A.M. but my wife, sitting across a table in a pink sundress, lit by a candle, hair falling to her shoulders, lifting against gravity. She closed her eyes, letting Ferran's chocolate dust settle and liquefy in her mouth.

And what did happiness taste like? Let me tell you. It tasted like seaweed and air. It tasted like watching your wife shorn of worry or care. It tasted like watching her face pass through every expression of surprise and mirth on the high road to euphoria, eating delicacies that she'd never eaten before, that exist nowhere else on earth.

Afterward, having finished champagne, having discussed nothing but food, having sat there until the restaurant was nearly empty and the moon had reached its apex and begun its descent again, we went to find Ferran, but he was nowhere to be found. Somewhere down in the real world our baby boy was sleeping, and we were told Ferran had gone to bed, too, up in his furnitureless room. It was possible. Or maybe he was respectfully absent, so as not to be embarrassed by what would have been our inevitable gushing. Either way, his nonpresence here was strange. His kitchen was silent and empty, the counters gleaming. The Pacojet sat unplugged in the corner; the silver foam canisters stood neatly in a row.

I imagined him in his room then, his head on a pillow or bent quietly over a book, his ever-moving mouth silent, his ever-darting eyes giving in to night, the sorcerer at rest. Of course he'd had no intention of checking with us after our meal. After all, what was he going to do with our happiness? It was ours. And so we kept it to ourselves as we traveled back down the mountain, passing the bent Johannesburg trees that made their own music in the wind, passing through the night into town, to our sleeping baby boy and each other, our world having ended and begun again.

EATING JACK HOOKER'S COW

GO WITH HIM. GO OUT INTO the feed yards with Jack Hooker. His daddy was a cattleman, he was a cattleman, his son today is a cattleman. Go out to the feed yards near Dodge City, Kansas, out into the stink of manure and the lowing slabs of cow, into the hot sun and rain and driving snow with Jack Hooker and know what it means to be a man.

First, a man looks like someone who's lived a while. Looks like Jack Hooker. Has a neck like Jack Hooker's, the back of it all tanned and crosshatched. A man has hands like Jack Hooker's, calloused but soft with pity on the rump of a steer he's sizing up for the slaughterhouse. He walks like Jack Hooker, with that same authority, that same plain movie-cowboy grandeur, his shoulders rolling slightly, his arms moving with the smooth swivel of his hips, his body blading through air as he crosses the parking lot of a motel. As if he might be there in body but always somewhere else, too—out in the yards, lost in an ocean of cattle.

See, a man like Jack Hooker looks on a heifer that stands twelve hundred pounds off the hoof and feels majesty. He shakes his hand on a deal that brings a new herd of a hundred head to his yard, and he feels grace. He sees God in a Black Angus that carries his meat in the flank. And he fights Satan himself when his cows go down with fescue, their tails, sometimes their feet, just falling off, littering the ground. What salvation is offered him here on earth, what afterlife, comes by seeing a glimmer of himself in a son who rises up in the yards like his daddy did.

And what everything comes down to for a real man like Jack Hooker is this one thing: America is a cow. It might sound funny if you're not from Jack Hooker's world, if you sit in those city offices trying to figure out how to take a piece of Jack Hooker, how to tax him and strip him bare, but America is a cow. And that's how America got to be America and that's what America is and that's what America will always be.

But now, here's where it gets tricky. Used to be you had a yard full of cattle. You fed them up to a good weight and herded them onto pots, the trailers that take them to the slaughterhouse. Honest work by good people. But now in those slaughterhouses, you can't find many people wanting to do the job. Jack Hooker did it once. Wasn't pleasant, but he did it. But now it's the Mexicans and those Asiatics. All these yellow and orange and black people stunning the cow and hooking it and flensing its hide. All these yellow and orange and black fingers inside every Angus and Hereford cutting them open, scooping out the viscera in slimy piles, all these yellow and orange and black hands sawing these cows in two, crushing up the bones, vacuum-packing their parts for the country to eat. That smell, that rancid, stomach-churning smell of melting cow, used to be a good thing, as good as the smell of money, but now it smells foul. Comes down on Dodge City like human flesh gone bad.

And what eventually happens here is that these yellow and orange and black people get a good wage—maybe eight, ten dollars an hour—and save up. Wait ten years, bide their time. And in that time, Jack has become a different man. He's out of cattle now, in semiretirement. Buys a motel with his wife, Beverley. But everything goes squirrelly in the late eighties, and Jack Hooker loses $100,000 in one of those bad S&L deals. Loses their house, too. Broke and homeless, they answer an ad in the paper: a Dodge City motel looking for managers. The Astro Motel. On the business card, it reads, THE SPACE AGE MOTEL. Has a little astronaut on a couch watching TV. Twenty-eight dollars for a single. The parking lot is full every night. Full of beef-jerky salesmen and crop adjusters and windmill collectors. The Hookers live in two rooms behind the front desk.

And then come the Cambodians, or whatever the hell they are. They come around with cash saved from all those years in the slaughterhouse, and they buy the two motels on either side of Jack and Beverley Hooker. Suddenly, they're surrounded by gooks. And Jack and Bev, they just manage the Astro Motel; but the gooks, they own the Thunderbird and Holiday motels. They gross more than $300,000 a year.

So go with Jack Hooker now. At sunset. Out into the empty parking lot of the Astro Motel. Look to either side, at your neighbors. They're holding your money in their yellow fingers. They own a Jeep Grand Cherokee and an Acura Legend and three other cars, and you have only your old Buick. Can you feel something building? Can you feel what a man like Jack Hooker feels? Maybe the difference between you and a real man like Jack Hooker is that he will tell you what he hates; he will honor his hate and unleash it and understand that his hate will come back on him, understand that he, too, is hated. For a real man like Jack Hooker realizes that he hates and is hated. And then, with the motel signs lit three in a row, tells you in so many words what he knows: Reckoning Day is coming. The gooks are eating his cow.

So this is your new life, Jack Hooker's life: Broken Coke machines and ice makers, broken Zenith TVs and GE air conditioners, broken Sylvania bulbs and Budweiser beer bottles smashed from the second-floor balcony last night by some wasted Mexicans, the jagged glass reflecting on the pool bottom. Just off the boat, says Jack Hooker in his gravelly drawl—you know how that goes. Then frowns. There's no special time when things break around here, they break all the time. Even now, things are breaking, and Jack Hooker's down on one knee, fixing them or picking them up.

Forget the bullet holes in the lobby window—the Astro is a family place. American owned. With two golden rules: (1) People want a clean room, and (2) People want a good bed. That's it. Built in 1965, when they set six metal beams thirty feet in the air, painted them blue, and hung a prefab, L-shaped motel from them. Today, there are still two scrunched-down stories and thirty-four rooms with alternating yellow and blue doors. An ode to another era, like some George Jetson space station, hovering just above the landlocked plain top of southwest Kansas.

Oh—and it's your life. You go to bed here; you wake up here. You eat here and make love here and may die here. Do you know what it's like to have ten thousand cows passing in pots every day, rumbling up your spine, lowing in your dreams? After a while, it doesn't matter how clean your room is, doesn't matter how soft your bed is—it gets to you, gets to Jack Hooker sometimes, too. But you do your best with it, make a family of the people passing through. In the old days, they came because they wanted to visit Dodge, soak up the lore of Boot Hill and Wyatt

Earp and Bat Masterson, came to see what was once known as the Wickedest Little City in the West. Whores, gunfighters, gamblers. Used to be a monument to everything that made this country great. Home to cowboys. American cowboys. So many once that you could hardly part them with a horse.

But now things have changed. Cowboys are dead. What's left is the rednecks and the bankers and the outsiders. The clientele at the Astro isn't tourists so much anymore: They stay at the chain hotels—the Holiday Inn Express, the Super 8, the Best Western—all those big conglomerates. Now it's the blue-collar people and traveling salesmen who keep the Astro alive. And Dodge City is losing its white majority—a quarter of the town is already Hispanic. And then you've got your Asiatics and blacks. Most all of them here for the slaughterhouse work, though they're branching out, infiltrating everything. Especially the Asiatics. One day, they'll have the country club, too, be up there playing eighteen like they were born to it. Scares you, scares Jack Hooker. There are gangs and killings and kids sniffing gold spray paint—what's called spooking. There's a rumor around town that some gangbangers are gonna kill a pregnant woman, as some rite of passage, and she'll have blond hair. And there's a law now against buying hogs and slaughtering them and hanging them from the trees in order to drain the blood. Do you know what it's like to drive around the corner and see dead hogs hanging in the trees? Different people, these Mexicans and Asiatics—crawling all over your world, closing you in. And the Cambodians—you can't help but wonder why they wander in front of your place all day long, eyeing you as they go.

Thankfully, your guests are mostly like you, helping make an island against the others. Occasionally, some will stick around—for a construction job out at the new Walmart site or maybe doing time at the slaughterhouse, like the rare black man in 107, a night-shift manager. Bev Hooker calls him my black man in 107 in the same way she'll say my construction crew in 117 and 119 or my British tourists in 120 or my Mexican gals when she refers to her cleaning staff, three women who speak very little English. To help them, Bev raises her voice and speaks slowly when asking for a cleaner toilet or a better-made bed.

And it almost goes without saying that Jack and Bev are two parts of a whole. Jack sometimes calls her Momma. Never felt the need to go looking after other women. Never once, in all those years on the road, buying cattle. Nights in Abilene or Wichita or Denver or Dallas or Shreveport. Out for a steak. Talking cows. A strong, proud man with a James Dean walk. Turned more than a few heads in his day, you can count on it. But just so lucky to have her. Ain't wanted another momma, he says. And Bev, she must have come straight up from a cornfield, born into this world with eyes like a clear twilight sky. That same blue. Some days, she might wear shell earrings and a shirt that looks like a big scallop. A prettier version of Shirley Booth. And her hair, swirled like cotton candy.

Some nights at sunset, Jack and Bev'll get out the lawn chairs, sit under the eaves of the front office, watching it all add up. People come and go. The woman in 106 is in the pool with her daughter, doesn't have a bathing suit, so wears her dress, soaked up to her armpits. A group of men shuffle around their pickup trucks in the parking lot. One brings a paper bag full of beer up to his room. Upstairs, there are a couple of windmill collectors: John and Johnny West, their real names, a father and son with their wives. On the road, looking for old farm windmills to buy and refurbish—and then do what with? Maybe keep around the yard. It's a dying thing, says Johnny, looking over at his wizened, fading father, who's nodding his head. We want to keep the old days alive.

Occasionally, some folks aren't so friendly. Like these two young troublemakers, two wire-rim liberals from Wisconsin who pull up in their VW van. When they ask Bev the price of a single, she tells them; then when they hem and haw, she brings the price down a bit—something she doesn't normally do. And still they take off, peeling out of the parking lot. Off to the Cambodian jungle, says Jack Hooker.

At night, Jack Hooker may sit behind the front desk, waiting for someone to need a room. He may sit and sit and sit. He may watch the cars picking up speed as they leave Dodge, off to somewhere better, maybe. Sensing they're on the final edge of town, somewhere between in-between and nowhere, the drivers just press a little harder on the gas pedal. Kind of shoot by in streams of red taillights out into endless fields of wheat.

It's early in the morning now, out on the edge of Dodge City. There is a woman, Bout Sinhpraseut. Follow her. Follow Bout Sinhpraseut up into the graveyard, under the cottonwoods. She's called Donna, but her real name is Bout Sinhpraseut. You can say it: *boot sin-pra-sit*. It's her name. She's not from Cambodia, as Bev and Jack think. She's from Laos—an entirely different country. Forty-two years old with four children, she left her home after the U.S. bombed it to rubble, after a civil war broke out, left it in 1981, fled seven days through the jungle with her family, then made her way to America. Now she owns the Thunderbird and Holiday motels in Dodge City, Kansas, on either side of the Astro Motel, her signs lit nightly with NO VACANCY while the Astro is only half full. Follow her now. She is climbing a knoll in a graveyard with headstones that have come up like pearled tongues in the first sun. Everything is quiet here. Follow her to meet her God and know what it means to be an American.

First, an American looks Laotian as much as an American looks Irish or Rwandan or wears a turban or won't eat Kansan hog for religious reasons or is quadriplegic. An American looks like Bout Sinhpraseut. Donna. A small woman with small hands and a mouth full of magnificently white teeth. Smiles like anything can be done, like a lighthouse of faith. Blinds you with it. And an American walks like Donna, in small, determined steps, with legs like pistons, driving her arms through the air, until she has covered a great distance by taking small steps. Walks this way when crossing the parking lot at the Thunderbird to clean rooms or heading up the highway past the Astro, under the suspicious eyes of Jack and Bev, to her other motel, the Holiday Motel, the cow-filled pots rumbling by at full tilt, spraying manure on the pavement at her feet. There in body but always somewhere else, too. Up here in the graveyard, with her God.

See, Bout Sinhpraseut came to this country and became Donna. And her children became Jamie and Johnny, Amanda and Sue. Do you know what it's like to give up your name and take another? Here's what it's like: One day, you're called Tommy and you live in, say, Wichita or Minneapolis or Atlanta, and the next day you're in Vientiane, Laos, and the people around you are speaking in a duck-quack rat-a-tat, calling you Inthaithiath. How do you even pronounce that? Only Donna's husband refused a new name, kept his old one—Boun. You can say it: *boon*. Once a French teacher in his home country, he finally gave up trying to learn English. After a while, just sat in his bedroom at night, watching Thai movies and reading Laotian books. My husband frightened, says Donna. He wake in morning and come out and say to me, How did we get here?

According to Donna, this is how: Leave your home in Laos, village called Champassak near Cambodian border, and go to Texas. You don't know anything, can't figure out the first thing about this circus, America—so you learn everything from scratch. When you open your mouth, folks in big, silly hats look sideways at you, hear only that duck-quack rat-a-tat. Everyone who's not a cowboy is either Chinese or Vietcong. They don't look kindly on you, either, tell you to go back where you came from. You live in a little apartment. You're packed in pretty tight, all six of you. Everything is a circus. Your little kids are afraid of black people in the streets, come home from school shaking, don't wanna go back. Scare you, too. Ask neighbor, Are they human or animals? Neither, he says. Just niggers.

Nigger—what does that mean?

You may be a short person, but you still have a big heart. And seen trouble before. Seen your brother poisoned and killed by Buddhists back in Laos and had two friends blown up by land mines. Ran through jungle with Communists firing at your back. You get your family out of Houston to Dodge City, and you go to slaughterhouse and work ten years. Hard work but good money. Husband work, too. Once he was a French teacher; now he scoops slime out of cows. Sometimes you're so sick of seeing the insides of cows, you don't think you can ever see another one— but still you come back. Some days, you're so tired you can't stand, but you still rise the next morning. Back to the slaughter- house. Back to whirring saw blades and sickening smell. The smell of melting cow bones. You can't really eat for ten years with that smell on you all the time. Just go on bleary-eyed, like some kind of prizefighter, just keep taking those steps, working the arms. And you start saving, too. Buy gold jewelry. Round $26,000 worth. That pretty good.

But now, here's where it gets tricky. You live in a trailer park surrounded by other recent immigrants—Vietnamese, Laotians, Chinese—and most of these people, they don't have bank ac- counts or insurance or anything like that. They work in the slaughterhouse and keep their money in twenty-four-carat-gold jewelry—hide it, like you, in the house. You're smarter, though, also have a bank account and some money stashed there. But then come home one day from work and the front door's open. Kids— Jamie and Johnny, Amanda and Sue—are tied up in the living room, and some men tie you up, too. They wave their guns and tell everyone to shut up and they take everything, all the gold, and then turn off the lights. They're gang members—Asian Pride or something, Vietnamese or Laotian, and even though you're one of them, they hate you because you work hard, because you're moving up. They take most of your ten years at the slaughterhouse, walk it right out the door for you. Take your American citizenship papers, too. Do you know what it feels like to be left sitting in the dark, tied to your own chair, watching your life walk out the door? Have you ever seen your own kids tied up and crying?

And in this time, Donna becomes a different woman; something begins to build in her, too. Can you feel it? She begins to hate, because now she really knows she is hated. And somehow, it makes her that much more determined. Get up and go to work again and again and again. Nearly starts from scratch and prays for God to reveal himself to her. And one day, he does. He just comes to her. Seems like he seven feet tall, says Donna. Weigh three hundred pounds. Name is Dwayne. Dwayne Price. Big white man, drives a Continental. Donna's giant, her God. Owns the Countryside Manor trailer park, where many of the Asians in Dodge City live, where Donna's family lives. Knows Donna's family, hears about its trouble. He's a big white man with a big car, in his early sixties, and he takes pity on Donna and tells her he's going to help her. He grosses about $15,000 a month from the trailer park, owns a six-bedroom house, got five bathrooms in it, and a wife who's twenty years younger and three daughters— all of whom he claims don't love him. Buy them all new cars and they still don't love him. So, on sunbaked days, with the stench of manure pressing down on the grain elevators and wood-framed houses of Dodge City, he cruises with Donna in his big Continental, a perpetual cigarette in his mouth, pricing out property. She has some money of her own for a down payment; he shows her how it all works. She buys the Thunderbird and then, with the first six months of income from that, buys the Holiday. Both of them are dumps, but they haven't met Donna yet. She knows how to clean.

Boun, Donna's husband, he's afraid of Dwayne's brilliance and his doctrines about money—how money invested becomes money earned, how risk turns to profit. But Donna, she has faith. She runs the Thunderbird; daughter Amanda runs the Holiday. Boun, he cuts the grass, moves heavy things. They are nervous and happy, and still they are hated. Sometimes, white folk drive in, then drive out when they see Donna at the desk: Some are vets, some maybe lost kids in Vietnam, some are militia members, some just feel like giving her the finger. There's a bullet hole in the lobby window here, too. When the hotels are full in the center of Dodge City, the desk clerks don't recommend Donna's motels. Dirty, they say. Try the American-owned place. Translation: Avoid the gooks.

Gook—what does it mean, anyway?

What eventually happens here is that Dwayne is stricken with cancer, and because he's more or less estranged from his own family and because he and Donna are now inseparable, Donna has him move into the Thunderbird with her family. Right into their living quarters, with its new shag rug and new TV and Walmart art on the wall. But he doesn't just move in, he moves right into her bed. Everybody think I was girlfriend, but wasn't like that, Donna says now. I do anything to support family, but I don't sell body.

Dwayne Price sheds weight, goes downhill fast, has a terrible hacking cough. In Donna's mind, seven feet, 300 pounds. But wasting away—250, 210, 170, 145, 120 pounds. She massages his great white back, sponges his wide white shoulders, feeds him when he loses strength. She curls onto the vast white suburb of his body and sleeps there, in his white light, in a cool white lane of sheets, so if he dies in his sleep, he dies with her arms around him, roped over his body knowing he was loved. Let his whole race mistreat her during the day; at night, she is here with Dwayne, whispering, dreaming up plans for the two of them to one day visit Laos. And what does Dwayne get from this? He gets to be a god. He gets love. He gets a dignified, deified death. And Donna? She draws power from him, or he gives it to her. And Boun himself knows this man is like no other man, knows this man has a special, otherworldly gift. He has taken them from the hell of the slaughterhouse, saved them from the cows, and delivered them to the Thunderbird—and Boun is, for once, less anxious. Yes, Dwayne is dying, but they are blessed. Boun stays in his own bedroom now, down the hall from Donna and Dwayne, watching Thai movies, colors pulsating over his body in the dark. He puts a picture of Dwayne up on his Buddhist altar, where he lights incense each night.

And then Dwayne passes.

So follow Donna now, under the cottonwoods, to the grave of Dwayne Price. Listen to her talk to her God. About how the Mexican whore is two-timing her husband in 225. About how the ice-cream-truck driver in 220 took all the towels when he left. About the bikers who broke the framed print entitled *Afternoon Punting,* of English ladies observing swans in an English park somewhere. Every little thing. Do you know what it's like to believe so deeply in something, in a race of people that most often hates you, in a country that is your country now and yet pulls up in your parking lot and flips you the bird? Maybe the difference between you and Donna is that she hates and understands that she is hated back. But more than that: She believes, too. She takes you to the graveyard, on a hill looking down on Dodge City, above the cows and the slaughterhouses and all the white people. This place where she goes every day to leave an offering of oranges or flowers at the foot of this marble headstone that she rubs again and again, like it's Dwayne Price's white back.

Midnight along Wyatt Earp Boulevard—comets of passing traffic, an occasional drunk stumbling along the shoulder. Stand in a place before Red's Cafe, near Iseman Mobile Homes, out on the edge, right before Dodge City turns back to a country of red dirt and wheat fields and feed yards again. Look across the street. See that stubby, thickly built man with muscular legs, wearing a weight belt and baseball cap, the one pedaling a mountain bike? Boun on a covert mission, on his way from the Thunderbird to the Holiday to check on daughter Amanda. But not just that: At the edge of the Astro parking lot, he teeters off into the dark shadow of a concrete wall. Sits a while on his bike, hand propped against the wall, feet on the pedals, counting. Can see Jack Hooker in the glassed-in lobby, but Jack Hooker can't see him. Jack Hooker is standing behind the desk, head down, reading something—a *National Geographic*. At this hour, in this light, Jack Hooker looks older than he is and younger, too. Boun never sleeps a night without knowing exactly how many cars are in the parking lot at the Astro Motel and reporting it back to Donna. The best way to beat your competition, said Dwayne Price, is to know your competition. Tonight's cars: Thunderbird, twenty; Astro, four. What more do you need to know?

Behind the desk back at the Thunderbird, fifty yards from where Jack Hooker stands reading his *National Geographic*, Donna is sitting behind her own reception desk watching *Married . . . with Children* reruns on TV. I like Al Bundy, she says. Like a lot. Funny funny things come out of his mouth. The laugh track laughs incessantly. Donna laughs, taking her cue from the laugh track. Those teeth—blinding. Now wait here a while and laugh with Donna. Wait until a man eventually comes in—got a swabby head of white hair and bloodshot eyes—and says he was a friend of Dwayne Price's and Donna's eyes light up. Can remember this man, a peanut salesman? Something like that, right? Vending machine, he says. Chuckles, Snickers, Kit Kats. It's after midnight, but at the Thunderbird the night is its own day, has its own constant neon bloom of light—people come at all hours, for all reasons—and Donna doesn't sleep that much anyway, not since Dwayne died. Miss him, says Dwayne's friend. He had a good heart.

Donna nods, pulls out a photo album. Hundreds and hundreds of pictures of Dwayne, in various stages of wasting away, a man in the stunned process of some final realization. *I'm going to die.* Even now, Donna keeps pairs of his oversized underwear piled in her bedroom drawers. Keeps his baseball cap and socks. Leaves offerings to him on Boun's altar. She is wearing one of his blue short-sleeved shirts now, comes down to her knees. Every night in the last year of his life, they slept together but didn't sleep together: Two people with apparently nothing in common went down into some river running beneath all of this stumbling, cursed, warring humanity and became one thing—not yellow or white or black or orange but just one pure thing. Donna didn't try to possess Dwayne Price's death—that was his alone. And Dwayne—he couldn't possess the other Donna, the one named Bout Sinhpraseut, the woman who led her family through the jungles of Laos with Communists shooting at her back. And neither of them tried. They just were. Donna helped Dwayne Price die, and Dwayne Price just showed her how to be an American.

So this is your life, Donna's life: sheets and towels and dirty toilets. Money, always money. Worry about kids. One daughter been hurt by her Vietnamese husband. When it comes to him, won't even acknowledge that word: husband. Errands. Every three weeks, fifty new towels from Walmart. Sheets and dirty toilets. Fuss over kids. Count money. Have Boun replace air conditioner in 218. Bring food to another dying man in 223, the one who stands behind his curtains, glassy-eyed, staring out all day, every day. Gonna die in that room. Worry about kids. Other daughter, the one off to university this fall, going to marry a Mexican who stayed at Thunderbird. Why the Mexican? Then give thanks in the graveyard, near the cottonwoods. Thanks to Dwayne Price. Remember where you were before him, where you're going after him.

Sometime, we get poor people here, says Donna. It rain, it snow. We give free room, some food. We get help when we were down. If people ring bell at 3:00 or 4:00 A.M., I get up and smile. I tell them prices. They come and say they were next door and Jack said, Don't ring our bell if you aren't going to stay. He grouchy. That not way to do business. She shakes her head, dissatisfied. Astro used to get good business, not so good now. We on the way up, she says. They going down.

Listen to her. Listen to Bev Hooker tell what happened and hear what she's really saying, beneath the words.

Seems there's been a disturbance in the night at the Astro Motel, and Bev is still flustered. See, she usually goes to bed around 10:00 P.M., then wakes before 6:00 A.M. to handle the early shift. Jack, he gets up when he wants but then handles the late-night. Still, he'll turn in around 1:00 A.M., and then if he hears the doorbell ring, or if Nikki, their sweet Australian shepherd with half-rotten teeth, starts barking, he'll get up and go out to see who's there. Problem is, Jack's become hard of hearing, confides Bev in a whisper. And the dog's deaf, too. So it's Bev Hooker who often answers the door, huddled in her bathrobe, out of the daze and blindness of sleep, her swirled perm of sandy curls a bit lopsided, opening the door to whoever comes off the highway, opening it to whatever they want from her. And they always want something.

Well, last night, late, the bell rings, and Bev stumbles from bed, puts on her robe, goes to the door, and sees some Asiatic guy jes grinnin' away. They look at each other for a moment from either side of the glass, and she could tell he was a kook. She thinks about calling 911, reaches back and puts her hand on the phone. The Asiatic on the other side, jes grinnin' away. Wearing some kind of pea-green jacket. And something makes her open the door. Reach up and draw back the dead bolt. Don't know why. Not usually such a risk taker, but it isn't natural for someone to be at the door jes grinnin' like a kook, especially an Asiatic. Puts his foot inside, says he is selling wind chimes. *Wind chimes?* You come back in the day, then we'll talk. Said it sharply then a couple more times before he got her drift. She bolted the door again and went back and lay awake in bed. She looks kind of shellshocked remembering it now, the morning after, and scared, too, as if it's a hopeless thing ever to try to understand the deep strangeness of the Asiatics. Makes you shudder to think what he really had in mind.

So, standing in the air-conditioned lobby of the Astro Motel with Bev Hooker this sweltering morning, have you really heard her story? What she's telling you is that it's a war out here, on the edge. She's telling you that someone is schlepping around Dodge City at 3:00 A.M., selling wind chimes or pretending to sell wind chimes with the idea of making money—one way or the other. Money—that's what everything gets reduced to. That's what everyone's fighting for out here. And when it comes to money, Bev says, no one can be trusted. Not even her own kind. We had white girls in here helping us clean once, she says. Big, fat white girls. They don't work. They'll try to cheat you. That's why we have Mexicans now.

Harder still for Bev to look at Donna and her people, so many of them over there—and not think of their greed, too, how they out-American the Americans almost, but playing the whole thing kind of dirty, by different rules: doing all the work themselves to cut costs, taking food right out of the mouths of white folk. What kind of neighbor is that? Started when they put those signs out. Before that, why, Bev Hooker talked to Donna. Donna would come over at first, sometimes bring cookies. Realized the Astro charged $28 for a single. Then, according to Jack and Bev Hooker, put that sign out. SINGLE, $26.95. See two signs now: one at the Holiday and one at the Thunderbird. False advertising, declares Bev. Draw people off the road, then say the cheap rooms are already full. Before that, yes, they spoke, though Bev confesses she didn't know Donna's last name, has so many vowels you don't know what it is. (You can say it: *sin-pra-sit*.) Now they don't speak at all. After Donna put her signs up, Jack Hooker went right out and put up his own sign: AMERICAN OWNED. Donna retaliated by buying a bunch of American flags, put them up everywhere. But I think we're having the last laugh, says Bev confidently. The wind out here just rips 'em right up, and she's wasting a lot of money.

Now picture Bev Hooker in bed just after her encounter with the Asiatic. It's five minutes past three in the morning. She is a good woman, a woman full of the earth itself, who a moment ago was sleeping soundly and is now wide awake and jittery. She is listening for a bump or a bang or a window being forced open, but all she hears is something distant and indistinct—maybe the lowing cows in Jack's dreams. And still she is afraid, feels hunted. It's hard to know what drives certain folk, what chemicals are inside people. Occasionally you find syringes in the next-morning rooms of the Astro. And there are people out there right now spooking and shooting bullets at one another. There are people next door—your neighbors—who'd sooner devour you than bring you cookies anymore. Somehow, they've entered the same bloodstream that keeps you alive.

So have you really listened to Bev Hooker's story? Have you figured out what she's really trying to tell you, herself? There's an Asiatic selling wind chimes at 3:00 A.M. out on the darkest edge of Dodge City, where the streetlights end, and no one, no one at all, can be trusted anymore. But what scares someone like Bev Hooker, what scares someone like you most, is this: Maybe the person you can trust least of all is yourself. See, when the Asiatic rang at the door jes grinnin' like a kook, you pushed back the dead bolt, and then you—you yourself—let him in.

Donna, behind the reception desk, in Dwayne Price's tennis shirt, the headlights off Wyatt Earp Boulevard flooding the Thunderbird lobby with pale white light, then emptying again, the colors and the things of the room—the oversized blue couch, the bubbling aquarium full of rosy barb and tigerfish—resuming their prior lives. Donna sits here now, will be sitting here this winter and spring and fall, as the pots rumble into town, ten thousand cows a day to the slaughterhouse, even as the wheat grows and is shattered and threshed and made into bread and bought at the store. To make bologna sandwiches, to put some hog between Wonder Bread for Donna's family. This place—this beautiful Thunderbird Motel—is home.

Wasn't at first. Was a pit, a bug-infested hole, cockroaches the size of your pinkie, crawling on your body at night. Dirty white folk sold it for $225,000. They angry, says Donna. Went belly-up. They never show us how to do nothing—how to register people, how to clean. They leave one day, lock the door, and go to Oklahoma. Had to spray the place for months to get rid of the roaches. Then Donna was full of sudden doom, thinking: It all a mistake. No matter what, we end up back in the slaughter-house. No matter how hard we try, we live the rest of our lives inside the cow. But Dwayne, he just holds everyone steady. The pool fills with litter and red dirt every day. Pour concrete in, says Dwayne calmly, get rid of it. Save on insurance, too. The gospel. Shows them how, one small step at a time. Work the arms. Clean the toilets. Get up and do it again.

Very hard at first. The former owner's daughter is still in town, works the night shift at another motel. When the rooms are full, she recommends the Astro Motel. Locally owned, she says, a nice white woman works there—Bev. We get lots of bad reports back from the other one, the Thunderbird. Dirty. When Donna hears this, her smile fades, anger rises, clouding her face. She big woman, fat, short, go with black guy, she says. Let's say compared to young girls, she not so pretty. She pretty ugly. Everyone have dirty words for me. Say my motel is dirty. Bev and Jack, they grouchy and old. Everyone say, Don't stay at Holiday or Thunderbird, but people come here and see how clean. People come here and say they saw sign next door—AMERICAN OWNED. Then ask, Are they American? If so, why need sign?

That's what boggles Donna. She's an American citizen, and she owns the Thunderbird. It's American owned, right? No, not even close. See what's happening here? Can you feel something building? Make someone feel dirty and eventually they're going to outclean you. Tell them they're not like you and they will become you. Put up a sign that says you're American and they'll already have a sign up that says we are, too: SINGLE, $26.95.

Out-American the Americans. Start with nothing and eventually you have a Trinitron TV and a new gold shag rug. You have a Jeep Grand Cherokee and an Acura Legend and a twin-cab Ford pickup truck. And yet something keeps you up at night. You're an American in Dodge City, grossing more than $300,000 a year from two motels, and you can't sleep. In the graveyard, talk to Dwayne about it. What's eating you? What? It's this: Frightened for your kids. Frightened even to let them go up to town. Gangs and kids spooking. Kids up there right now with gold-flecked nostrils, crazy-eyed, like they're from some long-lost tribe of the world. A Laotian just broke out of the county jail—in for killing another Asian. Tomorrow, they'll find him hiding under a trailer home, two snake eyes staring from the dark. Out at the slaughterhouse some years ago, three Asians were shot and killed in the parking lot with a .380, killed by another Asian over a four-dollar gambling debt.

That's what keeps you up at night. Almost helps to have a job like this, behind the desk at the Thunderbird Motel. People coming and going. Late, a white man from Ohio stops in with his son. Driving America on summer vacation—New Orleans, Big Bend, all over. Stopped in next door at the Astro, but prices are a little higher over there, will take a room here. Donna likes talking, talks to them. Pots rumble outside the window. When it comes out that Donna's from Laos, the man tells the story of some Cambodians in his Ohio town. The Tran family. Don't speak English, but they came to Thanksgiving dinner. Before eating, someone stood up and told the story of the Pilgrims: how they came on the *Mayflower,* nine weeks at sea, arrived starving and homeless and learned to grow corn and pumpkin from the Indians. The story was translated for Mr. Tran, and when he heard it, he smiled and exclaimed delightedly, Ah, you're boat people, too!

When Donna hears this, she breaks out giggling, beams a

big smile. Seems as if a great weight has been momentarily lifted from her shoulders. That right, she says, shaking her head, slapping the counter. We all boat people here, isn't that right?

Drive with Jack Hooker. Away from the Astro Motel. Away from Dodge City and the stench of a town stuck between a slab of meat and a frying pan. Forget the broken Coke machine, the futile phone calls to the distributor. Forget about the million decisions, ones that led to each room being outfitted with, say, the electric-pink Astro Motel flyswatters that read YOU'RE ON TARGET WITH US. . . . KILLS 25 PERCENT MORE FLIES. Leave it all and drive. Drive until you've driven beyond yourself. Into the heart of something else. Wheat fields and John Deere 9500 combines— all of it giving way to cows. To the amazing throw of feed yards across the plains, to the sharply cut pens and four thousand head of snorting, farting cattle. And the thing buried beneath it all, the secret of it.

On the way, look out at the wheat—a late-spring freeze and above-average rain have delayed the harvest. But these fields are a week away, golden and waving in a breeze. Their beauty fills Jack Hooker with a flicker of sadness. No such thing as the American Dream anymore, he says. You used to do business on your honor and good name. You could spend half a life building your good name, and the IRS takes it away. You know the story about the ten Indians? Then there were nine, eight, seven. . . . There's no American Dream left.

See, before you had anything, you had the Indians—the Kiowa, Comanche, Arapaho, and Sioux—and then the cowboys turned it all into America, made this country great. After that, you had the railroads and the bankers and then the feed yards and the slaughterhouses. If there were differences, it wasn't about

skin color. But see how it's changed now? America, the thing itself, is in bed with all the special interests and the conglomerates
and the outsiders. In bed with people like Donna. Rather help
her than its own kind. Look at these Asiatics in Dodge City: Got
their Asiatic restaurants and markets, got their own pool hall,
their own gangs. Drive Japanese cars. Damn shame.

Remember a day at the Astro three years ago, when a big
Continental pulled in bearing Dwayne and Donna. Dwayne
rolled down the window and asked how much for the motel.
Owner was there, said $450,000. Can have it if you can afford it.
But didn't really take kindly to the idea of a white man and his
Asiatic buying the Astro. Window went up, and they left. Then
Dwayne Price helped her buy the other two places—$550,000
for both of them—and went for the Astro's jugular. Sold out his
own people. That's the difference between Dwayne Price and
Jack Hooker: never occurred to Jack Hooker to sell out his people. Suspicion is that Dwayne Price was keeping Donna as his
girlfriend and worked out some underhanded deal for her, and
now Donna doesn't pay taxes. When Dwayne Price died, the joke
was that he died because he knew the authorities were closing in.

Still, do you know how it feels to have a hundred years on
this land, a hundred years of Hookers buried in this ground, then
have it taken from you, just ripped away by people who washed
up yesterday? Makes you feel sick, powerless. Feel like an Indian,
on a reservation somewhere. No American Dream left. Jack, at
the steering wheel, ponders a moment, wheat blurring in his side
window. Been thinking about joining the Peace Corps, he says.
Know much more than some college kid. Go to South America,
out on the pampas there. Could teach them a thing or two about
cattle. Wouldn't get near the Asiatics, though. Wouldn't share in-
formation with them. The Cambodians and their kind are worthless. First, there's too many of them: one in three people of the
world. Second, don't like jungles.

As soon as the yards appear, as soon as cows materialize on the horizon—Jack Hooker lets go. Seems as if a great weight has been lifted from his shoulders, exhales. His son walks out to meet you. Wears brown cowboy boots and a collared button-down and Wrangler jeans. Uncanny. Looks a bit like Bev in the face, but everything else is Jack. Father and son both stand with their elbows cocked, both have slight paunches that place equal pressure on the buttons of their shirts, both have pens in their left breast pockets, and both have the same sun-stroked, grooved skin on the back of their neck that shows an honest day's work. Except that the son may be a bit broader across the chest and has a full head of silver hair, you feel as if you're looking at Jack Hooker twenty-five years ago. Walks with a slight swivel of the hips. Out in the yard, lost in a sea of cattle.

Nearly a third of America's meat comes from southwest Kansas, says Jack Hooker. Now, a hundred years ago, maybe five million head come through Dodge City in as little as a decade. Part of the natural Santa Fe Trail. Old cowboys drove the cattle slow so the cows wouldn't lose weight, then loaded them on the railroad and sent them east for slaughter. Today, they leave on pots, go right from this yard, past the Astro Motel, to the slaughterhouse. Look at the country now, says Jack Hooker. The beautiful part is that it's still so strong, still so full of grass. You know why? Do you know the secret? Deep down in the earth, there's water running under all this. The Ogallala Aquifer. See, it starts with water, all this clear water running beneath the earth from South Dakota to Texas. Beneath rock and sand and gravel, millions and millions of gallons' worth. Running of its own sweet will.

Jack Hooker's son is the man who goes to Texas and Kentucky and wherever else and buys these animals—British Whites and Herefords, Charolais and Simmentals and Black Anguses. Huge, lowing creatures. Twelve hundred pounds off the hoof.

Some of them have the face of Christ himself. Drink seven gallons of clear water a day, eat corn and hay. Creatures of habit. Like us. Pick out a spot in the yard and never leave it. Pick a place at the trough to eat and always come back to it. Rub up against the same exact cows every day. Get in their way and you might take a horn. Some of the cattle get sold to the Japanese. Those folks have a slightly different standard for their meat, says Jack Hooker's son. Like theirs with a little more fat. Sometimes they come over to Kansas, to the yards, and handpick the ones they want, cameras looped around their necks. They're the picture-takingest people, says Jack Hooker's son, chuckling at the thought.

In the late afternoon, go up to the ridge with Jack Hooker and his son. On a rise at the edge of the yard. Blinding sun and blackflies, but they don't seem to touch the Hookers. They just stand there, the two of them, looking down on it all. Have you ever looked on miles and miles of cattle in a cast of orange light? Four thousand of them. Big, lumbering, beautiful things— mentality of a five-year-old. Have you ever seen the way the light plays on a herd, the way clouds come rolling in from California, and every one of them turns a different color? Looks like a museum painting of the Old West. Something behind glass.

Purdy, purdy sight, says Jack Hooker.

That's right, says his son. They're breathing in unison, and then Jack looks at you looking at the cows, then looks back at the cows himself and says to no one in particular, Don't get more real than that, does it?

It's been a long day at the Astro Motel. Bev's black man had a visit from his wife and child, or girlfriend and child, or whatever they are, and the three of them frolicked in the pool to escape the 100-degree heat. The white man in 109 saw them out there splashing around and came in and said to Bev Hooker, I see you let your help in the pool. Thought this was an American place. Both Bev and Jack know they have a problem now—they can't afford to offend their few paying customers—and Bev has suggested that they raise her black man's rates if he's going to have outsiders come visit and use the pool. It's only fair, right? Or am I prejudiced? she wonders. Don't think I am, but am I? Problem is this, says Jack, settling her: You let one in, then they just keep coming. Most colored folk make a lot of noise, he says. But now this man, he's a good man.

Sent Bev to bed with tornado warnings on the radio. Told her they'd work it all out tomorrow. Sleep well, Momma, he said. Now he's on the night watch. If someone comes in at midnight, one o'clock in the morning, he'll open the door and give him a bed. It won't matter what race or color, won't matter what he thinks about him in the bright noon of day, because he knows what it's like to be tired, knows what it's like to be without shelter on a stormy night. There are dead hogs hanging in the trees; there are kids spooking. When guests come through the front door of the Astro Motel, Jack Hooker will hand them the keys to one of his rooms and welcome them. Whoever they are, they'll sleep under the same roof as Jack Hooker tonight.

But no one comes. Wind starts up and blows the rain sideways, so fierce it feels like some kind of Old Testament storm. Cars keep passing, but no one stops. On their way to other motels. The bullet holes in the window have pooled with darkness now, and everything reflects back. Can't see the outside world, just hear it roaring. Look at Jack Hooker now, in the haunted lobby of the Astro Motel. Can you see him looking at himself? Do you see what he sees? Just a man—a man who hates and knows he is hated—turned ashen in the lobby light, standing with his calloused hands at his side, waiting and watching.

Meanwhile, behind the desk over at the Thunderbird,

Donna registers a trucker, a short, speedy white guy, and hands him the keys to 228. Clean room, she says, smiling. If you have problem, you come back and talk to me. Got ice machine right over there, too. You sleep well, okay? Al Bundy is on TV, and Donna laughs with the laugh track. She is wearing another one of Dwayne Price's short-sleeved shirts. Kids in bed. Boun in his room, watching a movie. Look at this weather, she says excitedly. Tonight, I bet we full.

She comes around to the front of the desk and tidies. Puts away the photo albums of His image. Goes to the aquarium, where she begins to feed the fish. Look at this woman Donna. She is now on her tiptoes, reaching her hand into a tank full of rosy barb and tigerfish. Can you see her? Clear water flows some-where in the earth beneath her feet, and she has her hand in the aquarium, among the psychedelic fish, so that part of her is in the water, too. Can you feel how cool it is? Can you see how clear? Outside, the wind is ripping her American flags, and there are more cars pulling into her parking lot, an endless wave of refu-gees washing out of the storm tonight. Look at Donna, Bout Sinhpraseut. She is smiling, feeding the fish. There are people with money coming to her door. She lets them in.

THE GIANT

ONE DAY WHILE LOITERING AT MY desk, I happened upon a news-wire story about a giant. The story was of the variety that appears from time to time, offering a brief snapshot of the oldest/small-est/fattest person on earth, a genre in which I take a keen inter-est. But there was something else about this one. The giant was reported to be thirty-three years old, residing in a small village with no plumbing in a very poor region of Ukraine. He lived with his mother and sister, who happened to be tiny. How he'd gotten so huge wasn't entirely known, because the giant wasn't interested in seeing doctors anymore. Something inside him had been broken or left open, like a faucet, pulsing out hormones as if his body presumed that it still belonged to that of a proliferat-ing pubescent boy. This apparently was the result of an operation he'd had as a child. Under the knife that saved him from a blood clot in his brain, his pituitary gland had been nicked. Now he was more than eight feet tall—and still growing.

In the article, the giant was pictured sitting at his small

dining-room table, reaching up to change a lightbulb at a height that a normal-sized person couldn't have reached standing. Another picture captured the giant in an unguarded moment, staring in astonishment at his hand, as if he'd just picked an exotic, oversized starfish from a coral reef. Near the end of the article, he said something that killed me. He said that his happiest hours were spent in his garden, because only the apples and beets don't care what size you are.

Beyond my admittedly voyeuristic interest in the facts of the giant's life—his huge hands, his constant search for clothes that fit, the way he traveled by horse and cart—that one comment brought with it the intimation of something heartbreaking and even a bit holy. It began a story: *Once upon a time, there was a giant who kept growing.* . . . And yet this was a real life. And what kind of life was it when you had to find solace among fruits and vegetables? Maybe he was an angel. Turned out of heaven, or thrown down to save the world. What other explanation could there be?

In the days and weeks after I'd read the article, the giant came back to me as I stood in the kitchen making dinner (did he use an oversized spatula to make oversized pancakes?) and while bathing my kids (how did he bathe if he couldn't fit in a shower or tub?). He returned to me in the lulls, while I was brushing my teeth or driving among a trance of red taillights. Maybe I cracked an egg when he did, and maybe I didn't and just believed I had.

Fall arrived. The leaves changed. I didn't forget about the giant; no, he'd only become more insistent. He was out there, and stuck inside me, too. Why? It made no sense, really. It was almost irresponsible. I was a father of two, and we had another on the way. I loved my wife, even more as her belly grew, as the cells split inside, but a part of me—my old self or soul or me-ness—had been subsumed by this new family of ours. I'd wanted it to happen, of course, invited it with eager if naïve willingness, but then there were moments when, perhaps like all parents, I found myself sunk down, overwhelmed, uncertain. Having children was its own kind of proliferation. You suddenly found yourself at the center of something that was growing wildly around you, all kudzu and blossom. Extra hands and feet and voices getting louder, a world of spoon-fed mush, babbling ditties, and dirty diapers telescoping into flung chicken legs, the all-purpose use of the word *No!*, and creative wiping. Sometimes I felt unable to form an adult sentence. Except this one:

It was time to see the giant.

I broke the idea gently to my wife, Sara, expecting the worst. Some guys take their getaways at a ballgame or Las Vegas. In my line of work, you can enable some of your most mysterious urges if only an editor says yes—and mine already had.

"Okay," she said. I could sense her mind whirring. A political profile in D.C.? Sure. A story about some interesting person in Europe? Why not. A giant in Ukraine—*why*? And yet she was disconcertingly zen. Maybe she was already imagining some future day with friends, a hotel stay with room service and in-house salt glows, what the Romans called quid pro quo and others call me-time.

So I packed a bag, said my goodbyes to the children—it never hurts any less—and made a beeline for the airport. There I strode straight up to the counter like a black-market arms dealer and bought a ticket to Kiev, the old-fashioned way. It may rank as one of the most pleasing things I've ever done. Maybe I was already imagining a fable in which some essential truth is revealed. Or maybe, under the guise of work, I was just hoping to escape, for a moment, what I was growing into and return to who I'd been. Either way, hadn't I earned a little me-time with a Ukrainian giant?

There was only one road leading to the giant—a ribbon of battered, unlined pavement wide enough for exactly two and a half
cars. Landing in Kiev, I was able to pick up a translator and a
driver whose beat-up black Audi smelled like the inside of a gas
tank. Before leaving the city, we stopped and bought a cake.
Somehow cake seemed like the right sort of gift for a giant, lest,
as giants sometimes did in fairy tales, he mistook me for a delec-
table morsel.

We drove west toward Poland and Slovakia, through all the
small villages inhabited by all the small and average-sized human
beings of the country. The people here—the babushkas and the
hunched old men—looked as if they might have been out mean-
dering on this same road three hundred years ago. Ancient and
ruddy-faced, they wore old wool hats and sat on the hard benches
of their carts, driving their horses, hauling their beets to market,
payloads of what looked to be purple hearts.

We followed the Teterev River, winding westward through
flatlands, and knew we were close when we came upon a town
called Chudnive, or "Miracle." The giant allegedly lived nearby,
in Podoliantsi, a tiny backwater of four hundred people, which
sat on a vein of blue granite. We drifted off the highway near a rail
yard, came over the tracks, which were lit by a string of indigo
lights leading to Minsk, then skirted the edge of an endless field,
finally turning right on a dirt road.

There was no WELCOME TO PODOLIANTSI sign, just a bunch
of hens running loose and the smell of woodsmoke. It was dusk,
without much light left in the sky, though the sun had come down
under the gloom and momentarily lit the land crosswise, throwing long, spindly shadows, catching a nearby cloud, making it
glow orange over the village until the last beams of light tipped

higher into space as the sun fell beneath the horizon line, like a spotlight suddenly diverted.

We asked directions to the giant's house from a woman at a well drawing water, and without a word she blushed and pointed ahead to another dirt lane. We turned and stopped before a stone one-story with a blue-painted gate. Apple trees loomed everywhere over the house. When we got out of the car, my eyes were slow to adjust to the shadows. There was mostly silence, some wind blowing quietly out across the fields rustling some faraway trees, until a hinge squeaked loudly, which caused the air to exhale from my lungs and my heart to skim seven or eight beats. I could feel a thudding reverberation emanating up into my body from the earth. *What was I doing here again?* Suddenly, a voice sounded in the dark: It had its own special reverberation, too.

"Dobryi den," the giant said from behind the gate, among the trees. He didn't boom it out in some fee-fi-fo-fum, but said it almost delicately, politely, so as not to startle anyone. He was behind the trees, and among them. Slowly, I could make out the low, interleaving branches and then some higher branches, with silver apples trembling there, on a level with the gutter of his stone house. And just above them, breaching, came the giant's head. It was enormous, and he ducked down to come to our level.

"Dobryi den," he said again. Good day. As if he'd been waiting. He was smiling as he undid the gate, teeth like mah-jongg tiles. He was tall. The top of my head reached only to his elbows. And he was wide. On his own, he was a walking family of four. My hand instinctively shot out, and he hesitated, then took it. Hand in hand, mine vanished in his like a small goldfish. He seemed to measure its weight a moment, considered its smallness, then squeezed. Yes, ouch—without realizing it, trying to be gentle—very hard! His palm was too wide to clasp fingers

around. Meanwhile, he was crushing certain fine bones I didn't realize I had. But I was doing what you do when you meet a real giant in a strange, faraway land: I was smiling like hell, nervously gesturing toward the cake in my other hand.

"*Dobryi den,*" I said. And these two small words were a spell cast over everything. Holding my hand, he ceased to be a giant at all. Rather, in his world now, I became the dwarf.

His name was Leonid Stadnik. He had a thicket of chestnut-colored hair trimmed neatly over the ears and hazel eyes that squinted ever so slightly. His feet were shod in black leather shoes, size 26, so large that later, when I tried to lift one, I needed two hands. When he walked, he did so heavily, with knock-knees and a precipitous forward lean, his legs trying to keep pace with the momentum of his upper body. He led me into the house, ducking and squeezing through doorways as he went, doorways through which I passed with an easy foot of clearance. His head brushed the ceiling that I couldn't reach without leaping.

We entered a cluttered foyer into the kitchen, where there was a small refrigerator, a woodstove, and various religious icons on the wall, including Saint Mary and, as he put it, "Saint Jesus." Leonid took me into a living room off the kitchen. Spanning almost its entire length was a bed—not a normal bed but one at least ten feet long, extra wide, covered with a green blanket of synthetic fur and, up near the pillows, three stuffed bunnies. There were heavy rugs hung on the wall, cheaply made Orientals, and several Soviet-era wardrobes along the near wall, spilling over with unruly swatches of fabric: exceptionally long shirtsleeves or stray pant legs, the world's largest gray suit, a bright sweater with enough wool to make a half-dozen sweaters. It brought to mind parachutes and gift-wrapping the Reichstag.

He offered me a chair and sat on the bed, reclining with his back against the wall. In the light, he was good-looking and boyish. He was perfectly proportional to himself, if no one else. If his growth surge had been the result of a surgeon's errant knife, he didn't technically suffer from gigantism, which is almost always caused by tumors on the pituitary gland. And he didn't *look* like other giants, with their heavy foreheads, prognathic jaws, abundant body hair, joints and limbs gnarled and misshapen. Also, unlike other giants about whom I'd read, his skin wasn't coarse or oily, and he was not odoriferous in the least. I don't know that he smelled at all, because the only detectable scent was that of the house, the land, the air here—of Ukraine—a strong, earthy, manure-laced, rotting-apple odor that suffused everything. It was the smell of agriculture, of human beings living partially submerged in the earth, in the mud and muck from which they originally came, and it wasn't at all unpleasant.

In the days leading up to my visit, I'd done some research. Being big—the kind of big that happened in the one foot of stratosphere above the seven-foot-six Yao Mings of the world and was the province of only an elite group of giants—was both physically and psychologically traumatic. Problems ranged from crippling arthritis to lost vision, severe headaches to sleep apnea, tumors to impotence. Many giants simply couldn't be supported by their enlarged hearts. To find one alive past fifty was a rarity; forty was an accomplishment. And many ended up living alone, on the margins of society, their only claim to fame being their height. There were websites devoted to tracking these people the way stocks are tracked: Hussain Bisad, a man from Somalia, was reported to be seven feet nine inches tall. Ring Kuot, a fifteen-year-old Sudanese boy, was rumored to be eight feet three. And until Leonid's emergence at eight feet four inches last spring, people generally assumed that Radhouane Charbib of Tunisia, at seven feet nine, was the tallest documented man in the world. Which was fine with Leonid, because he didn't want the title. To have it meant that it was only a matter of time before his body betrayed him. It meant an early death. It might be next year, it might be ten years from now, but the clocks were echoing.

Seated in the giant's house, I wanted to know everything. We began with the easy stuff. Leonid talked about his favorite foods, which included a dish of rice and ground meat wrapped in cabbage leaves called *holubtsi*. "I like sweet things, too—cakes and candies," he said. "I adore ice cream, like a child. Pancakes with jam. But I'm not demanding. We grow all that we use: potatoes, cucumbers, carrots, tomatoes, pumpkins, apples, pears, grapes, plums, cherries . . ."

The list continued, and he cut himself short, saying it would take another fifteen minutes to name everything they cultivated in their fields and garden and then differentiate between the categories of apples and cherries, the ten kinds of grapes and squashes. "You know, when I was in Germany, I could not understand why they live so well," he said. He'd traveled to Germany the prior spring, and not only was it the epic event of his life, but it remained a constant point of reference. "They have very bad land," he continued, "and we have great land. We have natural resources and the Germans don't, but they have a better life."

That first night, he talked while I marveled, as one marvels in the presence of seemingly impossible creations, whether they be exalted paintings or Thoroughbred horses. He sat hugging himself, in a red-plaid shirt and heavy brown slacks. When he raised a finger to make a point, it was dramatic, huge, as if he were waving a nightstick. He had a twitch in his left eye and a way of dreamily staring into space as he spoke that suggested he saw something there or was merely trying to see something through the opacity of his life.

Every once in a while, Leonid's sister, Larisa, appeared. She was elfin, under five feet tall, and looked more like a boy than a woman in her early forties. Her only nod to femininity was a *hustina,* the traditional Ukrainian scarf, that she wore over her head. At one point, she ferried plates of brown bread, fish, tomatoes, teacups, vodka glasses, cheese, and cold uncooked pig fat called *salo* to the table, as well as an unlabeled bottle of vodka. She didn't try to communicate with us, just nodded once and disappeared again. By this time it was very dark—and cold—and Leonid said she was going out to bring in the cows, which had been grazing somewhere at the edge of the village.

From another room came the sound of a television and the intermittent voice of Leonid's mama, Halyna. She was even shorter than Larisa, wrapped in crocheted blankets in the rounded, robust shape of a sixty-something babushka, her leg heavily bandaged. The family had suffered a shock in July when, while lugging a large milk jug up the front step, she had stumbled and fallen, the jug crushing one of her legs. "Mama tried to save the milk," said Leonid.

Not owning a car—not having the money to buy one and not being able to fit in anything smaller than a microbus—Leonid and his sister had driven their horse and cart miles to visit their mother in the hospital. This is how he'd been traveling for over a decade, and how people had been traveling here since before the birth of Christ. It was an investment the family made because Leonid couldn't bear the traumas of riding the bus—where he became a target of derision—and after his weight had destroyed several bikes. "My sister stayed near the horse, and I went to see Mama in her room," he said. "Then we shifted, and I stayed with the horse and my sister visited Mama. That's the problem with a horse and cart: Someone always has to stay with the horse."

After her release, Leonid's mama had returned home to her

bed, where she'd been for months ever since. But if there was any doubt, she was still very much in charge, barking orders, overhearing snippets of conversation, and shouting spirited rejoinders.

"Yes, Mama," Leonid called back.

"I know, Mama," he said.

"Okay, Mama."

We drank, all of us except Leonid, who claimed never to have had a drop of alcohol in his life. The vodka was very good, homemade from potatoes. I asked him how he could avoid drinking when his family made vodka this good. "It's a matter of principle. It's not that I don't drink. I do drink. Water, juice—cherry juice especially—but I don't drink alcohol. I have a motto: *Try to do without the things that you can.* Look at me. I've been broken by my height. Probably I would become a drunk if I started drinking."

He wasn't looking at anyone when he said it, but gazed out the dark window again—at something, or nothing. If people throw off vibrations, if certain people move molecules because of their words or actions or presence, Leonid sat in the room like a herd of buffaloes about to thunder. "In my life, I've done my best to become a normal person," he said, "to reach something. But because of my unusual body, I will never have a family or wealth or a future. I'm telling you, I've done my best. Everything that depended on me, I've done."

He was silent again, but his whole disposition had suddenly changed. "There's a saying here in Ukraine," he said. "'God punishes the ones he loves most.'"

I returned early the next morning. Leonid didn't seem to mind my presence or my questions, he just took me on as his little-man apprentice. He'd risen sometime after five, as he always did, and started by milking the cows. It was as dark outside as when I'd left him the night before—the air wrapped close around the morning bodies in cloaks of purple and black—and it was just as cold.

He put on his shoes at the door and walked across the flat granite patio of the inner yard, past two chained dogs rolling in their own feces, through the muddy passage between the small barn and the granary and the outhouse, past towering piles of stacked wood, and entered a room where LaSonya and Bunny, the cows, stood munching hay. Imagining him simply as a form moving through the predawn, one could say he was, physically speaking, a true behemoth. His back was several tectonic plates; his head was more rectangular than round—his nose was a straight, emphatic line; his chin, a mesa—but he didn't give the impression of being sharp-edged, willful, or stressed by these geometries. He was just 150 percent as big as the world in which he lived, and had figured out long ago that the only way to live in it at all was to remain absolutely calm—and to make himself as small and invisible as possible. Here, at home, was the only place where he was still Leonid the boy.

He towered over those cows as they chewed cud, and though he professed that they could be unmanageable, they grew still in his presence. The evening before, he'd said that one of his loves, one of his gifts, was the way he communed with animals, the way they fell under his sway. This was evident with the cat, called Striped One, who constantly sought him out, like a persistent lover, to have his ears scratched. But when it came to the cows and horses, the animals seemed to sense that, in this one case, they were in the company of a much larger being. So they became followers.

When milking, he used only his forefinger and thumb, because that's all that fit down there, squeezing out the teats, streams of white liquid clinking in a metal bucket. He sat on a stool, and because of his size, he had to reach down so far to the udder that he rested his head on top of the cows' haunches. I kept having an image of him, after he'd finished, hoisting the cow up over his shoulder just because he could.

Having once worked at the local collective as a vet, Leonid knew his way around a farm. He loved digging, the feel of the earth in his hands. But unlike others in the village, he was fairly well educated, having attended a local institute, graduating with honors. And yet his height had defined everything. At fifteen, he was closing in on seven feet, growing several inches a year. By the time he went to college, he was a full-fledged giant. He needed new clothes every four to six months, and finding them was nearly impossible. After he'd outgrown store-bought clothes, he turned to a local dressmaker. "Sometimes she was successful, and sometimes she was not," he said. His eyesight became poor, and his legs began to fail. He slipped on the ice and broke his leg. He got frostbite commuting the three miles to work and finally quit his job. By then, he'd long ago let go of his friends; he'd become afraid of crowds, afraid of anyone who might point a finger and laugh.

"I don't like to look at myself from the outside," he said. "I don't like the way I walk. I don't like the way I move. When I became tall, I felt shy and separated from my friends. A friend is a person with whom you can share your happiness and unhappiness. My best and most loyal friend is my mother."

When he spoke in his deep baritone, the trivial things he said felt metaphoric: "Lilies that don't work are more beautiful than any other flower in the world. But this is controversial." Or: "I wouldn't say I like to fish, but I like to look at people who like to fish." Or: "Everything depends on pigs and how fast they grow."

After milking, he took the buckets and emptied them into large jugs and then went out to meet the milkman. It was nearly ten before he made himself some rice and ground beef and rested for a while, reading the Bible.

"Here you're so busy," said Leonid, seated on his bed again. "You work until you see the moon in the sky, and that means it's evening. When I was in Germany, there were days when we didn't have to do anything; we had no special plans. So we could not wait for the end of the day, because there was nothing we had to do and nothing to do. Here every day seems very short."

Ah, Germany. He explained how a Ukrainian expat named Volodymyr, now living in Germany, had read an article and contacted him. It turned out that the two were distant relatives, and Volodymyr invited Leonid to visit Germany, all expenses paid. He arrived with a special bus and then drove him all the way through the western Ukraine and Poland to southern Germany, a two-day trip. At each stop along the way, the giant of Podoliantsi emerged from the bus as a great spectacle, to the awe of people who wanted his picture, his autograph, a few words. "You're a movie star," said Volodymyr. This was somehow different from the reaction he sometimes faced at home in Ukraine. In this case, the awe wasn't mean or intrusive; it was "cultured," as Leonid said. In one town where there was a festival that included carnival performers, he walked into a restaurant and sat down, drinking apple juice with Volodymyr. People assumed he was part of the carnival, too, and couldn't help staring.

If they were looking at him, Leonid was looking back. He shared their sense of awe, even if the source of his was the amazing things he saw around him. "There were so many bikes in the street," he said. "And the roads! Compared to ours, there is no comparison. I had a small table in my bus where I could put my glass with tea, and in Ukraine there was great movement and in

Poland a slight movement, and when we were driving in Germany there was no movement at all!"

He wanted me to know, however, that German roads and prosperity did not make Germany a better place. "When we went to Germany, we crossed the border, and even looking around, we could see that it's another country," he said in professorial tones. "Germany is a specific country. It is a strict country. Even the color of their buildings is usually gray, brown, some pale colors." He paused seriously, marshaling the full force of his memory. Surely few from Podoliantsi had ever been to Germany, and it was clear that some relatives, and maybe some of his mother's friends, had sat rapt through these recollections before, wondering what secrets he had brought back from abroad.

"The ornaments on the wall were different," he said.

At the end of each day with Leonid, I went back to Kiev, where, for me, the ornaments on the wall were different—as were my strange, empty hotel on Vozdvyzhenska Street and the late-night drunks lurching through the shadows. I thought about Leonid and how he seemed trapped inside something growing out of control. Not just his body but the effect his body had on the world around him. He was shy and sensitive, and his only defense had been to withdraw. In so many ways, he was still a child who'd missed so much of life: first love, friends, marriage, children of his own. He no longer had a profession, just a business card with a picture, one made up for him by Japanese businessmen who had come to visit, of Leonid towering over a seven-story building.

He was a full-time giant now, waiting. But for what?

I called home and spoke to my wife. I could hear the kids in the background. By being here, I hadn't escaped them at all; in that hotel room, they seemed everywhere. And yet, because I wasn't able to touch them—wrestling around with my son, Leo, or getting power hugs from my daughter, May—I felt myself floating in outer space. They were growing, changing, proliferating, and I wasn't there. I was here, halfway around the world, trying to find some notion of what I thought I'd lost, feeling all the more lost.

Over the days, the routine with Leonid was similar: I usually brought food and gifts. I gave Leonid's mother a scented candle and she responded happily, tickled, saying, "I've smelled one of these before and will look forward to smelling it again!" Then she barked to Larisa, "Matches!"

We spent many hours in the room with the big bed off the kitchen, chatting with Leonid, who sometimes brought a plate of walnuts to the table, crushing three or four at a time in his hand, then picking bits of meat from the serving tray of his palm. It was hard to say enough about his hands, to describe their power and enormousness. He was proud of them, the one thing he was unafraid to show the world. He also knew that if he ever hit someone with them, "that person would be dead," as he succinctly put it.

Larisa came and went, harried, rosy-cheeked. She regarded us openly, without expression, like an animal. A squirrel, to be exact. Sometimes she became impatient with Leonid's loafing and stood for an extra moment glaring at him—even muttering single words like "carrots" or "cows" to signify the task at hand—while he spoke on, oblivious, staring out the window into space. "I don't always have the will to pursue my goals," he said. "I force myself to finish very dull work. But my sister, she is persistent. She never gives up. I can give up, but she can't."

So that was her role, the sister of the giant of Podoliantsi. To work twice as hard while caring for her mother and brother. And that would be the role for the rest of her life, as both of them became more and more infirm. And Leonid's role, for us at least, was to reflect on his life, to offer it like some gilded manuscript, one with missing pages, of the things he'd actually missed in life and the things that were too painful to recall. He wouldn't discuss his operation at all, for instance, even when I pressed for details. "All you ask about is trifles and some negative moments in my life," he said, almost angrily. "Ask me about something gay and something happy, though I have few moments like that."

About his height, he said it was something he couldn't comprehend when he was young. He said everything seemed normal after the operation until one day, in ninth grade, the class was measured and the two-meter tape was too short for him. After that, he became acutely aware of people laughing out loud when there wasn't a block of empty seats on the bus and, unable to stand on his legs, Leonid would squat, as if over a hole in the ground. "One in a million would have survived what I survived on that bus," he said.

But somehow he did. He kept surviving.

And if God was punishing him, God had also kept him alive. Leonid had nearly died five times. In the first year of his life, he slipped into a coma and couldn't breathe. His parents bid their last goodbyes and made preparations for his burial—and he came back. When he was twelve, the Lord was more emphatic, letting loose the blood clot in his brain. Leonid couldn't move his hands or legs. To alleviate the paralysis, a risky procedure was performed inside the brain. Before he was put under, he remembered being wheeled through a ward of paralyzed children and then his parents saying goodbye once more. But whatever saved him that day doomed him to be a giant forever.

Realizing his fate over time, suffering the unbearable loneliness of giants, he twice tried suicide by hanging. ("My angels were awake," he said of those two attempts. "They did not want me to die. And my skeleton would not be broken.") And then, in his cart a few years ago, being pulled by his horse Tulip, he hit a rut. The cart toppled, and all 480 pounds of him were suddenly in the air, then beneath the heavy cart. What would have killed anyone else, what would have cleanly snapped a spine or neck, did not kill him. He came up from under the cart and went chasing his horse.

God had kept him alive. That's what he believed, so that's what the truth was. And he believed he'd been kept alive for a purpose. But what?

"I ask him, but He doesn't hear me," Leonid said. "The Bible says that those who cry in this world will then be happy in heaven. I'm not sure it will be like this, but I want to believe it. Secretly, I think those that suffer here will suffer in heaven, too."

"But why did God choose you for this?" I asked.

"I'm too tired to think about it," he said, finding the last bit of meat from the walnuts. "I used to think about it all the time, and now I don't want to think about it anymore. My future is only black."

Almost on cue, Larisa appeared again, muttering the word "apples." Her appearance was perfectly timed. Leonid smiled broadly and said, "Come," waving his hand for me to follow. "We'll go pick some." He forced himself to his feet and ducked through the first doorway, listing through the cramped house without so much as disturbing a spoon. He grabbed his coat and cap, squeezed through two more doorways, then went out into the day, which was still full of light.

Leonid was a prankster—and a giggler. He had a sweet giggle, very boyish and innocent. At one point, seated on his bed, he reached into his pocket, as if suddenly remembering something important, and produced a mobile phone, which he seemed to check for missed messages. With his pointer finger, he somehow plinked out a number. To give him his privacy, the translator and I began chatting, until her phone engaged, too, and she formally excused herself to take the call. She answered, *"Dobryi den,"* and then Leonid answered back from three feet away, in his booming baritone, *"DOBRYI DEN!"*

Watching the translator's surprise, his eyes became slits, his cheeks rose, and there was an enormous uplift at the corners of his mouth. His face, which was wind-chapped from so many hours in the garden, became its own planet. His ears, the shape and size of a hefty split Idaho potato, wiggled; his prodigious chin raised to reveal a patch of whiskers he'd missed while shaving; his two eyes were ponds of hazel water, suddenly lit by a downpour of sun. All the features of his face were complementary and, taken together, offered no clue that he was a giant. It's only when they were set against the rest of humanity that he became, in every way, more exaggerated . . . and, well, gigantic.

And yet his happiness was such a feathery, redemptive force. He had the same smile in one of the only pictures that still existed from when he was a boy—a picture that hung in a frame over his mama's bed, of a towheaded three-year-old with almond-shaped eyes. It had been taken on a special outing at the Kiev Zoo, one of the few times the family had been out of their village together, on a proper trip. It was sepia toned, as if taken a century ago.

Looking up at that little-boy face in the picture and then looking at Leonid's now was like watching the arc of an entire life being drawn between two points. More than anything, the primary experience of Leonid's life had been his growing, though his primary desire had been to go back to that moment when he was simply a child again.

"I was a little guy, and now I'm a big one," Leonid said when he showed me the photograph, his mama sitting nearby, still bundled in blankets.

"He was so nice when he was small," she said, with a touch of longing. "At least he has a suit for his funeral."

So it came down to this: On the day his life was saved by doctors operating on his brain, Leonid lost the ability to determine his own fate. On that day, he became chosen, as he pointed out—but he also became powerless. No wonder he was so dedicated to the Bible, reciting certain parables to whoever would listen. Long ago, he had thrown his life over to God, with his Old Testament temper, because nothing could explain what was happening to him. God was his hands and his feet and his mah-jongg teeth.

Maybe because of my size, mere mortal that I was, I had choices. And my god wasn't his god. In fact, I wasn't sure about who my god was. Maybe he was a feeling I got sometimes, a feeling that there *could* be a god. Or a glimmer I occasionally saw in the trees.

God was in the apple trees and red oaks or a bend in the river that we'd come upon yesterday where leaves fell into the current and were borne to the Black Sea in gold trails. God was the cows chewing cud and Tulip the horse pulling the cart and the dogs rolling in their own shit. God was the vein of blue granite running beneath the ground here and the milk in the jugs that pinned Leonid's mama, crushing her leg.

God was that moment when Leonid went out to pick apples and I followed. He used a stool, and I took a crude metal ladder and leaned it against the house. We levitated way up in the top boughs of the trees, and the apples thudded as they were dropped in the buckets. We were up in the trees, Leonid and I, and he began singing, in his own tongue, gently twisting fruit from each branch. His voice, that sweet song, sounded as if it came from some deep underground river.

The town of Miracle lay beyond him. Across the fields, a train sounded. God was the trees and the apples and the glowing clouds overhead. We were part of the same body, the earth as it was, as it had been created by some cosmic force. When I think of this, I still get that feeling, up there in that tree, that feeling of belonging to something sizeless.

I get that feeling of being up in the trees with Leonid, and everything that really matters, everything worth it, is up there with us, too: my children, his mama. All of our giants and dwarves. The apples are sources of warmth on that cold day, as if heated from within. To touch them was divine.

My time with Leonid was coming to an end. I'd gotten fleas—or something—from my hotel bed and was itching like a possessed maniac. When I'd filled the tub to wash, a flow of cold, smelly green water had eagerly obliged. Anyway, Halloween was approaching, and I would be returning to my kids, returning to watch them grow. And I was returning to one day set them free of this giant body, our family: to eventually put them on a bus somewhere so that they might come back and tell us of the ornaments they saw out there. I realized that once I left Leonid, I was really returning for good, that my next probable meeting with the giant would come some random afternoon at my desk, when I'd stumble across a newspaper item about his death, the tallest man in the world finally subsumed by his size.

Here were the basic facts: He would die having grown to eight and a half, nine, nine and a half feet, perhaps as the tallest man that ever lived, a title he'd never wanted. He would die a virgin, without ever having had a lover. Without having close friends, for that matter. He would die without children, having made it to Germany once, but no farther. It would have been many years since he'd been able to run or swim. He might or might not have a suit to fit him when he was put in his casket and lowered by the village men, at least a dozen of them, into the earth of Podoliantsi.

Until then, he clung to his otherworld, half made of dream and half made of manure. "I have no bad thoughts about the end," he said. He ate ice cream, sucked down a dozen raw eggs at a time, chewed cold pig fat, sang, and slept with three stuffed bunnies. He fell into bitter moods, cursed his God, then contritely read his Bible. He received his pilgrims and told them the tale of his life, hugging himself, gazing out the window, while Larisa came and went, muttering words like "beets" and "melon." He wasn't an angel or a beast after all, just a man, forming his beliefs from the body he'd been given. He said goodbye among the apple trees, where he'd first said hello, crushing my hand again, his face turning the colors of the leaves as we drove away.

But I remember him most vividly in a moment just before leaving. I went for a quick walk to see the cows. When I returned, I came upon him standing in the shadow of the apple trees, leaning against his gate, looking out from his stone house at the landscape, the red oaks on fire now, villagers using their wooden plows to turn the fields, the sun coming down just opposite him in the melancholic end of day. He had no idea I was there. He just breathed it all in. There was a presence behind his eyes—not just his enormous brain and eardrums, but *him,* his himness or soul or whatever. It was a moment where he just *was*. Contented.

He stood against the fence, and a neighbor child drifted by. The neighbors had cherubic boys and girls, blond and fresh and smiling, like he once was. Maybe, in another life, one of them would have been his own, light enough to hold up in one hand.

But now, hidden in the shadows beneath the apple tree, invisible, Leonid gently said, *"Dobryi den,"* which sent the boy skyward. He hadn't seen the giant there at all, and that was before factoring in that the voice belonged to an actual *giant* who happened to be his neighbor.

"Dobryi den," the boy said in a startled whisper. He looked up into the branches, gazed upon Leonid's face there, and stumbled. Then he put his head down and hurried on.

It took two days to get home. In the lounge at the airport in Munich, still itching madly, I realized that something smelled. Did anyone bathe in Germany? Yes, they did. It was me: I smelled like Podoliantsi, and I could tell people were thinking twice about sitting near me. I got up and found a terminal shower that I could use and stood in warm, clear water for nearly a half hour, washing it all away.

On the flight to Boston, I looked down on the world for any signs of life on land and sea, but from that height many of the fine details of the earth, including large houses and tankers, were simply erased. After landing at Logan, I waited in line, passed through customs, and again waited for my luggage to appear from behind rubber ribbons, trusting it would. The minute it did, I ran like a madman for the bus. I was so shot through with adrenaline, I was floating.

Soon the bus cloverleafed onto the highway. Two hours north now, to home, fitting neatly in my seat. When I saw this familiar land outside the window—fall here, too, flat land with its own forest flaring—and when I saw my wife, her stomach rounded against her sweater, and my daughter in funny pigtails there at the station, waiting, and I could finally touch them again, and when I lifted and held my little boy, Leo, in my arms again and felt my heart beating hard enough to know that I wanted to live a very long time, I took his hand up against mine, just to check, just to see what had occurred in my absence.

His hand lay in mine, and I felt its weight: the bones and the smooth, scarless skin so soft it didn't seem real. Mine dwarfed his, but still I held his hand up and inspected his fingers for a moment. He thought I was being funny, and he laughed, a little-boy giggle. His breath smelled like cookies. Yes, his fingers were bigger, and I was not frightened. Maybe the betrayals lay out before us somewhere in our murky future. Maybe we were all growing until someday nothing would work for us anymore. But I was not frightened. I was filled with joy.

It read four o'clock on the wall—on the East Coast of the United States of America—and at that very moment, some-where, the giant was sleeping on his oversized bed. His huge shoes lay empty near the doorway, his pants thrown over the chair. His enormous suit hung in the closet, waiting.

Soon he would rise to milk the cows, feed the pigs, pick the rest of the apples. In the dirt lane before his house, carts would come and go, bearing payloads of huge purple hearts. And there he would be, the giant, alone up in the apple tree, gently picking fruit, humming the notes again.

At the bus station, my children began singing.

DRIVING MR. ALBERT

IN THE BEGINNING, THERE WAS A brain. All of the universe was the size of this brain, floating in space. Until one day it simply exploded. Out poured photons and quarks and leptons. Out flew dust particles like millions of fast-moving birds into the expanding aviary of the cosmos. Cooked heavy elements—silicon, magnesium, and nickel—were sucked into a pocket and balled together under great pressure and morphed with the organic matter of our solar system. Lo, the planets!

Our world—Earth—was covered with lava, then granite mountains. Oceans formed, a wormy thing crawled from the sea. There were pea-brained brontosauri and fiery meteor showers and gnawing, hairy-backed monsters that kept coming and coming—these furious little stumps, human beings, us. Under the hot sun, we roasted different colors, fornicated, and fought. Full of wonder, we attached words to the sky and the mountains and the water, and claimed them as our own. We named ourselves Homer, Sappho, Humperdinck, and Nixon. We made bewitching sonatas and novels and paintings. Stargazed and built great cities. Exterminated some people. Settled the West. Cooked meat and slathered it with special sauce. Did the hustle. Built the strip mall.

And in the end, after billions of years of evolution, a pink two-story motel rose up on a drag of asphalt in Berkeley, California. The Flamingo Motel. There, a man stepped out onto the balcony in a bright beam of millennial sunlight, holding the original universe in his hands, in a Tupperware container, and for one flickering moment he saw into the future. I can picture this man now: He needs a haircut, he needs some coffee.

But not yet, not before rewind and start again. Not long ago. In Maine on a bus. In Massachusetts on a train. In Connecticut behind the wheel of a shiny, teal-colored rental car. The engine purrs. I should know, I'm the driver. I'm on my way to pick up an eighty-four-year-old man named Thomas Harvey, who lives in a modest, low-slung 1950s ranch that belongs to his sixty-seven-year-old girlfriend, Cleora. To get there you carom through New Jersey's exurbia, through swirls of dead leaves and unruly thickets of oak and pine that give way to well-ordered fields of roan, buttermilk, and black snorting atoms—horses. Harvey greets me at the door, stooped and chuckling nervously, wearing a red-and-white plaid shirt and a solid-blue Pendleton tie that still bears a waterlogged $10 price tag from some earlier decade. He has peckled, blowsy skin runneled with lines, an eagle nose, stubbed yellow teeth, bitten nails, and a spray of white hair as fine as corn silk that shifts with the wind over the bald patches on his head. He could be one of a million beach-bound, black-socked Florida retirees, not the man who, by some odd happenstance of life, possesses the brain of Albert Einstein. But, in fact, he possesses the brain of Albert Einstein, literally cut it out of the dead scientist's head.

Harvey has stoked a fire in the basement, which is dank and dark, and I sit among crocheted rugs and genie bottles of blown glass, Ethiopian cookbooks, and macramé. It has taken me more than a year to find Harvey, and during that time I've had a dim, inchoate feeling—one that has increased in luminosity—that if I could somehow reach him and Einstein's brain, I might unravel their strange relationship, one that arcs across this century and America itself—and, as well, figure out some things for myself. And now, before the future arrives and the supercomputers of the world begin to act on their own and we flee to lunar colonies—before all that hullabaloo—Harvey and I are finally sitting here together.

That day Harvey tells me the story he's told before—to friends and family and pilgrims—one that has made him an odd celebrity even in this age of odd celebrity. He tells it deliberately, assuming that I will be impressed by it as a testament to the rightness of his actions rather than as a cogent defense of them. "You see," he says, "I was just so fortunate to have been there. Just so lucky."

"Fortunate" is one word, "improbable" is another. Albert Einstein was born in 1879 with a head shaped like a lopsided medicine ball. Seeing it for the first time, his grandmother fell into shock. "Much too fat!" she exclaimed. "Much too fat!" He didn't speak until he was three, and it was generally assumed that he was brain-damaged. Even as a child, he lived mostly in his mind, building intricate card houses, marveling at a compass his father showed him. His faith was less in people than in the things of the world. When his sister Maja was born, young Albert, crestfallen, said, "Yes, but where are its wheels?"

As a man, he grew into a powerful body with thick arms and legs. He liked to hike and sail but spent most of his life sitting still, dreaming of the universe. In 1905, as a twenty-six-year-old patent clerk in Bern, Switzerland, he conceived of the special theory of relativity and the equation $E = mc^2$, a supposition that all matter, from a feather to a rock, contains energy. And with his theories that predicted the origin, nature, and destiny of the universe, he toppled Newton and more than two hundred years of science. When the first inkling of relativity occurred to him, he casually told a friend, "Thank you. I've completely solved the problem."

So complex were his findings that they could only be partially understood and verified fourteen years later. Then, of course, Albert Einstein instantly became famous. His mischievous smile beamed from newspapers around the world. A genius! A Nobel Prize! A guru-mystic who had unlocked the secrets of God's own mind! There were suddenly hundreds of books on relativity. Einstein embarked on a frenzied world tour, was fêted by kings and emperors and presidents, gamboling into the world's most sacred halls in a sockless state of bemused dishevelment. He claimed he got his hairstyle—eventually a wild, electric-white nimbus—"through negligence" and, explaining his overall sloppiness, said, "It would be a sad situation if the wrapper were better than the meat wrapped inside it." He laughed like a barking seal, snored like a foghorn, sunbathed in the nude. And then took tea with the queen.

Everywhere, it was Einstein mania. People named their children after him, fawned and fainted upon seeing him, wrote letters inquiring if he really existed. He was asked to "perform" at London's Palladium for three weeks on the same bill as fire-eaters and tightrope walkers, explaining his theory, at a price of his asking. "At the Chrysanthemum Festival," wrote one German diplomat stationed in Japan, "it was neither the empress nor the prince regent nor the imperial princes who held reception; everything turned around Einstein." A copy of the special theory of relativity in Einstein's scrawl was auctioned off for $6 million. And *The New York Times* urged its readers not to be offended by the fact that only twelve people in the world truly understood the theory of "the suddenly famous Dr. Einstein."

In the years to follow, Einstein's fame would only grow. He would vehemently criticize the Nazis and become a target for German ultranationalists, who waited outside his home and office, hurling anti-Semitic obscenities at him. When they made him a target for assassination, he fled to the United States—to Princeton, New Jersey—and became an American citizen. He was called "the new Columbus of science." David Ben-Gurion offered him the presidency of Israel (to everyone's relief, he declined). His political utterances were as good as Gandhi's. Before Michael Jordan was beamed by satellite to China, before Marilyn Monroe and the Beatles and Arnold Schwarzenegger, Albert Einstein was the first transglobal supercelebrity.

In the last years of his life, he was struck with frequent attacks of nausea, the pain flowering between his shoulder blades, culminating in diarrhea or vomiting. An exam revealed an aneurysm in his abdominal aorta, but Einstein refused an operation and anticipated his own demise. "I want to be cremated so people won't come to worship at my bones," he said. On the night before he died, April 17, 1955, lying in bed in Princeton Hospital, Einstein asked to see his most recent pages of calculations, typically working until the end. His last words were spoken in German to a nurse who didn't know the language, though sometime earlier he had told a friend, "I have finished my task here."

The next morning, April 18, when the chief pathologist of the hospital—our Harvey, then a strapping forty-two-year-old with Montgomery Clift good looks—arrived for work, Einstein's body was laid out, naked and mottle-skinned, on a gurney. "Imagine my surprise," Harvey says to me now. "A fellow up in New

York, my former teacher Dr. Zimmerman"—and an acquaintance of Einstein's—"was going to do the autopsy. But then he
couldn't get away. He rang me up, and we agreed that I'd do it."
Harvey says that he felt awe when he came face-to-face with the
world-famous physicist, the voice of conscience in a century of
madness, who had bewildered the world by suggesting that time
should be understood as the fourth, and inseparable, dimension.
Now he lay alone in the pale light, 180 pounds of mere matter.

Harvey took a scalpel in his hand and sliced Einstein open
with a Y incision, scoring the belly, the skin giving like cellophane,
then cut the rib cartilage and lifted the sternum. He found nearly
three quarts of blood in Einstein's peritoneal cavity, a result of the
burst aneurysm, and after investigating his heart and veins concluded that, with an operation, the physicist might have lived for
several more years, though how long was hard to tell "because
Einstein liked his fatty foods," in particular goose scratchings.

Working under the humming lights, his fingers inside Einstein's opened body, juggling the liver, palpating the heart, Harvey made a decision. Who's to say whether it was inspired by awe
or by greed, beneficence or mere pettiness? Who's to say what
comes over a mortal, what chemical reaction takes place deep in
the thalamus, when faced with the blinding brightness of another's greatness and, with it, a knowledge that I/you/we shall
never possess even a cheeseparing of that greatness?

Working quickly with a knife, Harvey tonsured the scalp,
peeled the skin back, and, bearing down on a saw, cut through
Einstein's head with a quick, hacking motion. He removed a cap
of bone, peeled back the meninges, then clipped blood vessels
and bundles of nerve and the spinal cord. He reached with his
fingers deeper into the chalice of the man's cranium and simply
removed the glistening brain. To keep for himself. Forever. In
perpetuity. Amen.

What he didn't count on, however, was that with this one act his whole world would go haywire. Apparently, word got out through Zimmerman that Harvey had the brain, and when it was reported in *The New York Times* a day later, some people were aghast. Einstein's son, Hans Albert, reportedly felt betrayed. Harvey claimed that he was planning to conduct medical research on the brain, and, in an agreement eventually struck with Hans Albert over the phone, he promised that the brain would be the subject only of medical journals and not become a pop-cultural gewgaw, as the Einsteins most feared. Sometime after the autopsy, Harvey was fired from his job for refusing to give up the brain. Years passed, and there were no papers, no findings. And then Harvey fell off the radar screen. When he gave an occasional interview—in articles from 1956 and 1979 and 1988—he always repeated that he was about "a year away from finishing study on the specimen."[1]

Forty years later—after Harvey has gone through three wives, after he has sunk to lesser circumstances, after he has outlived most of his critics and accusers, including Hans Albert—we are sitting together before a hot fire on a cold winter day. And because I like him so much, because somewhere in his watery blue eyes, his genial stumble-footing, and that ineffable cloak of hunched integrity that falls over the old, I find myself feeling for him and cannot bring myself to ask the essential questions:

Is Harvey a grave-robbing thief or a hero? A sham artist or a high priest? Why not heist a finger or a toe? Or a simple earlobe? What about rumors that he plans to sell Einstein's brain to Michael Jackson for $2 million? Does he feel ashamed? Or justified? If the brain is the ultimate Fabergé egg, the Hope Diamond, the

1. According to newspaper accounts following Einstein's death, mystery immediately shrouded the brain. Dr. Zimmerman, on staff at New York City's Montefiore Medical Center, expected to receive Einstein's brain from Harvey, but never, in fact, did; Princeton Hospital decided not to relinquish the brain. Harvey, however, also decided not to relinquish the brain, and at some point removed it from the hospital.

Cantino map, the One-Cent Magenta stamp, *Guernica,* what does it look like? Feel like? Smell like? Does he talk to it as one talks to one's poodle or ferns?

We conclude the visit by going out for sushi, and over the course of our conversation he mentions a handful of people he hopes to see before he dies. "Yessir, I'd really like to visit some folks," he says. They include a few neuroanatomists with whom he has brain business, some friends, and, in Berkeley, Evelyn Einstein, Hans Albert's daughter and the granddaughter of Albert. Harvey has wanted to meet her for many years. Although he doesn't say why, I wonder if he's trying to face down some lingering guilt, some late-in-life desire to resolve the past before his age grounds him permanently and, with his death, the brain falls into someone else's hands. Perhaps, too, he wants to make arrangements for someone to take over the brain, and Evelyn is going to be interviewed for the job. Whatever the reason, by the meal's end, doped on the incessant tinkling of piped-in harps and a heady shot of *tekka maki,* Harvey and I have somehow agreed to take a road trip: I will drive him to California.

And then, one afternoon soon before our departure, Harvey takes me to a secret location—one he asks me not to reveal for fear of thieves and rambunctious pilgrims—where he now keeps the brain. From a dark room he retrieves a box that contains two glass jars full of Einstein's brain. After the autopsy, he had it chopped into nearly two hundred pieces—from the size of a dime to that of a thick turkey neck—and since then he has given nearly a third of it away to various people. He parades the jars before me but only for a second, then retreats quickly with them. The brain pieces float in murky formaldehyde, leaving an impression of very chunky chicken soup. But it happens so quickly, Harvey so suddenly absconds with the brain, that I have no real idea what I've seen.

When I show up at his house a few weeks later in a rented

Buick Skylark, Harvey has apparently fished several fistfuls' worth of brain matter from the jars, put them in Tupperware filled with formaldehyde, and zipped it all inside a gray duffel bag. He meets me in his driveway with a plaid suitcase rimmed with fake leather and the gray duffel sagging heavily in his right hand. He pecks Cleora goodbye. "He's a fine Quaker gentleman," she tells me, watching Harvey's curled-over self shuffle across the pavement. He rubs a smudge of dirt off my side mirror, then toodles around the front of the car. When he's fallen into the passenger seat, he chuckles nervously, scratchily clears his throat, and utters what will become his mantra, "Yessir . . . real good." And then we just start driving. For four thousand miles. Me, Harvey, and, in the trunk, Einstein's brain.

Toward Columbus, Ohio. February 18.

We morph into one. Even if we are more than a half century apart in age, he born under the star of William Howard Taft and I under the napalm bomb of Lyndon Baines Johnson, if he wears black Wallabees and I sport Oakley sunglasses, if he has three ex-wives, ten children, and twelve grandchildren and I have yet to procreate, we begin to think together, to make unconscious team decisions. It seems the entire backseat area will serve as a kind of trash can. By the time we make Wheeling, West Virginia, it's already strewn with books and tissuey green papers from the rental-car agreement, snack wrappers, and empty bottles of seltzer, a hedge against "G.I. upset," as Harvey puts it. An old rambler at heart, he takes to the road like it's a river of fine brandy, seems to grow stronger on its oily fumes and oily-rainbow mirages, its oily fast food and the oily-tarmacked gas plazas that we skate across for candy bars and Coca-Colas while the Skylark feeds at the pump. By default, I take charge of the radio—working the

dial in a schizophrenic riffle from NPR to Dr. Laura and, in between, all kinds of high school basketball, gardening shows, local
on-air auctions, blathering DJs, farm reports, and Christian call-
in shows. Harvey is hard of hearing in his right ear and, perhaps
out of pride or vanity, refuses to wear a hearing aid, so I've
brought music, too, figuring he might do a fair amount of sleeping while, as designated driver, I might do more staying awake.
I've got bands with names like Dinosaur Jr., Soul Coughing, and
Pavement, and a book on tape, *Neuromancer,* by William Gibson.
Harvey himself is partial to classical music and reads mostly scientific journals and novels by Kay Boyle.

And although we are now bound by the road—Einstein's
brain, Harvey, and I—he studiously avoids all discussion of the
brain. Earlier, however, he ticked off twelve different researchers
to whom he had given slices. According to Harvey, one of them,
Sandra Witelson from McMaster University in Hamilton, On-
tario, organized his ephemera and articles on the brain into a
scrapbook, and he turned over nearly a fifth of the brain to her.
"She has one of the biggest collections of brains around," he says
proudly. "She gets them from a local undertaker." (Later, when
contacted, Witelson said that Harvey's assertions about her were
"incorrect.")

In most cases, Harvey has made it sound as if he himself
handpicked these people after reading their work, though by
some of their own admissions, a number of them had contacted
him first. One neuroanatomist, a Berkeley professor named Marian Diamond, had written a paper claiming that she had counted
in Einstein's brain a higher than normal number of glial cells,
which nourish the organ. The only other paper written to date,
by a researcher at the University of Alabama named Britt Ander-
son, stated that Einstein had a thinner cortex than normal. "You
see," says Harvey enthusiastically, "we're finding out that Ein-

stein's brain is more unusual than many people first thought." But a professor of neurobiology at UCLA, Larry Kruger, calls the "meagre findings" on the brain "laughable" and says that when Diamond herself delivered her paper, the audience found it "comical," because "it means absolutely nothing." (When I asked Diamond, a woman with impeccable credentials, about this, she claimed that Kruger had "a lack of inhibitor cells" and said, "Well, we have to start somewhere, don't we?")

Despite my expectations that Harvey will sleep a good deal, what I soon realize is that he's damn perky for eighty-four and never sleeps at all. Nor talks much. In this age of self-revelation, he eschews the orotundity of a confessor. He speaks in a clipped, spare, almost penurious way—with a barely perceptible drawl from his midwestern childhood—letting huge blocks of time fall in between the subject and the verb, and then between the verb and the object of a sentence. He pronounces "pleasure" *play-sure,* and "measurements" *may-sure-mints.* When my line of questioning makes him uncomfortable, he chuckles flatly like two chops of wood, "Heh-heh," raspily clears his throat, then says, "Way-ell . . ." And just steps aside to let some more time pass, returning to his map, which he studies like it's a rune. Through the window he watches Pennsylvania pass by: its barns and elaborate hexes, signs for Amish goods, the Allegheny Mountains rising like dark whales out of the earth, lost behind the mist of some unseen blowhole. He watches Ohio all pan-flattened and thrown back down on itself. And he blinks languidly at it. But never sleeps.

I admit: This disappoints me. Something in me wants Harvey to sleep. I want Harvey to fall into a deep, blurry, Rip Van Winkle daze, and I want to park the Skylark mothership on top of a mountain and walk around to the trunk and open it. I want Harvey snoring loudly as I unzip the duffel bag and reach my hands inside, and I want to—what?—touch Einstein's brain. I want to touch the brain. Yes, I've said it. I want to hold it, coddle it, measure its weight in my palm, handle some of its fifteen billion now-dormant neurons. Does it feel like tofu, sea urchin, baloney? What, exactly? And what does such a desire make me? One of the legion of relic freaks who send Harvey letters asking, sometimes begging, for pieces of the brain? One of the pilgrims who come from as far away as Japan or England or Australia to glimpse it?

For Harvey's sake, I act like I haven't given the brain a second thought, while he encourages stultifying state-long silences and offers the occasional historical anecdote. "Eisenhower's farm was in these parts, I believe." Or, "In the days of the canal . . ." The more the idea persists in my head, the more towns slip past outside the window, the more I wonder what, in fact, I'd really be holding if I held the brain. I mean, it's not really Einstein, and it's not really a brain but disconnected pieces of a brain, just as the passing farms are not really America but parts of a whole, symbols of the thing itself, which is everything and nothing at once.

In part, I would be touching Einstein the Superstar, immediately recognizable by his Krameresque hair and the both mournful and mirthful eyes. The man whose apotheosis is so complete that he's now a coffee mug, a postcard, a T-shirt. The face zooming out of a pop rock video on MTV's *Buzz Clip* for a song called "MMMBop." A figure of speech, an ad pitchman. The voice of reason on posters festooning undergrad dorm rooms. Despite the fact that he was a sixty-one-year-old man when he was naturalized as an American citizen, Einstein has been fully appropriated by this country, by our writers and moralists, politicians and scientists, cult leaders and clergy. In the fin-de-siècle shadows of America, in our antsy, searching times, Einstein comes back to us both as Lear's fool and Tiresias, comically offering his uncanny vision of the future while cautioning us against the violence that lurks in the heart of man. "I do not know how the Third World War will be fought," he warned, "but I do know how the Fourth will: with sticks and stones."

To complete his American deification, Einstein has been fully commodified and marketed, earning millions of dollars for his estate. Bought and sold back to us by the foot soldiers of high capitalism, Einstein's name and image are conjured to sell computers and CD-ROMs, Nikon cameras and myriad baubles. In fact, a Los Angeles celebrity-licensing agency handles his account.

But why so much commotion over a guy with sweaty feet and rumpled clothes? The answer is perhaps found in a feeling that Einstein was not one of us. It seems we regard him as being supernatural. Because he glimpsed the very workings of the universe and returned with God on his tongue, because he greeted this era by rocketing into the next with his breakthrough theories, he assumed a mien of supernaturalism. And because his tatterdemalion, at times dotty demeanor stood in such stark contrast to his supernaturalism, he seemed both innocent and trustworthy, and thus that much more supernatural. He alone held the seashell of the century to his ear.

Einstein is also one of the few figures born in the past century whose ideas are equally relevant to us today. If we've incorporated the theory of relativity into our scientific view of the universe, it's Einstein's attempt to devise a kind of personal religion—an intimate spiritual and political manifesto—that still stands in stark, almost sacred contrast to the Pecksniffian systems of salvation offered by the modern world. Depending on the day's sex crimes and senseless murders, or the intensity of our millennial migraine, we run the real risk of feeling straitjacketed and sacrificed to everything from organized religion to the nuclear blood lust of nations to the cult visionaries of our world and their various vodka-and-cuckoo schemes, their Hale-Bopp fantasies.

Thus Einstein's blending of twentieth-century skepticism with nineteenth-century romanticism offers a kind of modern hope. "I am a deeply religious nonbeliever," he said. "This is a somewhat new kind of religion." Pushing further, he sought to marry science and religion by redefining their terms. "I am of the opinion that all the finer speculations in the realm of science spring from a deep religious feeling," he said. "I also believe that this kind of religiousness . . . is the only creative religious activity of our time."

To touch Einstein's brain would also be to touch the white dwarf and the black hole, the Big Bang and ghost waves. To ride a ray of light, as Einstein once dreamed it as a child, into utter oblivion. He imagined that a clock placed on the equator would run more slowly than a clock placed at one of the poles under identical conditions. Einstein claimed that the happiest thought of his life came to him in 1907, at the patent office in Bern, when he was twenty-eight and couldn't find a teaching job. Up to his ears in a worsted wool suit and patent applications, a voice in his mind whispered, "If a person falls freely, he won't feel his own weight." That became the general theory of relativity. His life and ideas continue to fill thousands of books; even today, scientists are still verifying his work. Recently, a NASA satellite took millions of measurements in space that proved a uniform distribution of primordial temperatures just above absolute zero; that is, the data proved that the universe was in a kind of postcoital afterglow from the Big Bang, further confirming Einstein's explanation of how the universe began.

It would be good to touch that.

We disembark that first night at a Best Western in Columbus, Ohio. As we open the trunk to gather our bags, I watch Harvey take what he needs, then leave the gray duffel there, the zipper shining like silver teeth in the streetlight.

"Is it safe?" I ask, nodding toward the duffel.

"Is what safe?" Harvey asks back, gelid eyes sparking once in the dark. He doesn't seem to know or remember. He's carried the contraband for so long he's come to consider himself something of a celebrity. No longer defined by the specimen, he's the real specimen. A piece of living history. On tour. In his glen-plaid suitcase, he carries postcards of himself.

Inside his motel room with the brain, Harvey gathers the sleep of the old. Next door I am exhausted yet wide awake. I am thinking of the brain, remembering that after more than eight million people had marched to their deaths in the fields of Europe during World War I, Einstein's theory of relativity allowed humanity, in the words of a colleague, to look up from an "earth covered with graves and blood to the heavens covered with the stars." He suddenly appeared on the world's doorstep, inspiring pan-national awe and offering with it pan-national reconciliation—a liberal German Jew who clung to his Swiss citizenship and renounced violence. What better way to absolve oneself of all sins than to follow a blameless scientist up into the twinkling waters of time and space?

Another contemporary of Einstein's, Erwin Schrödinger, claimed that Einstein's theory of relativity quite simply meant "the dethronement of time as a rigid tyrant," opening up the possibility that there might be an alternative Master Plan. "And this thought," he wrote, "is a religious thought, nay I should call it *the* religious thought." With relativity, Einstein, the original cosmic slacker, was himself touching the mind of a new god, forming a conga line to immortality through some wrinkle in time. "It is quite possible that we can do greater things than Jesus," he said.

That, finally, was Einstein's ultimate power and hold on our imagination. Eternity—it would be good to touch that, too.

Kansas City, Missouri. February 19.

Across Indiana, Illinois, and Missouri, beneath scudding clouds and clear shots of sunlight, the chill air fragrant with manure and feed. We pass over the chocolate, moiling Mississippi, drive near the towns of Emma and Bellflower, Peruque and Auxvasse. We stealth through shadows thrown by crop dusters and Greyhound buses, up against wobbling fifty-three-foot truck trailers full of movie videos or broccoli or industrial turbines and, at one point, a flatbed with a Vietnam-era helicopter strapped to it. On this bright, windy day, we see the outbuildings and barns of the Midwest, where farmers stand in small circles eyeing their fields like nervous, hand-wringing fathers, repairing their threshers, turning the first soil, pointing to what's yet invisible, speaking in incantations: feed and fertilizer, moisture content and till depth. With each day's work, with each fieldside conference and hour alone in the air-conditioned cab of a supertractor, they will silently appeal to the circadian rhythms of some higher power for a perfect calibration of sun and rain, as well as for the perfect ascension of market prices to deliver a bountiful harvest. On the radio, we get the farm reports: Lean hog futures down five-eighths; feeder cattle futures up a half. Corn futures and soybean and cocoa, up an eighth, down a third, even. January sugar and March corn; September rice and December cotton—all of them attached to a momentary price that may right now be making someone rich as it bankrupts someone else.

"Look at that cow!" exclaims Harvey.

And it is quite a cow! On this afternoon together, something is beginning to happen out here among us, the three of us.

Time is slowing, it seems, or expanding to fill a bigger sky, a more open landscape. The got-to-be-there self-importance of the East, its frantic floodlight charge, has given way to a single lit parlor lamp. And under it, a cow or one silver tree in the wind or the rusted remains of an old tiller seems more holy, even mythic. It's not that the Midwest lacks bustle; it's just that away from the cities, the deadlines are imposed by the earth and its seasons. I slip off my watch and feel myself beginning to slow into Harvey time.

We are, in fact, retracing Harvey's route when he came west from New Jersey in the 1960s, after eluding those who desired the brain for themselves. Within weeks of Einstein's death, after it was reported that the brain had been taken from the body, a group of leading brain researchers met in Washington, D.C. It was an august collection of men: Doctors Webb Haymaker and Hartwig Kuhlenbeck, Clem Fox and Gerhardt von Bonin, Jerzy E. Rose and Walle Nauta. And necessarily among them, but perhaps regarded with a tinge of condescension, this slightly awkward, nervously chuckling half doctor, this Irregular Sock, this pathologist from a small-town hospital connected only by the same name to the hallowed halls and elite eating clubs of Princeton University. When Webb Haymaker, who represented the U.S. Army, demanded the brain, Harvey simply refused to hand it over. *Heh-heh.* When Haymaker got angry, Harvey didn't budge. And now who laughs last? Who's dead, each last one of them, and who's out here busting for California with the brain, inhaling Frosties and baked potatoes, hoovering Denny's pancakes and green salads and chicken noodle soup?

"Harvey didn't know his ass from his elbow from the brain," says Larry Kruger, who at the time was a postdoctoral fellow with Jerzy Rose at Johns Hopkins. "Harvey refused to give up the brain even though he wasn't a neuropathologist, and then all bets were off. I mean, what were you going to do with it, anyway? I heard he kept it in his basement and would show it to visitors. I guess some people show off a rare edition of Shakespeare. He would say, 'Hey, wanna see Einstein's brain?' The guy's a jerk. . . . He wanted fame and nothing came of it."[2]

Meanwhile, Harvey bristles at such suggestions, regards himself as destiny's chosen one, the man who forever belongs with Einstein's brain, for better or for worse. In a way, it is a tale of obsessive love: Humbert Humbert and his Lolita. But Harvey sees it more prosaically: "Yup, I was just so fortunate to be the one to walk in the room that morning," he repeats again and again. Prior to that April morning in 1955, Harvey's life hardly augured greatness as much as it did stolid servitude and an abiding curiosity in science. He had met Einstein only once, to take blood from him. Expecting his usual nurse for such a menial chore, the ever-lustful scientist saw Harvey and blurted, "You've changed your sex!" Summing up his years as a pathologist, Harvey says, "It was great to try to figure out what killed someone."

Sawed-off statements like these initially make it easy to, well, feel underwhelmed by Harvey. In part, it is simply Quaker modesty, a respectful reticence, beneath which lies a diamond-sharp, at times even cunning man who has survived over four decades with the brain. Harvey grew up in a Kentucky line of dyed-in-the-wool Quakers, then moved to Hartford, Connecticut, when his father got a good job with an insurance firm. Later, he attended Yale, where he contracted tuberculosis, then spent over a year in a sanatorium, and when he returned to school, he gave up his dreams of doctoring and turned to pathology because

2. Later, when I visit Kruger in Los Angeles amid the clutter of his office, which includes an oversized book entitled *A Dendro-cyto-myeloarchitectonic Atlas of the Cat's Brain,* he's a bit more judicious. "What [Harvey] did is probably illegal," he tells me. "I guess he must be a slightly strange guy. . . . Had he been smart, he would have given it up and moved away from it, but he was grandstanding, and I presume he paid a price for it."

"the hours were less demanding." He lists that year of sickness and the later revocation of his medical license as among the greatest disappointments of his life. Did he pay a price for the brain? Perhaps. He was soon fired from his job at the hospital and divorced from his first wife. In the next years he drifted through jobs at state psychiatric hospitals and medical labs, another wife, and then picked up and moved west to start a general practice in Weston, Missouri, which eventually folded. Later, he lost his medical license after failing a three-day test and was forced to work the late shift as an extruder at a plastics factory in Lawrence, Kansas. All of it after the brain, perhaps because of the brain.

Nonetheless, a life isn't one paragraph long, and we might also consider Harvey a happy man, maybe with each move feeling himself to be on to the next adventure, with each wife and child perhaps feeling himself loved. Still, I try to picture him standing before Einstein's body—in that one naked moment.

Only occasionally can you glimpse, through the embrasures of an otherwise perfectly polite person, the cannons aimed outward; only in a certain glint of light do the eyeteeth become fangs. We are driven by desire and fear. Only in our solitary hungers do we find ourselves capable of the most magnificently unexpected sins.

Lawrence, Kansas. February 20.

In the heart of America, a psychic vortex. We cruise through a neighborhood of picket fences and leafless trees, parking before a small red house, a four-room once built from a Sears, Roebuck kit, replete with bookcases of paperback horror fiction and wax skulls. Here lives Harvey's former neighbor, the soon-to-be-late novelist William S. Burroughs. It's both odd and fitting that the man who allegedly stole Einstein's brain once lived with said brain just around the corner from William Burroughs, the strange, kinetic father of the Beats, as if Harvey were an invention of one of his novels.

While their neighborhood encounters didn't add up to much—Harvey remembers one extended meeting—he treats their reunion with all the gravitas of the Potsdam Conference. Shuffling across the front porch now, Harvey clasps the old writer's hand, enunciating loudly, believing that the eighty-three-year-old Burroughs is equally deaf, which he isn't, then climbs up his arm until they are in a startled embrace, the two of them as pale as the marble of a Rodin sculpture. "REAL, REAL GOOD TO SEE YA!" Later, Harvey quaffs glasses of burgundy until he turns bright red; Burroughs, himself a bowed and hollowed cult hero and keeper of the Secret—his cheeks dimpled as if by the tip of a blade, a handgun in a holster over his kidney—drinks five Coke and vodkas after taking his daily dose of methadone.

"Have you ever tried morphine, Doctor?" he asks Harvey.

"NO. NO, I HAVEN'T," yells Harvey earnestly.

"Unbelievable. In Tangiers, there was a most magnificent, most significant drug . . . went there just to have the last of it. Last there ever was. Tell me about your addictions, Doctor."

"WELL, HEH-HEH . . ." But then Harvey keeps quiet about the brain.

Burroughs lights a joint and offers it to Harvey, who demurs, smoke swirling around his head like a wreath of steam from a Turkish bath.

"DID YOU BECOME ADDICTED BECAUSE YOU FELT PAIN?"

"I wish I could say that, Doctor, but no," says Burroughs, considering. "I became addicted because I wanted more."

Later, when the two soused men face each other for a goodbye on the tippy front porch—for no apparent reason, Burroughs now calls him Dr. Senegal—the writer lowers his voice and delivers a farewell chestnut, one that Harvey receives with a knowing nod, though it isn't clear he actually hears it. "What keeps the old alive, Dr. Senegal," advises Burroughs, "is that we learn to be evil."

And then we are out in the night, in a downpour, Harvey trundling toward the car for what feels like a small eternity. Behind him Burroughs sways, curling and unfurling his arms like elephant trunks, then assumes a position of Buddhist prayer—pale, delirious, still.

Toward Dodge City, Kansas. February 21.

We wake in Lawrence to a nuclear-powered snow, driving horizontally, starring the windows with ice, piling up until the Skylark looks like a soap-flake duck float in a Memorial Day parade gone terribly wrong. Everything is suddenly heaped in the frigid no-smell of winter, cars skidding, then running off roadsides into gulleys. The snow falls in thick sheaves, icicles jag the gutters. It feels like Lawrence is going back to a day, 500,000 years ago, when it was buried under hundreds of feet of ice.

We take shelter in our adjoining rooms at the Westminster Inn, are slow to rise. When we do, Harvey is bright-eyed and spunky as we find the good people of Kansas doing what they do in a blizzard: eating pancakes. The Village Inn Pancake House Restaurant—real name—is packed: college students and retirees, all flannel-shirted, how-are-yas ricocheting everywhere, steak-and-egg specials zooming by on super-white plates. Some of the old men wear Dickies work pants and baseball caps with automotive labels; the undergrads sport caps emblazoned with team names or slogans like WHATEVER or RAGE or GOOD TO GO.

Even in the no-smoking section everyone smokes—one of Harvey's pet peeves.

Our routine in restaurants follows a familiar pattern: Harvey meditates over the menu, examining it, dissecting, vectoring, and equating what his stomach really wants. I get a newspaper and usually skim through the first section before he's ready. Even as James Earl Ray is planning to go on *The Montel Williams Show* to plead for a new liver and two teenagers are indicted for the murder and dismemberment of a man in Central Park, there's an ongoing existential debate raging in Harvey's head: salty or sweet, eggs or waffles with maple syrup.

Occasionally, after a particularly deliberate order, he'll deliberately change it. Our waitress is a pathologically smiley KU student, well versed in the dynamics of a breakfast rush, the coffee-craving, caffeine-induced chaos of it all. She waits as Harvey takes a second look at the menu. It could be that an actual week passes as he clears his throat a couple of times, then ponders some more, but she smiles patiently and then chirps back. "Eggs over easy, bacon, wheat toast, home fries. More coffee?"

This town was once the setting for a Jason Robards made-for-television movie called *The Day After*. In it, the sturdy people of America's Hometown were blown to smithereens in a nuclear attack, and the few who survived wandered in a postapocalyptic stupor, in rags, bodies flowered with keloid scars. That Lawrence would become connected in the nation's psyche with nuclear devastation and that Einstein's brain, the power that unknowingly wrought the bomb, rested here for six or seven years is a small pixel of irony that seems to escape Harvey. When I ask him about it, he says, "Way-ell, I guess that's true." And starts laughing.

The truth is that Einstein himself was confounded by the idea that his theory of relativity had opened up a Pandora's box of mutually assured annihilation. In a 1935 press conference, in which he was asked about the possibility of an atomic bomb, the physicist said that the likelihood of transforming matter into energy was "something akin to shooting birds in the dark in a country where there are only a few birds." Four years later, however, the Nazis had invaded Poland, and Einstein, the celebrated pacifist, signed a letter to President Roosevelt advocating the building of an atomic weapon. When the letter was personally delivered to Roosevelt, the president immediately saw the gravity of the situation—that if the Americans had just decided to build a bomb, perhaps the Nazis, with great scientists such as Heisenberg, were well on their way to completing one—and ordered his chief of staff to begin immediate top-secret plans that led to the building of an atomic weapon. Sometime later, on a mesa in New Mexico, rose the Town That Never Was, Los Alamos, and under the guidance of Robert Oppenheimer came Little Boy and Fat Man, the bombs that would eventually decimate Hiroshima and Nagasaki, respectively.

Einstein, who was thought to be a Communist sympathizer by the FBI and an untrustworthy, outspoken pacifist by the Roosevelt administration, was not part of Oppenheimer's team. In fact, he had nothing whatsoever to do with the bomb, though even today his name is connected to it. The letter to Roosevelt haunted him and his family and, in one case, incited a physical attack against Einstein's son, Hans Albert. Writing to Linus Pauling, Einstein called the letter the "one mistake" of his life. When the bomb was dropped on Hiroshima—on August 6, 1945— Einstein heard the news after waking from a nap at Saranac Lake, in upstate New York. "Oy vay," he said wearily. "Alas."

When Harvey and I loop back on Interstate 70 heading west, the snow has slowed to mere ticks. In this single day, we will live through four seasons. Which can happen if one drives long enough with Einstein's brain in the trunk. Time bends and accelerates and overlaps; simultaneity rules. Heading north now to Lucas, Kansas, and a tourist spot known as the Garden of Eden, a spring wind suddenly whips across the prairie. Borne along on it, we rack up our first speeding ticket.

My strategy has been to keep the Skylark at seventy-five or eighty, scanning the road for cops, and when feeling luxurious or bored rotten to push it to eighty-five max. Which is precisely what I get nailed for—eighty-five in a sixty-five-mile-per-hour zone. The state trooper asks me to join him in his cruiser, and I don't try to defend my actions, the greed of speed. "Where you boys going in such a hurry?" he asks. Glancing through the windshield of the cruiser into the back window of the car, I can just make out the silver crown of Harvey's head, and I'm overcome with the desire to confess. It's not exactly as if we have a dead body in the trunk, but it's not as if we don't, either.

For some reason, though—perhaps out of self-preservation, for fear of losing the brain altogether—I simply say, "California." The trooper writes out the ticket, warns me against reckless driving in his state, and sets me free. When he turns off the road in the opposite direction, I hike the speedometer up to eighty and hold it steady.

We drive south to Dodge City, the Ogallala Aquifer under our wheels, huge cow-uddered clouds overhead. On the radio: steer calves and heifers for sale, Red Angus bulls, yearlings with good genetics and quality carcass. Later, Bobby Darin singing "Beyond the Sea," Harvey tapping a finger on his knee, the brain sloshing in its Tupperware. In this happy moment, we could probably drive forever.

By twilight, a nocturne of rain on the roof of the Skylark. We pass a pungent nitrogen plant, itself like a twisted metallic brain. Water towers gleam in the silver light like spaceships, telephone poles pass like crucifixes, and grain elevators rise like organ pipes from the plains.

Out here, too, just before Dodge City and a most delicious

slab of Angus fillet, before a night at the Astro Motel and a dawn that brings a herd of eighteen-wheelers hurtling for Abilene, we see a rainbow and come face-to-face with Harvey's blighted ambition. "I remember more rainbows in Kansas than any other state," he says, blinking his moist eyes at the brilliant beams of blue and green, orange and yellow. "I used to try to photograph rainbows, but they never turned out."

Somewhere east of Los Alamos, New Mexico. February 22.

A confession: Over the last days, at truck stops and drive-thrus, at restaurants and gas stations, I've kept our secret that we've got Einstein's brain stashed in the trunk, and it's taken its psychic toll. There have been moments when I've been alone with the brain—Harvey in a restroom or loitering before postcards on a spinning display—when I've opened up the car trunk and looked in, pinched the cold zipper between my thumb and forefinger, but then couldn't bring myself to unzip the duffel and unsheathe the brain. Too much of a violation, an untenable breach in our manly society, even as Harvey covets for himself the gray matter upon which our private Skylarkian democracy is founded. In fact, we've been together now for nearly five full days, and he won't show me the brain. When I bring it up in conversation, he doesn't want to talk about it. When I ask him what parts of the brain we're traveling with exactly, he says he doesn't know and changes the subject. It is as if I am trying to find the hidden center of his power. Which I am.

Leaving the Astro Motel the next morning, I unexpectedly spill my guts at the front desk as I return our room keys to the manager. I tell him we've got the brain in the trunk, adding that we're headed to California to show it to Einstein's granddaughter. The manager, an affable, middle-aged man, stops for a moment and looks at me sideways, realizes I'm serious, and tries to be hospitable. "Einstein, huh? That guy knew some things," he says, folding his arms, shifting his weight. "That guy really did have a brain. But I wouldn't have wanted to live with him. You know . . . a little weirdy." He spins his finger in a cuckoo circle around his ear. "I have a nephew who is kind of a genius, but he hasn't flaked off yet. I met a guy in California who was so smart he couldn't talk. He sure could tell you how to look at the moon, but he couldn't tell you how to tie your shoes."

I'm not sure that I feel better, though I know that, in his way, he has tried to help. But does he scribble down our license plate number as we leave?

In Liberal, Kansas, we eat at a glassed-in coffin of a restaurant called Mr. Breakfast. Old folks arrive in old, rusted Ford pickups, chain-smoking, hacking phlegm. Swab runny eggs with Wonder Bread toast, gulp mud-water coffee. Looking around—Harvey fitting right in among the chorfing, anonymous throng—one discerns that this is not a bunch racing toward the millennium, that the millennium may, in fact, only be a construction of the coastal power elite, a media-and-marketing event. Frankly, out in America, you get the feeling that America is dying. And along its highways and byways, the country seems less ready to leap into the future than it is already clinging to a sepia-toned past when America stood as the unencumbered Big Boy in a Manichean world of good and evil, capitalists and Commies. Even the neon oasis-pods of the interstate—the perpetual clusters of Wendy's, McDonald's, Denny's, and Burger King—are crowded with people strangely reclaiming bygone days, connecting themselves to some prior eating experience, reveling in the familiar.

We gas down into Oklahoma (through Tyrone, Hooker, Guymon, and Texhoma) and then the Texas Panhandle (edging the Rita Blanca National Grassland, through Stratford, Dalhart, and Nara Visa)—all of it flat, with oil rigs like metronomes. I've taken to photographing Harvey by various signs and monuments along the road, and when we drift by a huge wooden cowboy with two guns blazing out across the empty plains, Harvey poses between his legs. By the New Mexico border, the wood-frame farmhouses have transmogrified into adobe. In Tucumcari, almost on cue, there is red dirt and tumbleweed. We drive through ruts and washes, over tableland and mesa. Here the hills are testicular, the ancient mounds monslike, but all of it has a desiccated, washed-out sexuality, decayed from a time when this place was overrun by dinosaurs. We climb the crags that rim the Pajarito Plateau to Los Alamos—the gridded, repressed hothouse that wrought Little Boy and Fat Man. In the rush of cacti, my frustration with Harvey's Humbertness, with his protective zeal, has bled into a kind of benevolent respect, an idea that Harvey actually may be a revolutionary hero. For wasn't he the one who thumbed his nose at the great U.S. Army doctor, Webb Haymaker, upped the establishment, and legged it out West on an end around with the brain? Maybe he thought he was protecting the brain from the so-called experts, or saving the brain of one of the world's greatest pacifists from the clutches of the U.S. military. Wouldn't that make him the perfect Einsteinian hero?

After all, Einstein himself had nothing but disdain for authority, spent a life shirking it. In a letter to his friend Queen Elisabeth of Belgium that described the stuffy hierarchy of his adopted hometown, Princeton, he said it was "a quaint and ceremonious village of puny demigods on stilts."[3]

Perhaps this is why Harvey felt that Einstein's brain, one of

3. An accomplished philanderer, he also flouted the conventional morals of his day. "Einstein loved women," Peter Plesch, whose father was a close friend, once said of the physicist, "and the commoner and sweatier and smellier they were, the better he liked them." To live so completely in his head, he held the real world close—women, sailboats, a sudden meal of ten pounds of strawberries.

the most powerful engines of thought ever on earth, deserved a committed curator, an unpartisan keeper, an eccentric brother whose sole purpose would be to unlock the biological secrets of Einstein's brain by placing it in the hands of a chosen few. Einstein himself had called his brain his laboratory, and with it had pondered the blueness of sky, the bending of starlight, the orbit of Mercury. And maybe, if Harvey knew nothing else, he knew enough to make sure that Einstein's brain didn't get sucked into the maw of the System.

This is my line of thought as we zag through saguaro and scrub brush, in the shadow of the Jemez Mountains. When I look over at Harvey, he has momentarily nodded off for the first time all trip. I've sort of nodded off, too. On a straightaway, I look at the speedometer: We're going 115 miles an hour.

Los Alamos, New Mexico. February 22.

At Los Alamos, we visit the Bradbury Science Museum. Not unexpectedly, the first exhibit is Einstein's letter to President Roosevelt. Harvey stands before it, nodding seriously, then moves on. The museum is a three-room pavilion walled with text and grainy black-and-white photographs that detail the scientific, as well as human, challenges of building the bomb, while lionizing the patriotic men and women who contributed to the Manhattan Project. But the museum—and the culture of Los Alamos as a whole—is most glaringly defined by what its curators seem to have selectively forgotten about the bomb.

For what the Bradbury Science Museum doesn't show is an August 1945 morning in central Hiroshima, trolleys packed with people, thousands of schoolgirls doing community service in the streets. It doesn't show the B-29, the *Enola Gay*, floating above at 31,000 feet, then releasing four tons of metal, Little Boy, through the air. It doesn't show the side of the bomb with its autographs and obscene messages (one starts "Greetings to the Emperor . . .") and emblazoned with the crude naked likeness of Rita Hayworth.

What the museum forgets to show is the forty-three seconds of utter silence, the time it takes Little Boy to drop on the city, and then perhaps the loudest second of the twentieth century, a blast that equals 12,500 tons of TNT. It doesn't show ground zero, at Aioi Bridge, the birds incinerating in the air, people flaming like candles, others swelling like bronze Buddhas. And this is just the beginning.

It doesn't show the firestorm that soon pulverizes the city, the atomic winds that turn into a tornado in the north part of town. The nine of every ten people dead within a mile of the blast, the 200,000 people who will finally be counted dead, and the black, sticky rain, carrying radioactive fallout, that beats relentlessly down on the survivors. It doesn't show the naked man, skin hanging from his body like a kimono, with his eyeball in his hand. It doesn't show the 70,000 rubbled buildings and the people trapped beneath them. Afterward, it doesn't show Nagasaki and the 140,000 more Japanese who will die in like fashion. One can spend a couple hours in the museum—as Harvey does, finally exiting, exhilarated, buzzed about the wonders of technology—but this devastation remains invisible.

We spend the night at the ranch of some friends of mine near Cerrillos—a thirtyish couple, Scott and Clare. We share a terrific meal, and Harvey is particularly animated, fired on red wine, suddenly talking at length about the brain, about how he came by it and how, after fixing it with formaldehyde (his one mistake was injecting the brain with warm formaldehyde instead of cold formaldehyde, thus hastening its denaturation), he photographed the brain. "It's a real tray-sure," he says. "I've gotten to meet many famous people, many who knew Einstein."

After leaving the room to make a phone call, I return to find Harvey and Clare alone at the table, flushed with excitement, absolutely twittering about the brain. They lower their voices when I come in, raise them when I leave again. Later, I feel compelled to ask Clare some questions: What is Harvey's magic? Does the brain turn her on? Does she feel hypnotized? "He's a very, very interesting man," she says. "And for some men chivalry is not dead. Did you see him pull out my chair for me before dinner?"

Before bed, we take a hot tub. I'm confident that Harvey will sit this one out, but, no sir, he doesn't. Shambles out in a borrowed bathrobe and swim trunks, dips a toe in the boiling water. It's a pretty chilly night, stars glazed in the sky like cold coins on black ice, and it's hard not to worry about the physiological ramifications of dropping an eighty-four-year-old body into 104-degree water. But Harvey just throws himself in like a heavy stone. "OH, OH, HEH-HEH. WOW, THAT'S HOT. WOW, WOW, WOW!!!" We simmer for a while, and, chitchatting over the bubbler, it slips out that in my earlier absence Harvey opened the duffel for Clare, unpeeled the Tupperware top, fingered chunks of the brain, and expansively answered questions for her. Rightly or wrongly, this infuriates me. I want to say something about how unfair it is that I've driven two thousand miles so far and not been allowed to examine the brain, while Clare, doing nothing but being her friendly self, got to see the brain instantly. But when I look over at Harvey, he has his eyes closed, in a wonderful trance, his pale body streaming out from him underwater. I wait for as long as I can take it, really, expecting to outlast him as a kind of revenge. But damn if he doesn't seem to gain strength. Finally, grudgingly, I lift myself from the tub, from its magic eternal spring, and splosh inside, leaving him in the dark waters, keening softly with pleasure— ahhh, play-sure!—alone beneath the cosmos.

Near Kingman, Arizona. February 23.

We reach one of those strange moments in the course of every road trip, exhaustion spilling into a kind of ecstasy, towns darkly iridescent like trout in a river. All things—the strains of "Wild Horses" on the radio, the galactic motion of driving, the purple night—seem like one perfect, unalloyed thing, haunted through. Like Charles Lindbergh, who believed that there were spirits riding with him over the Atlantic Ocean, we feel the presence of ghosts. Approaching the Hoover Dam, I stupidly pass a VW Bug and by the hairbreadth grace of God just barely avoid a head-on collision with a lumbering truck. Its lights, broken out like jewels on the grill, spell MARIANNE, the name of my mother.

Las Vegas, Nevada. February 23.

The city is a coronation of brightnesses, like so much shattered glass thrown by the fistful over a sandy floor, a high-desert Hong Kong of possibility. "Sunday midnight is our busiest time of the week," says the woman who checks us in to the Excalibur Hotel/ Casino. "There's no freaking explaining it." We've driven to Las Vegas in a dopamine infusion of orange light, nerved on Coca-Cola, gorged on pizza, the Skylark smelling vaguely stale. The brain sloshing in the padded cranium of the trunk. On I-40 in Arizona, we passed a Navajo woman in a Ford pickup listening to the same radio station we were, pounding out a drumbeat on her steering wheel. Later, an embalmed moon, Hale-Bopp like a pale teardrop. When Einstein once visited the Hopi Indians near the Grand Canyon, they honored him with an Indian name, the Great Relative.

And now, in the casino at midnight, we stand amid bally-hooing hordes of pale-skinned easterners and leather-skinned westerners, bikers and accountants, cowboy-hatted and big-haired and bald as cue balls, imperial on free drinks, soaring on the oxygen-enriched air pumping into the casino to keep people awake, everyone taking a stab at Instamatic riches. Harvey seems overwhelmed, his sensibilities so jangled that he schlepps straight up to one of our cheesy eighteenth-floor rooms—rooms that are tricked out like a cardboard-castle set for a high school production of *Camelot*. He refuses help with his luggage, has the brain slung over his shoulder in the duffel, tosses it in the closet.

Wide awake, I go back downstairs and roam all night, remembering that Einstein put little faith in games of chance. About quantum mechanics, a theory that allowed for unpredictable outcomes, he once said that God does not play dice with the universe. Yet Las Vegas is all about dice. And all about a perverse kind of hope, too. One man at a five-dollar blackjack table, a short, tightly bundled guy who smells of lime aftershave, is abstractly addressing the male dealer in gambler clichés and porn-movie dialogue. "Oh yeah, baby! . . . Yeah, baby! . . . Give it to me! . . . Hit me! . . . Oh yeah! . . . Hold right there! . . . Feels good!"

Soon he's sitting alone. As are others like him. These are men so sunk down inside themselves that they don't give a prostitute working the place a second look when she cozies up to them. Personally, I'm feeling pretty good, lose some quick money at the roulette table, and then, feeling a little less good, regroup in the Minstrel's Lounge. Maybe I've been alone with Harvey too long, probably I need friends, but I find myself asking an older couple about Einstein. The man tooks at me suspiciously. "I don't know anything about him, really, and I don't care one way or the other. I'm just trying to have fun," he says in a Yankee accent.

"I don't know anything either," chimes his wife cheerfully. "Just that he was a genius or something."

After the hot-tub revelation, I no longer feel compelled to keep our secret. I am traveling with the man who owns Einstein's brain, I say, and we are going to California to show it to Einstein's granddaughter. The man folds his arms and looks at me straight on. "Whatever makes you happy," he says.

At an empty blackjack table, I ask a dealer, a Korean guy with a mustache, about Einstein. "I don't know anything about him," he says, "but that man over there should be able to help you." He points to his manager, a white guy with a mustache. He barely lets me finish before responding. "Haven't seen him in here tonight. Sorry, pal."

I try again, with the friendliest-looking man I can find. He's middle-aged and round-bellied, like his group of friends, all wearing Bucky Badger sweatshirts. I smile at them, ask their pardon, phrase my question more carefully this time.

Mr. Badger furrows his brow. "Why do you want to know?" he demands. "Has anyone ever told you about $E = mc^2$? Has anyone in this casino bothered to tell you that?"

I explain that in fact no one has, that I myself am traveling with Einstein's brain. At the mention of the brain, he doesn't miss a beat, becomes impatient. "Let's bury the damn brain and be done with it," he says, as if he's been in on the debate since day one.

I try one last time, a cocktail waitress with a tornado of blond hair. She stands in a short black-and-gold dress, looking like someone's risqué aunt in age denial at a Jersey Shore wedding. When I ask her if she happens to know what Albert Einstein is famous for, her jaw drops. "You're kidding?" she asks. "You must be kidding me. Is there a hidden camera around here? You're the fifth guy to ask me that tonight, and frankly I'm offended." Her voice is pinched with anger. "You know what? I do know who he is . . ." She and I have known each other less than twenty seconds, and yet it feels like our first married fight. "He invented the atom bomb, and I happen to think he's terrible."

In the morning, Harvey and I go for breakfast. There are huge lines trailing out of the Roundtable Buffet and Sherwood Forest Cafe, and so we watch a juggler dressed in green tights work the crowd—"Oh boy, whatta juggler!" says Harvey. Later, we gather our bags and head through the casino for the castle door. As usual, Harvey refuses help with his luggage, has the brain slung over his shoulder. We pause at a bank of slot machines. A group of grandmothers give Harvey a quick once-over, then go back to their spinning lemons and limes and sevens. I pull a couple of coins from my pocket. "For good luck," I tell him. Until now, Harvey hasn't been keen on gambling, but for my sake he slides a quarter into the slot machine and reluctantly pulls the lever. In a way, however, Harvey has been a high-stakes gambler all along, having risked everything on one bet many, many years ago. And even though his slot windows display only unmatched fruit, he leaves the casino with his own jackpot safely stashed in the gray duffel, his step oddly light as he slips over the Excalibur's rich purple carpet and out into the blinding sunlight and sand-papery air.

Los Angeles, California. February 24.

Down through the brown, low-slung, burned-out flats of the Mojave, passing the Soda and Cady mountains, along Ivanpah and Silver lakes, powdered white and dinosaur-bone dry, through the broken-winged, blue-shadowed towns of Baker and Yermo and Barstow, by the world's largest thermometer (electronically measuring temperatures to 140 degrees), then up over Cajon Summit—all of it like a grim, parched-mouth, sun-bleached day-after-Las-Vegas hangover until suddenly Los Angeles explodes in lush green palm trees and red taillights at rush hour, the California sky tilting ultraviolet over the Pacific. Harvey reads from the map the whole way, literally reads to me like it's the story of Job. We pass a gold-earringed woman driving a red BMW with a vanity plate that reads 2success. It seems every car here gleams with its own declaration of erotic or financial prowess: 8mill; orgaz; money. On the radio, we get an action-news update about a disgruntled circus clown who's stolen a car, busting for freedom on I-110. And, packed in, moving five abreast, having apparently passed our desirable exit some miles ago, we're completely lost for the first time all trip.

When we finally escape the highway, we're somewhere in West Hollywood, though we're looking for Santa Monica and the ocean. At a gas station, I approach a stocky, balding guy in short sleeves and a tie. He works for Kodak as a field engineer. He gives me directions and then asks where I'm from. Once he's registered our vitals, the expression on his face looks like a billboard for the country of the dumbfounded. "No fuck, you got Einstein's brain right over there?" he says. "No fucking way. Right in that trunk? The car with the little old man? Are you making a fucking movie of this? Holy fuck." He pulls out a business card with a picture of himself on it, sporting a full head of half-synthetic hair. "That was in my Hair Club days," he says, without hesitation. "You gotta put me in this fucking article. I'm the guy who gave you directions to the ocean. Einstein's fucking brain! What the fuck next? Aliens, right?"

About five blocks down, we realize that Hair Club has given us bum directions. We drift to the curb and ask help from the first person who appears on the other side of our rolled-down window: a cross-dresser in body-hugging black leather with thin, shaven legs that seem six feet high and a tiara of some sort in her hair. She bends into the window seductively and gives precise directions, then says, "Hurry now, y'all don't want to miss that romantic sunset over the Pacific." After a half block, Harvey glances once over his shoulder. "Well, we sure asked the right person," he says. We drive the brain down Sunset and Wilshire, Rodeo and Hollywood, and finally hole up in Santa Monica.

We've come to L.A. so that Harvey can meet one of the doctors to whom he once sent slices of Einstein's brain for research. Yet Harvey can't seem to reach him—can't even recall his name when I ask. Meanwhile, I've made plans to meet Roger Richman, the president of his own celebrity-licensing agency and the man who represents the beneficiaries of the estate of Albert Einstein, which itself is presided over by Hebrew University in Jerusalem. Richman polices trademark infringements, hawks trade shows for Einstein contraband, and decides just how the image of the physicist will be used in advertisements and on merchandise around the world. When I first called Richman from Kansas and told him that I was heading his way with Harvey and the brain, he was curt. "The brain is at the Smithsonian," he said. "And I'd rather not have you bring that man along."

And although the brain has never been near the Smithsonian, and is authentically still in our trunk, I'm forced to make up some polite excuse when I leave Harvey—something about seeing a friend. I drop him at the beach, where he finds a senior center and spends the day writing postcards, making pals, playing cards. Then I guiltily head over to Richman's Beverly Hills office.

Richman, fifty-three, is a big, powerful man with big, powerful ideas and a full head of thickly parted, natural hair. He wears a green short-sleeve shirt. He greets me by saying, "You got the brain with you?" And then he starts laughing.

He ushers me into his office, a spacious, cluttered room strewn with unlicensed celebrity products, and before we begin our interview he puts a tape recorder next to mine, turns it on, and, in this most self-referential of cities, announces that he is taping for the autobiography he intends to write someday. "I would like to say that I'm a marketing genius," he announces.

Richman proceeds to tell me the illustrious history of Richman. How, eighteen years ago, the son of Bela Lugosi sued Universal Studios for a percentage of profits made from the image of his father as Dracula. And although he lost the lawsuit, the judgment contained one paragraph stating that whereas the studio owned the rights to Dracula and the family did not have a right to control Lugosi's image, no one else had the right to appropriate it either. With that one paragraph, Richman set off for swap meets, stalking the stalls, picking up all kinds of items that illegally appropriated the images of dead stars. Then he went after the infringers on behalf of the families.

In 1983, he drove to Sacramento with the sons of John Wayne and Harpo Marx and the grandson of W. C. Fields, and together they argued before the legislature for a celebrity-rights act, which legally assured that no one may use the name, voice, or picture of a deceased personality without permission from the family. Then the group made the same argument in New York State, where they were called "a group of tribal headhunters" by a lawyer representing Time Inc. "It was the proudest moment of my life," Richman says.

What he's become in these past two decades is the Upholder of Dead Celebrity, the Protector of the After-Image. Among the estates he has serviced are those of Louis Armstrong, Jimmy Durante, Sigmund Freud, Mae West, and the Wright brothers, as well as a personal favorite of mine, Basil Rathbone. It's easier to have dead clients, Richman confides, because they don't cancel a million-dollar dress deal when they get a better offer for a clothing line of their own at Kmart.

Of all his clients, Einstein is the biggest. Richman employs five law firms domestically and as many abroad to police him, paying up to $40,000 a month for their services. He shows me a stack of papers, dictionary thick. "All of these are Albert Einstein infringements," he declares proudly. He shows me a famous photograph of Einstein sticking his tongue out. "We never allow this picture to be used," he says fussily. "You know people come back to me and say, 'Who are you to say that we can't use this when he stuck his tongue out and he knew photographers were there?' and I say, 'Hey, I'm running a public trust; it's incumbent upon me to protect these people.'"

Richman won't reveal how much money he and Hebrew University make from Einstein, but he admits it's more than from any other client. When I ask if the figure is in the millions, he simply says, "I wouldn't say millions." I remind him that Einstein never allowed his name or image to serve as a product endorsement during his life. "Money only appeals to selfishness and irresistibly invites abuse," the physicist said. "Can anyone imagine Moses, Jesus, or Gandhi with the moneybags of Carnegie?" So wouldn't he object to himself selling Nikon cameras now? Richman dismisses this idea out of hand and assures me that all the profits go to scholarships at Hebrew University.

Then, to show me just how bleak a world without Roger Richman can be, he leads me to a large cardboard box across the room. It's full of black-market desecrations—"horrible, horrible stuff," Richman says. A greeting card with Mae West urinating through an hourglass, one of Marilyn Monroe snorting cocaine. There's John Wayne toilet paper ("It's rough! It's tough! And it doesn't take crap off anyone!") and a vial of Elvis's sweat ("Now you can let his perspiration be an inspiration") and a box of cotton balls emblazoned with the words BRANDO'S BALLS. But the *pièce de résistance,* the *succès de scandale,* is wrapped in paper with rubber bands around it. "I always keep him in his house," says Richman. "I never take him out."

Richman places it in my hands, and I unwrap it slowly to

find eight inches of hard rubber topped by the smiley-faced head of President Ronald Reagan. It was this very dildo that Richman waved on the floor of the California statehouse to make his point—"I HAVE HERE IN MY HANDS A SEXUAL DEVICE," he bellowed to the shocked assemblage—and that pleases him.

Once the Gipper has been wrapped and replaced in the box, we tour the rest of the office. And Richman gallops on: "We're planning a major celebration of the millennium. We're doing mailings to advertising agencies reminding them that it's coming, that we represent all these people, that they should be celebrating this past century."

In order to put his own client list in perspective, Richman recently called the Screen Actors Guild and found that about eighteen thousand actors have died in this century. "How many are marketable today?" asks Richman, throwing his arms open in apparent disbelief. "Twenty! These are the most talented people that ever lived . . . but most people are here and gone forever. You know, you have your fifteen minutes of fame and that's it."

Finally I ask Richman why our country is overly obsessed with celebrity today, why celebrity, as much as a Vegas jackpot, has become the Jell-O mold of the American Dream. He begins by quoting Thoreau: "The mass of men lead lives of quiet desperation."

"They'll never be an Elizabeth Taylor," he says. "Their hopes are their dreams and their dreams are on TV and their dreams are watching these beautiful chests walking into the Academy Awards in gorgeous gowns and they live for that. That's why Communism failed. [It] never gave people any hope. That's why democracy has been so successful. The American Dream, it's based on hope . . . as long as you have money, you go right to the top."

He continues. "When I travel into the heartland of America—I go backpacking a lot—and talk about what I'm doing, oh, these people, they won't let me shut up. They just ask question after question after question. I'm like a hero to them. Around here, no one cares. Dead stars, oh, forget it. You're an agent for the dead, you're a joke, c'mon."

But Richman is convinced that he's having the last laugh, in no small part thanks to Einstein, who's gone global. In Japan, Einstein's image is used in a commercial for a video game called 3DO; in Hungary, his mug is plastered on billboards for a local telephone company; in South Africa, he advertises insurance. "He's the most widely recognized human being that ever lived," declares Richman. "In China"—where Richman has recently brokered a deal for Einstein T-shirts—"they're limited to one child per family, and every single parent calls their one child 'my little Einstein.'" He smiles at the thought.

"China is a cultural wasteland," he says emphatically. "They've never heard of John Wayne. They've never heard of Steve McQueen. They've never seen any of their movies. But Einstein, they know."

San Jose, California. February 26.

Harvey is to give a talk on Einstein's brain in San Jose. Before we left Princeton, he rooted through the letters he keeps in a shoe box—letters from an oddball collection of fans and groupies, critics and psychos, everywhere from Denmark to New Zealand, everyone from angry rabbis demanding the brain for burial to elegiacal schoolkids cutely waxing juvenile about trying to figure out relativity—and called a woman named Sarah Gonzalez, someone he doesn't know but who had written to him a few years ago randomly asking for a piece of the brain. When she heard from Harvey, she felt that the Lord God had intervened on her behalf. Ever since his call, she has been busy informing San

Jose of our arrival, contacting the mayor and the local media, trying to set up a dinner party for leading lights in the community,
and arranging for Harvey and Einstein's brain to visit with students at Independence High School, one of the biggest in the
country.

Gonzalez has reserved us rooms at the Biltmore Hotel, but
when we arrive around 2:00 A.M., out on some industrial edge of
San Jose, there's only one available room left, with a single bed.
"Why, I'm sure it's a big one," says Harvey with a nervous chuckle.

I ask for a cot. And by the time I roll it into the room, the
gray duffel is up on the television with the weather on and Harvey is snorkeling through his suitcase, each item of his clothing—
his silk pajamas, a 49ers sweatshirt, his slippers, and a dress
shirt—wrapped in cellophane. He has brought two suits for tomorrow, neatly folded like big bat wings in his case, a black winter worsted wool and a baby-blue leisure-type suit that puts me
in mind of a carnival barker or a midwestern aluminum-siding
salesman.

I collapse on the cot, and no sooner do I hit the pillow than
I'm wide awake. But I keep my head buried as Harvey putters
about the room. I can hear him running water in the sink, clear-
ing his throat, ironing. I can hear him rustling through his
cellophane-wrapped clothes, then perusing his various articles
on Einstein, preparing for his lecture. I can hear something that
sounds like an electric toothbrush. Before the sun rises, he finally
beds down, and his breathing slows and then grows deeper, like a
river running into pools. Instead of snoring, there's a sweet lowing in his theta-gasps for air, and finally it puts me to sleep, too.
When I wake to the crunching of Harvey eating caramel corn,
it's 8:00 A.M., and he's half dressed, having opted for the black
suit with black suspenders and a gray turtleneck, though the
weather is verging on summer. Sarah Gonzalez calls and announces that she's in the lobby, nearly an hour early. While Har-

vey primps, I go to meet her. She's the only person at the bar, busily doing something with her hands. When I come closer, I realize that she is pressing on a set of acrylic fingernails. For a moment, she doesn't notice that I'm standing there, and we both admire her handiwork. When she looks up, she seems surprised. "Oh," she says, extends an automatic hand with half new nails and half bitten ones, and peeks around me for Harvey and the brain.

Sarah Gonzalez is a short, pretty, quick-moving Filipino woman with black-and-gold sunglasses and an ostentatious emerald car. In her mood and mannerisms she reminds me of a brushfire in a high wind. She personifies the immigrant's dream. A former executive secretary, she is now the president of her own company, Pacific Connections, which markets biomass energy conversion—or, as she puts it, "turning cornstalks to megawatts." Next week, she tells me, she will be in Manila meeting with the Filipino president, Fidel V. Ramos, in hopes of bringing the gift of energy—more lights and televisions—to her country of birth.

When Harvey comes chugging out, she blanches, then starts forward. "Dr. Harvey, I presume," says Gonzalez, clucking and bowing her head. "I can't believe there's someone living and breathing who was so close to Einstein." Harvey has removed the brain from the gray duffel and now holds the Tupperware container in his hand, though the plastic is clouded enough that you can really see only urine-colored liquid inside. Suddenly, it feels as if we're not fully clothed. Even as Harvey palms the brain in the lobby, I feel a need to hide it. Gonzalez herself doesn't notice and rushes us into her Mercury Grand Marquis. She's a woman who enjoys the liberal use of first names. "Mike, what do you think of this scandal, Mike?" she asks. "This—how do you say?—campaign-contribution scandal, Mike?" She is perhaps the most persistently friendly person I've ever met.

Harvey sits in the front bucket seat, sunk down in the fine

Italian leather, the fabric of his own suit, by comparison, dull and aged; there's a tiny hole in one knee of his heavy suit pants. He clears his throat repeatedly and starts to chuckle. "Do you know a fella named Burroughs, William Burroughs?" She's never heard of him. Harvey tries again.

"Where does Gates live?"

"Bill Gates, Dr. Harvey? That would be Seattle, I think. Isn't that right, Mike? Seattle, Mike?"

"I thought that fella lived right here in Silicon Valley," says Harvey, hawkeyeing the streets suspiciously. A little later on, Harvey's more at ease, sets himself chuckling again. "Those are the funniest-looking trees," he says.

"They are palm trees, Dr. Harvey," says Gonzalez.

We are given a brief tour of "old San Jose"—a collection of Day-Glo houses that look brand-new—then stop at Gonzalez's house, a comfortable bungalow on a cul-de-sac where she lives with her husband and five children, two of them teenagers. A full drum kit is set up in the living room. One gets the impression that when this house is full there's probably nothing here but love and a hell of a racket. Meeting her husband, I retract her title and claim him as the friendliest person I've ever met. "Oh, Dr. Harvey, what does it feel like to be you?" he asks. He serves us cookies and milk. Finally, after photographs have been taken on the front lawn, we start to leave. Harvey reaches down and lifts a pinecone from the perfect, chemical-fed turf. He holds it up, admiring its symmetry, and for reasons of his own pockets it.

Then we drive to Independence High, where we are picked up by a golf cart at the front entrance and whisked a half mile through campus. Harvey delivers his lecture in a dim, egg-cavern room flooded with students and the smell of bubble gum. Some wear baggy Starter sweats or jeans pulled low off their hips or unlaced high-tops; some have pierced noses or tongues or eyebrows. Some are white or Asian or Latino or African American. A number of boys have shaved the sides of their heads and wear moptops or Egyptian pharaoh dos; a number of the girls have dyed hair, all colors of the rainbow.

The teachers shush everyone, but the hormonal thrum here defies complete silence, and there's a low-level sputter of laughter like a car chuffing even after the ignition's been turned off. And then suddenly Sarah Gonzalez is introducing Harvey, the gold of her glasses synonymous with success, and Harvey, shaped like a black candy cane, is stumping to the podium, looking every bit the retired undertaker. He clears his throat and chuckles and then clears his throat again. He runs his hands up and down the side of the podium and focuses on a spot at the back of the room, rheumy-eyed, squinting. These are the thirteen-, fourteen-, and fifteen-year-olds of America—hundreds of clear eyes reflecting back at him, brains obsessed with Silverchair, Tupac, Blossom, and Brandy—and Harvey seems at a loss, begins a droning, discombobulated, start-and-stop remembrance of Albert Einstein almost as if he's talking to himself.

"The Great Scientist would eventually come up with the equation $E = mc^2$, and how he did that I'll never know, heh-heh . . .

"He was a friendly person. Real easy to talk to, you know. Wore flannels and tennis shoes a lot . . .

"I was just real lucky to be at the right place at the right time . . ."

Einstein's animated face is projected on a screen, Harvey's impassive one beneath it. When Harvey senses he's losing his audience, he tells them about the autopsy, about the Great Scientist lying on the table and how his brain was removed. "He liked the fatty foods, you know," says Harvey. "That's what he died of." He starts slowly for the Tupperware and the entire audience leans forward in their seats, crane their necks, hold their collective breath. For the first time, there is complete silence.

He pops the lid and unabashedly fishes around for some of the brain, then holds up a chunk of it. It's almost like a dream—illogically logical, shockingly normal. My first real glimpse of the Tupperwared brain on this trip, and it's with three hundred other strangers. One girl squeals, and general chaotic murmurings fill the room. Kids come to their feet in waves of "ohhhhs" and "ahhhs." The smell of formaldehyde wafts thickly over them, a scent of the ages, and drives them back on their heels.

Harvey natters on, but no one is really listening now, just gasping at these blobs of brain. "I took the meninges off. . . . This is a little bit of the cortex. . . . He had more glial cells than the rest of us—those are the cells that nourish the neurons . . ."

They are transfixed by the liver-colored slices as if it's all a macabre Halloween joke. They are repulsed and captivated by the man whose fingers are wet with brain. Sarah Gonzalez stands up, slightly disheveled, flushed in the face. "Children, questions! Ask Dr. Harvey your questions!"

One swaggering boy in the back of the room raises his hand, seemingly offended: "Yeah, but like, WHAT'S THE POINT?"

Harvey doesn't hear, puts his hand behind his ear to signal that he doesn't hear, and a teacher sitting nearby translates: "He wants to know what the point is," says the teacher politely.

Harvey hesitates for a second, then almost seems angry. "To see the difference between your brain and a genius's," he shoots back.

The crowd titters. A girl throws a high five at her best friend. "Dang, girl."

The old man is cool!

Another boy in the back stands. "I was told, like, Einstein didn't want people to take his brain."

Again the teacher translates, and as soon as Harvey pro-
cesses the question he bristles. "Where are you getting your in-
formation?" he says.

"My world government teacher," the boy says.

Harvey ponders this, then responds, as if it's answer enough,
"In Germany, it's very common to do an autopsy and take the
brain out."

When the period ends, the students storm Harvey and the
brain. They want to know how long he's had it (forty-two years).
Whether he plans to clone it ("Way-ell, under the right conditions someday, I suppose it might be done"). Whether an evil dictator such as Qaddafi might try to get his hands on it
("Heh-heh-heh"). I try to get close, but the crowd is too thick,
the crush too great, and so I stand on the edge with Gonzalez.
Even as Harvey goes to leave later, a few students come up and a
boy says, "Yo, man, where you going next? Can we follow?" Harvey flushes with triumph, stammers that he doesn't really know
where he's going now, as Sarah Gonzalez leads him to a seat in a
waiting golf cart.

When we pull away, I wonder what we must look like to the
students waving goodbye. Harvey rides shotgun as always, with
the Tupperwared brain on his lap—a man beyond their own
grandfathers, someone from a different dimension in time and
space, really, lit down here for a weird moment at Independence
High, then away again, vanishing on a golf cart down the concrete
superstring sidewalks of their world.

Berkeley, California. February 27.

We've reached the end of the road. Evelyn Einstein greets us at
the door to her bayside apartment complex in a black jumper,
wearing two Star Trek pins and globe earrings. Nearly a head

taller than Harvey, she's a big-boned fifty-six-year-old though looks younger, with a short bob of brown hair. Due to a series of illnesses over the past few years, she walks in small steps and breathes heavily after the slightest exertion. She gives off an aura of enormous sadness, though her powers of humor and forgiveness seem to run equally deep. Despite the distress that Harvey's removal of the brain caused her father—Hans Albert—and the rest of the family, she has invited him to her house.

Evelyn is known to be the adopted daughter of Hans Albert, though the circumstance of her lineage is a bit clouded. Rumor has it that she was born as a result of an affair between Einstein and a dancer. And at least one doctor, Charles Boyd, believing the same, tried but failed to match the DNA of Albert's brain matter and Evelyn's skin, given that the brain sample was too denatured. Whatever the truth, however, her resemblance to Einstein, the mirthful play of light in her heavy-lidded eyes and the Picasso shape of her face, is uncanny. Evelyn herself ruefully says, "If you believe in what Albert said about time, then I'm really his grandmother anyway."

From her light-filled living room, you can see the skyline of San Francisco, Angel Island rising from the sun-flecked blue bay, Mount Tamalpais lurking in the distance. Among artifacts and antique clocks, Evelyn offers us seats. We have come a long way—almost four thousand miles, to be exact—and yet it feels like Harvey would like to be anywhere else but here. Evelyn sits down. I fall onto the plush couch, overcome with relief and exhaustion. Harvey remains standing.

Evelyn tells us about what it was like to grow up as an Einstein, how her life became an exercise in navigating the jagged shoals of her family. Her father had inherited a degree of his own father's cold distance—she refers to her grandfather only as Albert or Albie—and Evelyn found herself shipped off to school in

Switzerland. She came back to Berkeley for college, had a bad marriage, lived for a year on the streets, then later worked as a cop in Berkeley and afterward with cult members and their families. She has very few remembrances of her grandfather. Most of the letters he'd once sent her were stolen.

As she says this, Harvey still stands frozen in the middle of the room, speechless. Evelyn does what she can to politely ignore him, asks me innocuous questions about the trip, waiting for him to sit, too. But he doesn't. He just stands there, his arms limply at his sides. He breathes more quickly. Somewhere in his head, virulent, radioactive cells of what?—guilt?—proliferate and mushroom. He stands awkwardly in the middle of the room and just won't sit, can't sit, holds the brain in its Tupperware, trembling in his left hand. Having arrived here, does he now have second thoughts? Could he ever have imagined, those forty-two years ago when he cut the brain from Einstein's head, that he would ultimately present himself in the court of Evelyn Einstein's living room with the contraband in his hands?

The fourth time Evelyn offers him a seat he takes it. He laughs nervously, then clears his throat. "Real good," he says. Evelyn is talking about cults, how frightening they are and how what's most frightening about cults is that it's you and I who end up getting sucked in, how easy mind control really is. "All my friends say I should start one," she says, joking. "I could channel Albert. I mean, when Linda Evans channels Ramtha she talks like Yul Brynner. It's just hysterical. If this broad can channel a thirty-thousand-year-old guy, I can channel Albert."

Having summoned his courage, Harvey abruptly pulls out a sheaf of photographs and slides with cresyl violet stains of axons and glial cells, then plunks the Tupperware on the table. "Ah, brain time," says Evelyn, and Harvey just begins talking as if he's talking to the youngsters at Independence High School again.

"This is a picture of the brain from different aspects, olfactory nerve, and so forth." He pulls out a photo of Einstein. "I like to show this picture because it shows him as a younger man, you know, when he first came over to be an American. So many of the photos you see of him are when he was an older man."

"I have a lot when he was young," says Evelyn.

"You do? I'll trade you some," says Harvey.

"Did you autopsy the whole body?"

"The whole body."

"What was that like?"

Harvey pauses a moment, clears his throat. "Why, it made me feel humble and insignificant."

"Did he have a gallbladder? Or had they taken it out?"

"I think he still had a gallbladder. Heh-heh. Yeah, his diet was his nemesis, you know, because he lived before we knew what cholesterol did to the blood, so he probably walked around with high blood cholesterol, much of it being deposited in his blood vessels. That aorta, that was just full of cholesterol plaque."

Evelyn nods. "Yeah . . . well, of course, the European diet . . . my father and I would fight over fat. When we got a ham, we would cut off the fat and fry it, then fight over it. Bitterly." Evelyn smiles.

"And all that good goose grease," chimes in Harvey.

"Oh yeah. Well, in those days goose . . . well, goose is actually a lot safer than beef, a lot less cholesterol."

"Oh yeah? I didn't know that."

"It's a family that just adored fat," she says.

"I used to eat in a little inn up in Metuchen, New Jersey, where your grandfather would spend weekends, and they had these cheeses, you know, full-fat cheeses and nice wines."

"I don't know if he was into wines," says Evelyn.

"I never saw him drink it myself," says Harvey, forgetting,

then perhaps remembering, that he met Einstein only once. "Well, the innkeeper had a good supply of wine, and I thought it was for your grandfather. Maybe it wasn't."

There's some talk about the size of the brain. Evelyn contends that at 1,230 grams it qualifies as microcephalic—that is, smaller than normal—according to a 1923 edition of *Gray's Anatomy* in her possession, but Harvey insists that the brain was normal size for a man Einstein's age, given the fact that brains shrink over time. He lets her see some slides but seems unwilling to open the Tupperware. When I ask him if he'd show us pieces of the brain, he seems a bit put out, uncaps the lid for a moment, then almost immediately lids it. He offers Evelyn a piece—to which she says, "That would be wonderful"—then, curiously, never gives it to her. Evelyn appears perplexed, as am I. After all of this, it seems, Harvey has decided that there will be no show-and-tell with the actual gray matter.

"I'm amazed they didn't work with the brain earlier, right away when he died, actually," Evelyn says. Harvey gets uncomfortable again, stiffening into his pillar of salt. The words slow as they come from his mouth: something about the fissure of Sylvius, occipital lobe, cingulate gyrus. All of it a part of some abstract painting, some hocus-pocus act. "It took us a while," he says finally.

And then Harvey abruptly tries to end the meeting. "Way-ell, it's been a real play-sure," he says, taking us by surprise. And then he explains: Earlier, in San Jose, unbeknownst to me, he made a call to his eighty-five-year-old cousin in San Mateo and now insists that he must go spend the night there, assuming that I will take him more than halfway back to San Jose in rush-hour traffic. But to come this far for only half an hour? And besides, Evelyn has made reservations for us all to have dinner. But nothing sways Harvey. I suggest that his cousin join us or that we visit his cousin in the morning after rush hour. Harvey stands firm; then I stand firm. After four thousand miles of driving, I, for one, intend to eat with the daughter-granddaughter of Albert Einstein. Harvey gets on the phone with his cousin and says loudly enough so that I can hear, "The chauffeur won't give me a ride."

Ever the rambler, Harvey decides to take public transportation—BART—and then have his cousin pick him up at the station. And so he does. We pile into the Skylark and drive to a nearby station, Harvey in the backseat with the brain. Although Harvey and I will meet again tomorrow for a visit with the neuroanatomist Marian Diamond, and although we will share a heartfelt goodbye as I drop him off at the train station again (he on his way to the airport to fly back home, me off to visit friends), this parting feels like the real end of our trip. At the station, Harvey opens his case and presents Evelyn with a postcard: a black-and-white photo of himself looking pensive in a striped turtleneck, his ear the size of a small slipper, gazing sleepy-eyed at some form in the distance, some ghostly presence. "That's a very nice one," she says politely.

"Yessir," says Harvey. "Couldn't have been happier to meet . . ."

It all seems so anticlimactic, but so appropriate. So like Harvey. And then he's off with his suitcase full of cellophane-wrapped clothes, caught in a river of people drifting toward the escalators, spilling underground, the silver tassel of his hair catching the light, then his body going down and down into the catacomb's shadow.

It's not until after Evelyn and I have had dinner that we realize the brain is still with us. In fact, it's sitting on the car's backseat in its bubble of Tupperware, lit by a streetlight, slopping in formaldehyde. It has been there for three hours, as Evelyn told me over dessert about the ugly schisms and legal battles inside her family for letters left behind by "Albie." Given Harvey's well-documented guardianship of the brain, it seems impossible that he's just forgotten it, but then maybe not. Maybe, through some unconscious lapse or some odd, oblique act of intention, he has left it for us. A passing of the brain to the next generation. My giddiness is now rivaled only by my sudden paranoia. What if it gets ripped off?

"He left the brain?" says Evelyn. "Does he do this often?"

"Nope," I say, and suddenly we are smiling at each other.

We don't look at it right away—right there in full view of the strolling sidewalk masses—but drive back to Evelyn's apartment by the bay. I stop in front of the building with the Skylark idling. I reach back and take the Tupperware in my hands, then unseal the lid, and, in the dome light of the car, open the container.

After all these miles, all these days on the road during which I felt taunted by the gray duffel, the big reveal has arrived. Bits of the brain are pouched in a white cloth, floating in formaldehyde. When I unravel the cloth, maybe a dozen golf-ball-sized chunks of the brain spill out—parts from the cerebral cortex and the frontal lobe. The smell of formaldehyde smacks us like a backhand, and for a moment I actually feel as if I might puke. The pieces are sealed in celloidin—the liver-colored blobs of brain rimmed by gold wax. I pick some out of the plastic container and hand a few to Evelyn. They feel squishy, weigh about the same as very light beach stones. We hold them up like jewelers, marveling at how they seem less like a brain than—what?—some kind of snack food, some kind of energy chunk for genius triathletes. Or an edible product that offers the consumer world peace, space travel, eternity. Even today, the Asmat of Irian Jaya believe that to consume a brain is to gain the mystical essence of another person. But to be absolutely honest, I never thought that, holding Einstein's brain, I'd somehow imagine eating it.

"So this is what all the fuss is about," says Evelyn. She pokes at the brain nuggets still in the Tupperware, laps formaldehyde on them. A security guard walks by and glances at us, then keeps walking. There is, I must admit, something entirely bizarre about Evelyn messing around with her grandfather's brain, checking his soggy neurons. But she seems more intrigued than grossed out. "You could make a nice necklace of this one," she says, holding up a circular piece of brain. "This is pretty weird, huh?"

Watching her in the cast of dome light—an impression of her sadness returning to me, the thrill of adrenaline confusing everything—I'm overcome with a desire to make her happy for a moment. Without thinking, I say, "You should take it." Then I remind her that Harvey had offered her a piece earlier but had never given it to her. "It belongs to you anyway," I say. Weeks later, on the phone, she'll tell me, "I wish I'd taken it." But now, sitting back in the teal velour of the Skylark, she says, "I couldn't."

Instead, she puts the pieces back in the Tupperware, closes it, and hands it to me. She gets out of the car and heavily walks herself inside.

Which leaves just me and the brain.

The Flamingo Motel. February 28.

We, the brain and I, drive the East Shore Freeway to University Avenue—skirting the bay, all black and glassed-over, San Francisco on the other side like so many lit-up missile silos—and then head toward Shattuck Avenue. Although I'm exhausted, I suddenly feel very free, have this desire to start driving back across America, sans Harvey. On the radio, there's a local talk show about UFOs, an expert insisting that in February 1954, Eisenhower disappeared for three days, allegedly making contact with aliens.

It would appear, as we go from no vacancy to no vacancy,

that all the inns of Berkeley are full. All the inns but the Flamingo Motel—a pink, concrete, L-shaped, forties-style two-story with a mod neon rendering of a flamingo. A fleabag. But it's enough. A double bed, a bathroom, a rotary phone. Some brother partyers have an upstairs room at the far end of the motel and are drinking cases of Pabst Blue Ribbon. As I carry the brain up to my room they eye me, then hoot and toss their crushed cans over the banister into the parking lot.

Inside, I'm hit with an industrial-sized wallop of disinfectant. The room is the size of a couple of horse stalls with a rust-colored unvacuumed shag rug scorched with cigarette burns. A few stations come in on the television, which is bolted high on the wall. *Nightline* is getting to the bottom of the sheep cloning business. It's been a long day, and yet the brain has got me pumped up. I try to make a phone call, but the line is dead. I try to write some postcards, but my pen explodes. By some trick of the room's mirror, it seems that there are lights levitating everywhere. Finally, not quite knowing what to do, I go to bed. I put Einstein's brain on one pillow and rest my own head on the other one next to it, fewer than four inches away. Just to see. I've come four thousand miles for this moment, and now all I do is fall asleep. Light from the road slips over the room—a greenish, underwater glow—and the traffic noise dims. I can hear beer cans softly pattering down on the pavement, then nothing.

It's possible that in our dreams we enter a different dimension of the universe. On this night, it's possible that I suddenly have three wives and ten kids and twelve grandchildren, that I've become Harvey himself, that I open up bodies to find more bodies and open those bodies to find that I'm falling through space and time. It's possible that in some other dimension, I am Robert Oppenheimer and Mahatma Gandhi, Billie Holiday and Adolf Hitler, Honus Wagner and Olga Korbut. I am Navajo and Cambo-

dian and Tutsi. I am Túpac Amaru and NASA astronaut. I am a
scatterling, I am a billionaire, I am a person in a field in North
Dakota about to be abducted by a UFO. It's possible, too, that I
am nobody, or rather only myself, slightly dazed and confused,
curled in a question mark in a pink motel with Einstein's brain on
the pillow by my head.

When I wake the next morning, craving coffee, there is
only the world as I know it again—the desk chair in its place, the
wrappered soap in the shower, the brain sitting demurely on its
pillow, the Flamingo still the Flamingo, with cigarette burns in
the rusty rug. There's a sudden grand beauty to its shoddiness.

When I step outside into the bright early-morning sun of
California, I have the top off the Tupperware. And although later
I will return the brain to Harvey, I am for a brief moment the
man with the plan, the keeper of the cosmos. Do I feel the thing
that all totems and fetishes make people feel? Something that I
can believe in? A power larger than myself that I can submit to?
Salvation? Have I touched eternity?

I'm not sure. The beer cans strewn in the parking lot make
out the rough shape of America, surrounded by pools of sudsy,
gold liquid. And the birds have come down out of the sky and
they're drinking from it. Even now, the universe is filling with
dark matter. We are slowing down. Snowballs the size of jumbo
trucks are pelting our atmosphere. Perhaps a meteor has just
been bumped into a new flight pattern, straight toward Earth,
and we won't know anything about it until it explodes us all, as
meteors once exploded the dinosaurs.

But I am here now. In the now now. Day has come back up
from the other side of the earth, the birds have come down from
the sky. There are flashes of orange light, the air is flooded with
honeysuckle. I feel something I can't quite put my finger on,
something euphoric but deeply unsayable. Is it love or just not

hate? Is it joy or just not sadness? For a moment, all of time seems to flow through the Flamingo, its bright edges reflecting the past and the present, travelers packing their bags and rivering into some farther future. We are always driving with our secrets in the trunk, amazed by the cows and rainbows and palm trees. And do I dare to think that there will be no ending of the world, of America, of ourselves? I do. I really do. For in some recurrence, in some light wave, in some shimmer of time, we are out there now, and forever, existing, even as surely as Einstein himself continues to exist, here in my hands.

THE ACCIDENT

THE ACCIDENT—THE FIRST ONE—OCCURRED ON THE Wednesday night before Thanksgiving of my senior year in high school. It left one friend injured and one dead, and for a while afterward, the whole thing seemed so surreal and impossible that all we could do—friends, family, anyone connected but not in the accident itself—was try to re-create the simultaneities of that evening, the first person at the scene, the shock of the couple at the nearby house from which the call was made for an ambulance, and then: who called whom and who was where when they heard. Given our own shock, we couldn't imagine the parents of the victims hearing those first words: *There's been an accident . . .*

When the news reached my family that night, in that orbit of calls, my parents, perhaps like other parents among our friends, presumed their child might have been in the car, which wasn't the case, though might have been, had I made a different decision earlier that evening. For us seniors, it was a free night with no school the next day, a holiday from everything, including our cursed college apps. Mine was spent with my girlfriend, so I missed the pre-party, and then the ride to the real party. And so I missed the accident, too.

There were two cars, belonging to Jax and Flynn, driving from the beach north up through town to someone's parentless house. Riding with Jax was Seger, and with Flynn, Xavier. On a stretch of road by one of the town's country clubs, Jax lost control of his car, hit a telephone pole, and skidded a hundred feet into a tree. The crash drove the engine through the dashboard. The Jaws of Life were required to cut the bodies from the wreckage.

At that moment—as the first siren sounded, as the first numbers were dialed, as the bodies were gathered and rushed away—I was watching a movie/eating Chinese/on a bed with my girlfriend, I can't remember exactly. Lost in the oblivious haze of youth, I was certain, like millions of teenagers before me, that nothing would ever touch us there.

Until, of course, it did.

Growing up, we had this sort of unusual thing in our town: an ambulance service operated by kids. It's still there today, in fact—thriving. Then, it was housed in a defunct red train station that rattled every time a passing commuter train rushed by on its way to Manhattan. In winter, icy gusts came lunging through the walls. There was a garage with two ambulances, and off it, a cramped radio room. Inside the station was an open common area, where presumably tickets had once been sold, but which now hosted our training sessions and organizational meetings. Upstairs, there was a loft where the CPR manikins were stashed. Sometimes you'd forget and go up there at midnight to turn out a light and nearly have a heart attack at all those synthetic bodies laid out, staring dumbly at the ceiling.

The ambulance service had been founded in the seventies.

It was as if some Hollywood execs had sat around spitballing one-line pitches for after-school specials, until someone blurted, "*Emergency* . . . but with kids in charge." Of course, we had adult advisers, who played a vital role—and our both tender and mercurial fiftysomething patriarch, who cursed and yelled and berated everyone, calling them "boobie," in an attempt to gauge our toughness. And yet it was we teenagers who did the bulk of the work. We started in the radio room in ninth grade, and graduated to gofer on the ambulance in tenth, then went on to become EMTs and ambulance drivers. As an experiment, the ambulance had succeeded a little too thoroughly, and by the time I came along, there were about fifty of us who worked there in one capacity or another.

Still, there were those in town who wondered: Could a sixteen-year-old EMT (someone who had only recently learned to drive a car) really help at, let alone handle, the worst accidents? It became our job, then, to be overdiligent and professional so as not to let anyone down. On every night of the week, including weekends and holidays, a crew was "on duty" at the rickety station, where we'd run through checklists, train, sit and do homework, or just flirt and shoot the shit, pimply, hormonal teenagers that we were. From 6:00 P.M. to midnight, we acted as first responders, clad in our "whites" (a curious uniform choice for those dealing in blood) and orange fluorescent jackets. The rest of the time we carried pagers, in school, at practice, wherever. And our precious weekends were soon filled with fund-raising, chores at headquarters, and more training courses, including hours logged at a local emergency room. There, we were taught to regard each new accident with a sort of dispassionate intensity, no matter how extreme the circumstance.

Initially, however, I remember a lot of time spent blowing air into those synthetic manikins, real lip to synthetic lip, thrusting palms down on fake chests loaded with thick springs, and, at the end, paper readouts issuing from a slot at the ribs, a ticker showing the peaks and valleys that gauged one's efficacy at giving CPR. Repetition made for perfection on those fake bodies, though reality, I would soon find to my dismay, could be different. When the grandfather of the boy next door keeled over on the lawn, I lined my palm up on his sternum as I'd been instructed—and had succeeded at so many times before on the dummies—and with the first thrust, felt three real ribs give way.

When it came to treating victims, every kid at the ambulance had at least one call that remained indelible—maybe a multicar crash on the highway, maybe a cardiac arrest or a house fire or head injury—that introduced us to a world of grief we hadn't known before, that took us behind the veil of our town. I recall responding to a daytime suicide, at a house not more than a mile from my own, and when we spilled out of the ambulance and hustled through the strobes in our bright uniforms, hoping to save the overcast day, fix the wrong, piece back the body— crazy-competent mini-adults that we were—one unimpressed police officer stopped us short on the doorstep.

"You're not going in there," he said. When we insisted, he exhaled an exasperated sigh and added, "She slit her goddamn wrists in the tub, and you're kids, and I'm not letting you in there." I remember we protested, outraged that he'd called us kids, and we wouldn't leave the scene, waging our own quiet sit-in, until we were finally called off by an adult adviser. But even as we worked ourselves into a bruit, I had this nightmare image of a submerged naked body, blood streaming from her wrists, face twisted in some ghoulish rictus.

Half an hour later, I was sitting back in calculus, trying to figure out a derivative.

———

The night of the accident I returned home from my girlfriend's house to find my parents and my sixteen-year-old brother sitting grimly at the kitchen table, a scene that undoubtedly played out in other kitchens across town, too. My dad, who would have been in his late forties at the time—my age now as I write this— was a business executive who worked long hours, seemed to have boundless energy for house projects on the weekend, and made sure we were at church each Sunday morning, where he often volunteered as a lector. My mom, a country girl transplanted to suburbia, possessed a deep reserve of patience for her four wilding boys. Among them I was the oldest, recently sprouting up an inch taller than my dad, attaining full, moody man-boy status. In that moment, I knew nothing really, and was being told nothing. My parents said they'd drive me to the hospital; I said I could drive myself, but they were having none of it.

As we left to go, my brother pulled me aside. He also worked at the ambulance service, and had heard that the night's on-duty crew had left the scene with two bodies. When my brother said one of them wasn't breathing, I reflexively thought, *Don't let it be Jax*, and repeated that in my mind, imploring some higher power as my dad drove me beneath the sodium points of light on the highway. In the zero-sum of that moment, it didn't even occur to me what the inverse meant: *Let it be Seger*. And how guilty I'd feel for years after about it.

As a kid, I thought my town was a wonderland. The lawns were always freshly cut, gardens overflowing with explosions of color, the blue sky etched with mystical fans of ice from the planes that came and went from New York. Somewhere out there was the wild world, but here, we lived in our own disassociated nirvana, a place where a kid felt protected and free. We rode our bikes everywhere. We swung on rope swings and swam in pools, or at the beach. There was nothing really to fear, so my mom set us loose out the back door each day, and we raced through the woods, to some neighborhood yard where there was always a game of football or Wiffle Ball raging.

There, too, lived Seger, an athletic kid with blond hair and blue eyes. I remember one year splitting time with him at quarterback on our Pop Warner football team, the little guys with good hands who conveyed the ball to bigger guys, who then tried to run through, or over, the opposing team. Later, in sixth grade, we'd hung out with two neighborhood girls, meeting after school, loitering, trying out the first rehearsals of sexual attraction. He took the lead, with the confidence of having older siblings. The louder and funnier and more kinetic he was, the more I struck a pose of dumb bewilderment.

And then we sort of lost track of each other. He moved, to Jax's neighborhood, and they became close friends. I saw him here and there, but we didn't really overlap again socially until high school. By this time, he'd become starting safety on the football team—but had a sentimental streak, too. Late at night, at whatever party, he could be counted on to hijack the stereo, caterwauling at the top of his lungs to one of his favorite songs. "*And them good old boys were drinking whisky and rye . . .*" He sang that song every time—and it became a ritual that made everyone laugh. *Ah, there goes Seger again,* we said. *He sounds like a dying cat!* Only later did we realize the irony. He'd been singing about an accident all along.

At the hospital that night, the waiting area was flooded in bright light and the stench of antiseptic. I kept replaying this disconnected memory of a summer Sunday earlier that year—the full-color positive to the stark negative of this moment—when I'd gone with friends from the ambulance to a remote reservoir where swimming was illegal, the sort of prohibition that was too hard to resist. We bought beer at some shady package store and, once on the right dirt road, pulled over and climbed through a hole in the fence, then hiked into a pine-lined lake where we leapt from rocky cliffs into clear drinking water. It was one of those endless afternoons, jumping, swimming, sunbathing on the rocks, all punctuated by salty gulps of cold beer as the day unfurled, then curled back on itself. Every hour felt like a day, and I remember returning home that night, my skin still hot from the sun, feeling as if I'd been gone a week.

Now, here we were, perched on a cold November night, at what felt like a certain end, in a state of suspension, as the seconds flew. The news was eventually delivered. Seger's dad arrived, and heard for the first time about his son's death. He was handsome like his son, with a smooth face, but now his expression contorted, and he let out a high-pitched keen that made us all tuck our heads lower, knotting our hands over our stomach.

Afterward, we sat all night—our circle of friends—stupefied, empty. We were all, more or less, facsimiles of one another. We got good grades, played sports, would soon be off to decent colleges. And now we were marked, too, by this night. So we waited for the news about Jax, with the same sense of dread. When the sky shifted from black to purple, someone told us to go home, that there'd be more news in the morning. So we did.

We'd had a dead cat, of course—and our first dog (RIP, Buttons). There was my cousin Cindy who drowned when we were both five, but I'd been too young to comprehend. And my dad's dad, who I never really knew though wish I had, attached to some weird bag at the end. But the accident was the first time someone in my everyday life—someone on the bus, someone in the cafeteria, someone in my PE class—had just vanished. Up until that point, I'd yet to encounter a dead body on any ambulance calls. And now Seger's death led to the shock of that other question: Was Jax going to die, too?

No, it seemed, he wasn't. The morning after the accident he struggled back up to full consciousness. Despite severe injuries, he was able to talk to his family—and he asked to see me, too. We'd been friends for nearly ten years by that point, first thrown together on a Little League baseball team. I drove back to the hospital—alone this time—wondering if he was disfigured or what he'd say, the Thanksgiving Day traffic gliding with terrible normalcy.

When I was shown into the ICU, there he lay, hooked and wired, legs in weighted traction, wearing a neck brace. He was so pale I could see a network of veins under his face. He looked as if he'd just washed up on a limpid tide after the storm, having been a shipwrecked party to some unspeakable acts. His cheeks and forehead were pimpled with the buckshot of the shattered windshield. He struggled to raise his head. And I couldn't look away.

When I'd first met Jax at second base—we played the same position—he stood spewing flecks that sparkled in the bright sun, making a Tourettic sprinkler of spit. I took note of his oversized mitt (didn't he know that besides me he was the smallest one out here?), his untucked shirt, the points of sandy hair from the ridiculous shag beneath his maroon cap. He didn't quite fit in the frame—brash, misplaced elf that he was. Off the field he wore strange, moccasin-like shoes he'd gotten while living in Europe.

Jax was a blurter, a motormouth, a fantastic nicknamer, the

name capturing the thing in you that was your weakness, or your greatest exposure. For instance, there was another kid we knew who spoke in chopped-up, sputtering excitement, and as a young teen could often be found puttering around the Sound in his whaler, jumping waves. And so he became "Hooten, Hooten, Merrily." (I'm not even sure what it meant, but it was perfect.)

And Jax was fearless. I saw him dive madly at ungettable balls, and later fly into a rage at his older brother or the class bully, scary for the fury of his attack, his willingness to sustain a hail of blows if only to land one. Once he launched himself onto the hood of a moving car, trying to reach the driver, a boyfriend of his sister's. I saw him take flight many times from the wooden, paint-peeled railing at the pier, plunging into the warm water of the Sound, his wiry body in catlike adjustment to the force of pushoff, the midair moment of peace, then always that little spasm of joy as he crashed through the water's surface.

Now here he was, Jax, the once-mighty berserker, laid low. In legends, he would have been the knight felled by the act no one dared to make, the wading of some rough river, the arrow slung at the giant, the throwing of his body at Doom, sacrificing his life for something perhaps meaningless. But here, in suburbia, he'd marked the days of our boredom by stunts and diversions, driving, say, with only his knees, to his girlfriend's, over four miles of twisty road. Or jumping from a moving boat. Or laughing that laugh that was on you, and with you.

Everything in life held a joke, except this, right now. He rolled his eyes, trying to focus, smacked his cracked lips, unable to produce saliva for all the painkillers mainlined through the IVs needled in his arms. His tongue was swollen. He looked frightened, diminished. "I'm sorry," he said with difficulty, then fell back to his morphine pillow.

That was it. But he'd needed to say it, and wanted me to

convey it, to our friends—and beyond. Whatever had occurred on that night before Thanksgiving—and he had little to no memory of the accident—he took full responsibility for it. His eyelids fluttered shut, while I stood awkwardly, watching him sink beneath the surface, as if bearing witness to a drowning. Then I was shown out.

It happens sometimes with the dead. A magnetic field builds around their absence compelling silence—or, worse, repelling memory, driving it underground. Until, later, it rises again. And it always does: A drive past the spot in the road, or the cemetery, or the house where Seger lived—then didn't—and the recollection of a life, and the accident that claimed it, comes back in bony fingers.

So how do you pry yourself loose of the past? We were teenagers then. We knew everything—and nothing. As the story got stranger some of us acted out in unaccountable ways. There were those who disavowed the accident entirely, while others, like me, stupidly went looking for a second accident, to reenact—or atone for—the first.

In the days and months after Jax hit the tree, we regularly visited him in his hospital room, where uneaten meals came and went on wheels, where he floated on the fine chemicals that inhibited his pain. When their powers dimmed, you could almost feel him sinking, wincing, fighting. He couldn't move, couldn't get up to pee on his own. Already thin, he quickly lost about twenty-five pounds. He had skin grafts, gnarled, scarred, screaming-red attachments on his feet and his legs, both of which were badly broken. And yet, over time, as he regained his senses one by one, he tried to create a whole life up there: nurses who laughed at his jokes, a parade of friends that revolved through.

His mother and girlfriend were a ubiquitous presence, as were the wobbly, Day-Glo blocks of uneaten Jell-O perched on the nearby lunch tray.

Once, several weeks after the accident, as if recording the severity of a crash he knew nothing about, I drove by the body shop to check on the condition of his beloved sports car, the one that he'd paid for with money earned from odd jobs. But he pointed to a deck of glossy photos already taken by his brother. Fanning them in my hands, I found shot after shot of the ruined car. "It's still a miracle you lived," I told him, instantly realizing the larger cliché that everything you might say in such a situation sounded clichéd, which is when I shut up about all that.

Of course, Jax saw no miracle in his survival. Seger was dead, and he hadn't even been able to attend the funeral, the church pews loaded with friends who came as their own act of penance. ("The cemetery is my first stop when I get out of here," Jax kept repeating.) And there was no miracle because, he knew, someone would be made to pay.

Jax was a brutal realist. Hung like a tattered kite in the anti-bacterial blankness of his hospital room, held up by wires and sinkered lines, he awaited his fate. His body already broken, the blow would hurt less than Seger's death. But, still, it was a desperate way to think. He'd been reduced to an immobile fugitive whose faith rested on the fact that he would likely be charged for his friend's death.

One other thing about the dead: With them so, too, goes God sometimes. This is normal, I suppose, in the aftermath of tragedy: to question one's faith. But no matter how grim the circumstances, Jax never seemed to have done the same, for he was one of my few friends who didn't go—by choice or force—to church every Sunday. There'd been a summer night between our sophomore and junior years when we sat out on the pier, just the two of us, Jax reeling in bluefish. After he filled a bucket with them, and a school of thrashing bunkers moved on (they beat the water into a desperate froth above the blues that gave chase), we sat staring at the stars draped over everything and got into an argument about God. I said He existed; Jax said no way. We ended up in his bedroom, paging through his *World Book* encyclopedia, as I tried to press my case with "facts." The more I jumped from one entry to another—Noah's Ark, the Ten Commandments, miracles—the more absurd my "scientific inquiry" sounded.

"It's all made up," Jax said, laughing more at my stubbornness. "You're never going to find proof of Him in there."

At Seger's funeral they played another of Seger's favorite songs, with its lyric *Childhood living is easy to do.* People stood and said the right things. People—Seger's girlfriend and parents, family and friends—became distraught.

I wanted to show some emotion, too—because he would be badly missed—but there I sat, boiling at God/no God, while otherwise disembodied, bringing the dispassionate intensity of my EMT training to every detail so I could report it back to Jax. As if we were all part of one body that could be fixed somehow, as if we could tick off the checklist—airway, breathing, circulation—to find the hidden ailment stuck in the left ventricle, and be saved.

Soon, the enforced patterns of our quasi-martial school life reasserted themselves: We dutifully went to our classes, to physics (where the teacher prattled on about the inadequacies of highway entrance ramps, chalking on the board in a swirl of scribbles all the horrible ways you could die while entering the faster flow of traffic), and English (we were reading *Gatsby* now, the green light, the deadly car accident, the body in the pool), and calculus (as if to solve a proof might put the universe back together, reveal a different god). The swim season had begun, hours lost in bubbles, lap after lap staring at the black lane line of my own failing. And, of course, I continued riding the ambulance, showing up at random accident scenes to splint the broken femur or bandage the bloody hand.

There was a night when we were called to help a man hit by a car. He'd been thrown to the side of a busy main street, bloody and covered in slushy dirt. He was drunk and belligerent, and as the cars came and went, and the strobes lit his face, it slowly dawned on me that he was my old swimming coach, Mr. Wharton, a guy I really revered. When I told him who I was and reminded him that he'd coached me over hundreds of hours in the pool, he tried with difficulty to look me in the eye. How many times had he pumped me up, or screamed at me to quit slacking, or celebrated a come-from-behind win, all to show he cared? But on the shoulder of the road now, unable to focus on my face let alone stand in place, he said, "Why don'ya go f-f-fuck yourself!"

Much more polite was the concussed kid at the ice rink, who gently barfed on me when I bent over him, covering me with bilious warmth. "I'm sorry," the boy mumbled.

From his first return to consciousness, Jax had no memory of the accident, none whatsoever, but accepted his guilt as a reflex. Of course, we, his friends, didn't care about blood alcohol levels and toxicology tests. He'd made a bad mistake, was filled with contrition, and had our instant forgiveness.

But Jax's lack of memory didn't stop the police in their investigation, it drove them deeper. What exactly had happened that night became a nagging mystery. Pixels of rumor and eyewitness account began to resolve into the possibility of another explanation.

For instance, I had friends who, at the time of the accident, had just finished playing paddle tennis at the country club up the road. They'd heard the loud crash, and when they came out of the parking lot, they were startled by a car moving past them. Later, when piecing it back together, they kept wondering: Why was Flynn's car driving away?

But all these things soon became clear to Jax when the police chief paid him that awaited visit one day in his hospital room, offering a surprising theory that went like this: On that dark stretch of twisty road, as Jax zoomed north, Flynn's car went to pass, bumping the rear left panel of Jax's car, which sent him careening off a telephone pole, into the protracted skid that listed left to right, and hurtled his car into the tree.

Could it have been true?

When confronted with the theory, Jax was incredulous. According to the police transcript from the taped interview, he said, "I don't think any of my friends would do that. . . . First of all, [Flynn] and I are damn good friends."

(Beneath the fusillade of his verbal assaults, one of Jax's greatest redeeming traits was that he saw those in his inner circle as figures of unimpeachable character, as loyal as he. For all the sport he made of us—and we of him—he was absolutely blind to the deeper stamp of one's defect. His belief in his friends was so complete it verged on naïveté.)

Sometime around Christmas, however, Flynn's car was impounded, and the police would later say that paint found on its front fender seemed to match the color of Jax's car. By spring, Flynn had been charged with negligent homicide, reckless operation of a motor vehicle, and evading responsibility. The narrative that had Jax in a moment of singular teenage elation and irresponsibility now opened to another possibility: two cars traveling at a high rate of speed when one car passed on a tight turn and drove the other off the road. That is, as much as Jax had screwed up, maybe it hadn't been all his fault in the end.

So much of what happened in my town—the ancient town I knew and loved, the sprinkler-fed garden that existed during the Reagan Pleistocene in one of the outer rings around Manhattan—was never spoken of, or if so, only in whispered gossip. Affairs, eating disorders, teenage pregnancy, trips to rehab: Everybody seemed to know everybody's business, but it was cloaked and closeted. No matter how egregious or boorish the behavior or betrayal, to say it out loud, to reveal it beyond the social circle for which it was meant, was an affront almost as egregious. Every scarlet letter was partially hidden.

This is true of many places, or perhaps true of *every* place. No small shame accompanies the moment when our failings are made public—and it's with tense, bated breath that most wait for the unpleasantness to go away. However unsettling the news, a year, or two, or three, and it can be relegated to the snowdrift of memory and then forgotten, replaced by the new drama of the day.

As a child, I found this disorienting. The parents were whispering about *something,* something with intimations of pain or dread, dark fairy tales of some sort, but *what?*

The charges against Flynn made the story uncomfortably public, and soon the paper ran a long article detailing the events of that night before Thanksgiving; the strained, surreal situation at our high school of friends trying to pick sides, or figure out what to believe in the first place; and the tragedy of alcohol-related car accidents in our town. Was it suburban privilege, or our access to cars, or the dark, winding roads? The police captain was quoted as saying that, over the course of the past three years, a dozen young residents had died in automobile crashes. The pastor said he'd never seen such "tragedy with youth." The leader of a youth religious group claimed, "There's nothing but victims."

One night during our monthly organizational meeting at the ambulance service, in a room packed with fifty kids—everything coming to a standstill at twenty-minute intervals as another commuter train roared by—I found myself launching a prayer, the first, really, since the night of the accident. This particular evening included the awarding of special gold stars, reserved for the members of a particular crew for an exceptional call, our version of the Medal of Honor. The crew, as I remember it, had responded to a very bad crash on the interstate, had performed CPR under harrowing circumstances, and had brought someone back to life.

To be so recognized was the pinnacle, to have your name called to come down and receive a star from the ambulance service's founder, to be so distinguished for heroics among your own hypercompetent, wildly applauding peers. (We all knew they'd seen and done something we both hoped to and hoped *not* to.) It meant that for at least that moment the prophecy was true: You were so good, in fact, that you could raise the dead.

Dear God, I found myself praying, *give me something horrible and bloody. Let my next call be a multiple car crash with gasoline glugging all over the highway, or a cardiac arrest in a house fire, or a kid electrocuted on the railroad tracks. Let it be a shark attack or an alien invasion, whatever makes the best movie. Whatever is the most impossibly fucked-up, Lord. Just let me lay my hands on some big, honking, metal-twisted tragedy, so I can work my own miracle this time.*

Jax came out of the hospital with snow on the ground, then con-
valesced at home for a while. When the police asked to talk to
him, he went without his lawyers, against their advice, and tried
to answer what he could about the accident. Eventually, he returned to school on crutches, which later gave way to this clunky
stimulating device he'd sometimes wrap around his leg and plug
into the wall, what we called his "bone machine." He hobbled the
same halls as Flynn, but they studiously avoided one another now
while the various lawyers prepared for the criminal trial. Meanwhile, it seemed clear that Seger's family would bring a civil suit
of some sort, perhaps against all the boys. But, at least on the
surface, everything carried on, despite the awkwardness. College
applications were completed and sent out; no one got dumped by
his girlfriend.

Time accelerated. The snow melted, the season changed,
and our town bloomed: daffodils and forsythia at Easter, the dog-
woods and cherry trees not long after. Lawns turned green again,
the leaves drawing lush curtains over everything. The pier was
repainted, boats were put back in the Sound, their sails snapping
in the wind.

With the passage of time, Jax doubled his efforts to retrieve
some shard of absent memory. The most important night of his
life to that point, and he couldn't remember anything but leaving
Seger's house to go to a party. It was some cruel, cosmic joke. His
antipathies, guided inward by guilt, now had an outward target.
When Flynn pleaded not guilty to the charges, reiterating through
his lawyers that he hadn't been at the accident scene that night—
a version of events backed by Xavier, his passenger that night—
Jax became animated again: He could have forgiven them if they'd
admitted it from the start, but as they clung to their innocence,
Jax's fury grew.

It was simple: Knowing what Jax believed they knew—how could they have left him there? And where had they gone?

It was hard for him to concentrate on anything but the accident—it all went back to that stretch of road.

We drove it every night, in our minds. And Jax tortured himself with trying to remember. Eventually, in conversation with his doctors, it was agreed that he would visit a Yale psychiatrist who used hypnotism. It was maybe something Jax would have once regarded skeptically—and would be regarded skeptically by others—but what other choice did he have?

The session lasted nearly two hours. He left the psychiatrist's office not knowing anything, ostensibly hypnotized as he was—nor did his parents. The psychiatrist promised that, after reviewing the videotape, he'd send it along. Jax could only confirm what the psychiatrist had said, that things had gone "very well," whatever that meant.

A few weeks later the videotape arrived. Jax called, I drove down to his house, and we joined his parents to watch it for the first time. When Jax appeared on the television screen—or what I remember of Jax on that screen—he sat straight up, wearing a button-down shirt. His eyes were shut, and he seemed fairly relaxed, answering some basic opening questions. He was apparently already hypnotized, and the psychiatrist pointed out a needle stuck halfway into the flesh between his thumb and pointer finger, though Jax said he felt no pain and seemed to have no knowledge of the pin.

The psychiatrist then asked Jax to navigate the first four-fifths of the night in question: Jax described how Seger had loaded in with Jax at Seger's house, riding shotgun, how Flynn and Xavier followed in the other car. Jax led them up Ocean to Main; Main to Birch; Birch to the high school. Then the two cars emptied through the high school parking lot, turned left onto Coral, and took a right onto High. At this point, they were a quarter mile from the tree.

In the videotape, Jax, whose eyes are closed but tracking beneath the lids, seems at ease charting their progress. The psychiatrist leads him slowly, asks him to regard the action as though it's "a photograph." Jax is talking to Seger, music on the radio, streetlights passing in longer intervals now, speedometer needling twenty, twenty-five, thirty . . . Then he's on the straightaway before the curve with the maple tree, and the psychiatrist says, "Concentrate on your rearview mirror."

There are leaves skittering, dark branches overhead, a wedge of light before the sports car. He reaches to turn up the music, presses the gas. The lights are reflecting in the rearview mirror; he claims to see the other car right on his tail. He is talking to Seger.

He's talking to Seger. The music is blaring. Leaves are skittering. The road takes a turn. Music, leaves, dark branches. Seconds from hitting the tree, he looks in the rearview mirror, answers the psychiatrist. "I see [Flynn's] car," he says, "see him cut out left. He's getting closer. What's he doing?" For the first time, he seems to be talking not to the psychiatrist but to himself. "He's almost parallel," he says. "There's no way."

His eyes shut tight. He looks stricken, thin lips pressed together. And then his body rocks once, very hard.

Did it happen like this? If you'd seen the tape, you might have thought so, though there were doubters. At the very least, it gave Jax a narrative to which he could finally cling as the courts began to parse the evidence of what had occurred that night.

First came the criminal charges against Flynn that hovered over him for a year, ending in a courtroom drama that found Jax hobbling in on crutches and Flynn home from college accompanied to court by a dozen family members. Despite several eye-witnesses placing Flynn's car near the scene after a loud crash, the prosecutor admitted that it was "a difficult case to evaluate" and decided not to prosecute. He said his decision was based on the lack of reliability of Jax's account under hypnosis (especially since the theory that Flynn's car bumped his had initially been advanced by police), and the judge dismissed the case. Outside the courtroom, Flynn's lawyer said the ruling "completely vindicates my client" and that Flynn was headed immediately back to college.

In the wake of that dismissal came an array of civil suits that dragged along for years, yet after Jax's and Flynn's lawyers settled with Seger's family (for $100,000 and $300,000, respectively), everything whittled down to one: Jax suing Flynn for damages.

Nearly four years later, the newspapers covered that trial blow by blow. On the stand, Flynn testified that they'd been drinking 7UP and vodka at Seger's house, detailing the route of his travels, which was nearly the same as Jax's, claiming he'd never seen an accident and only learned about it twenty minutes later, after arriving at the party. Under cross-examination, when questioned about the possibly matching color of paint found on the fender of his car, he said, "I never hit [his car] before, nor any other . . . car." The paint smear, the director of the state's forensics laboratory testified, was "similar, but possibly not the same." There wasn't enough paint to allow a more complete analysis.

Other details emerged: They'd begun drinking around 6 P.M. and left for the party around 9:30. At an intersection well before the site of the accident, Xavier had jumped out of Flynn's car and run ahead to Jax's for matches, after which they traveled several "lengths" behind Jax before pulling away along a road leading to the party. Another eyewitness emerged, who testified that she had seen only Jax's speeding car near the scene before hearing the crash. So, had the police been overzealous in pursuing the case? In the end the jury found Flynn "negligent, but not responsible" and awarded no damages.

It was senior year, seventeen years old, the soccer and football season just over, a party in the offing. Could life have been any better?

At the end of the school year, just before prom, my prayer was answered: On a humid, cloudy night, I got my call. Already I'd racked up my cardiac arrest (that neighbor of ours) and a chaotic highway accident (an unsatisfactory broken femur), but this sounded promisingly bad.

We were summoned to a vast seawater farm with its rocky hillocks and ancient oaks, a place we knew for its Revolutionary War battles and midnight cow-toppling. This night, however, the darkness was almost a substance, and even as we directed our spotlight up into the trees, the rays were absorbed, leaving nothing to see. Eventually we came upon a car on the shoulder with its hazards blinking, someone who had witnessed the accident and rushed to help. The ambulance stopped, and I jumped out.

The way I'd dreamed it always involved saving someone. I would perform some suitable miracle, and later, in the most ridiculous part of the fantasy, my victim and I would become friends, exchange gifts, and, if she was pretty, maybe get married, her wheelchair being proof that I'd snatched her from sure death. Now, I ran over soggy ground to the car. I shone a flashlight over boulders and downed branches. The car was off in the trees, sitting a couple of feet back from the gnarled trunk of an oak, the hood accordioned to half its normal size. The driver's door was ajar and a dark figure loomed in back, the Good Samaritan trying to pull and hold traction from his awkward angle.

Despite his best efforts, the woman's head still lay facedown on the steering wheel. I could smell gasoline and manure—and gin and beer. I, too, was in an awkward spot, down on one knee inside the open front door. I positioned the flashlight on the dash and then, as I placed my hands over each side of her head, over her ears, with both my pinkies lifting from below her jaw, her face rose before me. Her skin was soft to touch but she was badly bloodied, and her nose, where there had been one, was now just a piece of bone. There was a clean hole in her forehead and something green and gooey seeped out. Her eyes, half shut, were white. She was groaning softly, rhythmically, the kind of groan that reflected a pain so deep it may not have been felt consciously.

I regretted my decision the minute I made it. And now we were stuck together.

It was going to be a long time before we could move her—we were going to need the Jaws of Life to get her out—let alone before she would see an emergency room. The girl, or woman, maybe in her midtwenties, had hit the tree going very fast, fast enough for her skull to have been punctured and brain matter to have seeped out.

I can recall a lot about the minutiae of that night, about how the firefighters arrived, lighting huge spots on the car, making it seem like day in that glade, and then the whining of the saw as they cut her out. Another ambulance arrived, with grown-up paramedics authorized to administer drugs, which they did, running lines from drip bags to the veins in her arms. There must have been two dozen people working, spectating, helping, at the height of the action. And then after they cut her loose, I remember standing on the back runner of the grown-up ambulance, standing there as they sheared the clothes from her body—her skin was pale, her breasts full—and put in more lines and an oxygen mask over her face, trying to stabilize her before leaving for the hospital.

Afterward, when the grown-up ambulance went screaming off, everyone took their things and quickly retreated. We were pretty shook up; someone on our crew was crying. The woman was in a deep vegetative state, on her way to death by morning. And we'd done nothing to change that. I myself came closest to a feeling when the clouds parted and the moonlight came down over everything, including the serrated wreckage, in thick, pale, silver beams, a moment that could have been godly but was nothing of the sort. The feeling was of betrayal, and shock.

Now, whenever my mind slips to such naïve meditations— these mock-heroic dreams of saving anyone from anything— I need only conjure that girl's face in my hands again. I need only hold that unmendable body close to realize how far I'd traveled from Thanksgiving. I got what I'd wished for, and I wanted to give it all back.

One last memory of that night: When I came home in my ambulance whites and orange fluorescent jacket, splatters of blood on my sneakers, my father was sitting at the kitchen table, his work arrayed before him in scribbles on the yellow legal pads he favored. I gave him a few details, leaving out the part about when the girl's parents showed up at the scene.

"It sounds pretty bad," he said.

"Yeah, it was," I said.

There was a pause, a long one. I couldn't look him in the eyes for fear it would all come out, all at once, in a great overwhelming gush, everything I'd held down. He might have already understood this. But I'd spent the year arming and armoring myself, and no one dared to approach anymore.

My father sat at the table, his face registering a father's concern. If he had something he needed to say—or a question to ask—he thought better of it. Or I cut him off, on my own at last.

"Good night," I said, putting my foot on the first step of the back stairway leading to my room, unmoving for a moment, then shifting my weight heavily to climb.

"Good night, son," said my father.

This past Thanksgiving marked the thirty-third anniversary of Jax's car accident and of Seger's death. For a long time afterward, you could see scars of the wreck on the trunk of the maple tree they hit, written in what seemed like Sanskrit. It was hard to look at; but for the few marks, the tree itself seemed to flourish, carrying no memory of that night.

Over time, the enormous trunk healed itself, its bark without blemish, and then one day it was simply chainsawed to widen the sidewalk. In all those years that the tree had loomed there—blooming its gaudy leaves in the spring, losing them like discarded twenties in the fall—I'd pass by searching for evidence that the accident had actually happened, that it hadn't just been a dream. I often thought to stop and touch the markings, like an archaeologist, though never did. When the tree suddenly vanished—only pale sawdust littered the spot—there came this rush of feeling: sorrow, elation, guilt.

In the years after, Jax built a hectic, successful career in finance. Sometimes when visiting home, I might drop in to find him hungover on a Sunday morning, on the couch beneath a blanket watching old horror films. Eventually, some time after the rest of us, he married and had children. A few years back, when I told him I wanted to write something about the accident, he said, "Write the truth, then."

It took a long while to write anything, because the truth seemed so cloudy and those involved had all been friends, and I believed, as someone had once said, there were only victims here. As I found, the magnetic field around the dead really does repel memory at first, too. But once I let it all back in, I couldn't shake Seger, the one who couldn't speak at all, the one who was suddenly everywhere. One newspaper article from the time of the civil trial detailed the courtroom testimony of a financial expert, who was asked to assess the amount of money Seger might have generated in his life. The expert said $1.3 million was a fair guess, which would amount to about $2.8 million today, but it seemed all the more tragic to reduce his life to a number like that. Give us any other number: YouTube videos sent or dogs owned, favors for neighbors or baby pictures emailed. Before the rock closed over the vault, I wish someone had speculated about what he'd found that night—God or no God—when he passed through the tree.

Perhaps we really are surrounded by the past, made prisoners of it. No matter how far we travel, how hard we try to forget, the scarred tree forever stands by the side of the road, if only in our minds. The only way to drive by is to set the past straight, once and for all, by remembering.

Talking to my brother, a lawyer now with kids of his own, I ask what he recalls about that night, and he says two things: (1) that the EMT from our ambulance service had told him something he couldn't ever forget: that Seger had been found with a shard of glass in his eye, and (2) that I had originally planned to join Jax and the rest of them on that evening, prior to the party.

If so, maybe I would have missed the opportunity to write

this down, as I have, which is the only way I can make sense of anything, or realize ultimately that there's no sense to be made of it: that once upon a time in a faraway town of emerald lawns, we grew up—and some of us lived. And some of us tried to turn away, but never quite could.

But most of all, if I'd been there that night, I couldn't tell you now that Jax, my old friend, can still be a beautiful pain in the ass and the truest person I'll know. If I were never to see him again, this would be my memory of him, of that year: the bucket full of blues, the encyclopedia without God, the energy of his wiry body flying, bowed in the sun, trying to remember why he ever wanted to leave this earth in the first place.

THE FIFTEEN-YEAR LAYOVER

MANCHESTER AND LONDON WERE DELAYED ON account of weather, and Tel Aviv was a faulty wing flap. Tenerife, Johannesburg, Málaga, and Marrakech had been canceled for various reasons, and stragglers from those flights were trying to figure out their next move on this humid, thunder-stricken night at the end of May. Some were arguing with the airlines; some were studying the ever-shuffling flight board; some were headed off to nearby hotels, parched and ready for cold gin and tonics to ease the dull throb of their long day. A few scanned the terminal mournfully, searching for the right bench or piece of floor to camp on for the night. Later it would make a good story: the purgatorial night spent in Terminal 1 at Charles de Gaulle Airport.

Meanwhile, the flight to Libreville, which was to leave in two hours, had brought a raucous horde to the Air Gabon counter, the women dressed in colorful gowns, a cacophony of clipped tribal dialects punching holes in the fabric of the terminal's white noise. The group, maybe two hundred in all, had materialized suddenly, as if by incantation, and would just as quickly vanish, in the silver gut of a 747 roaring southward over the desert for home. Like everyone in this place, they were apparitions, part of the incessant tide that rushed, then ebbed, that filled and emptied, filled and emptied—at moments leaving the airport a lonely beachhead, one that bore no trace of those who had just been there.

As the hour grew late, the terminal took on a nocturnal malevolence. To be inside this place was not unlike being inside the belly of a dying thing. Upon its completion in 1974, Terminal 1 had been hailed as a triumph, an architectural breakthrough built by Paul Andreu, who had proclaimed that he wanted the airport "to project the image of Paris and France as one of equality, and prowess in engineering and commerce." It appeared as a gray doughnut-shaped flying saucer—outer space brought to earth—with a burbling fountain at its open-air center. But over the years the fountain had fallen into disrepair and the water was shut off, revealing, behind its vapory curtain, a wreckage of rusted pipes and a cement shed, the inevitable artifacts of the future disintegrating, then becoming the past.

The whole world passed through this place, on the way to Paris, or from Paris, or simply using Paris to leapfrog to the next time zone. Disembodied voices called passengers to their gates, where they were delivered heavenward. Soccer teams and school bands tromped through, as did groups of old people wearing the same fluorescent T-shirts or church groups wearing the same baseball caps. They sat reading or photographing each other. They went for coffee or hamburgers. They wheeled by in wheelchairs. And then they were gone.

The longer you hung around in Terminal 1, the more mundane everything became. Had a herd of red oxen been unloaded from Jerba and wandered out of customs, it would not have been

such a surprise. Had a planeload of mimes come from Nurem-
berg, they would have registered only as part of the passing circus, hardly remembered afterward. In this context, a great deal
made more sense here than elsewhere, including perhaps Sir Alfred.

A friend told me about Alfred a few years ago, having heard of
him on the Internet. Initially, she believed him to be a work of
fiction: the man who had waited at Charles de Gaulle Airport for
fifteen years, on the longest layover in history. But then, the man
was real. It was said he could be found in the basement, near the
Paris Bye Bye bar. He'd be bald on top, with frizzes of wild hair
on the sides and four teeth missing, smoking a gold pipe, writing
in his journal or listening to the radio. It was said, too, that it
really didn't matter what time of day or night or which day of the
week one visited, for Alfred was always there—and had been
since 1988.

    The truth was that no one knew the whole truth about Al-
fred, not even Alfred himself. He was born in either 1945 or
1947 or 1953 and claimed to be Iranian, British, or Swedish. In
some ways, it was as if he'd been found in the bulrushes—or was
still lost there. For years now, he'd lived mostly on the kindness
of strangers, eating his meals at a nearby McDonald's, wandering
the terminal's white-tile floor as if it were his own cathedral.
Mostly, he passed time on the terminal's first level, in gurulike
meditation, on a red bench before a big, filmy plate-glass window
near a shop selling CDs. He sat in a tight envelope of air that
smelled faintly of regurgitation.

    Alfred's odyssey had begun when he was a young man from
a well-to-do family living in Iran and had ended here on an airport bench in Paris, by mistake. Twenty years ago, while living in

Belgium, he'd simply wanted to go to England by boat. But having rid himself of his identification papers during the voyage, he'd fallen into a twilight limbo as a nationless, unidentifiable person no one wanted, bounced from Belgium to England to France, where, finally, he'd been left stranded at Charles de Gaulle Airport.

He'd lived there ever since.

My first visit to Alfred came on the night of the Air Gabon flight to Libreville. I was staying for a time in Paris during a two-month stretch of intense travel. Adding it up, I'd spent nights in no fewer than fifteen different hotels, making me the frenetic opposite of Alfred. For me, the sheer speed of life had begun to strip it of its meaning. I imagined him to be some sort of mystic, sitting still on his Himalayan mountaintop, the keeper of monastic truths.

It was late, and the airport was empty and gave an air of exhaustion, of an animal too tired to resist the thing crawling up its leg. Going down a flight of stairs from the second level to the first, I nearly bowled over a young, tan flight attendant in a powder-blue hat who seemed in a hurry to get upstairs. After her, there was no one but Alfred.

If all the dramas of farewell and hello unfolded on the floors above, Level 1 was a kind of wasteland. What shops there were— a good number had closed in the past years—were shut up for the night. I walked quickly, following the circle of the terminal itself. Where the exterior of the building was gray cement, its doughnut-hole interior was all glass, so that you could look up and see three floors above you. On the second floor were the airline counters as well as six preliminary boarding gates that led to moving sidewalks, called electric tubes, that crisscrossed in the air, carrying travelers up through the open center of the terminal to the third floor, to more gates, called satellites, from which passengers disembarked for their flights. On the fourth level were the customs hall and arrival areas. I could see the electric tubes crisscrossing over my head, and in various windows all the way to the fourth floor, flashbulbs fired as travelers collected final photographic souvenirs of friends or family frozen in time.

And then there he was, laid out like a body in a sarcophagus, a snoring heap of human on a red bench, surrounded by a fortress of possessions. I counted several suitcases, six Lufthansa luggage boxes, two big FedEx containers—his life's possessions. There were clothes hangers and a collection of plastic beverage lids. On the table before him was a pile of McDonald's coupons. He was gaunt and angular. His skin was the sallow, almost purplish color of the white fluorescent light, except for the dark rings under his closed eyes. His sideburns and mustache were graying. The nail of his left pinkie was long and sharp, but the rest were neatly clipped. And despite the heat, he slept in a blue Izod windbreaker beneath a light airline blanket, a gift, it appeared, from a sympathetic flight attendant.

I made a lap, returned, and he remained absolutely still. The third time, believing he was really out, lost in some Giza of a dream, I paused before him, and as soon as I did, his eyes flipped open. He bore no expression, but then his face twisted as if he were in great pain or perhaps about to lash out; and yet before he could, before some unholy utterance issued from his mouth, his lids fluttered shut and he fell back to sleep—back, it seemed, to his own mysterious crater in an obliterated landscape.

Once upon a time, before facts were eroded by dreams, before the man destroyed and re-created himself, he had been a boy named Mehran Karimi Nasseri, happily living with five siblings in the oil-rich south of Iran. His father, a doctor, worked for the Anglo-Iranian Oil Company, while his mother assumed the duties of the household. By the standards of their country, they were rich and thriving in an area of Iran that was rich and thriving.

Mehran went to school, then college, where he took a psychology degree. But then, when he was twenty-three, his father died of cancer. While he grieved, his mother notified him that she was not his real mother, that he was, in fact, the bastard son of an affair between his father and a Scottish woman, perhaps from Glasgow, who had worked as a nurse for the Anglo-Iranian Oil Company. In order to protect her husband, who would have been sentenced to death by stoning for adultery, she had pretended the boy was hers. Now, in one blow, she sought to undo a life of lies. She banished him from the family. Mehran was still only a young man, smart and able, with a promising future. He was a person in forward motion who, until that moment, had known exactly who he was and where he was going.

Mehran argued with his mother, claiming that she *had* to be his mother. Wrapped into this argument may have been his father's estate and the inheritance that he felt was his due. Mehran threatened to take her to court, and her rebuttal was simple: with whose money? In the end, they worked out an agreement. Mehran would leave Iran to study abroad in England, where he would receive a monthly stipend.

In Bradford, England, he enrolled in a Yugoslav-studies program, happily toiling for three years, until one day, without warning, his stipend ceased. He tried to reach his family in Iran, calling and writing, but received no answer. With what money he had, he flew to Tehran, where he was detained, arrested, and imprisoned. He was informed that Iranian agents in England had photographed him marching in a protest against the Shah, which made him a traitor. It was the first of what would be three prison stays.

When his mother, now not his mother, found out about his incarceration, she paid the proper bribes to the proper authorities to secure his release, but again with a stipulation: He would be given an immigration passport, allowing him to leave Iran, never to return. Which is just what he did. Though he needed another country that would receive him, one that would grant him refugee status, his eventual plan was to travel to Glasgow in hopes of finding his real birth mother, who he believed lived there under some variation of the name Simon.

So he left. It's not known or remembered what ran through his mind as he boarded the plane that took him from Tehran to London, leaving his homeland and family behind. It's impossible to know whether he'd been struck so hard by these events that he'd already lapsed into dementia or amnesia, whether he felt betrayed and reeling in space.

Over the next several years, starting with England, Mehran appealed to at least seven countries for asylum, until Belgium granted him refugee status in October 1981. He settled in Brussels, working in a library, studying, receiving social aid. After saving some money, he approached the British embassy to make sure he could visit Glasgow with his refugee papers and was told there would be no problem. He purchased a ticket to England by boat, and once aboard, believing that he now occupied British soil because he was standing on the deck of a British ship, he placed his papers in an envelope and then in a mailbox on the ship, dispensing with them, sending them back to the Brussels office of the UN High Commissioner for Refugees.

This, of course, was an act of self-perdition that can't be explained and that immediately became the genesis of Mehran's woes. When he arrived in England and could show no papers proving his identity, he was sent back to Belgium, where, in turn, he was returned to England. To be rid of him once and for all, and playing a game of transnational hot potato with his fate, England then randomly sent him by boat to Boulogne, France, where he was arrested and sentenced and served four months in prison for trying to enter the country illegally. After his release, he was given eighty-four hours to leave France and, without a decent plan, went to Charles de Gaulle Airport to see if by flying to England he might have better luck.

He didn't. Arriving in London, he was detained and returned to France, where, out of money and ideas, he settled into life at Terminal 1. At first he was simply one of those stranded travelers, waylaid for a night on his way elsewhere—then another night, and another. But he didn't give up. He began soliciting fellow travelers for money—five francs here, a pound there—enough finally to buy a ticket. Two years later, he again went up the electric tube to the satellite, again he boarded the plane, again he landed in London, and again he was expelled.

Returning to Charles de Gaulle, he was arrested once more for illegally entering the country and sentenced to six months in prison. After his release in 1988, he returned to Terminal 1, perhaps out of sheer habit now, packed and ready but with nowhere to go.

So much had happened since his arrival, if not to him, then to the world at large. Reagan, Thatcher, and Mitterrand had given way to Bush II, Blair, and Chirac. Communism had fallen; Rabin had been assassinated, Manhattan had been attacked. As the years passed—through war and famine, AIDS and SARS—he sat near the Paris Bye Bye bar, gleaning bits from the radio, occasionally watching the television set that hung in one of the restaurants. He renamed himself Sir Alfred. He was motherless, fatherless, homeless, moneyless, sitting still in a place where humanity moved frantically. Alongside a river of tinkling cell phones and half-drunk coffees hastily disposed of, he chose to live his life—most of which was packed into Lufthansa boxes. He now insisted that he'd been born in Sweden and renounced all connections to Iran. He refused to speak Farsi. He refused to answer to his original name at all, even when his freedom was at stake.

For seven years, Alfred's lawyer, a bearded public advocate named Christian Bourguet, tried tracking down Alfred's identification papers in Brussels, the ones Alfred had mailed from the boat. Once he had those in hand, he in turn was able to procure from the French government a visa and a *titre de voyage,* a kind of passport that would have finally allowed Alfred to go to England. But when Alfred saw that the documents were issued for the Iranian national Mehran Karimi Nasseri, he became churlish, refusing to sign.

"Belong to someone else," he said in his Farsi-accented English, and so sealed his fate. On the temporary identification papers he held, both parents were simply marked by an X.

"I am an X, too," he said.

After watching him sleep, I went to see Alfred again the following day, about midmorning. The sun beamed in bright forms through the windows that looked out on the wrecked fountain and lit the shadowy corners. The first level was bustling with Monday travelers and, for a moment, seemed much less sinister, much more like your standard sterile airport, with bodies flowing past Alfred's table or up the electric tubes to the satellites. For his part, Alfred was pleased to have a visitor, probably would have been pleased to meet anyone who stepped out of the moving crowd long enough to say hello. He cleared a small table in front of him and commandeered a nearby chair. For a man who'd made a life of sitting still, he looked relatively fit, with strong-seeming arms.

When he spoke, however, his voice was weak, and he claimed he hadn't uttered a word in two months. Mumbling more to himself than to me, his words swam three-quarters of the way across the table, then back again. Occasionally, a cluster reached my ear. Everything he said cloverleafed back into his "case," though it was nearly impossible to determine what that case was—after all, his lawyer had solved his immediate dilemma by securing the papers that set him free. He vehemently claimed that Mehran Karimi Nasseri was free to go but that Sir Alfred wasn't. Soon I came to regard any mention of his "case" as short-hand for everything he had forgotten or chosen to forget, as code for a mysterious process of healing that called for the complete exorcism of the past.

He said he believed his real mother was still alive in Glasgow and that he would find her. "I hope not to be here by Christmas," he said with the pained smile and resignation of a man who'd most certainly be here by Christmas or who was simply talking about some Christmas in the far future, after a nuclear winter.

When I asked whether, after fifteen years of this isolation, he felt he'd be lost in the world if he left the airport today, he said in his clipped English, "No, why? Same world." When I insisted that, if anything, these past fifteen years had in some ways drasti-cally altered our daily existence—citing the rise of computers, cell phones, and the nearly instantaneous changes in everything from food to fashion—he said, "Not worried."

After about a half hour of this kind of chat, his excitement began to peter out into that preordained moment, one that would repeat itself again and again, when, as I still sat across from him, he would simply raise a newspaper between us, like letting down a curtain, and begin reading. So this was goodbye? To let him gently off the hook, I announced that I was going to stretch my legs, and was answered by a single rustle of the paper. Then I walked a bit, figuring it probably didn't matter when I returned to him, as his sense of time must have been more like that of an animal who moves slowly, gauging the day by light and dark, or months by the weather.

On another evening, I asked how he'd spent his day, and he said he'd listened to the radio for five minutes and had brushed his teeth. That was all he'd managed in fourteen hours. He sat in a dull torpor, occasionally rubbing his head or working his jaw muscles, that blank stare taking in everything and nothing at once. Travelers streamed past, sometimes stealing a glance at him and his fortress. "People pass me by but don't touch," he said cryptically. When I asked what he'd learned about human nature here, in a place so transparently full of emotion, he said, "Everyone has their own function. They are mostly indifferent." When I pressed him about what function he served, he said, "I am sitting here, waiting."

At first I was intrigued by the mere logistics of a life spent waiting. No matter how little one accomplished in a day, Sir Alfred had accomplished less. His life rode no discernible narrative arc, and he had seemingly embraced the absurdity at the center of existence to the point where his sitting in place seemed like a political protest, seemed so meaningless it had to have meaning.

Yet Alfred clung to a few self-made purposes: waking, shaving, protecting his nest. He rose between six-thirty and eight in the morning. He would yawn, stretch, and sometimes pull out a hand mirror, check himself, and maybe shave with an electric razor, right there on his bench. He didn't limit himself to shaving in the morning, though. He shaved after lunch or before bed; he shaved in midconversation or while spooning a McDonald's sundae, a McFlurry, into his mouth.

He had his choice of two nearby bathrooms; he preferred the smaller and quieter of the two because it was closer to his bench and had a shower. Even though his belongings blocked the red bench from intruders—and he used a table and chair to provide effective reinforcement—he still sometimes had to shoo people away, tired passengers looking to recline and, finding no comfort in the metal benches that had replaced the plush red ones three years before (all except Alfred's), mistakenly choosing to brush aside his mess and sit or lie down, at which point Alfred appeared like an offended rooster, bristling and crowing and kicking up dust. "Okay, my place," he said. "Out now, thank you."

On occasion, there were other things that organized his waking hours. Someone had recently given him a carton of Thai cigarettes, for instance, and every day he gave me a progress report on how many he had smoked and how many were left. He said he normally smoked only a few a day, though a rough count over one afternoon suggested he smoked a few more than that. There were times when lighting up must have constituted his day's greatest exertion.

Sometimes he made a trip to the bank upstairs, where he had his savings account. While he was gone, a shopkeeper would guard his belongings, though a number of his bags were merely stuffed with newspapers, some with articles related to his case. Still, he'd recently lost a collection, most valuable to him, of *Time* magazines, so there was an ongoing need to be vigilant. Stung by the loss, he told me he now limited his wandering. Even though the first level of Terminal 1 had spotty air-conditioning and though it was now sweltering, he hadn't stepped outdoors to get a breath of fresh air in a month.

"I dream sometimes of going through the window and reaching the sky," he said.

With an unimaginable amount of time on his hands—growing old, alone, and having to look only to himself for the answers to life's mysteries—Alfred created his own mythologies, a basic religious impulse. But Alfred's view of the world had more to do with how McDonald's had siphoned money from him when France converted from francs to euros in 2002, or how the French postal service conspired to no longer deliver mail to him from all over Europe—some of it containing money—sent by people who believed he was a symbol, one of courage, of bureaucratic bungling, of soulless modern life swallowing us whole, of our human existential dilemma writ large.

When a noticeable growth appeared on his head a few years ago, he blamed it on "coffee and fake cola products." He showed me a photograph of his head from 1999 with the incontrovertible proof of a large, unsavory bump, "just there, jellifying," he said. The airport doctor, a short, busy man with bad teeth whose office was less than fifty yards from where Alfred sat, had watched it grow. Finally, he intervened, taking Alfred from the airport— one of the few times he'd ever left—to a nearby hospital, where the growth was removed. Yet in Alfred's retelling of the incident, he had performed the operation himself, in the bathroom, as a kind of medieval bloodletting.

In fact, the longer he sat there, the less Alfred seemed to remember, or the more fantasy merged with the few events of his life, casting out all other bit characters. Rejected by humanity, he now rejected humanity. The outside world was simply extraneous. His mind was panes of stained glass, rearranged in some self-satisfyingly inscrutable design.

When asked what he could recall of his boyhood in Iran, he could conjure only three distinct memories:

1. He had lived in a stone house.
2. He had been held down in a chair and stabbed repeatedly by actors in a theater, who had tired of him

shouting out their lines when they forgot, though that had allegedly been his job.

3. He had nearly died in a car accident that never took place.

When pressed to fill in the details, he would only add, "A house like those in England" or "You have to ask them why they stab and stab" or "I jump and run."

When I asked to see his collection of photographs, thinking they might catalyze his memory, most turned out to be of inanimate objects in the terminal: the revolving door in a wild snowstorm; an abandoned suitcase the bomb squad had exploded, leaving confettied paper everywhere; a counter in one of the nearby shops that had been dusted for fingerprints after a break-in. The rest of the photos were of him, either standing solo, staring straight into the lens, or posing with various passersby, none of whom he seemed to remember.

When I pressed him to identify someone, anyone, he spoke to in the airport, anyone with whom he had a human connection, he claimed to have known one of the employees at McDonald's for four years. When I asked his name, Alfred said, "I have no idea."

It's possible that our most religious moments occur in airports rather than in churches. This is not blasphemy but a fact of modern life. Apprehension, longing, and the fear of complete disintegration—what palpably animates an airport full of passengers about to take to heaven at the speed of sound—is what drives us to our gods.

Over the course of a few weeks, I looked forward to seeing Alfred for perhaps no other reason than that he seemed glad to see me, too. In some ways, I came to see his dilemma as a question of faith. After so many betrayals, he feared the world beyond his red bench. The red bench was his hovel, home, and haven—and yet occasionally he made the motions of wanting to break free. One day, for instance, I found him checking the classified ads in the paper, declaring that he was looking to buy a car. Perhaps it empowered him to say so, but it seemed impossible: Sir Alfred behind the wheel, on his way to who-knew-where. As he squinted at the classifieds, I was struck by the poignancy of his circumstance, the strength—if delusion—of his hope, an abnormal man living out of time, attempting to take on the mantle of a normal life.

I asked whether he was angry about having lost fifteen years of his life in this black hole at Terminal 1. "No angry," he said. "I just want to know who my parents are." Are you happy, then? I asked. "I used to be," he said, "but now I'm stuck between heaven and hell." When I asked if he believed in God, he nodded his head as if he were drawing the letter *U* with his nose; that was neither yes nor no. "Believe in soul," he said. "Your soul is not separate from your function, but it is also more. Your soul is your dream, your dream life, your dream world, and it walks around with you, wherever you go."

Then he gestured to his kingdom of stuff, his bags packed with newspapers and magazines, with his meager clothing and pictures of exploded suitcases, with endless pages from his journals relating the day's radio news. "Nothing has changed for me except I have more baggage," he said. He leaned back and rubbed his head, where the bump had once been, with a kind of superstitious care. "But I'm prepared," he said. "Other people stay in this place for a couple of hours. They arrive and go to cars that are waiting, or buses. They come and go up the electric tubes to the satellites. When it's my turn, when I am called, I'm ready to go to the satellite."

Eventually I paid a visit to his lawyer, Christian Bourguet. During the reign of the Ayatollah Khomeini, Bourguet had been Iran's lawyer, had been the man who arranged Khomeini's Air France ticket from exile back to Tehran in 1979 and had secretly negotiated with the Carter administration for an end to the hostage crisis, an end he said that should have come about nine months before it did. On the wall was evidence of Bourguet's work during that time: a couple of framed personal letters from Jimmy Carter.

He told me that when he'd first met Alfred, the man had been quite lucid in the telling of his story, but that over time he had become "free of logic," and so his story kept changing. After Alfred suddenly asserted he was Swedish, Bourguet asked how he then had traveled from Sweden to Iran. "Submarine," Alfred said. Perhaps he was crazy now, but, Bourguet argued, he'd arrived there by increments. "Assume that you are twenty-three," he said, working a piece of clay in his fingers while chomping on the stem of his pipe. "You've finished your studies in psychology, your father dies, and at that exact moment, your mother says, 'I'm not your mother.' You have brothers and sisters, but not anymore. And because you're illegitimate, you're a nobody in your country. You have no rights. And so you ask, 'Who is my mother, then?' You leave your country, only to return to be imprisoned, and then leave with nowhere to go, whereupon you are imprisoned again—and then once more.

"In your mind, you have renounced this person and this name that was formerly you, but when, years later, you go to get what you think is your freedom, the papers identify you as that person. How strong does a man have to be to resist so many big shocks?"

But then, I wondered aloud, why not suck it up and simply sign the documents, then legally change your name forever? "Let me tell you something," said the lawyer, rocking back in his chair, a ball of flame from his lighter disappearing into a nest of newly packed tobacco. "He's not leaving the airport. He's no one outside the airport. He's become a star there. Or he feels like a star—and acts like one. If you come with a camera, he knows his best side. Otherwise, his personality has broken into pieces."

He sucked deeply on the pipe, placed the clay on his desk, and looked up, shaking his head in pity. "I'm afraid the sad fact is that he's now completely destroyed."

The last time I went to see Alfred, it was evening, and another storm had blown over Paris, the wind moving the leaves like so many small fluttering wings, lights falling in slick, watery dabs over pavement, over the Seine itself. Cool air came rushing to replace the humid day, but when I entered the terminal, the remnant of that hot day was still trapped inside. I proceeded with my routine, making laps on the floors above before seeing Alfred. I stood for over an hour in arrivals near an expectant group waiting for a delayed flight from New York City. I meant to leave after five minutes, but with each passing second I found myself further embroiled in the small dramas of each party—the little girl with a sign that read YOU ARE HOME, PAPA; the three hippie amigos playing guitar and bongos badly to everyone's annoyance; the woman, so prettily dressed in white, who already couldn't hold back tears.

Later I found Alfred sitting on his red bench, shaving. Behind him, through the plate-glass window, lay the wreckage of rusted pipes, a reminder that at one time something spectacular had occurred out there. It was late and empty again. The white-tile floor seemed to sweat; the scent of regurgitation hung in the air; and here was my guru, my holy man, my ayatollah, opening and closing his mouth, exercising his jaw muscle. Then he started to speak. "I don't smoke for three days," he said somewhat bitterly. That was it. That was all he could muster.

If anything, with each day Alfred was becoming another inanimate object in this airport, devoid of the things that make us human, including memories. Soon, I imagined, he would forget the stone house or being stabbed or the car crash that had never taken place. He would forget that there'd ever been a guy at McDonald's he once remotely knew or maybe even the exact reason that he still sat here.

Shortly, his newspaper came up between us and rustled once. Goodbye. People washed past on their way upstairs for flights to Hamburg, Dublin, Oslo. Instead of leaving him entirely, I walked over to the bar, bought a beer, and settled in a window a third of the way around the circle. I drank my beer and then another. From where I sat I could look up into the windows on each floor of Terminal 1. I could see through twenty-four different panes, and in each of them, twenty-four different scenes played out: people saying goodbye, sobbing, laughing, lost in meditation, confused, in focused transit. To have heard their thoughts would have been to let loose all the joys and woes of the world.

Across the way, Alfred readied himself for bed, then lay down and, despite the heat, zipped up his windbreaker and pulled his thin blanket over his body. After twenty minutes or so, he seemed as if he were lost in a dream: His legs rose up and his knees lightly bumped each other; then his legs went down again. He was someone out of a fairy tale, someone shipwrecked or lost or trapped forever in an unsolvable nightmare. And yet, stripped of everything, he was his own god.

Above, the electric tubes were lit brightly in the night, and from my vantage here in the basement you could see the crowns of people's heads reflecting off the glass ceiling of the tubes as they were lifted toward the satellites. If you sat long enough, looking down on the crowns of their heads, you could have imagined yourself an angel. And it occurred to me that if you sat long enough thinking such dangerous thoughts, you might never leave either.

THE MOST DANGEROUS BEAUTY

BENEATH THIS BLACK ROOF, ON A well-clipped block in a small midwestern town on the Wabash River, a professor opens his eyes in the dark, confused at first by an outline under the sheets, this limp figure beside him in bed. From some primordial haze slowly comes recognition, then language: *bed, sheets, wife* . . . *Andrea*. He kisses her and rises. He is fifty-eight years old, and he wakes every morning at this ungodly hour, in his finely appointed brick house with exploding beds of lilies, phlox, and begonias. After three heart attacks, he goes now to cardiac rehab. Wearing shiny blue Adidas sweats, he drives off in the family's Nissan. Once at the medical center, he walks briskly on the treadmill, works the cross-trainer machine, and then does some light lifting. It's a standing joke that if he's not there at 6:00 A.M. sharp, the staff should just put on ties and go straight to the funeral home. After his workout, as he drives to his house, the town glows in a flood of new light; the river bubbles in its brown banks as the flies rise; the lawns are almost too bright, green with beauty and rancor.

He feels better for this visit, more alive, another day on earth ensured, another chance to breathe in the smell of cut grass before a spasm of summer lightning. He takes Lopressor, Altace, and aspirin to thin his thick blood. Even now fragments accumulate, arteries begin to clog, his cardiac muscle weakens, slows, speeds again to make up time. There is so little time.

He wears his silvered hair neatly parted. A creature of habit, he's worn the same style of round tortoiseshell-frame glasses for thirty years. He drinks a cup of chai every afternoon of his well-plotted life at a café near his office at Purdue University, where he teaches medical illustration. He is a humble, somewhat conservative man, a Roman Catholic whose joy in the simplest things can be overwhelming, inexplicable. After his third heart attack, when they jammed tubes into him and he was pretty sure it was over, he became insistent. "Just tell me I'm going to mow the lawn again!" he said to his doctor. "Tell me I'm going to mow the lawn!"

These were nearly his last words.

If this man can be oversensitive and a bit obsessive, if he has an exact recall of the big and small injustices that have been done unto him—he keeps old hurtful letters on file—he knows he must unburden himself now, make peace with those in his life: wife, children, friends, colleagues. And with the vanished ghosts that roam the rooms of his memory: mother, father, brother.

And what of Pernkopf? What of Batke?

He can't fathom where to begin with the Book, now forever out of print, effectively banned. When considering it, he often conjures the language of some illicit affair: rapture, consumption, shame. And if he was betrayed by that lover, does it lessen all those days he spent in love? Ah, the Book, the nearly unbearable perfection of its paintings, and then, weltering behind it, armies clashing across the face of Europe, six million spectral Jews.

Under pressure, history splits in two: the winners and the losers, the righteous and the evil.

It's not like this man to act impulsively, to yield control, to risk missing cardiac rehab, to wander seven thousand miles from his dear doctor, but he does. He packs a bag with some old journals, drives from West Lafayette to Indianapolis, and gets on a plane. He travels eight hours in coach, through spasms of lightning, wearing his Adidas jumpsuit, hair neatly parted. Fragments accumulate; arteries begin to clog. He drinks some wine; he pores through his journals, these copiously recorded memories of a sabbatical he took twenty-three years ago, when he went on a pilgrimage to find the Book's greatest artist, when he still worshipped—yes, really, that's the word—the Book's achievement. He naps, wakes, reads his decades-old handwriting again. If he were to die on this plane, in a hotel lobby in Vienna, in the echoing halls of the Institute searching for some truth, will he have been cleansed? After all, he didn't do the killing or throw the bodies from the window. He didn't spew the hate that incited a hemicycle of fanatics.

No, his sin, if that indeed is what it is, was more quotidian: He found beauty in something dangerous. There are days when he can't remember how it began, and nights when he can't sleep, remembering.

A cloudy afternoon, Vienna, 1957. A man sits and smokes, a body laid before him. A creature of habit, he wears a white lab coat and a white polyester turtleneck, no matter what the weather. He is small, with a crooked nose and skewed chin that give him the appearance of a beat-up bantamweight. He has a lot of nervous energy, except when he sits like this. When he sits like this, he seems almost dead, a snake in the heat of day. Before him lies a nameless cadaver that was brought up from the basement of the Institute, from the formaldehyde pools of torsos and limbs, then perfectly prepared like this: an incision, a saw to the breastbone, the rib cage drawn open, the heart removed. He stares at this open body, looks down at the floor, stares some more.

In his right hand, he holds a Habico Kolinsky, one with long sable hairs, his brush of choice. On the rag paper before him, he has sketched some rough lines, has plotted his colors. And now, after this prolonged stillness, he bursts from his chair. He paints across the entire canvas, maniacally, almost chaotically. He lays in washes of color, gradually building the glazes. His hand darts back and forth. He goes at the bronchus and then the thoracic duct. With his tongue, he licks the brush and lifts off pigment to show phantasmic light on this internal landscape. He flicks turquoise here and there to make the fascia appear real. What he does is highly intricate, but at this speed it's like running on a tightrope. He is in deep space, underwater, gravityless. He works in a fever, shaking and levitating. Weeks pass, and still he stands before this painting, this body.

What is his desire? To be a rich man, to paint what he chooses, to hang in museums, to make love to beautiful women, but he is on the wrong side of history. And yet he isn't a demagogue or a war criminal. He is merely a trained fine artist who must paint dead bodies for the money—and that's what he will do, for nearly five decades of his life: brains, veins, viscera, vaginas. Perhaps his sin is quotidian, too: In 1933 he says yes to a job because he's hungry, and so sells his soul, joining Pernkopf's army of artists, which soon becomes part of Hitler's army. Now a silver light pours thickly through the tall glass windows. He lifts pigment, then swabs his brush over the *Aquarellfarben* cake. He expertly paints in the ascending aorta and pulmonary trunk, giving them ocher and purple colors. He creates this astral penumbra of arteries and air pipes, galaxies within the body. For one moment, he does it so well he vanquishes memory. It has always been just him and the canvas. And as certain as he will be forgotten, with each painting he believes he won't. He is the righteous one, the butcher's son made king.

They don't know how to treat him, this unusual specimen, this volcanic event. He shakes and levitates in his temporary palsy. It is the summer between seventh and eighth grades, 1957. Far away, in another world, an unknown man named Franz Batke paints in Vienna while this unknown boy, David Williams, has some sort of infection. His body has burst out with huge open sores on his face, back, and chest. The shots put him into a high fever that brings on convulsions. He is a supernova; he could be cursed.

Outside, the Michigan sun burns, it rains lugubriously, and then there is bright light on the panes again. The floor shines with menace. There is no explanation for this suffering. No treatment that the doctors can find. Inside him a cell has split in two. He is a boy who, by some internal chemical flood of testosterone and disease, is fast becoming something else, a different animal.

In the fall, he is released from his hospital cell. He lifts weights and runs the sand dunes by the lake to build his body back. He dreams of being the middleweight champion of the world, the kid from Muskegon, Michigan, hitting someone so hard that he separates the guy from his body. If only he could convert his rage to power and skill, it might happen. After school he takes a football and runs through the cornstalks in the backyard, pretending each stalk is a tackler. It is twilight now, and the boy has been running through these cornstalks for hours, for days. His shirt is streaked with blood from where he's been stabbed by the stalks, the scabs broken open, releasing pustulants from the body. When he heals, his skin will be runneled and pocked. He will always live a word away from that good-looking upperclassman, the one in the locker room who, before everyone, called him Frankenstein. It will take him decades to understand these scars and what has happened to him. What has happened to him?

Years later, after crossing an ocean in search of something he can't put a name to, he finds himself in a room with the old man, who smokes so many cigarettes it seems he is on fire. They talk about the thing they both love most: art. Sitting in that studio in Innsbruck, David Williams, the would-be middleweight champion of the world from Muskegon, Michigan, who speaks in faltering German, feels immediately at home with this Austrian, Franz Batke, who speaks no English and who, unbeknownst to him, is a former Nazi. How has this happened? Because they speak only of art. Williams will write in his journal, "I am truly beginning to see this man as a genius." After all, among the scarred carapaces of lost civilizations, among the ugly ruins and tormented dreams of history's fanatics, some beauty must rise, mustn't it?

Mustn't it?

The cell has split in two. There is no diagnosis, no explanation. Clouds cover the city, hyena-shaped, turning on themselves. The tanks are rolling, and the people come out of their houses, clutching bouquets to pledge allegiance to their invaders, without fully understanding. They throw flowers and sing. They are thin already, engraved by rib cages and dark rings beneath their eyes. It is not easy to understand. Their euphoria is blinding.

On this morning, Eduard Pernkopf rises at 4 A.M. He is a short, portly man with gray-blue eyes, dour and phlegmatic,

though not entirely humorless. He wears round glasses and dili-
gently reads his well-thumbed Schopenhauer. He has a scar on his
left cheek from a duel he once fought. It is hard to imagine this
particular fellow in a duel. And it is equally hard to imagine what
moves inside him—ambition, zealotry, some canted idealism?
Or is it just sickness? He has thyroid problems and crippling
headaches. A blood clot is moving slowly toward his brain. When
his first wife dies of tuberculosis at twenty-seven, he pens a symphony dedicated to her titled *The Pleasure and Pain of Man*. He
marries her sister. He smokes exactly fifteen cigarettes a day. He
comes to care about only two things: the Book and the Party.

The Book begins as a lab manual while Pernkopf is teaching
at the Anatomy Institute in Vienna. He needs a dissection guide to
help students better identify the organs and vessels of the body,
but he finds other anatomy texts outdated or unsatisfactory, and
he is a perfectionist. He soon has what seems like an impractical
dream: to map the entire human body. And this dream is what
leads to his life's work: an epic eponymous four-volume, seven-
book anatomical atlas, an unrelenting performance spanning
thirty years of eighteen-hour workdays. Here our mortality is
delivered in Technicolor, in eight hundred paintings that illumi-
nate the gooey, viscous innards of our own machine, organized by
regions: the Chest and Pectoral Limb; the Abdomen, Pelvis and
Pelvic Limb; the Neck; and the Topographical and Stratigraphical
Anatomy of the Head.

The group he recruits to paint comprises fine artists, some
of whom have trained for years and are known as *akademische
Maler*. At this time—the early 1930s—there is no work in Vienna. People scrounge for crumbs. Beggars line the streets. On
Fridays shopkeepers leave small plates of pennies out for the
poor. A rich person is someone who owns a bicycle, and the artists take their jobs willingly, thankfully. Perhaps in another place

and time, they'd be famous for their watercolors of Viennese parks or Austrian landscapes. But here they draw the cold interiors of the human body.

Pernkopf oversees these men and women: four, seven, nine, then eleven artists in all. Perhaps he is dimly aware that this moment may never repeat itself. Never again will social conditions warrant that so many talented fine artists gather together to detail the body, and never again will the art of medical illustration veer so close to that of fine art itself. The book will coincide with the discovery and refinement of four-color separation: All anatomical works before it will seem to be from Kansas, while *Pernkopf's Anatomy* will seem to hail from Oz.

For his part, Pernkopf directs the dissections and preparations of the cadavers for painting. These preparations can be exacting, hour upon hour spent pinning back skin on a forearm, scraping fascia from a bone, sawing skulls open to reveal a fine minutiae of arteries, the skein of veins beneath the dura. But he learns quickly: The better the preparation—the more fresh and vivid the viscera—the better the painting.

He is driven by ideas of accuracy and clarity. He stresses again and again: The paintings must look like living tissue, even *more* alive than living tissue, if such a thing is possible. He strikes a deal with a publisher named Urban & Schwarzenberg, which after seeing the early work is convinced that Pernkopf's book may one day be mentioned in the same breath as da Vinci's sketches of the body, Vesalius's *Fabrica,* or Sobotta's *Atlas der Anatomie des Menschen.*

Meanwhile, the cell has split. The Jewish diaspora of the late nineteenth century—one bringing thousands from southern Poland and western Ukraine to Vienna—has also now projected Jews into the highest reaches of society, causing deep-seated rancor. Anti-Semitism becomes commonplace. Even at the Institute, competing anatomical schools rise under one roof to segregate the Jews from their Austrian detractors, a student army of National Socialists. Passing in the halls, students come to blows.

For Pernkopf this violence is as it should be. From the moment he enrolls as a student at the University of Vienna, in 1907, at eighteen, he joins a nationalistic German fraternity, which becomes the foundation for his later fervency as a National Socialist, including his belief that Jews have corrupted German culture. Shortly after joining the Nazi Party in 1933—which is against the law in Austria at the time—he joins the *Sturmabteilung,* or Brownshirts, the underground uniformed army of Nazis. And then he waits.

Months, then years, pass. Life worsens. The institute is only a microcosm of Vienna itself, of Austria as a whole, of this entrenched hatred pushing up through the dirt of society. On March 12, 1938, Hitler enters the country uncontested, in an open limousine. He speaks from the balcony of the town hall in Linz to crazed flower-throwing crowds and claims his beloved birthplace, Austria, as his own—a blank-check Nazi annexation known as the Anschluss. In Vienna, where Hitler once made watercolors of Gothic buildings, flags bearing swastikas are unfurled. Some feel a rush of hope; others, like Sigmund Freud, who lives only four blocks from the Institute, pack to leave.

And so, on this morning, Pernkopf readies himself for the most important speech of his life. It is 4 A.M., the time he usually reserves for writing the words that accompany the paintings in his atlas. He scribbles in shorthand, striving to find the right intonations and arpeggios, giving words to some echo he hears in his head. Later his wife will type the loose pages, and then he will stand in the hemicycle at the Institute before a room packed with medical school staff, pledging allegiance to Adolf Hitler, in his storm trooper's uniform, a swastika on his left elbow. He will call for "racial hygiene" and the "eliminating of the unfit and defective." He will call for the "discouragement of breeding by individuals who do not belong together properly, whose races clash." He will call for sterilization and "the control of marriage." And finally he will praise Hitler for being a man who has found "a new way of looking at the world," as someone "in whom the legend of history has blossomed."

The speech becomes an overt declaration of war within the university. Jewish students will soon be thrown from the third floor of the Anatomy Institute to a courtyard below, and 153 Jewish faculty members will be purged—some will eventually be sent to concentration camps; others will flee. In this milieu of bloodlust, the bodies of those tried and guillotined after the Anschluss—more than a thousand in all, mostly political opponents, patriots, Communists, and petty criminals, among them eight Jews—will be stacked like cordwood behind the Institute, to be used as preparations for Pernkopf's sacred atlas. From the legend of these human limbs, his temple rises.

As a child, the boy obsessively draws. He draws humans and animals. He does crude landscapes in watercolor. When he holds a brush in his hand, when he puts that brush to paper, he becomes invisible. He cannot be seen. He has no history, no scars.

He becomes the first in the Williams family to graduate from high school, then goes to community college. In his freshman biology class, he sketches a frog, the insides of a frog, with amazing accuracy and clarity. When his instructor sees it, she tells him about universities where one can learn to draw the insides of frogs—and other animals, including humans.

David the artist may be an enigma to his factory-working parents, but his younger brother, Greg, is an aberration. While

David is short, stocky, and a loner, Greg is tall, angular, and out-going. As David has his art and science, Greg toys with the idea of becoming a priest.

If the brothers dwell in alternative realities, they uncon-sciously remain each other's lodestars, each other's partial reason for hope. For they have the same goal: to escape the blue-collar drudgery of gray Muskegon and a house that has slowly gone from Norman Rockwell portrait to Ingmar Bergman film, mother listing into alcoholism and mental illness, father bur-dened by some deeply hidden guilt from his own unspoken past. Each son is searching for some kind of euphoria to obliterate the pain of growing up in this house. At the age of twenty, David abruptly moves to Hamburg to live with a woman he has met when she was visiting the States and who loves him, his scarred self, something he once thought impossible. Greg finds theater and opera, then men and drugs.

Years pass. Greg moves to Detroit, New York City. David splits with the woman in Hamburg, returns home, is accepted into the University of Cincinnati's medical-illustration program, meets his wife, a schoolteacher, after being set up in a Muskegon bar. Shortly after they marry, he encounters the Book for the first time.

He remembers the exact particle reality of that moment. At the university, he lives in an almost obsessive world in which people spend a hundred hours drawing a horse hock or the ten-dons of a human arm, in thrall to brush on paper. One of his professors has purchased *Pernkopf's Anatomy,* a mythic work Wil-liams has heard defined as pure genius, and he goes to the profes-sor's office to see it.

The books are enormous, with blank green cloth covers. Inside could be almost anything—Monet's water lilies, pornog-raphy, the detailed mechanics of a car—but when he opens them, when the bindings crack and the dry-cleaned scent of new pages and ink wafts up to his nostrils, there appear before him hundreds of thick, glossy sheets, these wild colors, these vibrant human bodies!

It's an electric moment, a pinnacle, of which a life may contain not more than a handful. But it is more than just the bright frisson of discovery, the wordless awe before some greater fluency. If this is a book with emanations, with a life of its own, then perhaps what startles him most is the glint of self-recognition that he finds in its pages: While he sees the timeless past in the trenches and deep spaces of the body, he also, oddly—and he can't yet put words to this—sees his own future.

What he doesn't know yet, flipping through these pages, is that twelve years from now, as an associate professor, he will take a sabbatical and go in search of the Book, that he will find its last living artist, Franz Batke, who will take him under his wing, impart his lost techniques. He doesn't yet know that he will return again to Batke just before the old man dies—and learn what he'd rather not know about him. That he will write an academic paper about the Book for an obscure journal of medical illustration, in which he'll praise *Pernkopf's Anatomy* as "the standard by which all other illustrated anatomic works are measured." It will briefly help his academic career and bring him a measure of fame. But with it comes a backlash. He will lose friends, question himself, and be judged guilty of Pernkopf's crimes by mere association; he will refuse to talk about the Book, curse the day he first saw it.

If this is indeed a book with emanations, as he will come to believe, perhaps even his heart attacks can be blamed on it—Pernkopf, in white lab coat, reaching from the grave for one last cadaver.

———

The book is blindingly beautiful, an exaltation, a paean, and a eulogy all at once. Page after page, the human body unfolds itself, and with each page the invisible becomes visible, some deeper secret reveals itself. What is it?

Here is an eardrum, whole, detached from the vestibulo-cochlear organ and floating in space. It appears as a strange wafered planet. Here is a seemingly glass liver through which appears a glass stomach and then glass kidneys, all in a glass body, an utterly transparent figure, aglow. Here is a skull wrapped in red arterial yarn, and here a cranium packaged in the bright colors of the holiday season. There are eyes that look out, irises in bottomless depth, a disembodied gaze that is the gaze of poetry itself. There is an unpeeled penis, a pulsating liver the color of a blood orange, a brigade of soulful brains, levitating.

And then there are the drawings of dead people—cadavers, faces half intact, half dissected, skin drawn back in folds from the thoracic cavity, heads half shelled, showing brain. Consider Erich Lepier's watercolor of the neck. In nearly black-and-white-photographic detail, the dead man seems to be sleeping; the intact skin of his neck is supple, his lips are parted, his eyes half closed. His head is shaved, and he has a mustache. Even the fine hairs of his nose are visible. Inside him a superficial layer of the neck's fascia comes in two strange shades of color: a bluish pearlescent and a translucent olive green. The acoustic meatus, pathway to the inner ear, is visible, as is the mastoid process. Every changing texture is felt, every wrinkle recorded. Half of this dead man is in exact decay and half of him seems alive. The painting is its own kind of pornography, half violation and half wonder.

Or consider Batke's watercolor of the thoracic cavity after the removal of the heart. It's like gazing on a psychedelic tree of life: arteries, veins, bronchus, extending like complex branches inside their bizarre terrarium. Batke employs all the colors of the rainbow, these interwoven lines of yellow, blue, orange, purple, but invented and mixed by him, all these appear as new colors. The bronchus, which rises in the background, is striped and Seuss-like in white and umber. Although the painting's concern is the minute sorting and scoring of these air and blood tunnels, it still captures an undulating energy, fireworks, the finely rendered thrum of the body. The painting nearly takes wing from the page.

Page by page, *Pernkopf's Anatomy* is stunning, bombastic, surreal, the bone-and-muscle evidence, the animal reality of who we are beneath the skin. And yet, as incomprehensible and terrifying as these landscapes can be, as deep as our denial that life is first and finally a biological process, hinging even now on an unknown blood clot orbiting toward the brain, on a weak heart, on the give of a vein wall, the Book brings its own reassurance. Lepier's detached eyes, like spectacular submersibles, Batke's precisely wrought otherworldly vaginas, Schrott's abstract, almost miraculous muscles/ducts/lymph nodes, Karl Endtresser's bizarre spinal configurations—all of these slavishly striving for the thing itself while being regarded, through Pernkopf's eyes and those of the artists, as beautiful, nearly spiritual objects.

So what can be said about this Book? That its intentions are good? That it is a masterpiece? That each painting contains its own genius? And what if a number of these paintings have been signed with swastikas, what then? Is it possible that only Nazis and their myriad obsessions with the body could have yielded such a surprising text?

And what of the dead stacked like cordwood at the Institute, their body parts pulled down by pitchfork? Do the secrets revealed in the Book count less than the secrets kept by it? Does its beauty diminish with these facts or the political beliefs of its general and foot soldiers? In a righteous world, perhaps it should, but does it?

Shortly after the Anschluss, after thousands of Austrians have been conscripted for the front lines of a war against the world, after more and more Austrians have died of starvation, the euphoria fades, the master race begins to devour itself. And yet Eduard Pernkopf ascends, his name a *Hakenkreuz* and a haunted house.

He is first and foremost a scientist, believing, mimicking the racial politics of the Third Reich. Well received by the powers in Berlin, he is first named dean of the medical school, then *Rektor Magnificus,* or president, of the University of Vienna. Shortly after the Anschluss—March 12, 1938—he issues a letter to all university staff: "To clarify whether you are of Aryan or non-Aryan descent, you are asked to bring your parents' and grandparents' birth certificates to the dean's office. . . . Married individuals must also bring the documents of their wives."

Under his presidency, medical experiments are conducted on the unfit and retarded; children are euthanized. Somewhere in his building is the severed head of the Austrian general, the patriot Wilhelm Zehner, who in the first days of the Anschluss either committed suicide in political protest against the Nazis or was murdered by the Gestapo. Among the more than a thousand guillotined bodies Pernkopf claims for himself from the district court, he searches for the best, the youngest, the finest specimens of muscle and skin. He opens the bodies like walnuts, discards what won't serve him. Those he decides to keep go to the formaldehyde pools in the Institute's basement, floating there until needed for use.

So who is Pernkopf? If he's taciturn with his painters, it is because he maintains the utmost professionalism. A dreamer, an intellect, a lover of music, he is in the workshop early in the morning and late at night: He is simply an overwhelming presence. The Book becomes both his great unfinished symphony and, slowly, his madness. Whether or not he encourages them, some of his artists now sign their work to show their Nazi allegiance: Lepier follows his name with a swastika, Endtresser fashions the double *S* of his name as an SS lightning bolt, and Batke seems to do the same with the number 44 when he dates his paintings from 1944.

But even before the American bombs fall on the Institute— mistaking it for a factory, leveling half the building—even before the lot of these men are left scattered on the wrong side of history, half anesthetized by the past and half consumed by it, there is this one last moment in which they believe they are the righteous ones. These paintings of the human body belong to the highest expression of their Nazi idealism, but they exceed even that classification. If they save human lives—which they do every time a surgeon uses them to heal the body—each one is an act of salvation.

There was no note, but nonetheless he knows. He knows from a conversation they had the last time his brother, Greg, came from New York City to West Lafayette, when they sat on the front stoop drinking beers. They talked about everything, and Greg mentioned how he believed hedonism was the highest possible expression of self and that to die in an act of euphoria was the only way to really live. In context it was not alarming, nor really surprising. In retrospect it explained everything.

When he learned of his brother's suicide, David Williams drove four hours to Muskegon, straight to his parents' house. His mother was sitting in the living room shaking her head, and his father refused to believe it was Greg, since there hadn't been a positive identification. Someone had to go to New York to identify the body. "You work with dead bodies all the time," his father said, cruelly. "You can do this."

The next morning, the elder son flew to LaGuardia, then took a bus and walked to the morgue at Bellevue to see the younger son. The waiting room was crowded with people there to identify family members who had been shot, knifed, beaten, or killed by gang members. A very large black man in a uniform, an officer of some sort, brought him into a room with a curtained window. He asked twice if David Williams was ready, and the second time Williams feebly answered "Yes."

When the curtain parted, there was his brother, still tall and angular, lying on a metal dissecting table, in severe rigor mortis, with the back of his head resting on a wooden block, exactly like a cadaver in a gross-anatomy lab. But this was his brother—and there was no longer anything beautiful about him, only a pallid mask where his face had been, a lifeless slab in place of his animated body.

If his brother's death left no mark on the greater world, the rest of those dark days in 1978 are part of David Williams's personal history: how he fell into the arms of the large black man who carried him from the room; how he refused to sign a piece of paper that said his brother was found with needle marks on his arm; how he went to the YMCA to pick up his brother's belongings; and how, when he arrived back in Muskegon, his parents were in denial about their son's sexuality and about his suicide, an act that meant he could not be buried, according to Catholic rite, with the other generations of Williamses at St. Mary's Cemetery.

And it's part of history, too, that his brother, the person whose life most closely tracked his own, ended in the cold, unconsecrated ground of Muskegon, among the graves of factory workers, back in this place they both tried so hard to escape.

Not long after, on sabbatical, David Williams goes to see Franz Batke. He is nervous; he doesn't know what to expect. He leaves his family behind in Munich and drives to Innsbruck. He thinks it is no coincidence that shortly after falling in love with his wife, he first saw the Book, and now, shortly after his brother's death, he arrives in Innsbruck to visit the dying old man who is the last living vestige of the Book itself. But what is it that draws him here? He is looking for answers, yes, or perhaps merely reasons to live. And even if Batke's paintings hadn't changed his life—as they have—it is not so strange that a young man suffering loss might seek counsel from an old man who knows a great deal about loss.

What he finds is that Batke is a hermit living in a cell in self-imposed exile. Batke has come to Innsbruck from Vienna, leaving behind his wife, because Vienna represents the past to him, haunting him even now, defeating him, and after more than fifty years with his wife, he is not sure whether or not he still loves her. And he has come here because he has been offered work by Werner Platzer, the man who after the war and Pernkopf's death brought the last books of the atlas to fruition. Platzer, who is hard-driving with frantic dashes of intellect and craziness, has promised his friend Batke pay and living quarters in return for paintings to fill a new book on vaginal surgery.

So Batke lives in two rooms at Innsbruck's Institute of Anatomy, where Platzer is the new director. The old man never leaves, never goes out to take the air. Students bring him his food and sundries. Usually, he drinks ice water all day while he works. At night he has trouble sleeping, due to a bad cough, ominous and deep, which worries even him. Against his doctor's orders, he continues to smoke cigarettes. If he is smoking himself to death, the cigarettes may also be what keeps him alive for two more years because they give him something, besides painting, to do.

At first he is mistrustful of David Williams, thinking the American scholar has been sent to spy by the publisher or by someone else looking to profit from him. But slowly Batke realizes that the professor is here for seemingly no reason other than to watch him paint—and to be taught. It dawns on him that, even if he has been remembered by only this one American, he has still achieved a certain kind of immortality. Though they can barely communicate, they become closer and closer. They don't discuss politics, only art. And at the end of each day, Williams records another entry in his journal.

"Herr Batke fixes lunch—scrambled eggs and small pieces of pork and wurst. I continue to work on the vein—he says to paint the middle valve first and then add the dark and light *dich-weiß*. He wants me to stop using such small choppy strokes."

And "even in German, I understand him: 'Loosen up. It's no big deal.' I feel it finally beginning to happen. . . . I actually enjoy it physically—the way the paint floats around. I really think this way of painting can suit me. He also demonstrates a vein. He can still do it at 77 years old. He works for two and a half hours on a very small section."

Under Batke's eye, the body becomes beautiful again for David Williams. After the shock of seeing his brother as a cadaver, he perhaps retrieves some small part of Greg with each new painting. And yet, for all of the gemütlichkeit, for all the warmth David Williams feels toward the master, Batke himself seems broken. He has been stranded on the wrong side of history, and now he never leaves his cell.

Night after night, they sit up talking. Batke shows so many little kindnesses, serves food, cakes, wine. One day when David Williams's family comes to visit, he has presents for the children, charms the American's wife.

So how does one quantify the joy he feels when Batke speaks to him as a friend and mentor—as a father, really—when Batke tells him that he, David Williams, might be the only artist with the ability to paint like the old man himself, someone to carry on the mythic tradition handed down by Pernkopf? Or how does one share what it meant that last day in Innsbruck, to see Batke come downstairs and step outside for the first time in years, to stand in a downpour of sunlight, just to say goodbye?

Isn't there something to be said for these moments? Aren't they a part of this man and this Book's history, too?

The tanks are rolling, and the people come out of their houses, clutching bouquets to pledge allegiance to their liberators. They throw flowers and sing. After landing at Omaha Beach, the Allied army sweeps across France, liberating Paris, and breaches the Siegfried line near Aachen. Hitler flees to his underground bunker and commits suicide with his mistress, Eva Braun. The Third Reich implodes.

When American troops arrive in Vienna, they arrest Eduard Pernkopf and Franz Batke. Both are removed to prison camps, where they are placed in what is called a de-Nazification program, one in which prisoners are subjected to hard labor and a history lesson in the truth: movies showing the reality of the concentration camps, among other horrors of the war. Pernkopf, who is fifty-seven now, who has lived with visions of grandeur, is lost and broken. Still, he has visitors sneak in his work, at which he continues to toil during his three-year stay.

Meanwhile, at the university, the members of the old regime have been imprisoned or removed, and the school issues a letter to those still-living former Jewish faculty members now scattered about the world, inviting them back. Of hundreds, only one returns, a man named Hans Hoff, whose wartime travels have taken him from New York City to Baghdad. Well regarded before the Anschluss, he is put in charge of the Neurological Institute. When released from prison, Pernkopf is barred from

teaching at his own beloved Anatomy Institute but somehow fi-
nagles two light-filled rooms under Hoff's roof to finish his Book.
The atlas is all he has left—and all that keeps him alive.

In these tattered postwar times, with jobs scarce again, he is
able to regather his former artists and then add two more. He
works his eighteen-hour days, remaining wholly unsympathetic
to those who can't keep up. Among his painters, disillusionment
and internecine squabbles are now endemic. Batke and Lepier
represent opposite extremes, the improvisational versus the
mathematical, and both work to fill the Book with their own
work in order to bring more glory to it.

In 1952, Pernkopf publishes *Der Hals* (The Neck), but time
is short. A blood clot in his brain causes a stroke, and he dies on
April 17, 1955, before the completion of his last two books.
Werner Platzer, who is regarded by many as Pernkopf's scientific
son, finishes those.

Despite Pernkopf's long fall from grace, his burial turns out
the entire faculty. He is celebrated by fellow professors as a perfectionist, a stirring teacher, and the impresario of what many
increasingly regard as the world's greatest anatomy book. Some
of those present are former Nazis and some are not, but all who
have lived through the war now seem to bear their own burdens,
secrets, and sins, and clearly they regard Pernkopf as one of their
own. So they commend him to heaven.

The Jew, Hans Hoff, is there, too, in a black suit. But what
passes through his mind, what he says to himself as Pernkopf is
lowered into the grave, is lost now in the ash of all unspoken
things. Perhaps to stand there in the first place, on Viennese soil
again, he has already begun the difficulty of forgiving, or forgetting. Perhaps he marks the moment indelibly, unapologetically.
Creator, destroyer—let him lie beneath the burnt grass and dying
blossoms of his own history now.

One day, during the height of the debate over *Pernkopf's Anatomy,* a close acquaintance, a kind Jewish woman, approaches David Williams and says sharply, "Why would you want to be remembered for your association with this book, of all books?" He has no answer. Another time, in England, while giving a lecture at Cambridge on the atlas, he is confused when a Jewish woman breaks down in tears and is helped from the room, pained by how this man, this American, has found beauty in the ugliest of books. What sickness moves inside of him?

And there's more. He receives a letter from a distinguished academic, challenging his paper for its whitewash of history. "Have you not been struck by the fact, Mr. Williams, when visiting cemeteries in small Austrian towns, how many innocent young men lost their lives on the eastern or western front, but these originators of the Nazi mentality survived?" he writes. "As convenient as it seems to be, one cannot separate a man's professional work from his spiritual being."

Meanwhile, an oral surgeon at Columbia University Medical Center in New York City, Howard Israel, has referred to *Pernkopf's Anatomy* before every new surgery of his career. When he finds out about its past, he feels deeply betrayed. He researches the Book with another Jewish doctor, William Seidelman, asserting in a medical journal that cadavers from concentration camps may have been used in the making of the atlas. Their evidence: the appearance of roughly shaved heads and circumcised penises. When Williams is asked about this by a reporter from *The Jerusalem Report,* he disputes the fact, saying that when he asked Batke if death camp cadavers were used in the Book, the old man became enraged and denied it vehemently. Even famed Nazi hunter Simon Wiesenthal examined the records, and his conclusions seem to bolster Williams's side. The two doctors, however, take a dimmer view of Williams as one of the Book's greatest defenders.

Williams is not alone in his view of the Book. Following the publication of his paper, the two most prestigious American medical journals review *Pernkopf's Anatomy* and declare it in "a class of its own" and "a classic among atlases," with illustrations that "are truly works of art." Nonetheless, Williams increasingly feels isolated, doubtful. How could beauty have made him half blind? Is he, as it appears to some, a Nazi apologist? On public radio, he is asked how it feels to be the one benefiting from a Nazi text, and he fumbles for an answer.

He loses friends; he loses sleep; his heart begins to hurt. He meets several times with the local rabbi, who tells him that his sin may be one of perspective. He must imagine the unimaginable when it comes to the Holocaust, must feel the grief of that woman at Cambridge, assuming she may be like so many who lost mothers and fathers, sisters and brothers, children and spouses, in the ovens and dark chambers of places like Dachau, Auschwitz, and Buchenwald. How hard could it be to see that for some the Book is not a metaphor for beauty or salvation or transfiguration, that it's not the highest expression of what saves David Williams from Muskegon, Michigan, or erases his scars, or, in some complicated way, brings Greg back? No, for that woman at Cambridge, the Book is nothing but a dirty crime scene, violated bodies that might include her brethren. The artists are no better than vultures over their carrion. What affliction or hubris has kept that from him?

Three heart attacks and several angioplasties later, he is a different man, one who still lies awake at night thinking about the Book, but thinking about it from the point of view of that woman who broke down at Cambridge. He doesn't speak about *Pernkopf's*

Anatomy for years, though he follows developments from afar. Under pressure, the University of Vienna launches and concludes an investigation into *Pernkopf's Anatomy,* claiming in November 1998 that circumstantial evidence suggests Jewish cadavers were probably not used in the making of the atlas. Reviewing the hundreds of pages of findings, Williams is left unconvinced, believes the university administration has obscured the results to protect its reputation.

From some primordial haze slowly comes recognition. It is the spring of 2002, and in West Lafayette he now prepares to return to Vienna, to Munich. He packs his bags, and when he is briefly overcome with doubt, his wife says, "You are *Pernkopf's Anatomy.* A big part of that Book is who you are." So he travels eight hours in coach, through spasms of lightning. But this time he arrives aggrieved, angry, skeptical, confused, searching for truth—more, perhaps, as a Jew would. He has come to avenge the naïveté of his younger self and to make his final goodbyes to the paintings, for he is sure he will never see them again in this lifetime, nor perhaps ever have the desire.

In bright sun, beneath a heavy roof, the Institute occupies half a city block along the trolley routes and shops of Ringstrasse. The first time he came to Vienna, the weather was bad—rain, thick clouds rolling over themselves—and somehow the city seemed cold, less receiving, left him empty and alone. This time he feels more resolute. Somewhere, he hopes, in the locked rooms and forgotten closets, among the thousand cadavers used by a new generation of anatomy students, is a clearer answer to the past.

He meets with professor after professor. He is unfailingly polite, phrases sensitive declarations of fact as questions in his midwestern lilt. A few he meets are defensive; most, quite the opposite. A gentle old man, a former president of the university who knew Pernkopf, serves him tea and cakes. Later, he finds out that the old man was an SS officer. Many records, including those of the identities of a number of cadavers, were destroyed by the American bombs that brought down half the Institute. Others were tampered with by those looking to obscure their crimes. Exactness is elusive. Rather than thinking there's a cover-up here, David Williams begins to feel pity for these people, relentlessly driven back to an increasingly untraceable past.

One professor leads him through the Institute on a tour: They stand on the spot where guillotined bodies once were piled in ten-foot-high drifts and taken down by pitchfork for Eduard Pernkopf's use. They stand in the hemicycle, where Pernkopf headily praised Hitler and called on his colleagues to lead a new age of medical experimentation, a period that would come to include the sterilization of the mentally disabled and the euthanasia of nearly eight hundred "defective" children. They go to the basement, a dark, dank, spooky place, to look upon the formaldehyde pools that once held Pernkopf's cadavers. An attendant opens the lid on one of the pools, activates a hydraulic lift, and suddenly several bodies, bloated and pale, each one donated for use in the school today, appear from the depths on metal trays.

Somehow, on his last visit he had failed to mark all these spots, or perhaps unconsciously didn't entirely want to or feel he needed to. Now he does, shaking his head, grimacing.

Finally, he dines with a young historian, Daniela Angetter, the woman charged with investigating much of the University of Vienna's Nazi legacy. Her world is one of chilling medical experiments and severed heads, and she wears her work with a gaunt hauntedness and weary eyes. Allergic to protein and lactose, she eats potato chips at dinner while her husband, a plumber, eats blood sausage. "This has been horrible for me, to see dead bodies," she says. "I'm a historian, and to think that people were executed because they were starving and stole a pig and ate it. Would I have been strong enough to stand up? If you didn't conform to the Party, you were executed. I've stayed awake many nights thinking about these things."

Sitting there, moved by this young woman, believing her, David Williams comes to realize this: All these people are run down by ghosts, too. He is not alone in his confusion. After illustrious postwar careers, former SS officers serve afternoon tea; a new generation born thirty years after the war pores over the past, making amends for its grandparents. Even now, on a sunny spring day in 2002, on the eve of the anniversary marking fifty-seven years since the fall of Nazi Germany, students carry urns bearing the last discovered remains of victims at the university during Pernkopf's reign; the government calls for calm in the streets of Austria's capital, deploying fifteen hundred police officers to ensure that neo-Nazi demonstrators don't rampage in the Heldenplatz, the square where Hitler addressed hundreds of thousands of euphoric Austrians in 1938.

Here is an entire country living the events of the war over and over and over again. Later, in Munich, Williams spends an afternoon with his friend Michael Urban, the erudite sixty-three-year-old grandson of Eduard Urban, the man who first struck a deal in 1933 with Pernkopf to publish his atlas. Having inherited his grandfather's company, Urban sold it to a company that decided to cease publication of the Book. He believes it to be a troubled masterpiece, one that should continue in print with a foreword detailing the most harrowing events of its creation. Now, while the German quietly listens, the American attempts to put into words something that has troubled him, continues to trouble him on this trip: He wonders whether, by being friends with Franz Batke, by seeing the magnificence in *Pernkopf's Anat-*

omy, he is doomed. And yet he feels that to reject both fully is a sin of its own, a betrayal.

"David, there's nothing wrong with you," says Urban. "We are moving on two planes: the principal, everyday plane and then one made up of these overwhelming feelings and emotions. When we try to talk about this, we move into a wordless dimension." Here he pauses, runs a tapered finger over his furrowed brow, smiles weakly. "My father was at one of these mass rallies, the Goebbels speech at the Sports Palace in 1943, and he said his arm was up in a Nazi salute before he knew what he was doing. It was hysteria. It's inconceivable what people did to one another during the war. But you must remember: People endure."

The next day, he goes to see the original paintings. He is wary, excited, and nervous. Urban has arranged for the paintings to be delivered to the downtown offices of the publishing house. And he has also arranged for Werner Platzer, the man who finished the atlas after Pernkopf's death, to come to Munich to lead Williams through nineteen oversized black binders stuffed with eight hundred original pieces of art.

Platzer operates three cups of coffee ahead of the world. He doesn't eat; he doesn't pee. He just sits with the paintings, providing long discourses on each. And Williams sits with him, a student again, savoring every moment, but this time questioning, too. He asks Platzer why he thinks the Book is out of print, and Platzer shakes his head, incensed. "It's too good," he says. "The Book is too good." When Williams points to a painting that many feel is that of a Jewish cadaver with a shaved head, Platzer explodes. "What does a Jew look like?" he says. "Tell me. It is absurd. I wish you Americans ate what we ate then: nothing. Three days a week, I might not eat. I looked like this man here. Absolute nonsense."

Williams sits before him, unblinking, and presses his concerns. He believes the swastikas and SS symbols have been removed from some of the originals, as they were removed from subsequent printings of the Book, so a laborious hour is spent trying to locate the paintings in question. In the end, he discovers the symbols have been erased, and he seems troubled, angry.

And yet, when he comes upon a Batke painting of the inner ear, he holds it up and stares for a long time. "It's just so alive," he says softly, passing a hand lightly over it. When he sees another, of the chest, he says, "I'd give anything to have that hanging on my wall." The two men look at the Lepiers and Dietzes, Endtressers and Schrotts. They marvel at the near psychedelic colors and intricate brushwork. With each painting—with each proliferation of arteries, with each gravityless organ—the body becomes that exalted place again.

The viewing takes seven hours, and in the end he feels it all over and over: joy, curiosity, shame, awe. In person, in full color, the paintings still mesmerize. They still emanate.

But this time in their presence, he is not exactly euphoric. If he feels a deep sense of fulfillment in seeing these paintings one last time, he also feels a strange sadness. When it is over, when the sun dips below a building and a streetlight blinks on in the window, he is almost trembling. He pulls out a handkerchief, removes his glasses, and wipes his face. His hair is slightly disheveled. He exhales, looks once at the oversized binders against the wall, presses his lips tightly together, and then turns his back and leaves the room.

The old man sits and smokes, a bottle of beer set before him. He has a crooked nose and a skewed chin. Night pours through the windows of his cell. Sitting across from him is the American, fellow exile and good friend now, who has remembered him, who has made a pilgrimage to record a way of painting that will be forever lost with his death. It is 1980, and they have spent months together, eating, drinking, laughing. There is so little time. Though they don't speak fluently to each other, they have formed a bond through painting. And now they are drunk, and their conversation veers from art to the war.

The old man suddenly rises and disappears for a moment, then returns with a small cardboard box that makes a jingling sound. It is dust covered and full of medals, including an Iron Cross he won for valor on the Russian front, where he was shot in the groin. He passes the medal to the American, who feels its weight in his hand, turns it in the light, admires it. The old man, who trusts the young man now, who is being a little vain and showy, sad and funny, mentions that he is still proud to have worn his Brownshirt uniform. He says the Americans blew it, joining the war on the wrong side, and accuses the Jews of forcing the Americans to enter the war against the Germans rather than with them. He chides his guest for this. He describes his imprisonment and his days being de-Nazified. And David Williams, the American professor, listens, nods, and later writes in his journal, "The evening seems like a dream to me . . . perhaps it's the beer. This man who I have admired for so long—I should say his work—there is no doubt in my mind that as a painter he is a genius!!—this man reveals himself as a common Nazi, a Jew hater, a Brown Shirt. . . . Is it possible that all makers of great works of art are ultimately exposed as thus?"

And ever after, he will wonder: Who is this old man, this last living vestige of the Book? And what secret has he found after his life as a vulture at the side of carrion? It appears there is no secret. The Nazis have lost, and he is dying on the wrong side of history. The mouth is made for food, the penis for the vagina, the heart made to beat. Until it simply ceases. Death is no salvation. The only thing left is to paint.

On the wall above David Williams's desk at home today in Indiana hangs a painting by Franz Batke, near an old portrait of Eduard Pernkopf. Sometimes, at the end of the day, after mowing the lawn, he spends a minute gazing at them. But if asked why the pictures are there, David Williams shakes his head; he can't say why. But he doesn't take them down.

THE AMERICAN HERO (IN FOUR ACTS)

WHEN YOU FIRST CAME INTO THE country, it was on a Buffalo, a huge, silver-winged transport flashing through the clouds at three hundred knots. This was your commute, the way some people ride the train to work. You stood up in the cockpit, in baggy pants and a T-shirt, watching the earth glide beneath your feet. A flat, spectral wasteland, cyclones of red dust writhing up in some slow-motion manifestation of—what? the devil? Whatever it was down there, it was the opposite of Richmond, Virginia. It was the opposite of home sweet home. Your hands were shaking, just a little, but still—shaking.

Somewhere at twenty-nine thousand feet, near the fourth cataract of the Nile, near the spot where it was prophesied by a great chief that a wondrous bird would one day bring food to the starving Dinka, they asked you your name. South African pilots— big, burly yahoos with seven tons of maize in the cargo hold, Coca-Colas pressed between their knees, and a couple of porn mags thrown around the cockpit, but good guys—asked you your name. So lost in your head, you couldn't speak. Move lips, make sound: Ja-son. Yeah, Jason. Jason Mat-us. American. They smiled at that. Like: This fish is gonna get eaten alive.

Then the earth got bigger. Green spots became tamarind trees; brown dots became tukels, thatched huts scattered in groups of three and four—some of them burned out, some bombed, some lopsided and listing. Purple forms blurred through the bush.

Now the Buffalo hit the ground, bouncing down a potholed dirt track. You went back into the long, dark cave of the cargo hold, moving on automatic, and suddenly the hatch was thrown open. What hit you was roaring and mean, beams of bright light and a 120-degree blowtorch of heat that incinerated your breath just as it was leaving your lungs, so it seemed to come out of you like fire. What hit you was the smell of Africa, the dust and sweat and burned urine and sun-scorched blades of elephant grass.

Everyone took a step back when you jumped down, as if you were an alien, dust rising when your booted feet hit the earth near their naked ones, your body inadvertently hunched in ready position as if you were back at school on the wrestling mat. And then there was that weird microsecond when your eyes rose up, your head craned skyward. To these men who just kept growing! You looked up at them, these men. And they looked down at you. And you looked up at them. And they at you again.

Until a hand came through the air. Big peace, a voice said in another tongue. Big peace, said Jason Matus without hesitation, putting a hand back through the air. And the hands met there— one the blackest of black, one the whitest of pale white. Like shaking hands with midnight; like shaking hands with goat's milk. And the man held on to you, Jason Matus, and led you away from the plane, into his world now, and the crowd parted, these amazing faces, hollowed with high cheekbones, super-white eyeballs and teeth, foreheads scarred with tribal markings, bodies clean of

THE AMERICAN HERO (IN FOUR ACTS)

hair. You didn't even notice their ribs at first, the ballooned bellies and the bloated hands. At first, you didn't notice what the Dinka simply call the Hunger, though that's what you had come for. Just saw their faces, made sure you met their smiles and gazes. And then all those hands reaching for you. Men in sky-blue djellaba gowns fluttering from their stick-thin bodies like loose sails. *Mali madit.* Big peace, my brother.

Suddenly everything you once knew—well, it didn't matter here in southern Sudan. You were walking into one of the all-time great fucked-up situations on this earth. Famine. Drought. Genocide. For most of the last fifty years, a civil war had been raging between the Muslim government in Khartoum and its militias and then the Christian tribes and Ph.D. rebel leaders of the south, all chasing one another around with AK-47s, trying to blow one another's heads off. And millions of innocents running, too, fleeing from rape and slave raids and murder, escaping with nothing but their own skin and bones, set loose across the whole wide expanse of barren flatland like crippled giraffes. Hundreds of thousands dying from the Hunger.

The victims—but they were smiling when you jumped out of that Buffalo. Each hand you touched—it was as if you were being pulled from a fast current of water. So who was strong and who was weak here? Who needed help, anyway? You were young, though not altogether innocent. Tough, but one hour in this sun and you were lobster red. You'd backpacked for nearly three years. Out there in the world—eating at roadside stands in India and bazaars in Morocco, surfing in Sri Lanka, drinking the bad water, going native, wearing sarongs and hippie beads and dreadlocks. Yes, it was a phase, but wonderful how no one cared who your daddy was or where you'd gone to school. No, you started with only two things out there. Name and nationality. Jason Matus, American.

You were on a secret journey, a pilgrimage to find your true self by abandoning the comforts of home, by throwing over who you were supposed to be. When you were sick—amoebic dysentery, malaria—you lay in bed in faraway youth hostels, fasting, dizzy with fever, listening to the ocean and the voices in Arabic or Hindi or some language you'd never heard before drifting up to your window. When you were in Nepal, you trekked into the Himalayas without knowing where you were going, searching for epiphany, and then almost froze in your epiphany at eighteen thousand feet. When you read a book about the medicinal benefits of drinking your own urine, you drank your pee every day for eight months because—well, you sound like a madman now— because you thought it would make you whole, make you strong, give you back some essence of yourself that you'd somehow squandered for so many years.

But what were you looking for out there in the world, anyway? What did you *want*? One thing: to match your words with your deeds. That was it: Marry the thought, the word, and the action. Make it one single reflex based on good intention. In this big world of hurt, you thought you could make a difference. Be one pure, unalloyed thing. A place of refuge. Shelter. Like, Give me your tired and poor and huddled masses. Give them to *me*, man.

So here you go, hombre. Welcome to the Sudan, to civil war, to these naked kids crawling in the dirt at your feet, covered in flies, too spent to swat them away. Welcome to sleeping beneath trees, the ground so hot at midnight your T-shirt is soaked, then waking to twenty hovering faces, more Dinka kids touching your hair. And here's to shitting in shallow holes, no running water, and never-ending days in the brutal sun. Here's to wondering if that distant thunder happens to be bombs from government Antonovs or if those nightly gunshots—what you will come to call "a little night music"—mean it's time to get up and run.

No, this wasn't some Sally Struthers late-night commercial, this was the real thing. This was one rebel group killing people at a food drop and spilling their blood over sacks of sorghum. This was coworkers getting shot and killed, land-mined and kid-napped. This was guinea worm and Ebola and sleeping sickness and about five other nameless diseases that could liquidate you instantly. And this finally was eight, nine, ten thousand dying peo-ple at an airdrop, standing right smack on the big white X, and you, Jason Matus, trying to clear them before the cargo plane appeared, before it released fifteen tons of maize or high-energy biscuits from eight hundred feet, just slid it down rollers on pal-lets and let it waterfall out the back hatch of the plane. The Dinka—and other tribes in the south, the Nuer and Luo—seemed only to half understand the danger of getting pancaked by a pallet loaded with 110-pound bags of maize. They held their hands out, mimicking a bird, smiling at you. Didn't they under-stand that one mishandled toggle would send fifteen tons down on their heads? That thought drove you through the crowd like a lunatic, shoving and yelling and then looking up at the sky for some sign of the plane. *Jetki rot!* Move! Get back! Did you hear me? Pick up and get back!

And then later, soaked with sweat, taking refuge in the shade of a tamarind tree, you watched the glory of that first food drop, helped command it with the radio in your hand. "Whiskey Whiskey to UN Foxtrot 12, clear to drop." A powerful thing, to see that dolphin-nosed aircraft marked WFP—World Food Programme—appearing out of nowhere, roaring from Kenya across the great nothingness of southern Sudan. Like the cavalry riding in. Its contrail like an umbilical cord. The hatch lowering and then the food—just awesome the way it poured out into all that light and space and sky, like the loaves and the fishes. Beauti-ful, the way the sacks speckled the air, each one full of good Kansas corn, and hit the ground with a thud and then, as if they were full of living bodies, turned somersaults. On this afternoon, there seemed to be nothing but big peace and three hundred somersaulting sacks of maize!

Still, you knew nothing yet. You came across that field, a magic man with hairy arms who'd perhaps conjured a big bird to feed the Dinka. Yes, for a few of them, you were the prophet fulfilling the prophecy. When the porters had removed nearly all the food and stacked it neatly beneath a tree, you went into the field to inspect, to make sure all the maize from the broken bags had been scooped up. The sun was in your eyes, and you didn't notice the ten thousand people lining the edge of the field. You didn't notice the first wave of them, or the second, or the third, until it was too late. They were stampeding toward you—sprinting, yelling, rioting. Hunchbacks and women with shriveled breasts; clubfoots and bloated children waving empty gourd bowls. Their faces twisted in pain, their eyes bloodshot and wild. Like some kind of nightmare. They came for you, but then they didn't even touch you. They dove into the dirt at your feet; people were scrounging against one another for the few leftover kernels of maize, clawing the earth with their fingernails, bickering and breathing as one mass. So thin you could see the underworkings of their bodies, see right to their beating hearts.

And you—you just stood there, frozen, the hairs on the back of your neck straight up. You watched their fingers work the dirt, the curled-over kids gobbling raw kernels, hair yellowed from the Hunger. Even today, five years later, after five years in the Sudan, at the wise age of thirty, you still remember towering over them, holding yourself in until you couldn't anymore, until you thought you might be losing it. No, my brother, you didn't know anything until that moment, knew nothing at all about your place in this world until you—Jason Matus, American— stood among the people and were rendered completely invisible.

So wake now in Lorton, Virginia, invisible. Wake in this forty-five-year-old body with a walrus mustache, your waist thickening, skin loosening, the whole fleshy ornament of you beginning to schlump earthward. Rise in this cramped, brick two-bedroom among other cemented-together brick houses in a perfectly bland brick subdivision on a busy thoroughfare. Feel your way down the dark halls of your cramped brick house, past the photographs of your family—your wife, the teacher's aide; your teenage son with the blinding fastball—to the kitchen with flowered wallpaper and linoleum floor. Drink coffee at the oak table you refinished yourself, sitting in a pool of one-hundred-watt light, and then head out the door for the one-hour bus ride to Washington, D.C., to the old Annex II building and your job in the Congressional Budget Office. Like every day. Like every day before and every day after.

This is the grind, your nine–to–five-thirty as a low-level government bureaucrat. Your life of put-on-the-same-old-clothes and take-the-same-bus and drink-the-same-bad-coffee and unjam-the-same-damn-Xerox-machine. Like, Do we have enough Bic pens around here? See, you're nobody. Or you're everybody—but either way, you're invisible. Just another guy. The anonymous Joe up in the grandstand, hot dog in mouth, proudly watching his son pitch goose eggs into the seventh inning. Invisible—which is why sometimes January 13, 1982, feels like a dream, as if it all happened to another Lenny Skutnik who wasn't you, who wasn't twenty-nine then, with a newborn baby. That day, like every day, you woke, rose, and stumbled down the dark hall. You drank coffee. On the radio, clouds, some snow in the forecast. You were thinking: Snow? C'mon, this is D.C. You carpooled with your father, Marty, and some coworkers. At the office, you did the usual. Checked the copy machines, delivered the mail. Ate lunch in the cafeteria, a club sandwich, and every once in a while stole a look out the window.

By early afternoon, the snow was so thick it seemed as if the moon itself had blown up, was coming down in woolly clumps. Everything falling out of the sky but car fenders. Seemed impossible, but all federal workers were let out early. And suddenly you were heading back to the brick subdivision to shovel the walk. Some warm soup and television on the couch. Home sweet home.

But no. The interstate was snarled, a bumper-to-bumper crawl. Took one hour to get one mile. High drifts on the ground. Then, around 4:00 P.M., just as the light began to drain from the sky, you came to a full stop before the Fourteenth Street Bridge, just off the main runway of National Airport. There was a commotion; people were out of their cars, looking over the guardrail at the frozen Potomac. People began working their way down the embankment by the bridge, slipping and sliding—something urgent—and you followed them in that silver light, with bits of the moon falling on your head. You weren't sure why, but you followed them down with your father and the other guys in your car. Your understanding of this came retroactively—all these people in the snow, running—as if you were speed-reading a story.

In the river were six people—splashing, fighting for air, trying to hang on to the tail of Air Florida flight 90, scheduled from Washington to Tampa. The plane had lumbered slowly down the tarmac on takeoff, banked hard left, and just couldn't raise itself up in the air, fighting all that icy downfall. Skimmed the Fourteenth Street Bridge, took off several car roofs, decapitated a few drivers, knocked over a truck, then crashed through the ice and vanished. About seventy people were already on the river bottom, buckled fast to their seats. Never had a chance, those people. Never got the flight magazine out of the seat pocket or moved on to the peanuts-and-soft-drinks portion of this beautiful, sad life. Swallowed whole by the Potomac.

You saw this big gash in the ice, smelled the sickening smell of jet fuel, and you—you, Lenny Skutnik, government clerk—could see bodies floating around, human hands and legs trying to hang on to the wrecked tail of the plane like toddlers without water wings, one moment hurtling down a runway, then suddenly thrown tumbling into this slushy water. It didn't compute: your life, then these bodies. A bystander, a sheet-metal worker, was already down by the water's edge, and people were trying to tie a makeshift line around him. One woman was taking off her nylons to add to some jumper cables—her naked legs gooseflesh in that silver light. The sheet-metal worker had his coat and boots still on, and he began to wade into the river, thirty-three-degree water, sucked in hard, walked up to his knees, thighs, waist, walking as if he'd suddenly become the Tin Man, but that's as far as he got before a helicopter appeared and you all pulled him back in.

Now everything moved in horrible slow motion. More people were slipping and sliding down the embankment, maybe fifty on the shore, watching the helicopter hover over the dazed, iced bodies in the river. Up on the bridge, there were more people, throwing rope to yet another survivor, who was trapped beneath the ice, trying to punch up through it. Over the open water, near the plane's tail, the helicopter dangled a lifeline with an open-noosed strap. There were three men and three women there. One of the men just seemed to disappear beneath the surface—gone. Another struggled to shore, and then another made it, too. But one of the women—you could tell she was in trouble. Somewhere on the river's bottom were her husband and her newborn baby, and somehow she had popped up on the surface, completely lost and pale, with a broken leg and some dim understanding that she needed to keep her mouth above the waterline, though the rest of her, that broken body of hers, just seemed to want to sink back down to her family.

The helicopter lowered itself, blowing everything sideways, bossing everything silver. Rotor blades shot wind under the skin of the wreckage and flipped the woman over with a piece of metal from the tail, flicked her like an insect. Flailing in that open water, wearing red, she reached for the lifeline, grabbed it, but then didn't have the strength to hold on when the helicopter rose. Again and again, same thing. The pale woman somehow struggled up onto a slab of ice, wobbling, and the lifeline came down, and you saw her grabbing it in slow motion, excruciating, and her whole body dragged back in the water, her lame leg dragged behind her. But then she couldn't hold on, let go with one hand, then two, and fell back in the water, in one pathetic, stonelike splash, washed under by the deafening sound of the chopper, which itself had become some kind of demented bird in this slow torture.

And suddenly, impossibly, out of nowhere—you! Her head underwater, fifty people gawking from shore, fixed in place, the sky spitting moon, and you just went. Like, outta here! Boots off! Reached down and yanked them off and tore off the puff jacket, just ripped loose of that thing, down to short sleeves—the same shirt as other days—and just leaped from the bank. Didn't think, didn't care. Just out of nowhere, roaring, skipping minutes, slicing between them, speeding time in order to get to this woman before she vanished, too. Out of nowhere, you, in the drink, in that slushie, windmilling like a sicko, a slashing fury of strokes. A blur. Fifty people standing there, and you, like, That's it! Enough! She's coming with *me*.

You powered to her, six ferocious strokes through electrocutingly cold water, got to her at the give-up point, the sayonara-this-life split second, her eyes rolling back in her head. She was gone, unconscious and sinking, and you just grabbed her. You didn't feel anything. Not cold—nothing. Claimed her, took her back from the river. Pulled her head up, then pushed her to shore, like water polo. Handed her off to a fireman who'd waded in. Dragged yourself to shore on your own. Stood up, soaking wet, breathing—yes, breathing!—looked back at the wreckage, and, once you knew everyone would get out, started up the embankment, picking up your puff jacket, looking around for your carpool, thinking: Time to go home. Let's go.

But then some cops corralled you. Led you to an ambulance. You said, Is this gonna cost me anything? I don't make no money. Free, they said. Someone put a hand on your back, and you got in. Noticed for the first time that your feet were cold. Missing your watch and a pack of cigarettes.

That's when it began, that's when the other Lenny Skutnik was born, when you realized what you'd actually done. Then found out it had been captured by a camera crew on the bank. At the hospital, they gave you a warm bath and some food, and as you were getting ready to go, they asked if you would answer some questions from the reporters. The story was out, the lead already written: In the nation's capital today, a blizzard and a plane crash. Seventy-eight dead. A gaping hole in the ice, and debris floating in the water. Helicopters circling, looking for survivors. Rescue crews waiting on the shore to rush the victims to the hospital. The media already had that part down, had their victim, too: Priscilla Tirado, the woman in the water. Now they needed their hero.

So you answered a few questions: Why'd you do it? Something just told me, Go in after her. Would you do it again? Yes, I'd do it again. Simple stuff. Obvious. Time to get home.

But no one would let you go. There was just this great, gaping need for you—not the Lenny you, the brick-subdivision guy, the government functionary; no, they wanted the hero you, the part of you in them that they most needed to see and touch and believe in. The part of them that went diving into that icy water with you. On *Nightline*, Ted Koppel told you, It's not only courage—there has to be a certain kind of magnificent insanity about it all. You said, Something just told me to go in after her.

The morning shows, newspapers, magazines paraded into your living room. They made you into a soap opera star. Lenny and Priscilla, Priscilla and Lenny. Hero and victim, victim and hero. They hauled Priscilla's father-in-law, father of her dead husband, into your living room and tried to film him crying in front of you. You said, Wait a minute! Wait! Took him away from that camera, back into the bedroom. You wanted to beat the hell out of that network guy.

When people heard you lost your watch, you were offered a hundred new ones—then trips to Hawaii, Canada, Puerto Rico. President Ronald Reagan invited you to his State of the Union address, seated you and your wife up there in the balcony with his elegant wife, Nancy—nice, nice woman. President went drifting off on some yabble about American heroes, suddenly mentioned your name, and the whole place erupted. Democrats and Republicans leaped to their feet. Hear, hear! Lenny!

You got two thousand letters, some running deep with emotion. People wrote and said they were jumping up and down in their living rooms in front of their televisions, crying, screaming, watching that girl drown, saying, Do something! Do something! Some told you they had always been terrified to express their true feelings about anything in their real lives. Then suddenly they were jumping up and down in their living rooms, screaming, blubbering at the television. You came out of nowhere, dove into that dark river for them, pulled them out, too.

So that was it—you became public property, a character in your own life. Without wanting any of it, you were shot from a cannon, along the Icarus arc of American hero-hood. Didn't matter that every day, today even, there are people out there pulling bodies from some wreckage. That there's someone taking a bullet right now on some school playground. Seventy-eight people died in that crash. Hard to think of heroes when an image plays in your mind of that one survivor who surfaced in the wrong place, couldn't break through; people on the bridge saw his face pressed against that ice, alive, guppy-mouthed. And then he was gone.

No, the sweetest thing about that day wasn't the name they gave you—no, that seemed more like a joke—but when the day actually ended, when you got back to Lorton at about 2:00 A.M. Nearly seventeen years later, you remember it as if it were last night. Awesome tired. A little stiff. Everything in your brick sub-division was absolutely still and glittering with ice, strung yet with some Christmas lights, just solidly, beautifully there, and you started up the walk. Shoes crunching on the snow.

Never forget that: the clean smell of winter, the mysterious dark in all of those houses, and, inside, these men and women, your neighbors, drawn together, wrapped in each other, in their bedrooms sleeping—these mothers and fathers having begotten children who would one day beget their own children, and all of you wrapped together. Cemented together like these brick build-ings. A light was on in your brick house, you remember that. A woman in the kitchen and a newborn kid. Your family, Lenny Skutnik. And the moon—it just kept falling, kept swirling down on you. It was suddenly as if you were drawn by a fast-moving current, reaching for a lifeline, moving toward some deeper place. And then you were up the steps, through the door, lost in that hundred-watt light. Home.

Now melt the snow, put the leaves back on the trees, recandle the sun to an unholy burn, turn up the heat. Home is this weltering hole called Tamarind Avenue. Home is a cyclone of red dust rising off this dirty concrete, this slow-motion manifestation of the devil. This oven of junkies and prostitutes and gangbangers in West Palm Beach, Florida—all of them stumbling between the street and their shotgun-shack shooting galleries. Down on Tamarind Avenue, it's a war between good and evil.

Yeah, the devil is loose here—devouring your people, these good brothers and sisters. Every day, you wake up dressed for the war. You shave your head clean, wear a Tut beard. You batten black fatigues over this six-foot-three, three-hundred-pound mountain, this massive, immovable muscle that is you. You wear scuffed black army boots purchased at a military surplus store, hang an old African coin around your neck. Same likeness as you, see? You walk with a wooden staff, stride manfully among the masses, speaking your version of the Word: Who's up? God is up. Who's up? The Lord is up. Who's up? We up. Plain and simple. You're the pure-brother street preacher, known in these parts as Mr. Samuel Mohammed, the dude who shot one dope pusher four times at close range, then later burned down the neighborhood crack house. As you see it, both were acts of mercy. Yeah, mercy, my brother. Add that mercy to some TV face time, and it makes you what they call a folk hero.

But you're not anything as earthly as a hero. You see yourself as the messiah. The one that Dr. Martin Luther King, Jr., implied would lead the people to the Promised Land. The commander, see? The cosmic commander. Plain and simple. Out here, there's an affliction called urban psychosis. It's like guinea worm—it starts on the inside, in your belly, then eats its way out through the flesh. A murder a day. Rape and AIDS. The candies of choice: crank, horse, crystal meth. Makes for tremors and itchy trigger fingers; turns people into needling, screwing, wanting animals—dogs. Live down here on Tamarind Avenue, and you'll see bodies laid out like starfish under a purple sky after another drive-by, see bawling families doing a Saint Vitus' dance around their dead. Live down here, and you'll have some junkie roll you for five bucks, a SIG .45 pressed to your temple.

When you first came to Tamarind Avenue, you went to work at a laundromat, a place not far from the railroad tracks. You were college educated, played football at Jackson State, got a black belt in jujitsu, worked as a bodyguard for all of these big stars: Whitney, Boyz II Men, Luther. It was your job to suss out the succubus and incubus, to laser-beam the lowdown, petty psycho-freaks who gain celebrity by taking out a celebrity. It all fell to you, the big-boy gatekeeper, the pulling guard, the black-belt ass kicker. And now you, Mr. Samuel Mohammed, made change for the old ladies at the laundromat, turning their dollar bills into quarters, which were like tiny, silver pennies in your huge hands. But then you were preaching the Word, too: Watch it now! We comin' up! Victory must be ours! Constellations of sweat spread over your smooth head from the heat of clothes dryers as you were railing against social injustice, the bureaucracy, and fleshly, human weaknesses. Time to pick ourselves up, hear! Ain't no one gonna do it for us—no politician or white man, no one living in a mansion! Yeah, talk is cheap—chitter chatter, blither blather, politicking and overlooking! Plain and simple. Don't need no fleshly promises; we stand here on high ground, on the promises of the Almighty!

The day you shot that teenage dope dealer, well, that had been brewing for a long time. Next to the laundromat was a grocery store, and that's where, in broad daylight, these drug lords were cussing and selling crack and pushing prostitutes. You, Mr. Samuel Mohammed, sat with the old ladies as they washed and dried their pinafores and undergarments, their blouses and socks, talking to them about the Scriptures. And these old ladies, most of them were too afraid even to go to their mailboxes to get their Social Security checks, so when you heard the profanity outside, you approached these drug lords. One of them mouthed off— the boy was strung out, deep-fried—and there was a confronta- tion. A few days later, he came back and nailed you with Mace. And that's when he threatened to kill you, kill the messiah.

On Tamarind, a threat like that is as good as having done it. And the next time he found you at the laundromat, he was wav- ing a gun. That was his mistake, my friend, for instantly he was disarmed of his weapon, and without thinking, you turned it on him. Four shots that took him off his feet, blew him right parallel to the ground, floating up in the air and down again. Left him lying there leaking his own blood like thick oil. Then you prayed for him. On the very spot where you shot him, you prayed for him. Prayed to your Father. And so the boy lived. The Father heard the prayer of his only begotten Son and let the boy live— your first miracle. They took him away in an ambulance, and you never got charged. Cops didn't see it as mercy but self-defense.

So God was urging you to make a stand here—Jesus against the money changers. The guinea worm was everywhere: You had a young man die in your arms, shot in the head on the street. Made no sense. And now you were fixated on the incubus and succubus in this shotgun shack across the street—a slave quarter is what you called it. Later, in court, your lawyer would say you were afflicted with urban psychosis, haunted by ghosts. He would say that you snapped. But it was simpler than that: You woke one morning, bought a five-dollar gas container, filled it with un- leaded, stalked across the street to that slave shack. Some hapless bystander tried to stop you, three hundred righteous moving pounds of you, and you said, Move! And he moved.

Kicked down the door then, almost off its hinges. Doused the place with gasoline, splattered it until the house filled with that smell of high-octane salvation. Made sure no one was there, then lit a match and threw it on the floor. And the whole thing leaped with flames. A pyre. Fire funneling up the walls and cascading back down them; ceiling coming down in a rain of magma. Couch, chairs, garbage, termites—all of it shrinking on itself, consuming itself. You could feel the heat on your back as you walked away. An awesome heat. Heat hotter than the street, yeah. People were pointing at you, murmuring, but you didn't run— you just went back to the laundromat and prayed. Later, when you saw a cop car cruising the neighborhood, you flagged it down, said to the officer: I'm the one you need to arrest.

You were offered a bargain on a couple of felony counts: plead guilty before the judge and get a reduced sentence. Your lawyer, Mr. Sam Berry, chatted with you, accompanied you to court—a no-brainer, six years maybe commuted to two and a half—and when the judge asked you how you meant to plead, you said, without hesitation, *Not guilty*. Mr. Sam Berry cleared his ear canal, perplexed. Can't cop a plea if you say not guilty! That's legal cognitive dissonance. Mr. Sam Berry's mouth dropped. Like, What the hell are you talking about, man? You did it; you admit it! Let's cop a plea and be done! And you: Yes, I did it, but I'm not guilty. I'm not guilty on earth as it is in heaven. Aim to prove that, yeah.

So Mr. Sam Berry went to work. Everybody, it seemed, had heard about you. Calls came from the networks: You were their vigilante, what America needed. An anonymous supporter put up $15,000 for your bond. The little old ladies testified to your good name. A detective told the jury that what you did was wrong but admitted there were many who admired your guts, your honesty. Yes, you did it, but look around. It was your obligation. No help from the government, no help from the cops. After all, you had a responsibility to your people, to protect them and find them greener pastures. To carry them on your broad shoulders, to keep them from the mouth of the wolf. Plain and simple.

See, you came to Tamarind Avenue to destroy the wolf.

The jury exonerated you on the arson charges after less than an hour's deliberation. Go free, cosmic commander, take back the streets.

Which is where you are now—after these 37 years of your human life, after 259 dog years, after one blink of a cosmic eye— with the sun piercing your head on Tamarind Avenue, melting the asphalt. The sidewalk gives with each one of your oversized steps, Mr. Samuel Mohammed. The thud of your big leather combat boots sounds out a warning. *He is coming! He is coming!* Your fingers are the size of peninsulas; your biceps rise beneath your fatigues like two Vesuviuses. Walking staff is a redwood tree. You're a planet unto yourself.

You're so big, in fact, you must love yourself more, pride yourself with extra pride, gulp additional air, all in order to share your love with your earthly brothers and sisters. To bring them the Word. You must be prepared to lay down your life for them— and the more your life is worth, the more willing you have to be to lay it down. That is what the good man believes, the righteous man, yeah. Let them call you freak or hero, murderer or messiah, Mr. Samuel Mohammed. You're the massive one-man black-belt power attack. And on Tamarind Avenue today, where there once stood a slave-quarter crack house, there's nothing but an empty lot of dust and broken bottles. Lay it down on the shattered glass and red dust, pure, messianic brother, and call it the Promised Land.

Now check yourself one more time. Do you feel strong? Do you have two feet planted on this earth and two lungs that work? Say, a nice ranch house on a deepwater bayou in St. Pete Beach, Florida? Then it's true: You ain't a hero, sir. You're fifty-four years old and alive, but you ain't a hero. Fishing your days, watching these heartbreaking sunsets come down in indigo tracers over the Gulf of Mexico. How many times have you seen your reflection in the bathroom mirror and wondered what that ornate piece of brass in your bottom drawer rightly makes you, anyway?

Name: Gary Lee Littrell. Rank: command sergeant major first class, U.S. Army, retired. In khakis and colorful short-sleeves now. Square, open face, steel-blue eyes, trimmed hair, an impish grin, and a muscle in your jaw that pulses when you turn serious. Career military; solid as a fence post. Out this morning in the *Eagle Five,* an eighteen-foot fishing boat named for your call sign, out with your son—fine boy with the same exact eyes—reeled in six smart-looking trout, fried 'em up for lunch. Sit around in these twilights, out by the dock with a couple of friends who live in the neighborhood, telling fish stories, checking the water for the occasional manatee.

Your buddies each have the medal, too. You encouraged both of them to come to St. Pete Beach. They had their reasons for needing a new life. You said, Come on down and we'll get you set up. And now you sit out here together, beneath the palm fronds and American flag, drinking Cokes, talking fish at sunset, marveling at the manatees, big, white, ghostly things, gentle as can be, going extinct because these speeding prop boats slice them up in the water, gouge their backs. Really, just talking about anything but—Hey, it's a hot, humid one, ain't it? Lookee at that sky. Sure is gorgeous! But maybe you're all thinking it anyway: Not unlike Vietnam. Not unlike it at all, thank you.

See, the past belongs in the past, and yet much of who you are today is still back there, somewhere near Dak Seang, in Kontum Province, bordering Cambodia. A real place under a strange sky on a hot, humid night not unlike this one. In April 1970, you, sir, were a twenty-six-year-old American adviser moving with a ranger battalion of South Vietnamese soldiers and three other Americans, including Lieutenant Raymond Green, your soul-on-ice comrade in arms, your brown-skinned double. You drank with him, slept next to him, shadowed each other everywhere. You both had the smell of the country on you, spoke Vietnamese, ate your meals with the men. They were good soldiers, vengeance fighters, brothers.

Hill 763 rose from paddies through chokes of bamboo to a bald nub at its peak, most of it set beneath a double canopy of jungle, the kind so thick it turns day into night, creates its own cloying underworld. Nearly five hundred of you humped up, then settled down on that hill to clear a forward-fire support base. You established what you thought was a safe defensive perimeter. Until you heard the first mortar rounds—that sudden, sickening pit in your stomach—and when they hit, things got ugly fast. A burning, sulfury smell of flesh and powder. Bodies scattered everywhere across this sudden crater.

Your first realization was that Lieutenant Green, who'd just been next to you, was gone—not only dead but torn apart, no longer whole. Ornaments in a tree. Everything inside you went numb; gravity tripled and brought you to a knee. The two other Americans were seriously wounded, mortars and rockets sizzling up the hill, and, folks, it was just you now, you and maybe three hundred of your South Vietnamese brothers left to stand down five thousand Vietcong moving on your position. The odds did not favor you, Sergeant Littrell.

You'd seen other men just surrender, curl up out of fear in a bunker, wetting their pants, letting the gods have their way. But no, it wasn't even a decision; it was reflex: You decided to fight. Lifted your M16 and went forward, drove yourself through the air. Move feet, run. Go, boy! Through hails of gunfire and mortar attacks, you collected the injured, reorganized the battalion. You worked the radio until you had the damn thing shot out of your hands, found another and kept going. It turned dark, a sky with no moon, and you placed the wounded near a makeshift landing pad, then went out there waving flares and strobes to signal a medevac. That brought on enemy machine guns, fire so furious no Dustoff could land. Even then, you waved the light all night. Out there like some haw lantern, marking your position. A ghost who wouldn't fall. Faced with your inevitable death, you didn't see the Holy Spirit—no, somehow you *became* the Holy Spirit. Bullets passed through without touching.

Four days and nights without food or sleep—misery and things from a nightmare. Maniacal, sir—maniacal. Shots of adrenaline and morphine to stay awake, jacked right to the ceiling. Spoke in Vietnamese to your brothers. Rallied them, lifted them up. *Danh!* Fight! The enemy massed for three human-wave assaults, and you, Sergeant Littrell, went to where they were coming, could hear their voices yourself in the bamboo, a deep, spooky feeling, and called in air strikes to within fifty yards of your own body, five-hundred-pound bombs that knocked you off your feet. To the ground, then up again. Again and again. Just like a Sunday stroll.

People dying like so many lepers around you. And bodies. Bodies everywhere. Then, on the fourth day, in a delirium, beneath another hail of mortars, when the will to fight had begun to seep from your body, you accepted your own death, too. You didn't think about your mama, didn't have some private conversation with God. Didn't have to wonder if you'd been a good man. Or what freedom meant to you. No, you just let everything get peaceful. You just stayed inside yourself for a moment, let yourself fill some small space on this planet one last time, fill it completely; like coming home to yourself, the weight of your body on this earth, your two feet on the ground, your lungs sucking air. Then you opened your eyes.

And yes, as sure as you were going to die, there came the miraculous reversal, the deus ex machina, the cavalry! Vietcong still swarming up Hill 763 for your big send-off to the Promised Land, ambushing and mortaring, grenading and machine-gunning, and suddenly you had a sky full of American bombers. Radioed them down on your position. Flying now yourself. You were just a shadow lost in these deafening bomb blasts, calling in more and more and more. And every time a bomb dropped farther down the hill, you and your hobbling men scrambled into the new crater, surrounded by amulets, all these Vietcong body parts. You carried one of your injured men on your back, dragged two others. And you all kept moving. Until there was nothing but silence. Until you'd come down off that hill with 41 walking wounded—you, impossibly, were only dehydrated—and the choppers filled the sky on their way to recover your 431 dead.

Later, when they fixed a big steak that you couldn't touch because your stomach had shrunk on itself like a dead leaf and you were frazzled on morphine and adrenaline, about to get sucked into some tsunami of withdrawal—when the Holy Spirit finally departed your body—you couldn't remember half of what had happened up there, what you'd said on the radio, how you'd danced with the flares. You were empty. But then there was no language for what you remembered.

President Nixon put this Medal of Honor around your neck so you would never forget. The citation called you "superhuman." And yet you never felt weaker. Everywhere you went now, you were followed by the 431 dead men. Sometimes in the mirror, it was Lieutenant Green looking back.

So check yourself, sir. Lounging by the dock in St. Pete

Beach with your two buddies, Sergeant Frank Miller and Captain Ron Ray. Both medal winners, too. Lit upon by the enemy, their bodies grenaded and machine-gunned, each literally half dead, they got up off their backs and they fought. Maniacally. Driven by some reflex beneath the reflex. Now, like you, they have graying hair and thickening bellies. Even today, it's hard to know what the medal makes you feel: proud, thankful, strong. Imperfect, lonely, mortal. Days it makes you feel more like an outsider. Makes you feel like a fraud, because all the real heroes are dead.

But then lookee at this sunset, this sky full of indigo tracers and deep-coral colors. There's an American flag luffing in a soft breeze. There are two men at this table—Sergeant Miller and Captain Ray—who know without having to say. You just sit, drinking Cokes, telling fish stories. Talking about everything and nothing. Some nights, they've got your back covered, help carry you down that hill without saying anything about it.

There was one night out in this deepwater bayou when you, Command Sergeant Major Gary Lee Littrell, went to the dock alone, just stood there a while, watching the pelicans, trying to feel something. When you looked down in the dark water, you were surprised by two huge, white manatees looking back at you with those mournful, wrinkled eyes. As if they'd come from another world, silently floating there, as if they alone possessed some secret, wordless language. They were just hovering there, underwater, big, gentle animals with gouged backs. These vanishing, beautiful things showed themselves to you once and then were gone.

So it's now been five years in the Sudan, Jason Matus, and you've been given a Dinka name: *Majok dit*. A black bull with a white crown on its head. You've been offered gifts—ivory walking sticks and golden pipes made from bullet casings and goats, more skinny goats than you would ever know what to do with. They might be starving, but the Dinka will give you, an American, their last goat.

You came into the country as an innocent, and now you're experienced. The fish has grown strong even as some of your co-workers have been killed. You've waded through thick crowds at hundreds of food drops, reached out to clasp thousands of reaching hands, lost your mind in the heat, pushed and yelled for people to clear the drop zone, and been trampled in riots from the Hunger. You've sat in the dirt, covered in red dust, trying to assess caloric intake and the nutritional value of shea butter nut, lalob, wild rice, cassava, tubers, yams, and tamarind. You talk slowly, like Boris Badenov, yeah? Understand, my brother? Listen, what I say might save you.

Five years, the biggest airlift in history, and yet it's the same famine, the same war as when you arrived. The same starving people, fleeing their oppressors; the same boll weevils in the dust at your feet, kids scrounging for maize; the same skeletons at the feeding centers and shrivel-breasted women holding dead babies. You yourself have run for your life, sought refuge from the bombs out in the bush for two days until you waved your Mylar blanket at a search plane. Thought you might drown out there in all that nothingness. At one food drop, you were called away by some Dinka. They took you a short distance and pointed at something in the dust near a fallen woman, and you nearly threw up. She had miscarried trying to lug a 110-pound bag of maize. That stayed with you. That made you wonder: Are we doing any good here?

Some of your comrades don't think so. They say you've all grown cynical and tired. They say the rest of the world, those people sending money because of a commercial, are really funding the Stone Age, allowing these half-mad militia leaders to blow one another apart, keep everyone else down. Food has become a weapon, the reason for war. And no one wants to end the fighting, because everyone is power tripping and making good money on this thing. Everyone gets to be a hero. Even you, Jason Matus. Even you.

But . . . no. That makes you grimace. Sure, you're paid for this. But it's not as if you're pretending to be Mother Teresa. No, what pisses you off is the alternative: What happens if everyone packs up and goes home, leaves the Dinka and the Nuer and the Luo without maize and sorghum, unimix and high-energy biscuits? More people starve, more die. Is that the answer?

Sorry, you believe. It's been five years, and there will be more. See, there's a book you carry with you everywhere in your mind, by this guy Paulo Freire, who says conflict is the midwife of conscience, yeah? And that the ideal of freedom isn't just some chimera, isn't some bauble located outside of us, floating around like satellites in space. No, it's something we have to reach out and grab, something we must ingest and then, our stomachs full, use for our own completion. This isn't about money or heroes, my brother; this is about capturing freedom. This is about laying it down for the people.

And it's finally about this: the end of another long day. A strong, dusty wind has picked up. You're tired, Jason Matus, bone tired. You're feeling mortal beneath this African sky, this slow, heavy tide of silver clouds closing in over your head. Passing through villages on your way home, you feel beaten, alone, an outsider. Evening fires are lit. People are gathered by their tukels, circled around bags of food you helped give them earlier. They're placing great, golden handfuls of maize in huge, hollowed trunks that they use as mortars and pestles.

So lost in thought, you almost don't notice that the people are smiling at you. They're smiling and speaking to you. Mothers and fathers in fluttering djellabas. *Mali madit.* Big peace, my brother. And from somewhere below, armies of naked kids grab your fingers and carry you along, cheering and laughing, bellies blown out. They're excitedly jabbering in Dinka, asking you, this white ghost, to be their friend, and you're jabbering back in English, asking them to be your friend.

And that's when the pounding begins: these heavy, magnificent thuds—these thick, rounded branches pulverizing the maize. Crushing it for soup. There's pounding all through the country tonight, echoing like beating hearts. You can hear it now—everywhere. Listen. The fires are lit; the children are dancing. Do you know how good that sound is? Do you know how that feels, the way it moves the earth that moves your body? How deep and real? See, that's what a little night music can really sound like. That's when you know you've earned this night of sleep. So lay it down now, my pure brother. Lay it down and sleep.

CITY OF DUST

THE ONES LEFT BEHIND, THE SURVIVORS, remember it as a sound that had no context: the thunder of hoofbeats, thousands of them, or the strange, grinding gears of some monstrous runaway truck.

At Police Headquarters in Port-au-Prince, the chief of the National Judicial Police, a tall, slender man named Frantz Termilus, sat in a meeting with his boss, the superintendent, discussing the city's nagging kidnapping issue. Termilus was a tireless man who loved his job, whose forthright manner and faith made him a force for good. It wasn't just the number of medals he won; it was his attitude every day: He truly believed that with humility and industriousness the wild city could be tamed. And now, in midsentence, that otherworldly grinding came and drowned out his voice. Then Termilus was lifted and thrown hard, the office lurching abruptly—the floor levering illogically—tossing him, and the furniture, into the far corner.

The police chief pressed his hands against the wall to hold himself in place, even as everything crumbled and calved. It went on and on. And when the building stopped spasming, and he knew himself to be alive, Termilus reflexively shouted, "Praise God." He crawled, then, until he was free of the earthquake's rubble, a regal man on his knees. Like the others who were caught out—at their offices or schools, in their cars or the market or returning to their families—like everyone who couldn't know what was waiting for them beyond what they'd just survived, Frantz Termilus instinctively started walking home, his uniform powdered in a white chalk.

You could immediately tell a terrible thing had happened. Above him, the sky had gone almost entirely black from all the dust and dirt blown upward, like a shroud drawn over the city. A burning smell filled the air; the heat of the day felt hotter. The stunned silence had given way to wailing, a collective animal keening. The city that lay cupped in the palm of a hand was crushed. It had taken less than sixty seconds.

Termilus had a wife, two daughters, and a son. That morning, his daughters—Emmanuella and Talitha, who were eleven and twelve, and whose preternatural intelligence had caused their teachers to promote them to the seventh and eighth grades—had dressed their three-year-old brother, Benedict, each slipping a shoe on a foot and tying it for him. They shared everything like this. They were the kind of girls, pigtailed and smiling and outgoing, for whom an excursion to the beach, or for ice cream, often meant packing the car with friends; Frantz at the wheel often marveled at the sweet jabber of children.

Now the city existed as a parking lot of hastily abandoned cars—some with their engines still running. Hurrying along one avenue after another, Termilus saw arms and legs dangling from the compacted buildings, limbs set at oblique angles, the dust-covered dead appearing as ghosts, some staring with open-eyed vacancy or grimaced expressions. The wandering survivors, too, were caked and stunned. To pass one was to see your own reflection, some strange mix of horror and elation. Two houses in a row might have been leveled while a third might have remained untouched, the line between life and death a couple of feet. And everywhere Termilus saw the living frantically digging, often with bare hands, for their kin or neighbors, hoping to pull a miracle from the mess.

Around each new corner came new horrors. Up the mountain, in the wealthier section of Pétionville, the Hotel Montana—one of the ritziest in town—collapsed, instantly trapping hundreds, including many Americans, some of whom had just arrived, on their way to the patio bar to watch the sunset. In the Bourdon neighborhood, beneath the collapsed seven-story United Nations complex, nearly one hundred others were lost, a multinational corps of diplomats and workers. In the poor neighborhood of Carrefour, the bowls formed by the mountain had given way, and the packed-together houses dominoed one into the next, taking entire families as they went. Meanwhile, in downtown Port-au-Prince, the National Palace looked like a flattened soufflé. Nearby the cathedral had split like a ship on the shoals, the facade collapsing first, stained glass shattering, then the roof, falling on a dozen members of the choir as they sang inside.

Termilus walked two miles, then three, then four, seeing sights that even a year later would make him tremble and weep. In his house, the daily routine was always the same: The family woke—or he woke the girls, who loved to sleep. They ate breakfast, and Frantz went to work. His wife ferried the children to school, the day unfolded, and when school was out in the late afternoon, his wife picked everyone up. Then Frantz returned, and they were a family again. Now, he oriented himself toward that normalcy: It was late afternoon. He was returning home.

When Termilus came upon his own house, he saw that it was still standing and felt a palpitation of hope. But when he opened the door, he saw only his wife. There is a French word for someone whose mind has been destroyed. *Fou*. She looked gone already, hovering before him in a trance. Benedict, she managed to say, was accounted for at his preschool. But she had been running late all afternoon, having gone to register the girls for English-language classes. She'd left them with the principal of the school. "You picked them up, right?" she said.

He left her then, wordlessly—and started walking again, with new purpose, another eight miles across town to the girls' school. Talitha and Emmanuella: It would be enough to see them—alive, injured, even dead—just one last time. It was getting dark, and there was no wind, or traffic, to envelop the wails. It would be months before the dead could be counted. And even then estimates would vary, but at least one hundred fifty thousand people were killed.

Downtown at the ministry of justice, Micha Gaillard, one of Haiti's leading politicians, was buried alive beneath pillars and stone, where he would stay for almost two days—like so many others who were unextractable—dying slowly, as his friends and finally his teenage son came to converse through the rubble, to say their goodbyes. Meanwhile, the archbishop, a man devoted to the poor, a man whose shyness sometimes caused him to stutter, had been indecorously pitched from his balcony. And the vicar-general, a natural joker, had been trapped beneath the same building, sending a cell-phone message saying he was alive, but was later found dead, sitting in a chair, a eucharist in one hand, a cross clutched in the other. At another church, the Brazilian humanitarian-aid worker and pediatrician Zilda Arns Neumann, whose work focused on children and pregnant women (and led to a Nobel Peace Prize nomination, as well as comparisons to

Mother Teresa), had just given a speech, after which she was erased by falling debris. She was found the next day, identified by a sandal.

Grief is a walk to the ending you already know, and during the seventh and eighth miles, a feeling overtook Termilus, a wish for only one thing: that he might stumble upon someone he knew in the streets—anyone—just to grab hold of the living and tell them the truth: that he loved them. Why hadn't he ever said so before?

When he came to the school, there was no school. All four stories had come down. And everything all at once left his body— all the hope and energy he'd mustered to match the horror—and even now he couldn't say how long he stood there, gazing upon the gravestone of that school.

He still stands there.

But that night, when he finally walked back through the city—now all the survivors, fearing aftershocks, were in the streets, some singing by candlelight, preparing for night, forming circles around the children to keep them from the *loups garous,* or werewolves—when Frantz Termilus took his place in the street and survived that first night, and the first light of morning broke over the carcass of Port-au-Prince, and he saw the other mothers and fathers, some of them digging again in the rubble for their own children, he picked himself up. His wife would go on believing for weeks that the girls were alive, somewhere, and though their bodies wouldn't be recovered for seven months, he knew that God had taken them. And left him.

There was no phone service, but it wasn't hard to know that the city was bedlam. Word of mouth traveled: Hospitals had been destroyed. There were no services, no potable water. The prison had broken open—and now five thousand inmates were loose, including all the kidnappers. There were caches of weapons that needed to be secured. And there were more children, trapped, orphaned, injured. He was on the verge of being consumed by memory, but instead of mourning before that pile of rocks, he dusted off his shirt—his badge, the epaulets. He straightened his uniform and went to work.

THE SUICIDE CATCHER

THE BRIDGE ROSE UP AND AWAY from the city's northwest quadrant, spanning the great Yangtze River. And yet, from the on-ramp where the taxi let me off that Saturday morning, it seemed more like a figment of the imagination, a ghostly ironwork extrusion vanishing in the monsoon murk, stretching to some other-world. It was disorienting to look at, that latticed half bridge leaving off in midair, like some sort of surrealist painting. It gave off a foreboding aura, too, untethered and floating, and yet it couldn't have been more earthbound—and massive. Later I'd find out it was made from five hundred thousand tons of cement and one million tons of steel. Four miles long, with four lanes of car traffic on the upper deck and twin railroad tracks on the lower, it transferred thousands of people and goods to and from the city every day. But now the clouds clamped down, and a sharp scent of sulfur and putrid fish wafted on a dank puff of air. Rain slithered from the sky. There, before my eyes, the bridge shimmered and disappeared, as if it had never been visible in the first place.

Its formal name was the Nanjing Yangtze River Bridge, and it served one other purpose for the masses: At least once a week, someone jumped to his or her death here, but a total was hard to come by, in part because the Chinese authorities refused to count those who missed the river, the ones who'd leapt and had the misfortune of landing in the trees along the riverbank, or on the concrete apron beneath the bridge, or who were found impressed in the earth like mud angels, two feet from rushing water. Perhaps such strict bookkeeping came in response to the fact that China already posts the highest sheer numbers, about two hundred thousand "reported" suicide cases a year, constituting a fifth of all the world's suicides. For a long time, the Communist government simply ignored the problem, hoping it would go away, or maybe thinking in the most Darwinian terms of suicide as its own method of population control. One recent case highlighted just how the Chinese bureaucracy tended to deal with prevention. In the southern city of Guangzhou, workers had been ordered to smear butter over a steel bridge popular with jumpers, in order to make it too slippery to climb. "We tried employing guards at both ends," said a government official, "and we put up special fences and notices asking people not to commit suicide here. None of it worked—and so now we have put butter over the bridge, and it has worked very well."

In Nanjing, the bridge remained butterless, even as the city spit out its victims. Nanjing was now just another one of your typical six-million-person Chinese metropolises, one of the famous "Three Furnaces" of China because of its unremitting summer heat. Daytime temperatures regularly topped ninety degrees here—due to hot air being trapped by the mountains at the lower end of the Yangtze River valley . . . and, oh yeah, *because all the trees had been chopped down*—and the sun rarely shone. Meanwhile, the city continued to explode in the noonday of the country's hungry expansion. The past was being abandoned at an astonishing rate, the new skyscrapers and apartment buildings replacing the old neighborhoods. Everything—and everyone— was disposable. Schisms formed. The bridge loomed. Loss led to despair, which in turn led to Mr. Chen.

I'd come through thirteen time zones just to see him. Once free of the taxi, I began trudging, a quarter mile or so, the bridge trembling under the weight of its traffic, piled with noisy green taxis and rackety buses, some without side panels or mufflers. Unlike the suspended wonder of Brooklyn or the quixotic *ponts* of Paris, this couldn't have been mistaken for anything but stolid Communist bulwark: At its apex, the bridge was about 130 feet above the water; was built with two twenty-story "forts," spaced one mile apart, that from a distance had the appearance of huge torches; and contained two hundred inlaid reliefs that included such exhortations as *Our country is led by the working class* and *Long live the unity of the people.* A brochure claimed that the bridge was both the first of its kind designed solely by Chinese engineers, and also "ideal for bird-watching." People teemed in both directions. Umbrellas unfurled, poked, and were ripped from their rigging, leaving sharp spiders dangling overhead. As I registered the passersby—their eyes fixed downward—everyone seemed a candidate for jumping, marching in that mournful parade.

He was close now. I could tell by the banners and messages— some were flags, some were just scraps of paper—that fluttered earnestly from the bridge. *Value life every day,* read one. *Life is precious,* declared another. His cell-phone number was emblazoned everywhere, including graffitied stamps he'd left on the sidewalk, ones I tried to decipher beneath the blur of so many passing feet. And then Mr. Chen came into view, conspicuous for being the only still point in that sea of motion . . . and the only one sporting a pair of clunky binoculars, the only one watching the watchers of the river.

He stood at full attention at the South Tower. Perched off

one side of the structure was a concrete platform surrounded by Plexiglas, a capsule of sorts where yawning sentries did their own dubious monitoring of the bridge through a mounted spyglass, as if conducting a sociological study at a great remove. The sentries looked like kids, while Mr. Chen, who stood out front on the sidewalk, among the people, looked every bit of his forty years. He had a paunch, blackened teeth, and the raspy cough of an avid smoker—and he never stopped watching, even when he allowed himself a cigarette, smoking a cheap brand named after the city itself. He wore a baseball cap with a brim that poked out like an oversized duck's bill, like the Cyrano of duck bills, the crown of which read *They spy on you.*

Six years earlier, working as a functionary for a transportation company, Mr. Chen had read a story about the bridge in the paper, about bodies raining down to their end. Soon after, he quietly took his post at the South Tower. Ever since then, when not working his job, he'd been up on the bridge, pulling would-be's from the railing. According to a blog he kept, he'd saved 174 jumpers—and in the process had been hailed as one of China's great Good Samaritans. Of those he saved, some small number met near the bridge every year around Christmas to celebrate their new lives and ostensibly to offer their thanks. As part of the ceremony, they calculated their new ages from the date of their salvation. In this born-again world, no one was older than six.

Back home I'd stumbled on Mr. Chen's blog one day, reading it in jumbled Google translation, and became riveted by his blow-by-blow of life on the bridge. There'd been the husband and wife who'd jumped hand in hand. There'd been the man dressed in black, floating there on the water's surface as a boat tried to reach him, until the current finally sucked him away. Another fellow had been pulled off the railing, back onto the bridge, and in the fight that ensued—one during which Mr. Chen had to enlist the help of others—the man had bitten his tongue in half and nearly bled to death on the sidewalk, leaving Mr. Chen covered in blood.

Mr. Chen's blog entries were sometimes their own desperate pleas: *Lovelorn girls of Henan, where are you?* read one. But more often they were a subdued, pointillistic chronicle of the day's dark news: *. . . Middle-aged man jumped off bridge where the body fell to the flower bed: died on the spot. . . . Speaking in northern accent, man gave me a cigarette, said: Alas! Wives and children. . . . A woman in the southeast fort jumped in riverbed, dead on spot. . . . Next to statue at southwest fort, man died jumping to concrete, one leg thrown from body, only blackened blood left behind. Meaningless life!*

And yet standing sentry among the hordes, Mr. Chen seemed a bit comical, or his mission seemed the ultimate act of absurdity. How could he possibly pick out the suicidal on a four-mile-long bridge? Were they marked somehow, glowing only for him? As no one seemed to pay him any attention, he was forced to take himself twice as seriously. And he was so engrossed in the Kabuki of his work that it occurred to me how easy a mark he might make for a practical joker tying shoelaces together. Had his heroics only been a figment of his imagination? Was he as unstable somehow as his jumpers? And was he serious with those binoculars, especially with visibility reduced to fifty yards or so in the murk? When I introduced myself, he waved me off. "Not now," he said gruffly. "I'm working."

Then his binoculars shot up to his eyes, sheltered by the bill of his cap, and he fumbled with the focus knob while gazing deep into the masses, searching, it would seem, for that fleeting infrared flare of despair, for the moment when he'd be called into action, ready for his hero moment.

One's reasons for being on the bridge belonged to the mysterious underworld in all of us, but to choose to die so publicly, so dramatically—turning languid flips or dropping straight as a pin—was something I couldn't quite understand. After all the humiliation one suffered, all the monotonies and losses, the erasures and disintegrations, after being constantly consumed by society, was it a small reclamation of the self? And what would it feel like to fly, to prove you could? The mere flicker of that idea seemed almost too dangerous to consider. If you let it in, is that when you started to feel the pull of this other force? Could it be stopped?

There were the Stoics, who justified suicide, and the Christians, who condemned it. There was the honorable *seppuku* of samurai, and the cowardly cyanide of Nazis. And there were suicide's other famous practitioners: Virginia Woolf, entering the River Ouse with a heavy stone in her pocket; Walter Benjamin, overdosing on morphine in a hotel room in Spain in the belief that he was about to be turned over to the Nazis; Sylvia Plath, turning on the gas . . . and then, later, her son, too, by hanging. Meriwether Lewis shot himself in the chest; Kurt Cobain, in the head. There were Spanish matadors and Congolese pygmies. Auntie Em from *The Wizard of Oz* and Tattoo from *Fantasy Island*. William James, the great humanist philosopher, tilting dangerously close to self-annihilation, wrote his father, "Thoughts of the pistol, the dagger, and the bowl began to usurp an unduly large part of my attention," and later proclaimed, "I take it that no man is educated who has never dallied with the thought of suicide."

Those on the bridge weren't dallying anymore. They'd come, one after the other, to jump, their lives reduced to this single sliver. Beneath the hum and blare of traffic came that insidious sucking sound. How could just one man stop it?

———

Mr. Chen appeared to have a very strict routine on the bridge, no matter if it was snowing, blowing, or broiling heat. He stood at full attention at the South Tower, where a large percentage of his encounters came within the first one hundred meters past the fort, in that area of the bridge that spanned from the riverbank to the river itself. "In so much pain," he would tell me, "they jump the second they think they're over the mother river. And a lot of them miss the water."

His routine called for maintaining his station for about forty minutes out of every hour—then he fired up his moped, an unconvincing contraption on the verge of breakdown, and putted off down the sidewalk, weaving between walkers, like John Wayne astride a miniature Shetland pony. These were his rounds, up and down the bridge, motoring out one mile to the North Tower and then turning back. If he sniffed trouble out there, he might linger—in some cases might be gone hours—but today he reappeared a short time later, stitching deftly through the crowd, then kickstanding his Rocinante and resuming his same exact position, his same exact suspicious disposition, his same exact focused gruffness beneath the bill of his cap. Though he was stout, with plump hands, he held himself like a much bigger person, like the one he felt himself to be when on the bridge.

The sky roiled and spit, as if we were lost inside some potion. Again, the scent of diesel and fish. After fifteen minutes or so, I had a splitting headache, and yet Mr. Chen stood nearly stock-still, unfazed, scanning the crowd with binoculars. His life was a grand monotony, but in his stillness and stasis, the possibility for calamity existed in every moment, and that's what kept him coiled and at the ready.

Mr. Chen would later describe a recurring nightmare that went like this: Someone was up on the railing, and he was sprinting as fast as he could to save the jumper. Over and over, he would arrive too late, as the body pushed from the railing to the hungry maw below. He said that he'd been visited on the bridge by a foreign psychiatrist who asked him if he might draw a picture of whatever came to mind. So he did: of a large mountain disappearing up into the clouds, which the psychiatrist interpreted as Mr. Chen trying to carry the weight of the weightless sky. Or something like that. Mr. Chen was fuzzy on the details and didn't have much time for this nonsense. The encounter smudged into the same colorlessness of every other colorless moment in the colorless flow of time on the bridge.

The rain had let up and the fog shifted, though the weekend traffic had worsened—the city dwellers heading out to the country, the country dwellers heading into the city. I meandered out on the bridge for a moment, away from the tower and the armed sentries and Mr. Chen, who didn't seem to care a whit about me unless I planned to jump. As I gazed downriver, in the easterly direction of Shanghai, a shipyard with an enormous crane appeared in the near distance while a temple loomed with its wooden pagoda on a hill. Skimming the river's brown, roiling surface came a steady, dirgelike stream of barges loaded with lumber, coal, containers, and sand. The view into its muddy waters was not for the faint of heart. There were two ways to die from here: on impact with the water's surface, which at sixty-five miles per hour is like hitting concrete, the shattering of bone and internal organs, the instant blackout and massive bleeding, the general pancaking and dismemberment of the body—or by drowning, by somehow surviving the impact and waking underwater, swept away in the current, unable to muster a frog kick given the various possible combinations of broken pelvis/femur/back/jaw, etc. Below, the waters eddied and swirled, etching a secret language on the surface. When a train passed, the whole bridge seemed to buckle and sway, causing me to clutch the railing.

One of Mr. Chen's blog entries was simply entitled "Girl's Tears." It told the tale of a girl from the country who'd come to the bridge, not far from this spot here, to end her life. It started with the observation that tears shed by girls were like tears of angels "that come from disappointment—or was it regret?" This was a runaway, said Mr. Chen, and she stood "tummy railing," looking down at the water, despondent. When Mr. Chen approached, he gave her three options: (1) leave the bridge, (2) call emergency services for help, or (3) let Mr. Chen take her to his house, where she could live for a time with him, his wife, and their daughter. Mr. Chen took her phone and called her belligerent boyfriend, and as he spoke to him, she climbed the railing to jump. He seized her hand; she pulled away, climbing higher on the railing, teetering for a second there. He tore her from the railing, but as the police arrived, she ran into traffic, then tried to disappear in the crowd. The police apprehended her and took her away. It was over just like that. One second he could feel her breath on him; the next she was gone, and Mr. Chen, tough as he was, claimed to have burst into tears.

"Next day called number," he wrote on his blog. "Always unanswered."

The reason Mr. Chen was in the business of saving lives now was that as a boy, he'd learned what it meant to go unanswered. There is a saying in Chinese he used to describe this condition, that he never possessed "mother's shoes." With those words, he threw back an oversized shot of a potent grain alcohol. "Getting drunk loosens the tongue," he declared empirically, then refilled our teacups as we sat together in a tight, crowded restaurant near the bridge. He clinked them in a toast and tossed another mini-bucketful into the back of his throat, where, according to my simultaneous research, everything caught fire and napalmed down the gullet to the stomach, where in turn it flickered and tasered a while, like rotgut lava. We had left the bridge for lunch, and he had insisted that I drink with him. Sensing we might be in the midst of a transitional relationship moment, I joined him in the first few rounds but then thought better of it—there was no doubt this guy was going to drink me under the table—and eased off. He laughed when I did, a disparaging laugh, wondering aloud at what kind of American I was.

Our party now included my translator, Susan—who had been born in Nanjing but raised in the United States—and a wordless man who had suddenly appeared, ostensibly a close friend of Mr. Chen's, called Mr. Shi. We'd arrived at this "family restaurant" sometime after noon, after we'd all left the bridge together, Mr. Chen on his moped and the three of us on foot, taking endless flights of stairs down through the South Tower to the ground, where Mr. Chen was waiting to ferry us, one by one, on the back of his moped to the restaurant. I didn't know where to put my hands, so I grabbed the bulk of his shoulders.

We sat down to filmy glasses of beer and a clear, unmarked bottle of grain alcohol, and saucers of peppers and tripe, tofu soup, noodles, and fish stew. Mr. Chen and Mr. Shi began smoking Nanjings until we were wreathed in smoke. Overhead a fan lopped away off-kilter, on the verge of unscrewing itself from the ceiling. The walls of the restaurant were sepia colored, plastered with old posters, Buddha sharing the wall with a liquor ad. The hissing sound of the wok—onions and chicken and squirming mung beans—agitated beneath the clatter of plates and the hoarse voices of men (there were no families here, only workmen) huddled at the eight or so tables, heads sluicing with liquor, too.

Mr. Chen explicated his opening statement. See, in the old

times, before "the Communist liberation," a great deal of pride was connected to these homemade textiles, for both parent and child. The shoes and socks were a declaration of individual love in a country obsessed with the self-effacing collective. His own mother had always been an erratic presence, but after his parents split when he was eight, she disappeared for the better part of a decade—and so, too, did his "mother's love," as he put it. That's when he went to live with his grandmother, in a village outside the city. Widowed at eighteen, his grandmother served an important function in the village: She was a peacemaker and therapist of sorts, if utterly unschooled. It was from her that Mr. Chen had learned the fine art of persuasion. It was from the incompleteness of his own family that he'd built this not-so-secret life as the defender of broken humanity. And the weight of the task had become its own burden.

"I've aged terribly in my six years on the bridge," he said, again clinking teacups with Mr. Shi. "To age!" He drank and then admitted that he had a lot of gray hair, due to the weather and stress—stress on the bridge, stress at work, stress at home. He caught me gazing at the thick, black, spiky forest matting his head. "I've been dyeing it for years," he said.

He sat back, removed his glasses, rubbed his eyes with the backs of his hands. He poured another glass, this time hesitating before drinking, and spoke again as he stabbed a piece of tripe, then began to chew. On the bridge, he said, there were three types of jumpers, and they had to be dealt with either by force or finesse, by blunt words or wraithlike verbiage fashioned into a lasso. Mostly they came peaceably, but sometimes it was a donnybrook. The first category included the mentally unstable or clinically insane. In the frenzy of letting go, these were the ones who might take you with them, grasping onto anyone as some proxy for "mother's love." So—Mr. Chen would charge them like a dangerous man himself, wrestling, punching, kicking, doing whatever was necessary. "I'm very confident in my physical strength," he said. "Since I have no psychological training, my job is to get that person off the bridge as quickly as possible." Whereupon he might take him or her to "the station," which, as it turned out, was an in-patient psych ward at the highly reputed Nanjing University, one of the few places in the city where the suicidal could receive professional care and treatment.

The second category was the emotionally fragile, the wilted flower, the person who had lost someone—a husband, a child, a wife, a parent—or suffered from some sort of abuse and saw no way to go on. If the potential jumper was a woman, Mr. Chen's strategy was to try to bring her to tears, for that often broke the tension, and once emotion poured forth, he might grab for her hand and huddle her away. Men, by contrast, were both simpler and trickier. You forked one of two ways. Either you told him bluntly that you were about to punch him in the nose if he didn't step away from the railing, or you did the exact opposite: You approached in a nonthreatening, even companionable, manner, offering a cigarette to the figure lingering too long by the railing, and from there steered him to a place like this restaurant, where together you could drink grain alcohol and really talk, something that wasn't so easy in a culture that still held fast to a Confucian ethic of stoicism.

The final category, he claimed, included the ones who "failed really hard, or too often." Usually men, these would-be jumpers had often lost a great deal of money and weren't feeling so wonderful about themselves anymore, especially when their failures were thrown into relief by those riding on the heady high seas of the new China, driving fancy cars, wearing designer clothes, smoking expensive American cigarettes. Mr. Chen then pointed to Mr. Shi and said, "He was one of those."

Mr. Shi, a thin man of thinning hair, blinked laconically through the smoke. Though the stage was set for him to unspool his tale, he showed no interest in taking up the story. "Later," barked Mr. Chen. It was strange, and not a little confusing, how gruff he could be while making himself, and those around him, so vulnerable. When more plates of food arrived, he shoveled beans and noodles, fish and broccoli onto his plate, then lit upon it all as if it were prey, gobbling and drinking, then gobbling some more.

I regarded him again in this dim light. He was unabashed in his mannerisms, a man who seemed to live so fully inside this hexed world of suicide that he had little time for polish or polite chitchat or getting-to-know-you. When I asked if he had heard of the famous Hollywood film *It's a Wonderful Life,* in which Jimmy Stewart plans to end his life on a bridge until an angel named Clarence saves him, he cut me off by shaking his head. No, he didn't care about movies or my attempts to draw fatuous parallels. Nor were we kindred spirits: Simply showing up did not confer membership in the club. He barely bothered to look at me when responding to my questions.

In turn, I soon found myself growing anxious there in that restaurant—very anxious—watching Mr. Chen and Mr. Shi drain glass after glass. My mind suddenly seized upon the notion that this was a Saturday, the busiest day on the bridge, and here we sat. However absurd it had felt to be standing on a four-mile bridge, thronged by thousands, trying to pick out jumpers, I felt a sudden onrush of dread at not being there at all, as if the welfare of all humanity depended on our vigilance. Part of it had to do with the effect of the grain alcohol. And part of it was fatigue—the result of all those time zones to get here. In that loud, hot space, I felt simultaneously this desire to stand and leave and yet to lay my head down and rest. The irrefutable truth was that nothing—

neither butter nor Mr. Chen——would dissuade the jumpers from coming: So what was the point of being here at all?

That was the question that occurred to me now in that mung-bean-and-hooch restaurant, that hole-in-the-wall, listening to the guttural rebukes of Mr. Chen: What was I doing here at all, in a place where people came to kill themselves, seven thousand miles from my home and family? This wasn't an assignment that had been given to me. I'd chosen it. I'd come as if there were some message here, some fragment to justify, or obliterate, that slow bloom of doubt in my chest. But now I could feel the pressure under the soles of my feet: The bridge ran under me, too.

If you dig deep enough into the past, almost every family has its suicide. My maternal grandmother once told me the story of a relative dating from the nineteenth century: a young woman fresh from Ireland, a Catholic who'd married a Protestant. She was isolated, living with her husband's family in upstate New York, in the region known as the North Country, and her life became a slow torment from which there seemed to be no escape, even after bearing a child. Her beliefs were pilloried and belittled. She slowly unraveled. One day she put rocks in her pocket and stepped into a cistern, where she drowned.

But such events didn't just belong to the past——or to some mythic country, either. From my own suburban hometown, I remembered a sweet, shy kid, roughly my age, who seemed incapable of any sort of demonstrativeness, who drove himself to the Adirondacks in winter, purchased a coil of rope along the way, found a sturdy tree, and hanged himself. I had nightmares about that boy, shagged in ice until his father found him and cut him down.

And the neighbor down the street, found in the bathtub . . .

And the kid who ran his motorcycle into a tree, an accident but for the note left behind saying that's exactly what he intended to do . . . And so on. Even in suburbia, suicide had seemed like its own opaque parable, the never-happened, glossed-over secret.

I came upon the story of a boy, a British art student named Christian Drane, who'd photographed suicide spots in England for a school project—including a bridge in Bristol, where he was approached by a stranger who wondered if he was all right—and then hanged himself in the Polygon woods of Southampton. No one could believe it. He'd made everyone laugh. He had a tattoo on his arm, representing his family. Afterward, his girlfriend told an inquest that Christian was the happiest person she knew, "cheeky, spontaneous, excitable." He whisked her to Paris for her birthday, wrapped her in "fairy lights" and took her portrait. He posted other photos from his project online: other bridges, subway stations, and Beachy Head, the chalk cliffs of Eastbourne, the most famous of English suicide spots. Each bore the moniker "Close Your Eyes and Say Goodbye."

The photograph of Christian that accompanied many of the news stories showed a boy with mussed-up hair and pierced ears with black plugs, looking impishly askance at the camera. Had the pretense of the project emboldened him, or was "the project" merely his eventual suicide? His final note, which no one claimed to understand, read: "To mum and anybody who cares. I have done something I can never forgive myself for. I am a bad person. I am sorry."

The Yangtze ever beckoned. And its pull was finally felt at the family restaurant by Mr. Chen, who abruptly stood, grunted, walked out the front door like a superhero summoned by dog whistle, then fired up his moped and went swerving off, his *They spy on you* double-bill back on his head, binoculars dangling around his neck. Left in his wake, we—Susan the translator, Mr. Shi, and I—straggled back to the bridge in a slow-motion amble. It felt good to be in the open air again, somehow cleansing after all the smoke and noise.

Bent like a harp, Mr. Shi was the kind of gentle man you instantly wanted to protect, to shield from life's bullies or from the falling monsoon rain that now switched on again. It seemed to pain him to have to speak. He was too slight for his somewhat dirty slacks and pale blue dress shirt—and carried himself with so little swagger he seemed resigned to the fact that he interested no one. Except *I* was interested. I wanted to know what Mr. Chen had meant when he'd identified Mr. Shi as one who'd failed really hard. Mr. Shi squinted at me as he lit a cigarette and then started to speak, hesitated, and started again. He said that several years back, his daughter had been diagnosed with leukemia. He'd borrowed money for her treatment and had fallen tens of thousands in debt, even making the desperate blunder of engaging with a local loan shark.

When he went to the bridge on that fateful day, he loitered by the railing long enough for Mr. Chen to lock in on him through his binoculars, and then this man was suddenly standing next to him, saying, "Brother, it's not worth it." After a while, Mr. Chen got Mr. Shi to smoke a cigarette and coaxed him off the bridge, down to the family restaurant to drink and talk, whereupon Mr. Shi's entire story poured forth. Mr. Chen listened closely, trying to understand as best as possible Mr. Shi's predicament, and then began to formulate a plan. Mr. Chen would speak with the loan shark and all the other vengeful parties in the matter. He'd negotiate a truce, a repayment plan, a job search. He insisted that Mr. Shi meet him the following day, at his workplace at the transportation company, where he often welcomed the weekend's forlorn and misfit to his desk, a recurring gesture that had left his bosses exasperated and threatening to fire him. He'd given Mr. Shi hope and friendship (though details of the repayment plan were murky), and Mr. Shi had found a way to begin life anew.

In this moment of sheepish intimacy—Mr. Shi had a habit of making eye contact, then looking away as if embarrassed—he reminded me of something Mr. Chen had said: "The people I'm saving are very, very kind. They don't want to hurt anyone, so the only way they can vent is by hurting themselves. In that moment when they are deciding between life and death, they are much simpler, more innocent in their thoughts. They almost become blank, a white sheet."

In a way, Mr. Shi was human pathos writ large; in another, he was the smidgen of hope that caused the caesura before jumping. It struck me as odd, however, that it required a moment like this, walking with him now, to realize that while the deeper, more ancient brain was at all times in dialogue with death, and while that dialogue asserted itself into one's conscious mind from time to time, the frontal lobe was a powerful combatant in self-denial. No matter what declivities I'd found in my own life, I'd always thought of suicide as something occurring over a divide, in the land of irrevocable people, when evidence suggested again and again—sweet Mr. Shi, right here in front of me!—that wasn't the case at all.

We climbed the South Tower stairwell back to the bridge and found Mr. Chen again, standing sentry, and he proffered us a slight if somewhat cool nod. He seemed so alone, standing there; even his wife and daughter knew little of his life on the bridge. They didn't know he'd once been stabbed in the leg; they didn't know the emotional storms he'd weathered on those days when he lost a jumper. ("I want to give them a clean piece of land," he said, using a local turn of phrase. "I don't want them worrying.")

Now the rain galloped harder; a sea of umbrellas popped open, moving south to north and north to south. Then, as quickly, the rain stopped and a low-lying monster cloud filled with a muggy kind of light and a crowding heat blanketed everything. One wondered if there'd ever been blue sky in Nanjing. Below, the barges glided downriver in the same stream that carried fallen trees and clumps of earth in the direction of distant Shanghai. While Mr. Chen scoured the crowd, Mr. Shi crouched under the shelter of the fort and lit a cigarette. Cars and trucks and taxis came and went, honking horns, the taste of fuel and smog thick in the air.

Another reporter appeared on the bridge. Young and wearing a flouncy miniskirt with white high heels, she held a device that looked to be the size of a pen, which acted both as her tape recorder and camera. It seemed like secret-agent stuff, but she announced herself to be a student from Shanghai, here to do a big exposé on suicide. Softened a bit by alcohol and the spectral vision of youth itself, Mr. Chen intermittently answered her questions, allowing that the hours between 10 A.M. and 4 P.M. were the most likely for attempts and that his method on the bridge boiled down to intuition. "I'm looking for their spirit as much as their expression and posture," he said. Then he made a grand show of getting on his moped, kicking it to life, and put-putting off on patrol, John Wayne again on his Shetland pony.

We both stood watching him go, the young woman and I, until he disappeared behind tatters of sky-fog that had come loose. In his absence, I was buffeted again by a wave of ennui, this crescendoing sense of uselessness. But then the young student reporter turned to me, beaming with bright eyes, and blurted in broken English, "What angel is he!"

There are always two countercurrents running through the brain of someone contemplating suicide, much like the currents working at odds in the river itself: the desire to escape and the dim hope of being saved. The mind, having fixated on suicide as an option, might take signs of encouragement in everything: cloud formations or rough seas or a random conversation. In the failure of the mailman to arrive. Or the store sold out of a particular brand of cereal. As the mind vacuum-seals itself to its singular course of action, and as the body moves in concert—as suction takes hold and begins to claim its molecules—the only solution to the inevitable chain of unfolding events, the only possibility of being saved, is an intervention of some sort, a random occurrence or gesture. The hand on the shoulder. Then, the mind that has held so long and fast to the body's undoing might shift, and unburden, and deaggregate, in some cases, almost instantly. Recidivism rates for those mulling suicide are low for all but the severely depressed. Help someone focus step by step across the bridge and he or she will be less inclined to ever return.

In my reading, I kept coming back to William James, brother of Henry, journeying across the European continent in 1867, his despair at feeling a failure, the pull of ending it all. In his Norfolk coat, bright shirts, and flowing ties—"His clothes looked as if they had come freshly pressed from the cleaners," a contemporary once said, "and his mind seemed to have blown in on a storm"—he decamped to Berlin, and took the baths at Teplice, in what was then Bohemia. Later, plagued by intense back pain that had migrated to his neck, he took the hypnotic drug chloral hydrate as a sleep aid, and tried electric-shock therapy, which failed to provide relief. In his deepest depression, he felt he'd arrived at a terminus. And yet he withstood the urge of self-annihilation, never again contemplating suicide. A friend of his, a woman named Minny, who helped encourage him through his troubled time (then died herself at a young age), reminded him in a letter of the proposition ever at work: "Of course the question will always remain, What is one's true life—& we must each try & solve it for ourselves."

Now, in the country that brought the world 20 percent of its annual suicide victims, I stood awaiting Mr. Chen's return while breathing in the particulates and invisible lead chips of progress. Time came to a very still point in the late afternoon, and I ambled out onto the bridge with Susan, the translator, realizing that whatever vision of Mr. Chen's heroism had brought me here in the first place, it was folly to think I'd actually ever see him save someone.

Susan was telling me about a family acquaintance who, years back, had jumped from the bridge in winter (most suicides here occurred in the fall and spring). Bundled in many layers against the elements, she had gone to the bridge in distress, climbed the railing, and leapt. One hundred and thirty feet down, at the speed of sixty-five miles an hour, she had hit the river, but if it was the angle or the specifics of her swaddling, if it was will or fate, she had lived, survived not just the fall but also the currents and hypothermia and, most of all, the killer flotsam. Every once in a while, for whatever reason, someone was indeed spit back out—but what I wanted to know was this: Having returned from the river, was she happy now, had she found in the aftermath her true life, solved the thing that had first gone missing in her? Susan considered the question. "I think happy enough," she said, "but who knows?"

Just then, as silence fell between us, a man lurched past in a blur of green. We paid him no mind, really, until he was about twenty steps beyond, out where the bridge first met water. Once there, he stopped, put both hands on the railing, and just like that, threw a leg up. The green man's body rose, and now he was hooking his ankle on the top bar, then levering himself from vertical to horizontal until he lay on top of the railing. People streamed by, apparently unaware, staring down. The green man began to push his way over the railing, at which point I knew that I was not dreaming and that he was going to kill himself. I shouted, and then burst toward him, sprinting past Mr. Chen's posters and flags.

The green man began shifting to the other side, listing as if on the curl of a wave, half of him letting go into space. Reaching him, I reflexively planted a foot against the concrete base of the railing, latched an arm up and over, then wrenched his body as hard as I could while I pushed back from the railing. His body, which was as limp and resigned as if he'd been filled with sawdust, came tumbling back into the real world, where he assumed the full proportions of his humanness again. He had a very tan face and rough hands. He reeked of alcohol. Even before we'd hit the ground, he'd blurted something in Chinese, and then repeated it as I held him in a tight bear hug, readying for a struggle that never came.

"I'm just joking," he implored. He had the supplicant, bedraggled demeanor of a man at loose ends. "I'm okay, thank you. . . ."

Shocked back into the world of the living, the green man didn't wait for the question; he just began talking, in a fit of logomania. "The reason I tried to kill myself," he blurted, "is because my father was in the army. . . ."

His story seemed disjointed, and more so because Susan was trying to do three things at once—translate, call Mr. Chen, who was not answering, and figure out how to get the attention of Mr. Shi, who was stationed back at the fort, casually smoking cigarettes. A crowd began to gather, an airless huddle. The man went on. "My father is ninety and very sick. We lost his documents in a fire, and we have no money to care for him. The government needs proof that he was in the army, but we are a family of soldiers. I was one, too. . . ."

Mr. Chen had said that people become innocent again on the bridge. They become simple and open in a way that they never otherwise were in real life. And here I was, bear-hugging a man in green coveralls named Fan Ping, trying to crush some spirit inside him that had opted to, in Mr. Chen's words, "dive downward." He was talking to me earnestly, though I didn't understand a word. He was a child, needing someone to understand. His eyes swelled, and two streams of water released over his smooth, rounded cheeks. I don't know, but it didn't seem like crying, exactly. It was like something done less out of grief than reflex. With my arms around him, hands chained, I could feel his heart thudding into mine. His breath of stale spirits filled my lungs. When I looked down, my shoes were his, two terribly dirty, scuffed sheaths of cheap, disintegrating leather. We could barely stand as we swayed together.

Fan Ping said that he was thirty-seven years old and that his mother had died three years earlier. He worked for a gas station, Sinopec, and made $400 a month. He was one of those known as a *guang gun,* or "bare branch," unmarried, a victim of demographics in a country where tens of millions of men went without wives. "What am I supposed to do now?" he said.

The crowd of onlookers registered their concern and curiosity. Some in the back were laughing, unsure of what indeed was transpiring, or just made nervous by it. I had an irrational second of hating those people in the back, of wanting to lash out, but all that really mattered was keeping my body between Fan Ping and the railing, in case he made another lunge. Eventually

Mr. Chen appeared and dismounted from his moped. On cue, the crowd parted while Mr. Chen stepped forward, invested with the power and understanding of all the nuances at play here. Fan Ping started his story again—*army ... sick father ... dead mother ... gas station ... so sorry to try to kill self*—and Mr. Chen asked me to let go of the man, something I wasn't at all inclined to do. Then he pulled out a camera and took Fan Ping's picture, which seemed at best like an odd way to begin and at worst like a major violation of the man's privacy. Then, glaring straight at Fan Ping, who stood slumped and dirty, with bloodshot eyes, Mr. Chen spoke.

"I should punch you in the face," Mr. Chen said. "You call yourself a family man . . . a son . . . Chinese? If your father hadn't been in the army, and if you didn't try to kill yourself just now, I'd punch you. You're not thinking—or are you just shirking your responsibility? I really would like to punch you now. Hand over your ID. . . ."

Fan Ping seemed utterly flummoxed, reaching into his pocket and fishing out his identification card. Mr. Chen made a show of studying it, then derisively handed it back—was this a diversion, part of a new therapeutic method?—and in the same brusque tone asked what in the world was he thinking, coming up here like this? Fan Ping replied that he wasn't thinking at all; he just didn't have the money necessary to care for his father—and that his life boiled down to this vast, sorrowful futility.

Mr. Chen sized him up again, with a withering look. I could see part of Fan Ping's blue sock poking through the worn leather of his shoe. "Yes," said Mr. Chen dismissively. "We all have our troubles."

Watching Mr. Chen face off with Fan Ping in that gray late afternoon was like watching twin sons of different mothers: They were both short and round. Mr. Chen asked Fan Ping where he lived. A country village outside the city. Mr. Chen asked how he'd gotten to the bridge. By foot, from his job. The conversation went on like this for some time while slowly Mr. Chen's tone shifted from outrage and aggression to a more familiar, fraternal concern, even sweetness. "I promise you that there's nothing we can't fix," he said, "but first we have to get you off this bridge." Then later: "I'm here to help you." In his dishevelment, Fan Ping didn't seem capable of movement, as perhaps he hadn't entirely given up on the idea that had brought him here in the first place. And Mr. Chen intuited this. He moved in closer and clasped his hand, a special shake, a locking of pinkies that meant brotherhood, then didn't let go, dragging Fan Ping to the fort and a bus stop there while the crowd followed. He arranged for Fan Ping to meet him at his office first thing Monday morning. He wrote the address on a scrap of paper and stuffed it into Fan Ping's pocket. He punched the digits of Fan Ping's cell-phone number into his own device.

"You promise you'll be there," Mr. Chen said.

"I will," said Fan Ping.

"Unless you try to jump off the bridge between now and then," Mr. Chen deadpanned. It wasn't quite a joke, but Fan Ping laughed, as did several in the crowd looking for some sort of release—and then Mr. Chen made it all okay by laughing, too.

Meanwhile, the student reporter from Shanghai grabbed me, tottering on high heels, and asked if she might conduct an interview. Not waiting for an answer, she began peppering me with questions, compensating for my lack of Chinese with her almost-English: "Do American engage in this so-called suicide event?" . . . "From bridges is always the favorite, no?" . . . "Does American—you—have fixes for problem?" . . . "Do you also enjoy *Sex and the City*?"

I couldn't even pretend. My hands, which rarely shake,

were shaking. And I floated from my body, watching Mr. Chen and Fan Ping walk ahead, watched—from some high, hovering angle—as Mr. Chen placed the man on a bus and Fan Ping squished down the aisle in his disintegrating shoes and took his place by the window, looking straight ahead. The bus gurgled, backfired, then lurched forward, gone in a plume of gray smoke. That's when some part of me came tumbling back down to myself. I turned and strode back out on the bridge to the spot where Fan Ping had readied to die. I came to the railing, peered down once more to the dark, roiling waters, and felt as if I might regurgitate my lunch noodles.

There would have been no way to survive that fall. And for some reason, standing there, I felt a sharp pang of loss, though no one had been lost. I felt I'd been a step too late, though I'd been one step ahead. It wasn't Fan Ping I was thinking about; it was all the other lives—within me and disparate from me—that had been lost. Yanking Fan Ping from the railing hadn't offered a stay of any kind; instead, it brought death nearer. Mr. Chen wasn't a caricature but a bearer of so much imminent grief. I was bound to him by a feeling Mr. Chen had elucidated for me earlier, a feeling of standing in a spot like this on the bridge, after an incident like this, hovering between heaven and earth, "heart hanging in air."

Back at home, the months passed, and so the day-to-day reasserted itself. And yet sometimes, randomly, Mr. Chen appeared in my mind, standing guard at his station at the South Tower, scanning the crowd. And on those few occasions when I found myself describing what had happened on the bridge to friends, I could hear my voice retelling the story of Fan Ping, and it sounded preposterous, even delusional. It sounded as if I might be a man of comical self-importance or full of conspiracies, the sort who wears a hat that reads *They spy on you*. Soon I stopped mentioning it altogether. After Fan Ping pulled away on the bus that day, I had joked with Mr. Chen about catching up to him on the big scoreboard of lives saved.

"It's 174 to 1," I told him. "Watch your back."

He smirked dismissively and said: "You're only given a half point for that one."

As it turned out he was right again. He already knew what I'd later find out. That is, if I'd ever imagined saving someone from a bridge, it probably would have been a fantasy bathed in altruistic light, in which I . . . SAVE . . . A . . . HUMAN . . . LIFE! But then it slowly dawned on me: I'd tried to stop Fan Ping merely so I wouldn't have to live with the memory of having watched him fall. My worry now was that he would somehow succeed in trying again.

So I contact Mr. Chen. He tells me that on the Monday morning after Fan Ping tried to kill himself—the morning that the two men were supposed to meet at his office—Mr. Chen arrived at work and his boss promptly fired him. He then left the office building and went to his station at the bridge, not so much because he was despondent but because that was where he felt he belonged. All the while, he dialed Fan Ping's number over and over again, but the phone was out of order. And remained that way, all these months later.

There's nothing to do now, says Mr. Chen, but wait for him to come back. Rest assured, he'll stop Fan Ping. Even as he's recently saved a father, and a few students, and a woman with a psychiatric problem. He knows what Fan Ping looks like. In broiling heat and blowing monsoon, he's out there, ever vigilant, waiting in his double duck-bill, scanning the crowd for Fan Ping—and all the others, too, who might possess thoughts of a

glorious demise. He assures me he'll be waiting for them all—
and you and me as well—binoculars trained on our murky faces,
our eyes sucked downward, trying to read strange words off the
surface of the murky river below.

The only question remains: Can he reach us in time?

11:20

Before it walked the parking lot, its crippled feet scraping the silence of that seventy-in-April spring day, before it lurched past the saplings bent once in the breeze, and before the sun flooded the wide, emerald windows of the library in a featureless building as featureless as the instant Colorado landscape in which it rose. Before the glass front doors were drawn back, reflecting nothing—no face, no figure—and the low, reassuring, under-water sound of voices, students at lunch or in choir or suiting up for gym, was met by the voice of something else, something piti-less and blank. Before Patrick Ireland, a real boy, was shot in the head and lay paralyzed on the right side of his body under a table in the library, playing dead though he half was. Before Lance Kirklin, a real boy, had his jaw blown off and had to communicate by squeezing hands, and before Daniel Rohrbough, a real boy, lay sprawled on the stone walk among the saplings as students leaped over him like cows fleeing from some medieval abattoir. Before the glass doors of that featureless building shattered and the pipes

burst and alarms sounded and the sprinkler system went haywire, before freaked students packed oxygenless closets or scur-
ried up into ceilings or hid in lockers. Before all the shirtless,
hairless boys were herded out of Columbine High School, hands
over their heads, looking pale and stricken and, well, like little
boys streaked with blood, their shirts having been used as wraps
and tourniquets on the bodies left inside. Before all the stunned,
gasping girls huddled in trembling circles, holding each other,
well, like little girls suddenly with no mother left in the world.

Before night fell and the dead still lay inside that booby-
trapped high school as a final affront, lay like the pinions of a star
around the killers—and what could the scene of that terrible
midnight have looked like?—before the media horde arrived
with its Aggreko generators and deep-space satellite dishes. Before the blame and the signed caskets and the psychedelic mountains of flowers, and before the angry, indignant promises for gun
control, for safer schools, for policing the Internet, for really caring about our kids, there was 11:20 on a Tuesday morning.
Eleven-twenty in Columbine valley, what used to be farmland
rising to the Front Range of the Rocky Mountains, in a place
where the American Dream lives in strip malls and stucco-and-
drywall housing developments. Eleven-twenty on a day when the
season makes a turn: Columbine High School, its windows like
microchips, its saplings showing first leaves. The wide baseball
fields bursting green. A dog barking, a plane passing lazily overhead, leaving a contrail trace of its progress. And for one last
time, at 11:20, everything in its place: goofy, pimply, smart,
beautiful, heartbreaking, not-yet-grown kids writing papers on
Thoreau.

Afterward the snow fell—for three days. It blew into the
backstops like huge, broken moths. Two hundred investigators
combed the high school sarcophagus while dozens of media cam-

eras like more guns were trained on a hugging boy and girl, the uncle of a dead girl in a leather coat and combed hair searching out any journalist he could find for an interview. "Death by may-hem," he kept repeating into microphones. Afterward, in a local diner, two older patrons argued about Wyatt Earp and Doc Holliday—who the better gunfighter had been. At a convenience store, a boy in a green bib sat behind the counter, bawling.

I myself stood for a while at the memorial, stood before the stuffed animals and flowers and purple Magic Markered messages—all of them trying to call back 11:20—and walked the police line that surrounded Columbine High, walked out over the baseball fields, snow up to my shins, until I was a good peg from the front door. It was silent but for the whine of generators. The shattered emerald windows to the library had plywood sheets fixed over them. And hundreds of cars sat in the lot: pickup trucks and Acuras, a motorcycle and someone's mom's old Dodge.

Inside that building, everything was exactly as it had been just hours before: computers and lights still on, lunches half eaten, books turned to the last page read, the college application of a girl who was shot, its final check mark made, the pencil lying next to it. That's what's most hard to imagine: how, in midsentence, in the throes of some idea, in the beginning of some meaningful life, that girl was entered by some dark, crippled thing and became a memory.

It was sometime after eleven, and, standing there, gazing out over the parking lot and beyond the school to the new houses with their new cars and the new living rooms with their new rugs, you could have actually imagined this as any other school day. Everything seemingly in its place. A dog barked and a plane passed overhead, but this time it sounded like the roar of a monster.

MR. NOBODY

HE COULD HAVE BEEN ANYONE, STANDING in that Lisbon hotel lobby. He wore a black suit and black tie with black shoes. His hair was jet black. His eyes from a distance seemed black, too, but perhaps it was merely the reflection off the glossy grand piano near which he stood. He could have easily passed as a financier or a diplomat waiting to take an important meeting, to report back to a man in a glass office in one of the other European capitals, someone of equal breeding and power who might then direct this man here to enjoy a night in Lisbon and carry on in the morning to Brussels, Berlin, or Geneva, to the next high-level meeting for whatever concern they mutually held at stake.

Just by looking at him, you might have perceived the meticulous if anonymous tailorings of a person from whom a certain power flows. And that lobby—with its well-appointed sterility—flowed with others of the very same disposition. It was impossible to know his country of origin or who he might be. The nails were manicured; the tie held a perfect dimple. His image reflected off the windows, off the Lisbon night outside, parts of him, angles of him hovering there that gave no sense of the whole. I would find that he spoke with a pure English accent, echoes of Yorkshire. It was only when he smiled as I crossed the room, both our hands outstretched, that I saw he was wearing braces.

It was July in Lisbon, when the heat was absolutely "beastly," as he put it. Our meeting had involved a tenuous exchange of emails played out over several months. "My story is very complex, I would also think very interesting," he had written. "I can vouch for it not being in any way banal. I would even venture to say that it is much more than you can imagine considering the social and philosophical implications. The fact is that I don't feel the need to tell it. There is something about me that upsets people."

If he didn't need to tell it, I wondered, why then was he writing any of this in the first place? And what could be so upsetting? "If your magazine's deontology allows you to arrange for a 'representation' fee package for me," he wrote, "I would be ready to meet with you. I don't want to meet anyone of consequence while I am penny counting and I can't even afford the taxi fare. It would not be an obscene sum, and it would not be paying for an interview, so you would not have to struggle with your journalistic conscience." When I had refused—it *was* paying for an interview—and wished him luck, he wrote back, "I would have been surprised and very suspicious had you given me an immediate and positive answer to my enquiries regarding certain financial matters." He told me others had been more than willing to pay, but he assured me that they were not the kind with whom he wished to consort.

So with whom did he wish to consort now?

I knew he was a man who had lived under at least five aliases. I knew he had allegedly traveled under false documents and been jailed. I knew that he was a vegan and a lover of tea. I knew a great deal of confusion surrounded his circumstance and that his amnesia had supposedly left him with no clue as to where he came from. He was a man either running from or trying to recover his past. It all depended on what you wanted to believe.

Seven years earlier, he had landed in a Toronto hospital, badly beaten, with those manicured fingernails. By then he'd already borne several other names, but in that hospital he supposedly had muttered the name Philip Staufen to the attending nurses. When the vintage of that moniker came due, he turned himself into Keith Ryan. His e-mail address read Mike Jones. And I knew him now by yet another name: Sywald Skeid (pronounced *Zie*-wald *Sky'd*).

"I don't go in for all that American informality," he'd told me. So I began by calling him Mr. Skeid.

So here was Mr. Skeid, a man who had claimed to know virtually nothing about his own past, aground in Lisbon—"a dreary place," as he put it—as he'd formerly found himself aground in Toronto ("the dregs") and Vancouver ("beautiful but for my life there") and Nova Scotia, where he'd lasted out a ten-day hunger strike at a county jail. If one had tried to determine the line of his perambulations—of his true history—before the moment of his beating and subsequent memory loss, one's finger might have fluttered back across the ocean, tracing dots from London to Paris to Rome. One's finger might have flitted up to Germany, floated across the border to Hungary, and—trailing back in time and over the flatlands—passed another border into a sort of oblivion. . . .

I will say this about our mysterious Mr. Skeid: Despite the gust of *froid* he emanated, I, along with an entire nation, had been immediately drawn to him. Not to the man by the piano in the lobby of the expensive hotel, but the one we'd met five years earlier. While connecting through Toronto on a business trip in June 2001, I fanned open that day's *Globe and Mail,* and there, occupying the upper fold of page 3, was his face, or rather the face of Philip Staufen, under the headline BIZARRE AMNESIA PUZZLE TRAPS MAN.

In a photo that accompanied the story, Philip Staufen looked to be in his midtwenties, boyish, with a pronounced nose and shaggy blond hair and dark eyes, one of them trailing slightly to the right. His mouth was set in a grim line. He seemed beleaguered and lost, like a stray. Living on $525 a month of state assistance, he said his days were spent reading sonnets at the public library.

The article outlined his attempts to gain Canadian citizenship and went back to the beginning of his story, or what was known of it. The more I read—and afterward, the more of everything else I could find about this Philip Staufen—the more the tale took on an utterly fabulist air. In November 1999, Staufen had first appeared at a Toronto hospital. He arrived with a broken nose, unable to walk. The labels were missing from his clothes, and he had no idea who he was or what had happened to him.

Had it been a mugging? A hate crime? Self-inflicted?

At some point, he'd called himself by the name Staufen, but police officials failed in trying to match it, or his fingerprints, to anyone in various databases at home and abroad. The only certain facts about him were these: He was white, five feet nine, and 150 pounds. He was unusually tan, had muttered something about Australia, and, later, was diagnosed with postconcussion global amnesia.

His case became a cause célèbre, and though he was a young man, it carried with it the intimation of every child ever separated from his family while roaming the mall or the neighborhood or Disneyland, the primal fear of that separation. And of course, a country responded to that fear. Who couldn't feel for a wounded fellow human trying to find his lost family?

"I am quite depressed and would like to leave Canada in search of my identity or be able to lead a decent existence here if given the right to work and travel," he wrote the court in his appeal for citizenship. Further, he stated that he had a digestive disorder, couldn't sleep, and had been forced to the brink psychologically—a choice, as he put it, between "suicide or becoming a criminal," neither of which, he hastened to say, were options. "My life is senseless," he wrote.

On May 28, 2001, the court denied his application, primarily because of the same ambiguous question Philip Staufen seemed to be asking himself: Who was he? And if a majority of amnesia cases are transient—that is, one's memory returns within a short duration of time—and Philip Staufen showed no permanent brain injury, why after eighteen months did he still remember nothing at all?

Initially, a detective named Stephen Bone from the Toronto police department was assigned to the case. He was the first to meet Staufen in the hospital, to take his fingerprints, to call upon a linguist, who determined that Staufen had a well-bred English accent with notes of Yorkshire. Because the boy with no memory genuinely seemed to want to find his family and because Bone, then a twenty-two-year veteran of the force with a still-intact gift of empathy, genuinely wanted to help, photographs were circulated around the world through Interpol. Newspapers in Yorkshire and Australia—among other places—ran articles about the amnesia victim the press soon dubbed "Mr. Nobody." A couple of documentaries were made and aired abroad; news reports circulated in the United States, where, it was said, Philip Staufen hoped to one day hitchhike coast to coast.

After living in Toronto for a year—moving from shelter to

shelter, being taken in by Good Samaritans touched by his story (a young couple, a God-fearing spinster)—Philip Staufen moved on to Vancouver, where he met the public advocate, who took his case pro bono. Manuel Azevedo was one of the city's high-profile human-rights lawyers. An imposing bearded man with Portuguese roots, he accepted Staufen at his word and allowed him to move into the basement of his family home in December 2000. Six months later, when the court denied Philip Staufen a birth certificate, Mr. Nobody undertook his first hunger strike in protest. With utmost belief in his client, Azevedo likened Philip Staufen to Bobby Sands, the Irish Republican who died after sixty-six days on a hunger strike to protest prison conditions. "Weak, depressed, and paranoid . . . Philip Staufen will surely die," wrote Azevedo in a press release. "Canada will not be remembered for its compassion toward this man, but rather its indifference."

Despite all the attention focused on our man during those first years of his Canadian incarnation—or, as he might put it, incarceration—and despite all the hopeful mothers calling to claim this Staufen as their runaway son, no one emerged with a credible shred of evidence about who he really might be. No one could make a match.

When I later asked him whether the "Mr. Nobody" label ever bothered him, he said, "No, why should it have? There are two things about me. First, I am a very happy person, though I've lived an unhappy life. And second, I'm happy until I have to say my name, which carries a great deal of negativity for me. What troubles most people is that I want to be anonymous, without an identity. To them, this idea seems absolutely dangerous."

It was true: Our Mr. Skeid *did* seem dangerous. Even there in the lobby at the Ritz, he conveyed an air of passivity and menace,

each by turns masking the other—and masking deeper still a pre-
sumption, a serrated sense of entitlement. In an e-mail before my
arrival in Lisbon, he urged me to bring my bathing trunks because there was a quite nice spa at the hotel. "I might want a
swim," he wrote. His was a priggish kind of self-obsession. It was
inconsequential whether *I* might have wanted to swim—or could
swim at all. I would merely facilitate his desire.

But arrogance alone didn't constitute danger. And as far as
I could tell, he wasn't mingling with arms dealers or underworld
figures. No, what was most unsettling about our Mr. Nobody
was the idea of him, the affront he posed, the ghost he made
moving among the rest of us corporeal beings, the cipher he presumed to be in the lobby at the Ritz. Here we were, creatures so
weighted down by our own identities, trapped beneath our own
monuments—the record of our every purchase, trip, and rented
movie, the sum of our online aerobics—that we'd lost the strands
of our freedom.

Our predicament now narrowed to this possibility: We, as
human beings, possessed less and less mystery. Who in this world
could dream of being as light as air, as traceless as smoke, as unidentifiable and invisible as this man here? Who among us
wouldn't consider, at least for a moment, the potential joy of
being released, in one swift blow, from all the back matter of
one's own life?

Mr. Skeid's story fulfilled a central escape fantasy for those
who indulge such fantasies: that a life could be exited through a
series of closing doors that might lead somewhere completely
new and alien, without fear of past recriminations, debts, or
crimes. That is, you might pass through a portal on one side of
the world and arrive in a hospital bed in Toronto, Canada, with
manicured fingernails and dyed blond hair, not knowing who
you'd ever been—and perhaps not caring to remember.

But even then, it wasn't quite so easy to be Mr. Nobody. As

the weeks passed after his hunger strike, the curiosities and suspicions began to accrue. Even if his memory loss was permanent—which would have been extremely rare—even if he couldn't reach back to reclaim his family, there was still, despite massive publicity efforts, no one who came forward. Not a soul. And then this Mr. Nobody, who professed to want to find his family, who swore that his condition was driving him to the brink of suicide, refused all medical help and counseling. Even Detective Bone began to wonder why, when they spoke over the phone, Mr. Nobody failed to show much interest in the detective's attempts to locate his identity or kin—and worse, soon ceased to cooperate at all with the authorities.

When I asked Mr. Skeid about the souring of these prior relationships, he was succinct. "People only want to help you when they have power over you," he said.

Yes, he said, he had refused medical help, but only because he was offered electroshock therapy and hadn't wanted it. And yes, he refused to accept a special minister's permit, one that would have allowed him the right to live, work, and attend university in Canada, but only because he thought he deserved a birth certificate instead. He came to see the outpouring of help from Good Samaritans as an insult, and he didn't hesitate to let people know. It became a repeating pattern: He would push until he'd reached a cul-de-sac, though he claimed he wanted only what was his "by right of law."

In the summer of 2001, a call came to Detective Bone from England. It wasn't exactly the aristocratic connection some had expected but a publisher of pornography who claimed to have known Staufen. Further investigation turned up a photographer who claimed to have taken nude shots of him. They characterized Mr. Nobody as "the ultimate chameleon" with "a plan to get to America." They told Detective Bone they knew that Philip

Staufen went by a different name, the one on another passport he carried at that time: Georges Lecuit. It was alleged that this Georges Lecuit had made several gay pornographic movies—with titles like *Exposed* and *Crush*—posed for nude pictures, and worked as a masseur in a gay bathhouse in London called the Pleasuredrome.

The photographer produced for Bone a waiver that this Georges Lecuit had signed by means of which he was paid $300 for test photographs. To cap it off, one of Britain's leading forensic facial reconstruction experts said that there were striking similarities suggesting that Mr. Nobody and Lecuit were one and the same.

These revelations came roughly a month before Mr. Nobody was to marry. In yet another twist, he'd proposed to his lawyer's daughter. She was a thin, short-haired twenty-two-year-old named Nathalie Herve, who worked in her father's office as a secretary. Mr. Skeid described her to me as "very innocent," which may have been part of the attraction—as well as her shy beauty. But then, given that it's much easier to obtain citizenship as the spouse of a Canadian citizen, was it love or convenience?

"I didn't choose to fall in love," Nathalie told one reporter at the time. "It just happened."

"I wouldn't say it was love," Mr. Skeid told me later. "It made sense for us to live together. I just wanted to prove to myself that I could be a friend to someone, something I hadn't been able to do before. There are so many opportunities to betray and so few to be loyal. But she never had the intellectual capability to understand me."

Mr. Skeid admitted that he was genuinely shocked when people questioned whether his marriage was a sham. He recalled a conversation he'd had with a customs officer assigned to his case who asked him point-blank if he was gay. "I told him to mind his own business," he said.

The British and Canadian tabloids made their usual tawdry hay about Mr. Nobody's alleged pornographic past, but by then most Canadians had heard enough. For them, Staufen's amnesia tale had become untenable and preposterous. "Oh, for the sweet, sweet taste of amnesia!" wrote one citizen to an online magazine. "To forget my huge complicated life, my husband, children, responsibilities, relatives, to banish them in a mugger's blow! . . . Mr. Nobody wake up and do something with your life! You bitch like a medieval poet. . . . Live you fucking idiot!"

Was it possible that the man in the movies, the one who had the physical attributes of Mr. Nobody, who had a profile that seemed to explain a part of Mr. Nobody's murky past, wasn't in fact Mr. Nobody at all? After reviewing the evidence, Nathalie Herve, one of those in the best position to compare, stated for the record that this porn star wasn't her husband.

As for her husband—the one who would have known for certain—he simply couldn't remember.

Before our meeting at the Ritz, Mr. Skeid had spoken one sentence to the media, though reporters had stalked him in the streets of Vancouver and Halifax, at his various places of residence, at the gyms where he worked out. On May 7, 2004, reporters jostled in a pack, shouting questions as he emerged from jail in Nova Scotia. Fresh from his ten-day hunger strike, with Nathalie by his side, Mr. Skeid wore his black suit, with his hair now dyed black. He wore fashionable dark sunglasses and a dark beard as he made his way quickly through the scrum. "Can't you understand that I don't want to have anything to do with you or anyone else?" he said to the cameras—and then disappeared into the bright sunlight.

The detainment was a result of the work of Detective

Bone—a man who, to this day, Mr. Skeid thinks of as "one of the best I met in Canada." In his investigation, the detective had come upon a police report filed in Paris by the real Georges Lecuit, claiming that his passport had been stolen during a break and entry on August 17, 1998. Had the thief been Mr. Nobody?

Meanwhile, during 2003, Mr. Skeid and Nathalie Herve had made a series of moves—from Ottawa to Montreal to Halifax, where they had landed in September—in order to escape the increasingly "bad energy" of Vancouver. And it was here that they were called to the immigration office, and on the grounds of the French Lecuit's six-year-old grievance Mr. Skeid was detained on suspicion of theft.

The problem was that the real Georges Lecuit had no interest in pressing charges against the amnesiac, and despite the fact that Mr. Skeid had once allegedly been in possession of a stolen passport, there was no evidence that he'd done anything wrong. Eventually, the immigration board ruled that there was no basis for holding Mr. Skeid, and after those ten days in jail, he was released.

Was he a fraud or a victim, a man of the world or one who had been irrevocably injured by it? Was it possible to be all at once? At the very least, Detective Bone pointed out, he'd traveled under false documents. But was he really the bogeyman— "the vegan Hannibal Lecter," as Mr. Skeid later put it—that the media now made him out to be?

Because Nathalie had dual Canadian and Portuguese citizenship, the couple decided to relocate to Lisbon, to escape the scrutiny of the media and to see if Mr. Skeid could lawfully establish citizenship there, again as the spouse of a national. Nathalie traveled ahead to prepare for her husband's arrival; Mr. Skeid stayed behind to secure the proper papers for his own travel but ended up stranded. Finally, after a year, in March 2006, he left, as he said, "on a laissez-passer travel document with another name than Sywald Skeid."

And now here he stood before me, reflected and refracted, hung among the lights and blackly aglow in the lobby at the Ritz. I happened to be passing through Lisbon on business, so our meeting was really just to be a dinner, a mutual tryout. We sat for a drink in the lobby bar.

His health was of utmost importance to him—"I want to look good someday in my coffin," he said, grinning—and so he worked out at a local gym, ate well, and rarely consumed alcohol. He spoke in low guttural syllabics but swallowed every fifth or sixth word, as if he weren't exactly sure of himself at first or, rather, was being intentionally obscure. Every once in a while, he got caught on a word, a near stutter that may have been nerves, because after this night it never appeared again.

For the sake of rarity, he ordered sake, and when they didn't have it, he called for a fresh juice, asking after the ice, whether it was made from tap water or spring water. He seemed adversarial, especially with waitstaff—or a bit bullying, a civil kind of bullying—sometimes directing them to the point of exasperation. "Would you pour common tap water into any drink of quality?" he asked rhetorically. His being a vegan complicated our dinner plans, but he had a place with a patio in mind. He called ahead and while speaking to the maître d' gave a mock-disparaging look at my jeans and short-sleeve shirt—the disparity in our uniforms being something for which I'd already apologized—and asked if a dinner jacket was required.

Later, on the dinner patio, he loosened a little. I listened closely to that low rumble, his voice in a timbre that found occasional disguise behind the clatter of silverware, the scrape of a chair across the patio. He was quoting from Shakespeare. "What's in a name?" he said. "Hitler's real last name was Schicklgruber.

Names are not famous in and of themselves. They become famous by propaganda."

We paused to look at the menu. "There's a bottle here," he said, pointing to it on the wine list, "one that I shared once with a friend. It is a very good wine, and it would not disappoint you." My eyes flitted to the price—over three hundred euros. Since I was buying, he wondered, how much did I have to spend?

My employers, themselves partial to the odd bottle of fine wine, probably wouldn't have batted an eye. At the very least, I could have justified the importance of watching an amnesiac drink a bottle that held such memories for him, which in and of itself raised a question about his memory. Nevertheless, I felt manipulated. He'd made it oddly personal, a referendum about his own worth. I tried to ignore the question, but he pressed, testing *my* power now. "Not more than a hundred euros," I finally said, feeling every bit the discomfort he'd forced on me.

In everything, I would soon find, he took control—wardrobe, restaurant choice, encounters with waiters, the ordering of food. "I'm a domineering personality," he said. Knowing his history, though, I was paranoid about being played, in some complicated manner involving the potential emptying of my bank accounts by identity theft. He said he'd read everything he could find that I'd written, he'd found photographs of me online. "You've gone through three phases," he said. "The shaggy you, the respectable author you, and the CNN you, in suit and tie." He said he knew more about me "than you can imagine." But he hardly hid one of his ulterior motives. He stated part of it bluntly in an e-mail. "You may help my cause," he wrote, referring to his attempts now to become a Portuguese citizen, "as people here tend to be impressed by an American journalist."

At the table, when I asked about his memory—and whether it had returned—he was evasive. Yet when the subject of those

"British chaps" came up, the ones who'd alleged his participation in pornography and possibly prostitution, instead of being defensive or forgetful, he seemed the opposite. "Everybody has a lot of sex," he said, "unless you're particularly ugly." In his case, it apparently occurred in front of a camera, for which he had no regrets, sex being natural and nothing at all to be embarrassed about. "I'm a child of nature," he said. "Those who watch it should be asked why *they're* watching it—and why *they're* embarrassed." Anyway, he continued, pornography wasn't a violation of the law. And when the tabloids got hold of the story, they turned it into theater: Can we embarrass the porn star? What will he do next?

I sat listening. So was this an admission? I took it as one, but later he emphatically insisted he'd put the whole business to me hypothetically: that, without confirming his participation, he had no problem with the *idea* of someone being paid to have sex in front of a camera. And later still, he claimed: "I suppose I spent time with those who were not of my own intellectual level and became a Pygmalion to them. The kernel is this: The life I lived could justify acts much worse than the ones attributed to me."

But mistakenly or not, in the infrared of that moment I thought I picked something off of him, something that might sound naïve: Beneath his self-constructions, there was a flicker of bravery. And something else: Behind the bluster and the slightly absurd power plays, inside this human being skimming from country to country, "riding energies," as he put it, there was another person—the oversensitive boy, the confused melancholic, the isolated dreamer—a figure I spotted out at sea, as the poem said, not waving but drowning.

When I returned again to Lisbon and the Ritz—this time in late October—the lobby was still under occupation by the same thinlapeled brokers of influence, but this time our Mr. Skeid greeted me much more casually, in cargo pants and a short-sleeve Polo shirt with a turned-up collar. Gone for the moment was any adversarial posturing, any reason to suspect his intentions. In fact, he had summoned me back to tell his story, no holds barred, to play to his audience of one, me, by chatting, lecturing, cajoling, and mining the dramatic moments.

"The truth is my best disguise," he said. "I can remember places, energies, pictures, smells, but I can't sit at a table and say, 'I remember this, I remember that.'"

He was relaxed, smiling, welcoming me to the country of Skeid with notes he'd made on tablet pages, an agenda of his thoughts, of what he wanted me to know about him, of those figures with whom he most identified. He said this might be one of the best ways to understand him, by understanding these other people with whom he most intensely identified: the directors Ingmar Bergman and Lars von Trier, the billionaire reactionary writer Taki Theodoracopulos, the politicians Boris Johnson and Christoph Blocher, the exiled English poet Shelley, and the unnamed protagonist of Knut Hamsun's *Hunger*. ("One of my great accomplishments," he said, "is that I've lived that protagonist's life in a way only a few people in this world can understand.")

At one point, when he opened his date book, I saw that he had neatly written: the elsewhere.

What did it mean?

"I know who I am," he declared. "I know the true color of my blood."

The story that followed came in a rush that seemed to last three very rainy days. He'd show up at the hotel in the morning, having walked I assumed, and his love of tea ("It has its own inner life, as opposed to the sadness of coffee") was what then guided our path through the seven hills of the city, traveling by taxi from teahouse to vegan restaurant to the Ritz. He forbade me to tape our interviews, so I wrote everything in my own notebook until my hand cramped. Never once in the telling did he show an emotion—and at the end of every night, he walked out through the automatic doors, past the besuited men coming from meetings and dinners, some with women on their arms, and headed back to his spare studio apartment in downtown Lisbon.

"People think I'm crazy or a liar or both," he said as we drank from our first pot of rose tea that morning at the Ritz. "They can't believe that someone who speaks well can be in a position of fragility, which is a pity."

He claimed that he'd suffered a very real breakdown in Toronto, that he still didn't know how he'd come to be in Canada in the first place, nor the hospital, but that he'd been terrified. He gave up his fingerprints to the detective and waited to be revealed as "a murderer or secret agent or felon." He remembered the nurses saying, "He can't be a street kid—look at his fingernails!"

He said that his recent past had returned to him in shards, but the chapters of his early story seemed linear and detailed. "I came from Romania," he told me, "a place I loathe. My family had nothing, but I was picked up for my musical talents in kindergarten. I played the violin, and I lived among the Communist elite in a special school that I attended, but I was poor. I had one dress shirt that I cleaned and ironed every night. I was never free among these people, though they had no culture whatsoever. I never felt poor or inferior or that I needed help, but people disliked me—perhaps because I spoke my mind.

"I have a memory: this evil apparition, a teacher, and everyone is running, and the only one left is me. I remember this teacher approaching me at school. I was maybe ten. I remember him looking up and down the hallway to make sure no one was

about, and then he hit me as hard as he could in the stomach, just
because he could.

"After seven or eight years, it came time for a big test to see
who would move on. There was dictation and theory, on which I
scored ten of ten; a part where we were graded for group singing, for which we all received the same score; and finally I had to
play the violin. It was only me and the Communist nincompoops,
my teachers, in a room. I was given a low score and wasn't allowed to progress. And that's how they ruined my life the first
time."

He said his name had been Ciprian and that he'd grown up
in the Romanian city of Timişoara (pronounced Timi-*shwara*)—
under the repressive Communist regime of the dictator Nicolae
Ceauşescu, himself the architect of grand delusions—where he
lived until the age of nineteen. He was born to parents who
worked as common laborers. He said his father was a drunk. "I
have a memory of not existing," he said, "of having no room to
call my own. I remember waking with people lying around me. I
remember windows shattering—and sleeping outdoors, counting stars. . . . My mother didn't have the courage to leave the
crazy man who ruined my life." He said his father also beat him.
He said he might have had a sister.

According to him, the only affinities left to him in Romania
were nature and music. He claimed the happiest day of his life
was the moment he heard the strains of Richard Wagner, by mistake. "When I heard his music—it must have been on the sound-
track of a movie or something—I knew that this wasn't me, the
boy living this life, that there was someone else inside me and a
place beyond this place, where I might belong."

His other recollection of joy, the only one conjured from
the landscape of his home country, included no image of other
people: It was a memory of standing by a rushing river in the

mountain village of his grandmother, the peaks looming beyond. Just the boy and the river and the mountains, for that one moment: pure.

Somewhere around the age of eighteen, Ciprian was conscripted into the army, and without being able to specify anything in particular about the experience, he said it was a year of hell that "broke" him. That's how they ruined his life a second time. When he came out, he fled the country in the months before Ceaușescu's fall, traveling to Germany to visit a friend there. He returned to Romania after a year, stayed for several months, and then left for good, never to be heard from again. "I had no one," he said. "The easiest thing was to leave the country. There was no betrayal."

When I pressed him for a specific memory of leaving Romania—the country he now referred to only as "R."—he was typically vague. I thought he might have felt relief, happiness, or perhaps a moment's regret. But all he remembered was crossing in a car to Hungary, on the way to Germany. There were other people there. He claimed he felt nothing. I expressed disbelief. Finally, he looked at me calmly, from across the wreckage of empty teacups and skewed crockery adrift on the table between us, and said, "What do you want me to say: I had an orgasm and saw a rainbow?"

Mr. Skeid came in dichotomies. He could be funny, controlling, fascinating, and monotonous. He could be principled, dubious, evasive, Zen, and exhausting—sometimes all within the same sixty seconds. I'm quite sure I'd never met anyone like him. Some nights I'd go back to my room with my head spinning from all the philosophizing, with a sense that he'd been patronizing or insulting. ("You remind me of Adriano Celentano," he told me. "You have that same forced smirk, though you're much, much less ugly than he is.") And then some nights I went back wondering what must have happened to him as a boy, feeling half sorry for him— only half—before stopping myself with the thought that he would have hated even that much pity.

Within the constellated mind of our Mr. Skeid, there may have been the underpinnings of a good old-fashioned narcissist, but he wasn't without a conscience: He professed to wanting to be good, to trying to live in a pure way. He'd even retrofitted Mr. Ripley's famous motto—"I'd rather be a fake somebody than a real nobody"—to suit his predicament. "I'd rather be a fake nobody than the real me," he said.

In order to transcend his station, he believed he needed to free himself of his Romanian past. He needed straight teeth and a better nose, which he'd submitted to two operations since it had been broken—what the press had called his "nose jobs." ("It's a decent nose, but it's not Hollywood," Mr. Skeid told me.) He wanted a piece of paper that declared him a citizen of some other nation, with a name other than Ciprian, a worthless coin chosen, he said, "by those who mistreated me."

"I lived twenty years in a repressive regime, and when I got away I was still trapped," he said. "People would have liked me if I were that chap from R. trying to make good: 'Oh, he speaks so well. See the monkey play the piano.' But I've too much pride for that."

His pride was what made Mr. Skeid's isolation seem insoluble. No one was better than he; very few were worth letting in. His most ardent friend was himself, and he spent days roaming the interior hallways of his person. He cited his greatest accomplishment as having eradicated the Romanian language—"an ugly thing"—from his mind and having made English the internal foundation of his linguistic-spiritual world. He could switch between six or so languages with varying fluency but simply couldn't remember his mother tongue. When he heard it, he claimed to be struck by a pounding headache.

He confessed that during this most recent year, when he and Nathalie had been separated, she'd found someone else. ("She couldn't stand the test of living with me," he said.) The irony was that the other man was from Romania—and while they weren't formally divorced yet, they no longer spoke, which dashed all plans for Mr. Skeid to procure Portuguese citizenship through his wife. "I didn't expect her to be monogamous, but she had done nothing to prepare for my arrival," he said. "I had no apartment. It would have been fine for the three of us to live together until I'd had time to find a place." In his mind, it went back to the teacher, the father, the military commander, and now even his wife—all those who were trying to strip him of his personhood, his birthright, his freedom, his destiny. He fancied himself someone who would have made a good lawyer, actor, musician, writer, politician—and there were probably other roles he might have played to seamless perfection besides that of masseur—but as a passenger in each country, he never bothered to try.

When I asked about the source of his money—especially after he revealed that he read twenty newspapers a day on his new Apple laptop, that his shoes cost $500, his braces $1,200, and that he still received the occasional manicure—he smiled and allowed that credit cards had helped him and Nathalie, until they declared bankruptcy. Not a great amount owed, something less than seven thousand dollars. Now he was living off a loan that he intended to pay back shortly, once he had the right papers.

"I'm arrogant but not illogical," he said. And whom was he hurting? He hadn't put a gun to Nathalie's head to force her to spend on his behalf. They'd done it together, as husband and wife, like millions of other couples spending into debt. "Even being bankrupt is a science. You can do it the right way or the wrong way," he said. As for the loan, it had been given willingly.

As easily as Mr. Skeid had been able to discuss the setbacks in his life, as vividly as he seemed to recall them, the decade from 1989 to 1999 marked the lost years, the ones he was unwilling to discuss. Were these the years during which he'd shared that three-hundred-euro bottle of wine, then sunk so low as to have pilfered someone else's passport? Were they the years of sexual awakening? The years during which he'd refined his existential philosophies? There was only one memory from that time that he would allow.

It occurred in France, perhaps in the early 1990s. He remembered stopping at a spot on the way from Cannes to Saint-Tropez. He'd come to see the sea, on this fabled, glitzy coastline, and stood at an inlet. Out over the water were lights on the other side, people's houses, and he began to wonder about those people.

"I was by the Mediterranean," he said. "I realized that people didn't appreciate my gifts, and I was looking at the sea and wondering if I could cancel all that. I was wondering how, given my past, I could achieve a family, a good job besides washing dishes, a life of holidays. I very seriously contemplated the notion of suicide. This goes back to Japan, where suicide isn't a negative thing but rather, if one wants to protect one's karma, it's better for them to leave. I'm a good swimmer, so it was hard to kill myself. I didn't even try. But I had to kill myself either literally or figuratively. I had to break from my past even as the physical world demands papers and history, even as there is the continual demand for your name."

As we made our rounds in Lisbon, we visited a Japanese restaurant that Mr. Skeid favored. He said it was run by a friend, and he phoned her one afternoon to see if the kitchen was still

open for a late lunch. When we arrived, he spoke with her, jok-
ingly. He could be very disarming in this mode. He could be
charismatic and generous with his good mood and had a funny,
sarcastic sense of humor. His friend called him by his Romanian
name, Ciprian, and when I asked him about it, rather than answering directly, he told me his past had recently come back to
haunt him—he'd been speaking to a lawyer over the phone,
someone in Bucharest, who ostensibly spoke English and was
going to help him secure a passport. He now had a copy of his
Romanian birth certificate. When it had arrived, he'd been rattled to discover that he was thirty-six years old, six years older
than he'd thought himself to be.

The idea was that since Romania was entering the EU, Mr.
Skeid would try to get a Romanian passport and move to Dublin,
Oslo, or Geneva, somewhere he might be able to establish residency. In order to receive a Romanian passport, however, he
needed to prove residency in Romania. For maybe a thousand
euros total, he could get it done—someone would rent a flat for
him and then appeal to the bureaucratic powers for the document in question. He was deeply ambivalent about this: It was
much more than he was willing to pay.

When I proposed that he accompany me back to Romania
in order to straighten out the passport business, his response was
curt: *never.* What, then, I wondered, if I were to go, to find the
family he'd lost seventeen years ago when he left? Would he object? "It doesn't bother me if you want to see my parents," he said
at his most Zen.

I had him write their names in my notebook. So was he
sending me as his proxy? Or did he doubt I'd ever go?

The connection in Milan was a short, brisk walk to a small
plane—and then, with the hum of propellers, I felt myself lifted

up over the Alps, which were snowcapped and hovering eerily like a bloom of behemoth jellyfish in the morning sun. The plane skimmed the countries of Slovenia, Croatia, and Hungary. The land flattened and emptied; a tiny horse and cart appeared below. I could almost smell manure wafting from the earth to that height. "I never had a home," he'd said. "I never had a name. I never had the peace of having a place for me. I was born in the wrong place, to the wrong people, and never lived free."

So he'd made himself into a German, a Frenchman, an Englishman. He tried to become Canadian and Portuguese. And finally, aground in Lisbon, he'd reached another dead end. He could have been anybody—and had been—and now he was nobody. "I don't exist," he kept repeating to me. "I can't be betrayed."

The airport at Timișoara was nothing but a cracked tarmac and a low-slung gray block building—the remnants of another time—toward which we walked after deplaning. Inside floated a crowd, albeit a small one, that familiar beam of expectant faces one sees upon exiting customs almost anywhere in the world. I spied a man and a woman, huddled close together—and they looked back at me without looking past. The man was thin, slightly stooped, with tufts of hair on either side of his head and smooth skin on top. The woman was about forty, with dishwater hair and a kind if tired face. I'd later find she hadn't been able to sleep for the week leading up to my arrival, but what I noticed first was that one of her eyes trailed slightly to the right.

Like her brother's.

They pushed toward me and we embraced. As if I were the brother himself. His sister's name was Daniela, and for seventeen years she'd assumed the worst about Ciprian. Seventeen years without a word from him—and then, ten days ago, came a call from America. The voice at the other end had belonged to my friend's grandfather, a man born in Romania, who spoke fluently, calling on my behalf. He'd been kind enough to find a listing that had led to Daniela.

They would tell me later that they'd been confused and overwhelmed, happy and shocked. They attributed that call to God. It was a warm, hazy Tuesday in November, and they were taking the afternoon off from their work at the radio communications firm where Daniela's husband, Stefan, was a technician and Daniela was a secretary. Their only son, Razvan, who was nineteen years old and spoke perfect English, was in class at the language college and would join us later.

Daniela was tentative, polite. Her dress was simple, of the anonymous Eastern European variety. She wore no perfume, put on no airs or affectation. We walked the parking lot in a bit of a daze, trying to think of what to say first. It was seven miles or so to the city, and we rode in their small car. Both could speak English well enough for us to communicate the basics. Daniela had so many questions, and after waiting a polite modicum of time, they came flooding: Where was Ciprian? What did he look like? Was he okay? Was he healthy? What was his job? Was he married? Did he have the correct papers? Had he any trouble with the law? Would he be coming home soon?

She regarded me as a dear friend of Ciprian's—as well as a friend of hers. But more, I think she saw me as a deus ex machina come to rectify years of grief. She had already called me "a good man," whereas her brother, quoting Wagner's *Das Rheingold,* had said, "I only trust your greed." Over the course of our days together, she listened carefully to everything I could think to tell her: He was fine despite the head injury, worked out often, was married (or at least not divorced yet). She had an open, curious expression, one of trying to understand. And at the same time, no matter what odd twist the story took, she seemed to recognize the strength of her brother in all of it. Sometimes her eyes would well with tears, and then she would fight to hold herself together, to put everything back inside that placid, resigned body of hers. When she finally couldn't hold her emotion, she cried so politely that it seemed she wasn't crying at all.

"*Why* does he keep changing his name?" she asked. "Can we write his wife, our sister? Will they have children?"

They wanted to start by giving me a tour of Timișoara. Once past the rings of Communist construction, the blight of soulless apartment blocks, it was a beautiful downtown, full of Hapsburg-era buildings and a number of remarkable squares and churches, including an Orthodox cathedral that served as a central landmark. Timișoara had always been Romania's most Western city, the first in Europe to have introduced horse-drawn trams and then electric streetlights. And it was the place where the bloody revolution that led to the downfall of Ceaușescu had begun in December 1989.

One of the first stops was Colegiul Național de Artă Ion Vidu—the music school. We walked the narrow, slightly dilapidated toothpaste-colored halls. Children of all ages were afoot everywhere. "He was quiet," remembered his sister. "He liked to read and listen to music. He didn't get into trouble, at least not here." The plangent strains of violins could be heard emanating from behind closed doors, the tinkle of a piano, a trumpet blast. There was only this outward evidence of joyful, noisy learning. One had to go back in time, passing through decades, to retrieve the days of the Ceaușescu regime: the rationing and curfews, the abolition of religion and private property, the renaming of cities and streets, and fishburgers—only fishburgers—for sale at what passed as restaurants. The rigidity and daily persecutions of Communism had stripped the people of their dignity and identity. Holidays were erased, street names changed. People were forced to live double and triple lives. Was it this hallway here where Ciprian had received the punch from his teacher? Or this one here? Or was it, rather, all in his mind?

Daniela could remember that, after school, she and her brother were rarely permitted to play with friends but practiced the violin two to three hours at home each day. She allowed that her mother, who had worked in a bread factory, always had a special affection for Ciprian. "She did everything she could for him," Daniela said. "And he was such a smart, sensitive child. Even when he was fifteen or sixteen—when he was very sad, he would cry." It was the violin that his mother hoped would propel her son beyond their consigned life. Ciprian: He'd been named for a Moldavian composer.

About her father, Daniela said he was a decent man, too— one who also loved his son—except when he drank. He began his career as a shoemaker but then worked in the meat-processing business. We drove into an older section of the downtown, along a street of brick row houses, and ended up in front of the family's old domicile, or the door that led back to an inner courtyard and a long stablelike building with three or four apartments, what she called "a wagon house." They'd had three cramped rooms in their apartment—which, taken as a whole, was the size of what my room had been at the Ritz—and Daniela admitted that "things did not go well when my father was drunk." She said alcohol was his illness, not every night but often. And he was doomed by a lack of tolerance: When he did drink, he got drunk fast. And then things flew, windows broke, no one was safe. Their mother was beaten, and Ciprian, who objected to his father's behavior, was beaten, too—with a belt.

I believed her, of course. I walked the perimeter of the courtyard, trying to place myself in the shoes of that sensitive boy, the dead one now, the one buried beneath all those names and identities. There would have been four families jammed into

these apartments, with everyone living on top of each other, all
living tightly circumscribed lives, always under the weight of
Communist suspicion.

So when the objects flew, had Ciprian slept the cold night
over here by the stone wall, under the stars? Or was it over there
in the corner, under the porch roof?

The next day, Daniela wanted to take me to visit her—and
Ciprian's—parents. While still exuding calm, she appeared that
morning more ragged, with deeper rings beneath her eyes and
her hair a little more limp. Perhaps this was the effect of having
stayed behind in Romania—having lived a hard life here—or
perhaps it was the price she'd paid for having lost a brother to the
world beyond and being revisited by him now, through me.

We drove to the edge of town and parked the car, then
walked two blocks along a high wall with the traffic racing past at
breakneck speed. Sharp horns sounded; the loud trucks bore
extra-heavy loads. We came through the gate to the cemetery and
ambled to the back, to a small mountain of dead flowers. Daniela
tidied and decorated the sarcophagus that held both her parents.
She lit candles, placing them fastidiously in bottle caps, and fussed
with the flowers. Ciprian's mother had passed away in 2000, to
the end believing that she would see her son again. Daniela told
me that there was a very popular television show in Romania,
one that reunited lost family members, called *Surprise, Surprise,*
and her mother thought many times about calling with his name,
but then thought better of it, wondering if her Ciprian might be
in prison somewhere—or worse, she might find that he'd died.
Sometime later, when I reached an old friend of Ciprian's from
his high school years in Romania, one who himself had emi-
grated, he said, "Every time I went back to Romania, I went to

see her. She could not understand his anger. She lost her mind, really. She died of suffering."

His dad died two years after his mother. Later in life, Daniela said, he'd tried to limit his drinking, realizing the pain it had caused his family, and yet still could not be trusted: For her son Razvan's birthday parties growing up, he was never invited. But then, she remembered him in the family wagon house, an old man with a destroyed liver, standing at the window, wondering about his son. Filled with self-recrimination, he felt that his family was keeping Ciprian's whereabouts secret, and he pleaded for some word about him. "Have you heard anything?" he said over and over again.

I listened to all of these revelations feeling that uncomfortable combination of voyeurism and vampirism, its own form of greed. Here I was, walking through someone else's life to steal it for a moment, to assume it, reshape it, and resolve it somehow, all things that I knew I would never accomplish in the end. It wasn't just that the patterns of abuse here were so ingrained, so historical and repetitive, and that Mr. Nobody's own personal tale was trapped in this larger irrevocable pattern. But it was that I, having been sucked into the vortex of his person, having given him every benefit of the doubt, still couldn't balance how he might have killed off his entire family. How was it that he claimed not to remember their faces?

Had he ever felt anything? Perhaps the truth—the only real truth about Mr. Nobody—was the eerie depth of his emptiness.

I would have believed this if it hadn't been for that last evening with Daniela in Timişoara. We'd gone shopping together to buy food for a special dinner, then returned to their three-room apartment with its kitchen, a living/dining room where Daniela slept on the foldout couch, and a bedroom where father and son slept together. They'd saved this visit for last and seemed almost nervous to have me here, but why? Daniela held up a finger to signal that I should wait; then she descended some metal stairs to a dank basement and returned with a cardboard box.

She placed the box on the coffee table and reached in. Now that I myself seemed to be family, she told me that the final split had come as a result of "a small argument." Ciprian had been working as a chef in Germany, at an Italian restaurant, and was making more money in a month than Daniela and Stefan together earned in a year. When he returned home briefly, his mother mentioned that perhaps he should think about buying a house in Timişoara, and for some reason that set him off. He packed his bag and left. Later, he sent his sister all of her letters back. And they never heard from him again.

"When you see him," said Daniela, "tell him we love him— and that our lives are too short not to know each other." Though I'd warned her of his recalcitrance when it came to being in direct communication with them, she couldn't help herself. She imagined a scenario in which she might have a chance just to lay eyes on him once more, maybe from across a store. "What if we were to bump into each other on the street?" she wondered aloud. "Would we recognize each other?"

But the reality of her world was so stark—and she seemed so wrung out by it—that her expectations always made their correction. "Even if he wrote us one e-mail a year, one line," she said. "Just something telling us he's fine and where he is."

She reached for the box, from which came photographs, poems, and letters, all of them belonging to Ciprian, the boy who'd been left behind. Could this have been what he meant by "the elsewhere"?

There were pictures of Cipi as a baby, lying naked on a table. Here was Cipi on his father's lap, a modest Christmas tree hung with ornaments behind them, his handsome father gazing easily at the camera. Here was Cipi on vacation at the shore, year after year with his mother and sister, dressed as a cowboy, a sailor, an Indian. Here he was, standing stock-straight, dressed in his fine clothes, playing his violin in a school recital. There were pictures of Cipi growing older, sprouting up. At the end of high school, according to Daniela, he took an entrance exam to study languages at college. There were hundreds who took the exam in hopes of getting one of four spots. Ciprian hadn't made the cut. Nonetheless, in all the pictures of his graduation, he appeared singing and smiling, arms slung around friends, of which he seemed to have many.

It was his letters, especially those from the military, that seemed to capture the depths of his despair, the culmination of his disillusion. "He was someone who was used to showering once a day," said his sister, "and the military ruined him." Remembering his own military service, Stefan said, "They tried every way they could to degrade you. That's how I lost all my hair."

Ciprian's letters often began with the salutation "Dear ones." He sent happy birthdays to his parents and sisters, pleaded for his father to come visit. He was conscripted for a year and a half, and during that time he was forced to harvest crops and do field work. He underwent the psychological torments of a new recruit, being broken and made into a cog. "I've only been here a week," he wrote, "and I've already had all my fingers destroyed. . . . After two months of this, I won't be able to play the violin ever again."

In a letter to his sister, he concluded with the words: "From the first day here, something in me, like a flame, was put out.

"Happy Birthday. Love, Ciprian."

One imagines the boy as he was then: nineteen years old, presenting a hard countenance but broken inside—and if he stayed, his life was over. In Romania, every person became the exact stamp of his neighbor. If you had an inclination to experiment—with your ideas, sex, religion, or dress—you ran the risk of prison and torture. Devoid of professional prospects, Ciprian would have been forced to take a job—one of the unglamorous sort—perhaps like his father, in meat processing. Or whatever the state decided. He would have fallen under the weight of one identity, and would have died with it. Trapped, he might have easily fallen into the tar pit of too much drink, passing along what had been passed to him: an age-old rage. Sooner or later, he'd find his resting spot by the pile of dead flowers in the cemetery, another victim of ideological consumption.

And so he came up with a plan. If a Romanian citizen living abroad were to issue an invitation to another national living back in the home country—an invite for that person to come and visit—the state could issue temporary travel documents. For some, it became a means to escape: The invited party might arrive in Germany and, once settled, send an invitation back for a friend, who would come and then send for a friend, and so on. Soon you were all living illegally abroad on flimsy, often expired Romanian travel documents, which entailed its own very real risks. But at least you were free of Romania—and at least you could eat meat again instead of fishburgers. So Marius, who'd moved to Germany, sent for Ciprian, who later sent for Adrian. When Ciprian had arrived, he'd found a job cooking in an Italian restaurant. He read the Bible under the covers at night with a flashlight, so as not to bother anyone. Was he still a believer or merely grasping for the last of his faith?

So began the lost decade. After another year—after returning to Romania one last time and leaving angrily, with that exhale of finality—he moved to Paris. Now twenty-two, he joined Adrian, who had moved to France straightaway. Fourteen years later, Adrian was still there when I reached him by phone. I told him I was trying to recover the memory of his friend, and when I mentioned him by name, he said, "Ciprian? You're calling about Ciprian!" He could barely contain himself. "You saw him? How is he? Where is he? Will he see me?" Adrian remembered their shared fear at not having papers beyond the temporary travel permits they'd been issued, the fear that they'd be found out and either sent back home or imprisoned. Adrian recalled how Ciprian—whom he said would "always have a special place in my heart"—became someone different in Paris.

"In a way, he was one side of everyone," Adrian said, "the rebel that most don't have the courage to be. He didn't have any limits. He just said what he said. I really respected that in him." According to Adrian, during this time Ciprian read the Romanian philosopher Emil Cioran, who wrote obsessively about suicide. He renounced his family—and shortly, too, his country. "Work is prostitution," Ciprian declared to Adrian. One day he appeared at the bar where Adrian worked. "He came in with a guy," said Adrian, "and the way they were talking, the way they were together, it was different. In Timișoara, he only went with women." So now that had changed, too.

After a year of their living together, Adrian finally had had enough. He bristled at the criticism, especially when his friend felt no qualms about living in the apartment for free while Adrian worked so hard to pay for it. "I was part of his story; I was his friend," said Adrian. "He didn't have any reason to fight with me except to find a reason to go away, to claim that I was just like the others who had let him down."

And then Ciprian left, never to be seen again. Adrian thought about him often while carrying on: He married, divorced, studied photography in Prague, and returned to Paris as a professional photographer. "Ciprian was there when I needed someone the most," Adrian remembered. "But he was against everything all the time. His desire was to be different. He didn't care about money. I would never say he wanted to be 'famous.' That's a word I would never use. He just didn't want to waste his life doing stupid things."

The last Adrian heard, he'd gone to Italy—but where? Mr. Skeid couldn't, or wouldn't, recall. So he'd moved like a wisp over the Continent, hoarding his papers and whatever documents enabled him to cross this or that border, filling his brain with books and Wagner, formulating his opinions on everything—his slightly disconnected unified theories—while, as he had put it, making himself into a Pygmalion to others of lower intellect.

Where, and with whom, had he consumed that expensive bottle of wine?

"I won't answer any question that may jeopardize my freedom," he said.

After Italy, how had he made it to London?

"I can tell the truth, but I can't be made to answer," he said.

So which was he, the one they said was a grifter and a fraud or the one who'd been a victim?

"Remember, I don't exist," he said.

It was fascinating to think so. If one were to believe the facts and allegations that constituted the only known record of our man—the polish of his accent, the testimony given by alleged friends and acquaintances, as well as the version presented by the Canadian authorities—he arrived in England with the passport of Georges Lecuit, taken by theft or cash, moved to London, engaged in various versions of selling his body, grew tired of the scene there after some years, and left with a plan to get to America, where, he'd allegedly claimed, he planned to make more pornographic movies.

Then he was found in Toronto. Beaten and traumatized. From that point forward, his memories were vivid again. The nurses hovering over him in the hospital, the time spent living in the rough Downtown Eastside section of Vancouver, his wedded life with Nathalie, the alleged injustices visited upon him by the politicians of Canada, the bureaucracy, the guards at the jail—he could recall specific conversations, the number of days in his hunger strike, the people who had taken him into their homes out of pity.

"My time in Canada proved one thing," he said. "It's a hypocritical dictatorship with a genocidal past."

And here he stood now, in the lobby of the Ritz, on our last night together. What incarnation was this? His eighth or ninth? How many times had he committed some figurative suicide to be here now, to purify himself, standing there with his air of superiority and vulnerability, with his new teeth and his new nose, living in this world of his own ideas that defended the boy who had once come so easily to tears? In what cul-de-sac would he soon find himself stuck again?

He was being funny—and, as he admitted, a bit snobby. He thought the tapestries on the wall, the ones of supposed "museum quality" depicting centaurs, were "absolutely shabby." Speaking of Nathalie, he said that she was probably happier now, with a man who might be more sensitive to her insecurities, even if he was from Romania. "I'm so full of myself," he said. "I consider it compliment enough if I decide to be with someone. I don't need to say anything." He spoke of Wagner, of the difficult circumstances of his great hero's life, the last of nine offspring, his father's low station. "He had all the odds against him, lived most of his life with little money. He once said, and this isn't verbatim: 'At first, I tried not to be anyone at all. Then I tried to become someone. And then someone better.'"

It was maybe ten or eleven o'clock, and I was beginning to feel nauseous there in the lobby at the Ritz, amid the onslaught of all those fashionable suits, all those fine, hollow men residing in their various vacuums of power. Certainly no one was as he seemed, everyone had his secret, but I was beginning to feel exhausted by trying to figure out *his*. Tomorrow I'd be on a plane, heading home to resume my life, and he'd be in his apartment, still shipwrecked here in Lisbon, lashed to the rigging.

We shook hands, our Mr. Skeid and I. "In a funny way," he said, "you know me better now than anyone." And again that feeling of pity, that exact thing he didn't want, registered inside me. I wanted to say something to him then—something about how a smart and able person such as himself could still make something of his life if only he'd *try*. I wanted to reiterate what he'd just said—that a stranger such as myself knew him better after these four days in Lisbon than his mother, father, sister, or wife ever had, and how could that be?—but thought better of it. It merely would have angered him, for he must have felt he *had* made something of his life. Or found something, something approximating freedom. His image reflected again in the gilded elevator doors, statuesque and absolutely generic. I stepped aboard, and he courteously wished me safe travels; then the door closed between us.

I rose to my room with a sense of relief, while I imagined his leave-taking, how he may have lingered for a moment, in his cargo pants and collared shirt and $500 shoes. He could have been anyone, except that he had no reason to be here any longer, a spell dematerialized. I imagined him stalking the marble floor past the concierge desk to the sliding door that would have heralded the entrance of those returning to their finely appointed rooms: the diplomat squiring his new lady friend, the businessmen back in a congratulatory pack from a gluttonous dinner and the gracious flow of money from some client's pocket to theirs.

He would have glanced once at the knot of their ties, the fabric of their suits. He would have noticed the leather of their shoes and the size of their cuff links, registered everything he considered their birthright and destiny—and all that hadn't been his.

And then, once and for all, he would have disappeared from the lobby of the Ritz—as he did then—lost once more in his spin of lights, the welter of night.

NEVER FORGET

THERE WAS A SAYING IN KHMER from those times. The people would caution that a body "was fading away." They would say: "Be careful or your body may disappear."

On the day the man, Chum Mey, was reunited with his wife (thinking her already dead), how could he have known that she had just seventeen more hours to live? They were prisoners of the Khmer Rouge, herded into different groups, in the last hours of the regime, chaotically fleeing the Vietnamese. Even now, he remembers first seeing her again, the heightened metabolic state of happiness, and though he revealed no emotion (even the act of smiling—something Cambodians do so readily—was thought by the Khmer Rouge to be unrevolutionary), he watched her carefully as she walked ahead with their small son, both dressed as he was: in black pajamas. When the guards were at a distance, he spoke to her once about the scenery.

They did not touch.

At that time—during the nearly four-year reign of Angkar lasting from April 17, 1975, to January 7, 1979—the killing was so random and widespread across Cambodia that death became a near certainty, especially if you were sent to the prison camp known as S-21. While the odds were roughly one in four of dying—and worse depending on your demographic (for instance, adult men died in much higher percentages)—your chance of survival at S-21 was .04 percent.

Or put the opposite way, the odds of your death were 99.96 percent.

Before death, though, a prisoner confessed, over and over again, until he'd named sometimes hundreds of "traitors," in order to stop the pain of torture. The man who would soon lose his wife and who, as it turned out, was a mechanic with dexterous hands had been named and arrested, taken away blindfolded to the place where fifteen thousand others were sentenced and exterminated in nearby pastureland famously known as the Killing Fields. But then, as fate would have it, he would emerge as one of only seven survivors from the prison camp. He became living proof that somehow surviving the absolute certainty of your own death can be as horrific as murder itself. For in the end, you're the only one left to carry the memory of fifteen thousand terrors.

The man was forty-four years old when the body of his wife disappeared, the same age as I am right now. There is no equivalence; this is only a fact.

And one other: At this same age, though I have three children, he'd already lost four.

From the Book of Atrocities, the evil fable begins like this: Once upon a time, a group of men educated in Paris and steeped in Communist ideology had a dream for their homeland. To create a Cambodian society that surpassed the greatness of Angkor, the kingdom that reached its pinnacle under the god-king Surya-varman II in the twelfth century with the construction of Angkor Wat. From the jungles—where their leaders had fled to escape the repressive measures of Prince Sihanouk in 1963—they fought a guerrilla war, led by a soft-spoken, enigmatic schoolteacher named Saloth Sar. These Communists, however, did not believe in gods, kings, or culture, but they were good at biding their time. In the vacuum of power left after the eight-year American bombing of Cambodia, they swept east across the lowlands to the capital, Phnom Penh, finally wresting control from the corrupt U.S.-supported regime in 1975. (The premier, Lon Nol, had already fled to Hawaii.) Their first act was to evacuate the city, hurrying the populace under the pretense that the Americans were coming to bomb again, emptying hospitals, setting millions of people—including the elderly, lame, and pregnant—walking on the roads that led to the countryside, a scene of hunger and corpses straight out of Brueghel.

What the Khmer Rouge had in store was a radical agrarian revolution, one with the professed aim of completely renovating society while giving the peasants a better life, of evening the rewards and feeding the hungry, of bringing a rational and utilitarian nation-state into being. At first, without the world knowing their real intentions, they were partially applauded, even by American journalists and politicians. Prince Sihanouk assured our Congress that the Khmer Rouge would establish "a Swedish type of kingdom," and Senator George McGovern believed that the new regime would be "run by some of the best-educated, most able intellectuals in Cambodia." But almost immediately the Khmer Rouge's revolutionary pretenses gave way to the sickening irrationality of brutes. In that first spasm of violence, everyone wearing glasses was killed. Everyone who spoke a foreign language was killed. Everyone with a university education was killed. Word was sent to expats living abroad to come home and join the new Cambodia; when a thousand or so arrived on special flights from Beijing, they were killed. Monks, so revered in Cambodian society and long the voice of conscience there, were killed. Lawyers, doctors, and diplomats were killed. Bureaucrats, soldiers, and policemen, even factory workers (who in the minds of the Khmer Rouge were equivalent to industrialization itself) were killed.

In that first moment, the lucky ones were directed to keep walking to their home villages—some traveled for months this way—where they were sorted, sent to collectives, and worked from sunup to twilight. A person's worth was eventually measured by his ability to move cubic yards of earth. "To keep you is no profit," said the executioners to the unworthy before killing them, "to destroy you is no loss."

Chum Mey, the man who would survive S-21 but lose his wife, realized that the troops first entering Phnom Penh were mostly lost boys from the jungle, dirty and ragged, with blank expressions, who within hours of being greeted as liberators by cheering crowds turned on the masses with their AK-47s. In the south of the city, they fired warning shots; in the northwest sector, they fired on people. Never having seen toilets before, the soldiers drank from them as if they were cisterns, shat on the floor, wiped themselves with sticks that they left strewn about abandoned houses.

It was April, the hottest month. Fires ringed the city, the roads were so packed you could progress only in baby steps, parents were separated from their children, the sick and old laid themselves down, moaning. The man had his wife and children. At night he went down to the river to get water for them and found himself standing on bodies, and then in the water surrounded by bodies, so thick in places you couldn't drink.

Funny, a repugnant memory such as that clung with an almost humid fondness now, thirty-five years later, for as horrible as the moment was, his family was still gathered about him. When he carried the water back, there was still thirst to quench, voices calling for their father and husband: Here, *Pa*! Here! Terrible things gathered around them, but lying down for the night, he could whisper to his wife: *Is this really happening?*

The leaders of the revolution were designated Brother Number One (Pol Pot), Brother Number Two (Nuon Chea), Brother Number Three (Ieng Sary), and so on. And they were nothing if not ambitious in trying to build a new society. The Brothers abolished courts and banks. They abolished money and holidays and love. They abolished time and history, setting everything back to Year Zero. And they abolished the four things Cambodians hold most dear: family, village, food, and Buddhism. Those who hailed from the city were branded with the designation "New People," versus "Old People," who were from the country. New People were the ones most often punished. The entire populace was forced to wear black pajamas, the women Maoist bobs. So secretive were the Brothers that for a year no one knew who was running the country. Until Saloth Sar emerged under his new revolutionary name of Pol Pot, it was as if the faceless godhead Angkar decided all.

When it came to song, workers were only occasionally allowed to sing from a menu of revolutionary anthems like "Struggling to Build Dams and Dig Canals" or "Bravery of Construction Revolutionary Soldiers" or "Best Wishes to People in Northwestern Zone." But a jingle secretly murmured by workers at the time spoke the truth: "Angkar kills but does not explain."

On the road from Phnom Penh during those first days, a Khmer Rouge cadre said to Chum Mey, the man with dexterous fingers, who would soon lose his wife: "See nothing, say nothing, do nothing against Angkar and you may survive."

I first went to Cambodia in 2002, primarily, as it turned out, to change diapers. My wife had work in Phnom Penh, and thus left with her driver and translator early each morning and returned late each night, while I took care of our firstborn son, who was two at the time. Initially I thought we'd have some cultural moments out in the city, but soon realized that we were destined to spend an abnormal amount of time eating grilled cheese sandwiches by the pool.

When we ventured out of the hotel, I pushed him in a stroller down a sodden sidewalk along the Mekong River, drifting with the hordes to the center of town, to a park there, where under a brutal sun, in the sticky, soaking heat, one could ride an elephant for a dollar. With son in arms, I climbed a rickety metal ladder, sat warily on the huge beast (his legs were chained to each other), and one with the pachyderm now, we lumbered the circumference of the park while my son, in silent panic, clutched me like a snake-spooked chimpanzee. Everyone—the mothers clutching their own babies, the fathers hand in hand with their daughters—pointed and smiled at us.

Back at the hotel, we ate our sandwiches, swam in the pool, went to bed. We understood nothing, of course. Our ignorance was willful. We tried to sleep but couldn't. I lay awake, remembering all the smiles in that park. Why had everyone been smiling? It made me suddenly paranoid. Was there something I hadn't known about that elephant, that park, that set of operators? Was the joke on me? And if so, what was the joke?

Or had they merely smiled because they could?

I was to have one afternoon to myself in Phnom Penh, after my wife had completed her work. I scoured the guidebook—the Silver Pagoda, Wat Phnom, a drink at Le Royal—but got stuck on S-21, the famous prison camp located in a former school called Tuol Sleng. Even *Lonely Planet* couldn't bring itself to recommend a visit to the site, which had been turned into a museum. Here's what it said:

"Altogether, a visit to Tuol Sleng is a profoundly depressing experience. The sheer ordinariness of the place makes it even more horrific: the suburban setting, the plain school buildings, the grassy playing area where today children kick around balls, rusted beds, instruments of torture and wall after wall of harrowing black-and-white portraits conjure up images of humanity at its worst. Tuol Sleng is not for the squeamish."

So that's where I went.

It was silent when I arrived, and I was trying to gauge that silence at the same time that I was guarding against it, with the same active ambivalence I've had visiting other holocaust museums and concentration camps. The mind proceeds with trepidation: How bad will this get? Which is another way of asking: Just how deep and dark are we? And: Am I willing to participate, even if just bearing witness? Which itself is a defense: *bearing witness*. After all, we are the animals, too, bearing witness to our accomplishment.

Tuol Sleng had all the gulag charm of any nondescript concrete-block three-story building complex blooming with mold, humidity stains, and the sickening presence of evil in the unwashable blood marked into the umber-and-white-tile-checked floor. People, tourists like me, moved through the old school in ghostly rounds—as if the guards of yore—and in the background, seemingly far away, came the low rustle of the city.

S-21 had been directed by a man named Kaing Guek Eav, whose revolutionary name was Comrade Duch (pronounced *Doik*). Once a teacher of mathematics, he'd first been conscripted by the Khmer Rouge to run a jungle prison camp, where he'd studiously refined his ideas about torture, and was then put in charge of S-21. It was here that he condoned "living autopsies" (the slicing and flaying of victims); that he demanded the extended use of torture to obtain confessions (including near drownings, the removal of toe- and fingernails followed by a dousing of alcohol, electric shocks applied to genitals, suffocation with plastic bags, and forcing prisoners to eat human excrement); that he ordered the murder of at least fifteen thousand people, who were taken to the Killing Fields and shot or bludgeoned (with iron rods, shovels, and axes) and then dumped into mass graves.

Operating from 1975 to 1979, S-21 became the most infamous of 196 such prison camps the Khmer Rouge established throughout Cambodia, primarily because so many of its prisoners were the purged party loyal—and because Duch's methods were so stunningly brutal. In 1979, when the Vietnamese drove the Khmer Rouge from power, they happened upon Tuol Sleng because of the stench of rotting corpses.

Now Tuol Sleng was a museum—and perhaps the most potent symbol of the Khmer Rouge's dystopia. As I crossed the courtyard, the leaves of the palm trees and banyans shifted benevolently in a breeze, and detaching the scene from its history, one might have imagined this courtyard at a swank hotel in Honolulu: pleasant, tropical, hushed. But instead of someone taking drink orders, there was a billboard posted with security regulations from Duch's time. They began with their own warm welcome: *1. You must answer accordingly to my questions. Don't turn them away. 2. Don't try to hide the facts by making pretexts this and that. You are strictly prohibited to contest me. 3. Don't be a fool for you are a chap who dare to thwart the revolution.*

From the Book of Atrocities: The Way They Killed, Part One. Prisoners were hooked up to a pump and IV line and had all their blood drained for use in the hospitals. According to witnesses, the breathing turned to gasps, then wheezing, until the victim's eyes rolled back in his head, leaving only the whites. Bloodless, the corpses were then thrown into pits.

At Tuol Sleng, you drift from room to empty room. Here stands that iconic rusted frame of a bed, used to bind prisoners. *(6. While getting lashes or electrification you must not cry at all.)* Here the bolts that helped shackle up to fifty prisoners at a time, in holding cells, the bodies laid out on the floor like soon-to-be-gutted tuna. *(7. Do nothing, sit still and wait for my orders. . . .)* In some rooms are photographs of the very same rooms, taken by the Vietnamese on the day they discovered the prison camp, a decomposed body left on the bed, a slit neck bled out in nearly black puddles. There are shackles and metal boxes that once held excrement for feeding.

There's a map of Cambodia on one wall, made from three hundred skulls, and barbed wire on the upper balconies, put there after a rash of suicides to keep the prisoners from jumping. But it's the empty eeriness of the rooms that fills the imagination; the tranquility that calls up the shrieking opposite. *(8. Don't make pretexts about Kampuchea Krom in order to hide your jaw of traitor.)*

Located on the first floor of the middle building are some of the most famous death masks in the world, those black-and-white photographs taken of living prisoners upon admission to Tuol Sleng. And yet the captured already know they're dead. *(10. If you disobey any point of my regulations you shall get either ten lashes or five shocks of electric discharge.)* The fear and resignation, the dark epiphany that the flashbulb brings—some have already been beaten, some have babies clinging to them, some stand unflinching, in their last moment of public dignity before Duch's men have their way—is made more poignant by the fact that they are trapped inside an unsolvable koan. Their confusion is writ large beneath their defeat. What they're about to confirm, during the hours and days of interrogation that will soon follow, is that there are no right answers. That they have become victims, as one visitor put it, of an "irrational radicalism" or, more plainly, of an absolutely absurd universe, one in which the sanctity of the body is torn down again and again to a diamond-hard point, void of ideals and emotion, where ultimately dying becomes less painful than living.

Among those who died under Duch were members of the Khmer Rouge's own Standing Committee (caught in the spin cycle of Pol Pot's ever-increasing paranoia, more and more high-ranking officials were thought to be turncoats) and at least eleven Westerners: four Americans, three French, two Australians, a Brit, and a New Zealander. How any of them ended up at S-21 in the first place must be seen as a horrifically random act of cosmic bad luck. In the case of two American men who were sailing from Singapore to Hawaii, they mistakenly ended up in Cambodian waters and were apprehended by Khmer Rouge patrols.

Besides these special cases, the killing at S-21 was indiscriminate and nearly complete (99.96 percent), including the equal-opportunity elimination of laborers, teachers, factory workers, artists, monks, diplomats, cyclo drivers, and on and on. When one thinks of the loss of life, one wonders again at those who made it out alive. (There were seven.)

One way was this: The Party, in imitation of Mao's cult of personality, decided it needed portraits of Pol Pot, and two of the prisoners happened to be painters. Thus they were offered the chance to paint for their lives. (On the list of those to die, next to the painter named Vann Nath, Duch had scribbled the words: *Leave for using.*) Meanwhile, the prison camp needed a good mechanic, and in the case of Chum Mey, the man who would lose his wife, he knew how to fix things with his dexterous fingers, and his turn to die coincided with a broken sewing machine used for repairing the guards' uniforms.

And so the spinning wheel's needle landed on the sliver-wedge that bore their names—and that's why they lived.

The Way They Killed, Part Two. To make love out of wedlock meant certain death, and a boy who had just reached puberty, who was confused and desperate, was caught in the act with a water buffalo. The next day everyone from his collective—from the youngest to the oldest—was gathered. The boy was paraded before the crowd, strung up, then taunted, tortured, and killed. As odd as the case sounds, survivors of the Khmer Rouge recall public executions—full of redress and mockery, disembowelment and cannibalism—as being part of the daily schedule. "Better to destroy ten innocent people," was another saying, "than to let one enemy go free."

A visit to S-21 leaves an inconsolable feeling. It rides with you in the taxi back to the unreality of the hotel, through the streets of Phnom Penh, buzzing with markets and families, with the ramshackle grandeur of golden stupas and crumbling colonial architecture. And yet somewhere still behind it, one rearrives at the skeleton: the images just after the Khmer Rouge took the capital, a city drained of all human life, the colonial buildings empty and echoing, the pagodas ransacked and used to hold grain, piles of television sets and radios, burned cars and all other machines of modern life strewn in the streets, twisting columns of smoke rising from the wreckage. Behind the normalcy of today, even the veneer of progress, lurks that desolation (. . . it is still happening).

In my case, the aftermath of a visit to S-21 left me with (a) a suffusion of paranoia and (b) a feeling of utter futility. It was the futility that stuck with me, though, the gut-wrenching realization that somehow the Khmer Rouge had gotten away with their experiment and that they had razed a country of its lawyers and leaders, intellectuals and activists (all those who might have had the expertise and wherewithal to hold them accountable for their crimes). By "smashing" (their word) the populace, by pathologically replacing the individual with the collective (and making sure that the collective knew how to do only one thing: grow rice), they'd instilled a paralysis and fear that had so far, thirty years later, saved them from retribution. They'd effectively lobotomized their own country.

It was astonishing, really. In the annals of the century's great crimes against humanity, the Nazi leadership had been tried—and many of them executed—in fairly short order, as had the

Japanese war criminals. Guilty parties convicted of genocide in Rwanda, Iraq, and the former Yugoslavia were imprisoned and in some cases executed. Those responsible for apartheid in South Africa were subjected to a truth commission, which at least demanded confession and supplication.

Meanwhile, after being forced from power, the Khmer Rouge leadership set up on the border of Thailand, in the jungle stronghold of Pailin. From there, Pol Pot and his minions carried on their killing (including taking the lives of Western backpackers visiting the Angkor Wat temple complex) and tried to muster a second revolution. (It was said that between ordering the murders of his top lieutenants, Pol Pot, who was never pursued as a criminal, enjoyed cognac, Pringles, and reading *Paris Match,* a French celebrity rag.) During this time, the Khmer Rouge continued to occupy Cambodia's seat at the UN and receive foreign delegations in the jungle. The regime was so deeply entrenched that even the United States couldn't cut final ties until 1991, a decade after learning the worst about it. Meanwhile, a number of high-ranking Khmer Rouge leaders were invited back to Phnom Penh and given villas by the government.

The mystery to me, and many others, was also a pique: What was the exact purpose of all this accommodation? And more: When was someone going to pay?

Not long after returning from Cambodia that first time, I had coffee with an editor in Manhattan. As happens at such meetings, we discussed "big stories" that seemed to have been overlooked by the media, even though we *were* the media. When I brought up the untried Khmer Rouge leaders, pointing out the 1.7 million dead from nearly thirty years ago, his eyes glazed. It wasn't his fault, of course. He was hardly alone on the topic. Yes, horrible— but no. More than that, he wanted to talk about Hollywood.

"What people tend to miss," he said, "is that George Clooney's much more than an actor."

They did not believe in gods, kings, or culture. In fact, it's fair to say that in spite of their Communist doctrine, they believed in very little at all except a very dark, dominating kind of nihilism. They abolished schools, sport, toys, free time. They banned words like *beauty, colorful,* and *comfort* from the radio. They separated all children seven or older from their parents, placing them in packs called "mobile units" to help with the rice harvest. (It was a "vagrant life," said one survivor, "like that of a plant floating in the ocean.") They abolished happiness, as it was their supreme belief that in order to purge individuality, the people must be made to suffer; having suffered, they would be devoid of dreams and expectations. That is, without minds of their own, they'd be perfect revolutionaries.

The Khmer Rouge were so busy killing people, they didn't mince words. Here are a few of their sayings:

"He who protests is an enemy; he who opposes is a corpse."

"Angkar has [the many] eyes of the pineapple."

"Hunger is the most effective disease."

It's still happening, *Pa.* You're an old man now, and it is still happening. The thugs have turned out the nearly two million residents of Phnom Penh, and as you walk along that road with your whole family, and as others lie dying, as others are shot and beaten and literally steamrolled (one body you see has been mashed by a truck to the thickness of a pancake, oozing clear syrup and viscera), your youngest contracts a high fever, then diarrhea.

You bury her one night in a heavy rain and keep going.

Sometime during that death march, the soldiers demand that all the mechanics identify themselves. You are guileless and want to please in order to save your family. They assure you that your family will be safe, and when they pull you from the line, you look back once at them. Then you are sent to the city, where you begin that first month repairing the boats they use to transport Khmer Rouge soldiers up-country along the Mekong. Your next assignment is two years in the capital, scurrying through the empty streets, going from abandoned house to abandoned house, retrieving and then fixing, by your count, forty thousand sewing machines—forty thousand broken belts and bobbins—all of which go to the factories where the women work, making the same black pajamas that you will be wearing on that day in the future when your wife disappears.

The Way They Killed, Part Three. If someone required killing, it was common practice to kill their children. If a parent died of starvation or disease, the children might also be killed. At the Killing Fields, babies were held by their feet and smashed against a designated tree, the Baby-Smashing Tree. Duch would later admit, while explaining why he ordered the death of so many children, that those who came to S-21 with their parents were seen as dangerous agents, potential enemies of the state who would ultimately seek revenge for the death of a parent. "You must pull the weed at the root" went the saying. Or: Kill now before you, too, are killed.

Everyone had a theory, real or half-baked, about why it had been nearly impossible to bring the Khmer Rouge to justice. For some,

American guilt rode high on the list. That is, the Americans were loath to reexamine the sordid details of their eight-year secret bombing of the country—which killed somewhere between 150,000 and 500,000 civilians—and were unwilling to accept their role in the destabilization of society that led to the rise of the Khmer Rouge. For others, the prime minister, Hun Sen, didn't want his own Khmer Rouge résumé dredged up. ("We should dig a hole and bury the past," he was quoted as saying in 1998, rejecting the idea of trials.) And then the international community didn't seem to have much desire for it, either; being resource poor and of no geopolitical advantage, Cambodia had nothing to offer. Meanwhile, the money that was earmarked for eventual trials, money that poured in through various NGOs and foreign governments, created a lucrative cottage industry for certain corrupt local officials who were motivated to drag out the process as long as possible.

And yet as time sludged forward, an agreement was finally forged in 2003 between the Cambodian government and the UN to inaugurate the Extraordinary Chambers in the Courts of Cambodia for the Prosecution of Crimes Committed During the Period of Democratic Kampuchea, or the ECCC. A formal indictment followed in 2007, charging Duch with crimes against humanity as well as war crimes. In addition, the top Khmer Rouge leaders who remained alive were arrested and imprisoned, including Brother Number Two (Nuon Chea) and Brother Number Three (Ieng Sary). But until Duch took the stand in February 2009, to begin the first trial, there were still those who doubted such a day would ever come—and others, mostly those born after 1979, who didn't understand why there should be a trial for these mythical old men at all. Why did it matter? Or: Was it better left forgotten?

In writing the introduction to the trials in a handbook distributed to the Cambodian people, Hun Sen put it most simply.

"The crimes of the Khmer Rouge period were not just committed against the people of Cambodia," he wrote, "but against all humanity."

December 9, 1970: Feeling frustrated by the changing tide of the war in Vietnam, Richard Nixon calls his secretary of state, Henry Kissinger, to discuss closing down North Vietnamese supply routes through Cambodia. "I want everything that can fly to go in there and crack the hell out of them," says the president. "There is no limitation on mileage, and there is no limitation on budget." Throughout the conversation, Nixon seems agitated, peeved. "The whole goddamn Air Force over there farting around," he says. "It is a disgraceful performance. . . . Get them off their asses and get them to work now."

Minutes later Kissinger is speaking to Alexander Haig: "I just talked to our little friend," says Kissinger. "He wants a massive bombing campaign in Cambodia. He doesn't want to hear anything. It's an order; it's to be done. Anything that flies on anything that moves. You got that?"

On the transcript, the response is described as follows: "Couldn't hear but sounded like Haig laughing."

Over and over and over, in past, present, and future, it's happening, has happened, will happen again. Like this:

In 146 B.C., the Romans attack Carthage, jealous of its wealth and refinement. After giving up their weapons to avoid war, the Carthaginians are asked to abandon their beloved city, and when they refuse are set upon, beaten, and burned alive. Over the course of a week, Roman soldiers employ all manner of killing—using swords for stabbing and spears for impaling. They loft bodies from rooftops to the cobbles below and bury children and old people alive or stampede them beneath their horses. According to one account, bodies are torn asunder "into all kinds of horrible shapes, crushed and mangled." When the Carthaginian commander, Hasdrubal, finally surrenders, his wife appears before him at a burning temple with their children, and, reproaching him for his cowardice, she slays her children, tossing them into the fire and plunging in after them.

Witnessing it all, the Roman commander Scipio clasps the hand of one of his lieutenants. "A glorious moment, Polybius," he says, "but I have a dread foreboding that someday the same doom will be pronounced upon my own country."

Or in other words, our own genocide forever comes next.

Before returning to Cambodia during the phase of Duch's pretrial hearings, I was reading a lot. Books about Pol Pot and the Khmer Rouge. Books about torture and genocide. I sat in a room, in the middle of winter, ice shagging the windows, staring at pictures of the Brothers Khmer (oddly bloated while everyone else starved)—and some of their victims (fed on teaspoons of gruel; you could see their ribs). I read and took notes. By the time I recorded the details of one horrific happening, it was subsumed by the details of the next. It was hard to accept the incomprehensibility of the feat, the sheer creativity of Angkar's sadism. But there it was, in the pictures taken at S-21, in the still-alive faces auguring death.

During this time, I thought that perhaps if you applied logic (for instance, a syllogism) to something illogical (for instance, a genocide), you might reach, well, the beginning of understanding. One afternoon, poring over my notes, a couple of disparate lines unmended themselves, floated up, and spun down again. It was a beginning:

Language is the only means to reconciliation.

Pain destroys language.

For those in pain, there is no means to reconciliation.

My first morning back in Phnom Penh, I met at the hotel with a defense attorney for Comrade Duch named François Roux. The ECCC was set up in such a way that for every Cambodian attorney, there was also a corresponding international attorney. Roux shared his defense duties with a Cambodian lawyer named Kar Savuth, who himself had lost two brothers and nearly his own life to the Khmer Rouge.

Roux had spent thirty years doing this work, traveling the world from Rwanda to French Polynesia to defend the accused. He'd defended José Bové, the man who tore down a McDonald's in France protesting genetically modified crops. Here in the United States he'd helped save the so-called twentieth hijacker, Zacarias Moussaoui, from the death penalty. "I like being on the side of the accused," he said. "I find it edifying."

At the hotel, he waved off the sumptuous five-star buffet, a cornucopia of pancakes and dumplings, *pho* and shrimp lo mein, and instead drank a single cup of orange-pekoe tea. He was a diminutive, impish man with quick, intelligent brown eyes, clad in a slightly ill-fitting black blazer and ironed white shirt. He'd spent so much time in Cambodia lately, he'd taken a little house to live in, and he found his life completely entwined with Duch's, whom he met with every day. Yes, they had formed a bond, he said, a client-attorney bond, but a human bond nonetheless. "I wouldn't say we are friends," said Roux, "but we have an understanding, a very good understanding."

I wasn't sure what that meant exactly. Was Roux here to act as an apologist for Duch, to report that he'd looked into the man's soul and seen something that the rest of humanity had somehow missed? Somewhere along the way, Duch had converted to Christianity, but thirty years and fifteen thousand dead bodies later was it okay to say, "Oh yeah, that stuff back there, that was a big mistake"?

I'm sure it wasn't the first time Roux had been confused with one of his clients, and he tried his best to explain, but for a moment I stubbornly, irrationally, held to my own simplistic syllogism:

> Duch was evil.
> Roux had a bond with Duch.
> Roux had a bond with evil.

The Frenchman's mouth kept moving—"due process . . . accepted responsibility . . . true justice . . ."—but I lost track of what he was saying. Only later, when I went back to the transcript, did I hear his voice again, almost plaintive in its individuation.

"I'm only here to try to make something fair out of something unfair," he said.

At S-21, when Duch had been omnipotent, when it seemingly hadn't occurred to him to question his own actions or seek expiation from his god for the sins he was committing, he preferred whips and electric shocks to waterboarding in order to keep his prisoners alive.

To an interrogator under his command, he gave these words of advice: "Beat [the prisoner] until he tells everything. Beat him to get at the deep things."

———

At our meeting, Roux had spoken eloquently about how it could be that we might allow someone like Duch back into "our human community." He went on to point out how the trial would allow his client to make his amends with the Cambodian people, how the criminal was always bigger than his crimes, that Duch had undergone a conversion. He was now a Christian, but more than that he was *changed* somehow.

Changed how? By sudden guilt? After the Vietnamese had poured into Phnom Penh in January 1979, effectively ending the rule of the Khmer Rouge, Comrade Duch had stayed at S-21 until the final second in order to oversee the killing of the last of the prisoners (the ones photographed by the Vietnamese, bodies bound on the rusted metal bed frames, throats slashed, bled out on the umber-and-white floor); then he'd disappeared into the jungle, eventually making his way to China to teach Khmer. Later he worked for Pol Pot as a bureaucrat and then taught school again in a small village, where he was regarded as a good teacher with a mean temper. Sometime after his conversion, he became a lay minister and worked in the countryside with the Christian relief agency World Vision, which is where he was found in 1999, under an assumed name, by a young journalist whose own initial visit to Tuol Sleng had led him on a personal manhunt for Comrade Duch. Would he have ever come forward if he hadn't been discovered?

I admit I had a hard time buying the tale of his full conversion, especially from the French defense attorney whose advantage it was to sell that particular narrative, however passionate and personable Roux was, however much I trusted Roux's intentions and his absolute faith in the process of justice. "Every case needs someone to defend," he had said. He implied that even someone like Duch could be saved.

But if, as Roux insisted, the criminal was always bigger than his crime, I wanted to know this: Wasn't the victim much bigger than both?

Roux, who was rushing to catch a plane to Rwanda, insisted that I speak to Kar Savuth, the other defense attorney. And so we set a meeting for a few nights later at the hotel bar. In 1994, Savuth had taken his oath as one of the first lawyers in Cambodia after the Khmer Rouge, completing a dream that had been delayed twenty years: He'd been a law student when the Khmer Rouge came to power in 1975. Instead of seeking revenge, a victim of the Khmer Rouge was defending them.

When he arrived at the bar, I would have guessed him to have been anywhere from forty-five to sixty-five years old (he was seventy-seven), wearing a gray shirt and gray slacks, sporting a gold watch and diamond ring, and carrying three cell phones, which he laid out before him on the table. We took a seat in the far corner with my translator, a woman named Veasna, and beneath the rotating paddle fans that hung from the ceiling, drinking seltzer, Kar Savuth wanted to make something very clear. He saw himself as a medical doctor, with Duch as his patient. He understood his obligation to his client. But he was not willing to forget.

He was not willing to forget how they'd killed his brothers.

He was not willing to forget how they'd killed his cousin's entire family.

He could not forget his own feelings of survivor's guilt.

He could not forget watching a woman killed in front of him, her liver removed, cooked, and eaten by the soldiers . . . then her hip meat . . . then her breast.

Kar Savuth sat on the cushion edge of the rattan chair as he spoke, straight at attention, his face a mask. He said all of it without a trace of emotion. His strength seemed almost severe. When he himself had been interrogated, he told them he was a cyclo driver, and then they asked him the distance between two hospitals in the city. A month later, three months later, a year, and three years later, they asked him the same question over and over again. What is the distance between the two hospitals? If he'd changed his answer, they would have killed him.

And of course he remembered nearly starving to death, being so sick that his hair had fallen out. He'd playacted that he was clumsy so they might take pity—and ever after, he'd been clumsy, unable to relearn how to ride a bike, for instance. He'd even unlearned how to read. "It took a long time to become a human being again," he said.

And yet, he said, when he first met Duch, the former Khmer Rouge commandant had cried, overwhelmed by guilt, then gathered himself, pointing out that the first commandant of S-21 had been killed and that he knew it was only a matter of time before he himself would be killed, too. Duch asked Kar Savuth a question: If they told you they were going to kill your family, what would you have done?

And Kar Savuth said, "I would have done exactly what you did."

There have been many myths about the trials: One is that the Cambodians don't want them, that the two-thirds of the population born after 1979 think of the Khmer Rouge as a scary bedtime story they'd rather not hear, while the other third would rather not recall the actual horrors they actually survived, suffering still as they are from PTSD and ungovernable fear. Another is that they won't be able to handle the trials, that the idea of Western justice is foreign enough to the populace at large that a sentence other than life in prison (the death penalty is forbidden) will spark violence. And yet these misreadings—or half readings (of course, a third of the population *does* live in fear, but their Buddhist faith prohibits revenge killing)—by outsiders are just a continuation of centuries of *farang* misapprehension.

Despite the constant whiff of Western condescension that has hung over the country since the French made it theirs in 1863, the years leading up to the trials, and now the first trial, the Duch trial, have forced an important if uneasy reckoning. And in large part that reckoning was begun for his people by Youk Chhang.

Chhang was sixteen when the Khmer Rouge controlled the country and his sister was murdered before his eyes. Accused of stealing rice, she had her stomach slit open to prove her treachery (there was no rice there) and died a slow, painful death. After that—after becoming a refugee and making his way to America, to Texas—all Chhang wanted was revenge, Buddhism be damned.

An English teacher who befriended him, and who couldn't help but notice his anger, gave him a book about Cambodia by a man named Ben Kiernan with an inscription in her hand that read: "My friend Youk, Happy birthday. May you understand your country's history and may it help your dreams come true. . . ." As it turned out, Kiernan was a professor at Yale, Chhang sent him a letter, the two became friends, and when Kiernan received a half-million-dollar grant from the U.S. government to research the Khmer Rouge, he bought Chhang a plane ticket back to Cambodia—leaving Friday, January 13, 1995, a date Chhang will never forget—to begin compiling what became the largest archive of evidence chronicling the Pol Pot regime and what became the foundation for the prosecution of its leaders. Without the two of them, it's fair to say there might not have been any trials at all.

"He changed my life," says Chhang of Kiernan today, sitting among the piles of books and folders, dossiers and files in his cluttered office on the third floor of the Documentation Center of Cambodia. Chhang, forty-eight, wears a white pressed shirt and chinos. Before he had a staff and assistants, he worked virtually alone, going from village to village with a field recorder, interviewing victims but also interviewing the Khmer Rouge cadres (the farmers and shopkeepers, the teachers and laborers who executed, quite literally, the commands of their superiors). In the process, and as he collected letters, documents, ephemera of all sorts, he was able to map Angkar and its chains of command, the web of killing and unapologetic doctrine. In some villages, murderers and survivors lived across the street from each other, and he'd interview both—sometimes in each other's presence. But of the more than ten thousand Khmer Rouge cadres he and his fellow researchers have interviewed to date, only one has ever admitted to killing anyone, and in that case only "five or six people."

"We haven't begun to reintegrate ourselves with each other," says Chhang. "And that won't happen until the victims accept ownership of the atrocities—and the perpetrators claim responsibility."

In a rare interview at the end of Pol Pot's life, he rejected the idea that he had ordered a genocide, that he had anything to do with the deaths of nearly two million people, claiming that it was the work of unhinged elements—radicals, the Khmer Krom, the Vietnamese, et cetera—and that his conscience was clear. "When things get quiet, I go to bed at 6 P.M.," he said. "I sleep under the mosquito net by myself. My wife and my daughter live apart from me. Sometimes I do nothing, putting up with mosquitoes and insect bites. I get bored, but I'm used to it."

But Pol Pot had wrought another kind of stark loneliness.

One mother, feeling herself being sucked away by Angkar, dying slowly in a work camp, turned to her daughter and said, "You will have to learn to live without me now."

On the surface, Chum Mey had a typical story—if one measured such stories by torture endured, family members lost, atrocities witnessed, if one could ever accept the ingenious methods the Khmer Rouge had of robbing people of their dignity. Now he was an old man who no longer had the eyes or dexterity to repair sewing machines, and he walked slowly, carrying all of those invisible things bundled on his shoulders.

And yet he was almost natty, wearing a white watch cap, gray wool pants, a button-down short-sleeve shirt, and, from the country that produced garments for some of the world's best-known labels, a faux Versace belt. His face was open and almond-shaped, his eyes brown. He betrayed no hint of having been blindfolded for two straight weeks or stripped and hung like an animal from the crossbar as they'd whipped him with electric cords. I forced out the image of that metal bed and the pliers they'd used to remove his toenails or the electrodes they'd put to his ears until they'd shocked him unconscious. He'd begged a twenty-year-old kid to let him live (the boy called him by the vulgar form of you, *hein*). He had no idea what CIA or KGB stood for, but they wanted him to confess to being an agent for one or the other. He prayed to the spirits of his mother and father to protect him. On the day the other mechanics, his friends, were taken to the Killing Fields, there'd been a broken sewing machine. And here he was, one of only seven to have survived S-21. How many times had he wondered why he'd been permitted to live?

As it was, he'd been too afraid to meet me in a public place.

He claimed his life had been in danger for years, all because he'd been willing to tell his story, and there were those, the relatives of those headed to trial, who wanted him silenced. Who could question his paranoia? Who could blame him for relaying the intimate details of his trauma as if he were watching himself from very far away? So there we sat in Veasna's living room, in her new white house in a subdivision at the edge of the city as the land movers and bulldozers groaned outside, adding another walled ring to Phnom Penh as they excavated the skeletal past. Then, suddenly, the machines went silent. Lunch.

Chum Mey looked at his watch, worn on the wrist of the hand that the Khmer Rouge had broken when he raised it to block the bamboo stick whistling toward his face. He looked blurrily at the frosted-glass window as if trying to see out, unsure perhaps whether it was his eyes or the window itself that disallowed transparency.

"Eleven o'clock," he said. "This was always the time of day when the screaming was worst of all."

The Way They Killed, Part Four. Death became a pestilence: arbitrary, ravaging, and contagious. And it became a strange performance, too, the killers trying to outdo each other: At S-21, living prisoners were cut open with knives and scorpions were let loose inside their bodies.

The man painting the same image over and over, feverishly, incessantly—*green stroke, black stroke, the flesh-colored*—his name was Vann Nath. He, too, had lost a wife and his children. He, too, had been shackled at S-21, until they released him (*leave for using*) and brought him downstairs to a room where there were two other painters and a sculptor. He was given paints and a canvas and three days to regain his strength. He was handed a photograph and asked to make a "realistic, clear, correct, and noble reproduction" of it. He did not know, at first, that it was Pol Pot. For weeks, he woke at dawn and worked until midnight. When Duch arrived to evaluate his first painting, Vann Nath knew quite well that his life hung in the balance. The commandant looked at it for a time, then asked the opinion of another, who said it didn't exactly match the photograph.

"It's all right," responded Duch.

And that's why he lived.

I'd met with Vann Nath at his art gallery, which was attached to a restaurant his family ran on a busy street. Clad in a dirty gray dress shirt and green pants, he was sixty-three years old now, with a head of snowy hair, baleful eyes, bushy eyebrows, and a caramel complexion. During his time at S-21, he'd produced eight portraits and one sculpture of Pol Pot. After surviving the Khmer Rouge, he'd kept painting, feverishly, incessantly, but this time he depicted the scenes of torture at S-21. He painted Pol Pot's dystopia: the sweltering cellblock with fifty bodies in shackles; a prisoner having his fingernails removed in a torrent of blood; the whippings and near drownings; the starvation and degradation; throats slit and babies taken.

He had remarried, as many of the survivors had. After the decimation, after the sudden disappearance of the Khmer Rouge (one S-21 survivor, Chim Math, said her first act after freedom had been to eat three bowls of rice and then to break down weeping), they'd clung to each other; they'd tried as hard as they could to put it all behind them. But Vann Nath still had nightmares about Duch.

"For me, it's the wound that can't be healed. I knew the meaning and deepest horror of the Khmer Rouge. I lost my wife and children. When I think about it, I lose all my energy, all my bearings. It's only my grandchildren that can take away the deepest wound now."

"He who protests is an enemy; he who opposes is a corpse." One starless night, late, I went out to the hotel pool after the lights had been shut off, with that Khmer saying rattling in my head. While the courtyard was silent, I could hear the faint late-night noise of the city, like the distant breaking of glass. I lowered myself into the warm water and floated for what seemed like an hour, trying to process all the raw data of genocide as I did, and yet I felt nothing. No sense of agency or emergency. No point of connection. No language in the end to describe the fugue state that the country seemed to inhabit. Hyacinth and smoke mingled in the air. Cambodia kept passing me by in windows, but there was no way through. I felt utterly defeated: Who was I kidding, being here, as if to find a unified theory, practicing my own unknowing brand of exceptionalism—as if only I could understand? I floated like this for some time, letting it all stream out until I emptied my mind, until drifting off in the deep end, until Duch's question came back: If you'd been threatened with the death of your family, what would you have done?

What *would* I have done?

The Way They Killed, Part Five. There were so many ways they killed—it goes on and on—and none were ever tender. No method was somehow better than any other, more humane or considerate. This was murder, of course, but of the most heinous sort. Their acts came from the darkest part of the soul. In this instance, there was a soldier with a knife who cut the clothes off a pregnant woman. A deep incision was made in the flesh of the belly, there were screams and whispers and, finally, the stillness of death. That is, what came next, what was taken and hung by the neck, was as innocent as the act was unspeakable. They hung it with the others, in rows along the rafters, to ward off evil spirits. These were called the Smoke Children.

Chum Mey sat in silence for a moment, looked up from his watch at 11:01 A.M., and began speaking again, at first in a dull monotone. He spoke directly to Veasna and only occasionally met my eye. When I asked him questions, he sat looking straight ahead at the window. Then he spoke.

As the Vietnamese approached Phnom Penh, locked in a room with twenty others, you could hear bombs going off, and then you were herded with the last group from S-21, up the same road that you had disastrously traveled when evacuating Phnom Penh nearly four years earlier. At about 7 A.M., your group met up with another group of prisoners being herded by the Khmer Rouge, and in that group, in one of those strange moments of fate, were your wife and son, whom you hadn't seen in a very long time.

You watched her carefully as she walked ahead with your small son, both dressed as you were: in black pajamas. When the guards were at a distance, you spoke to her once about the scenery.

You did not touch.

By nightfall, it was clear you were being led to your deaths; members of the group were taken away, then gunfire erupted. When they took your wife and child, she screamed your name.

She screamed it over and over and over again: They want to kill us! Chum Mey, *run!*

Her voice stopped when two reports filled the air. And then you ran.

There can only be so much unmending of the body before one turns away.

In Long Beach, California, ten years after the war, at least 150 female Cambodian refugees were diagnosed with psychosomatic blindness, an otherwise incredibly rare occurrence. Doctors were perplexed: Their eyes were fine, yet they couldn't see. According to the therapists who studied the group, their blindness was "linked to a dissociated cluster of primitive meanings, horrific images, and behavioral responses or muscular representations loosely organized around the incomprehensibility of the events and the desire or 'need not to see.'"

As one survivor put it, "My family was killed in 1975, and I cried for four years. When I stopped crying, I was blind."

Ultimately, Duch, too, disappeared: into the jungle, to China, back to the jungle again. And then, unlike those he ordered to be tortured and murdered, he reappeared. He became a Christian. He was haunted and repentant. In 1999 he was arrested and later given counsel; François Roux and Kar Savuth were chosen to defend him.

By the rules of the ECCC, the pretrial discovery phase called for the accused to return to the scene of his alleged crime and stand before his accusers. And so on a February day, amid the rusted bed frames and bloodstained floor, Duch had stood before Vann Nath and Chum Mey and a group of other guards and survivors. He seemed so small, said Vann Nath afterward. But the painter was still filled with such fear, he couldn't look him in the eye.

And yet however one chooses to look upon it, something remarkable happened that day. Duch tried to speak to them as human beings. "I ask for your forgiveness," he said. "I know that you cannot forgive me, but I ask you to leave me the hope that you might," he said before breaking down on the shoulder of one of his guards. And after everything that had transpired, after all the atrocity, one of those gathered said, "I've been waiting thirty years for those words." But the other survivors said nothing.

When the ECCC officially commenced this past winter and Duch took the stand to begin a trial that will likely last until the new year, he looked tired. His face was swollen and his eyes were red. He sat at a raised podium while Kar Savuth and Roux sat slightly below in black robes and frilled white neckerchiefs. To hear Kar Savuth tell it, Duch has spent an awful lot of time crying over the past year.

So far, in the first phase of the trial, the defense's strategy has seemed somewhat straightforward. Duch denies little, shares what he can, tries to set the record straight. He has discussed his reasons for employing torture ("I never believed the confessions I received told the truth," he said. "At most they were 40 percent true") and the killing of babies ("I didn't remember it until I saw the pictures, but I am criminally responsible for killing babies, children, and teenagers"). He has discussed his beloved leader ("Pol Pot was a murderer. He was the greatest criminal father of Cambodia") and the fact that, steeped in Khmer Rouge propaganda, he honestly never knew that torture was illegal, had never heard of the Geneva Conventions until he'd been charged.

And he continues to apologize. Discussing the fact that he tortured two prisoners himself but asked his minions "to smash" many others, killing them by cutting their throats, he has said, "The burden is still on me—it's my responsibility. I would like to apologize to the souls of those who died."

Meanwhile, Roux and Kar Savuth continue to insist that Duch is being scapegoated, that he should be released from prison, that it's really Nuon Chea—Brother Number Two, the one from whom Duch ultimately took orders—who bears full responsibility for the deaths of hundreds of thousands of innocents. They claim their client faced execution if he didn't follow instructions. They seem to ask the same question Duch asked Kar Savuth when they first met: *What would you have done?*

And yet if this is the beginning of Comrade Duch's redemption, as Roux so insists, one wonders if he, the steely commandant of S-21, will finally have the stomach for it. Or if the ruination he sees in the mirror will finally crush him, too.

A Final Syllogism:

> For those in pain, there is no means to reconciliation.
> For those in pain, there is no means to reconciliation.
> For those in pain, there is no means to reconciliation.

In Veasna's living room, Chum Mey needed money to get home. He said he'd moved six times since the start of the pretrial hearings and now lived quite far away. He put on his white watch cap. His once-broken hand was crooked. His eyesight was going. Veasna offered him a ride, but when he refused, she gave him a few small bills.

Earlier I'd had a meeting with a top-level diplomat who'd said that the best Cambodians might hope for now was that this generation, both the perpetrators and the ones who had been so traumatized by the Khmer Rouge, might die off, and with them gone the country might start over again, afresh.

And here was one of the last of that generation, fading before me. The man who'd lost his wife and children, *Pa* to his family, the one who'd gone house to house in the ghost town of Phnom Penh collecting sewing machines to fix, the one who'd lost virtually everything and now moved again from house to house in utter fear and paranoia to keep ahead of his supposed enemies—how could one ever reach this man?

Veasna had something upstairs that she needed to retrieve before we left, too. So I went to the door and waited for Chum Mey to catch up. I was thinking about all the buried pain, everything I would never understand. Cambodia kept passing in windows. Yes, George Clooney was more than an actor. And here, halfway around the world, the room was blinding white, and since I couldn't speak Khmer, since I had no words, I didn't know what to do but keep smiling as Chum Mey approached. And *he* kept smiling, shuffling toward me, until I realized he had no intention of stopping.

Did he see me at all?

The old man kept walking, slowly, subtracting the space between us, until all of a sudden he came walking into me, our bodies pressed against each other, a trace of hyacinth and smoke in the city air, and he wrapped his arms around and rested his head on my chest.

Enough.

THE MAN WHO SAILED HIS HOUSE

LATER, LOST FAR AT SEA, WHEN you're trying to forget all you've left behind, the memory will bubble up unbidden: a village that once lay by the ocean.

Here are the neatly packed homes with gray-tiled roofs over which the mountains rise in rounded beneficence, towering over lush rice fields that feed a nation. Here are the boats that fish the sea, in all its blue serenity, and the grass in all its green. There is such peace in this picture of abundance: lumber from the mountain, rice from the field, fish from the deep ocean. People want for nothing here.

This village woven together by contentment is yours, Hiromitsu, and it is here, in the memory of it whole, that you know yourself best, the fourth-generation son of rice farmers. Here among a hundred wooden houses is the concrete one your family built. The house is made with metal pilings, which by your calculations will stand any high tide or errant wave. On your verdant plot a mile from the sea, a garden bursts with peonies, outbuildings sag, a koi pond teems. Here you live with your wife, Yuko, to whom you daily profess your love, and your parents, whom you still honor with the obedience of a child. In the barn are the pigeons you adore, for there's no more beautiful sight in the world than a flock mystically circling deep in the sky, then suddenly one breaking for home, wings aflutter, straining, as if to say, *I'm here*.

In this cage lie the chuckling pigeons, and in this barn of theirs, your happiness. Against the wall are full bags of rice seed—and from outside you can hear your wife's voice calling your name. *Hiromitsu.* Night falls—and in the bedroom you lie beside her. You will remember this later when trying to keep yourself alive: falling asleep one last time by the body of your wife in your house, beneath its roof of white tin, in the shadow of the sea.

Rise now, Hiromitsu, man of men, and accept your fate this day in mid-March 2011, a hint of sulfur in the salt air. Five-thirty A.M. and frigid, the first priority is, of course, the pigeons in the barn. Fresh water, their corn-wheat-and-barley mix bought from the shop. The wire cage holds all thirty iridescent heads bobbing as they hungrily peck. Out in that barn that holds your happiness, you often speak to them (*How did you sleep?*), call them by name, promise them their daily exercise (*We'll fly this afternoon*). When you were a child, they called you the Father of Pigeons as an insult, as if you would have no heir but these pea-brained winged things.

Down the driveway—past the koi pond and garden with the now-bare apricot tree and dormant peonies, past the greenhouse in which the rice seedlings grow—you turn up the road, past your tightly packed neighbors, past the nearby shrine, an ancient wooden building, then along Route 6, the sea to your right, all the way to your job in the lumberyard, your small white compact zipping between the lines—and twenty minutes later you're through the gates.

After hellos, you take your place in the first shed, running tree trunks through the table saw to make rough boards, the fanged blade in ceaseless rotation, throwing sawdust and the good, clean scent of cedar. Not an hour into the shift and your calloused hands are chapped red. But even this is familiar, an unspoken lesson taught decades before by your father in the rice fields: Work without complaint. Apply one's mind to the task at hand until everything else has been obliterated.

By noon, the sky has opened a little; a thin sun shines; clouds skim. And yet the cold gathers around you in the shaded shed, running the blade with stiff fingers. *One o'clock, two o'clock.* You watch the hours. Three is break time, in the wood-paneled room with the warm woodstove. Hot tea, rice crackers, and candy suckers. *Two-fifteen, two-thirty.*

At two forty-six, something rumbles from deep in the earth, a sickening sort of grinding, and then everything lurches wildly, whips back, lurches more wildly still. The cut boards stacked along the wall clatter down, and your first move is to flee the shed, to dive twenty feet free onto open ground and clutch it, as if riding the back of a large animal. Time elongates. Three minutes becomes a lifetime.

When the jolting ends, stupefaction is followed by dismay— and then a bleary accounting. Already phones are useless. The boss, Mr. Mori, urges you to rush home to check on your wife and parents, but fearing a tsunami, fearing a drive down into the lowlands by the sea, and trusting the strength of your concrete house to protect your wife and parents, you at first refuse. There are ancient stone markers on this coast, etched warnings from the ancestors, aggrieved survivors of past tsunamis—1896,

1933—beseeching those who live by the water to build on the inland side of their hubris or suffer the consequences.

The road is unbroken at first, until the third mile, where a depression has swallowed a rectangle of asphalt. There are downed lines and fallen trees—and yet the rice fields, fallow and unfazed, look exactly as they did this morning. The closer you come to home, the more alarming the damage grows: houses crumpled, windows shattered, sinkholes gaping.

Down near the shore, you pass a car heading inland, an old couple who appear to be *your parents,* whom you spy but do not exactly register in the fog of urgency, as you accelerate past the wooden shrine, through the dense neighborhood of houses, and turn finally into your drive. Immediately you observe that the storehouse wall has come down, and so have the tiles from the roof. Beams are cracked. The fertilizer barrel lies on its side. The walkway to the barn, however, has been meticulously swept.

Bounding up the stairs, you throw the door open to find the drawers have slid from the bureaus and the floor is snowed over with documents, receipts, and invoices. Your daughter, the one who lives in Tokyo now, in a mosaicked picture frame, your favorite heirloom, lies among shattered pieces. The Buddhist altar has been upended, the statue evicted. Everything once on the table litters the floor, including a bottle of wine. Out of all this mess, out of all the meaningful fragments in disarray, you can only think to bend down and pick up that meaningless bottle, replace it gingerly on the table. Your wife—where is she? Now your parents return, your father with that grim expression that belies his fear, beseeching you to follow them to your uncle's house on higher ground, just as Yuko's car glides down the driveway. She's been working out, of all things, at the gym. Her face is rosy. She says she only felt the quake as a tremor, had no idea of the damage until she got this far. She carries her worry well hidden. In the back of her car are the four twelve-pound bags of rice seedlings that need to be moved to the barn, and though you know the risks of dallying, rice is your history, your patrimony. You send your parents on their way with a promise that you will follow close behind. And some bifurcation of mind allows you to see a neighborhood—*your* neighborhood—damaged but still standing, on a quiet, mendable afternoon like any other.

So, let it be just another afternoon. Your parents leave. Yuko begins moving the bags from the car to the barn while you, Hiromitsu, take three cans of energy drink from the refrigerator and a box of caramels, go upstairs to assess the damage, then step out on the second-floor terrace. You don't look out to sea, not once; you stand staring at the mountain, Kunimi, in the distance. And now you can hear her downstairs, inside again, and now comes the creak of the bathroom door. Comes the sound of running water. Comes this vision of the mountain, placid, immovable—and then, to your right, to the north, within twenty feet, drifts the whole house of your neighbor. The house is moving past as if borne by ghosts. When you turn left, to the south and the garden, everything is as it's always been, dry and in place. When you turn back the other way, you can see only this coursing field of ocean.

And that's when you know you've been caught out, that you've squandered what time you had, that you must trust this house of concrete you've built to stand up to the sea. Your wife joins you on the second-floor terrace, reporting that she, too, saw the neighbor's house wash away. "We should run," she says, but you say, "It's too late." And then: "We'll be fine." Her arms circle your waist and lock there, while you stand stock-straight, gazing at the mountain, without daring to look back at the sea.

These will be your last words to her——*We'll be fine*. And you've already departed your body when everything seems to break beneath your feet and a roaring force crashes over you.

This force is greater than the force of memory, or regret, or fear. It's the force of an impersonal death, delivered by thousands of pounds of freezing water that slam you into a dark underworld, the one in which you now find yourself hooded, beaten, pinned deeper. The sensation is one of having been lowered into a spinning, womblike grave. If you could see anything in the grip of this monster, fifteen feet down, you'd see your neighbors tumbling by, as if part of the same circus. You'd see huge pieces of house— chimneys and doors, stairs and walls—crashing into each other, fusing, becoming part of one solid, deadly wave. You'd see shards of glass and splintered swords of wood. Or a car moving like a submarine. You'd see your thirty pigeons revolving in their cage. Or your wife within an arm's reach, then vacuumed away like a small fish. You frantically flail. *Is this up or down?* Something is burning inside now, not desperation but blood depleted of oxygen. What you illogically desire more than anything is to open your mouth wide and gulp. You scissor your legs. In some eternity, the water turns from black to gray, and gray to dirty green, as you reach up over your head one last time and whip your arms down, shooting for the light.

What you see when you explode into the air is a world swarming with burbling black water where one hundred homes once stood, pushing you inland on an oily swell. The mountains keep racing nearer. You're submerged up to your neck and carried with the current, flying by treetops, electrified by the cold water. It takes a moment to locate yourself here, to confirm that for the moment you're still living in this thin line between water and sky. In the frigid flow is half a roof, which just so happens to be yours. Frogging forward, you close the gap, try to lift yourself aboard, but your heavy clothes drag you down. You try a second time. And a third, arms wobbling until you fall back, exhausted. On the fourth attempt, you propel enough of your body out of the water to beach on the roof, then wriggle the rest of yourself to momentary safety. This is when you're overcome by two feelings: relief (*I'm alive!*) and disbelief (*Where has the whole world gone?*). The wave now surfs you deeper inland, over the homes of Mr. Yoshimura and Mr. Takahashi, Mr. Banba and Mr. Yamamoto (though the water is impenetrably black, you know this village by heart), and just when your forward progress slows (over the roof of the old-age home and the place where the hospital once stood) and is about to reverse direction, you think to jump, understanding that this may be your best opportunity to survive before the wave rushes back or another one speeds forward. The arm of a crane lies just ahead, at the water's edge, and yet you hesitate a second too long. The reversal of water begins as a sucking sound that gains intensity, amplifying, and then you're flying, faster and faster, backward over the village on a carpet of black water, to a line of froth where land and ocean formerly met, the mountains receding in a shot, and with them, everything you once thought immovable and holy. Where are you being taken? And what awaits you there?

So it is that you slide out into this nothingness. Tendrils of smoke rise from the country at your back; fires dot the coast. The slim chances of survival and the utter, certain loss of everything you call home makes you delirious, almost slaphappy. Hard to imagine that at 2:46 P.M. you were at the lumberyard, cutting boards, looking forward to your midafternoon break, and now at the hour when you'd normally be flying your pigeons, you're instead being pulled out into some watery oblivion under a low ceiling of gray cloud, a disconcerting smell of diesel on the air. Your body thrums with such adrenaline you feel nothing now. No thirst or pain, no fatigue or cold, though you've just been thrown into the ocean in March and are now exposed to near zero temperatures.

Your first thoughts turn to Yuko, how you're certain she's alive and certain she's dead, too, how your mind continues to hold these opposing ideas with the same fervor. On the one hand, in some myth, you'd like to believe she's become a mermaid. Or she was gently lifted and placed onshore, where she awaits your return like a seafarer's wife. On the other, doomed from the start, she was struck by a concrete pillar and went tumbling with the others. Or the watery hand held her down until she was motionless. And even as you play these scenarios, you're also imagining your parents, and how you're going to explain this to them, explain how, in the end, you happened to live while she disappeared, all because you didn't heed the tsunami warning—and their warning, too!

This line of thinking may kill you. It's vital to empty your mind of memory and remorse—the birds, the house, her—the might-have-beens (. . . *fingers loosening, then raking your body as she was swept away*), because you're an amnesiac speck who survives by the grace of some force you suspect may be circling to crush you. Be ready.

All your clothes—the two pairs of pants, the shirt and purple top, the green down jacket, even the watch on your wrist—all of it is intact, on your body, if drenched. The tsunami has taken more than twenty thousand lives, but from you, only your left shoe. And those caramels you stuffed in your pocket. The three cans of energy drink, mercifully, are still there.

At sunset, sky in scratches of purple light, a gnawing in your gut tells you it's dinner, so you crack open the first can, drink, then, head tilted back, try to lick out the last drop. The roof is perhaps twelve feet by six, of corrugated metal nailed to wooden beams, your raft at sea. Last night, you and Yuko slept beneath it, and now you perch atop it on the sea, above the goblin sharks and bodies and whatever else lurks below. Salt water laps up the sides, and any sudden movement immediately sets it seesawing. Sit still, in the middle—and as time passes, let the contrite sea bring gifts from the dead. This makes you giddy, too, the gifts. First it brings a red marker. Then the torn pages of a comic book, a manga, its hero, Captain Tsubasa, kicking a soccer ball with superhuman force. It brings some sort of red container that used to hold paint. It brings a tatami mat woven together with string, a broken radio, and a white hard hat. All of which you fish out of the murk. The hat (*To whom did it belong?*) immediately goes on your head, the marker in your hand. You imagine the dead offering you these things from underneath the sea. Hunched over the ripped comic, you test the marker on the damp page and write the following words in the margin: *On March 11, I was with my wife, Yuko. My name is Hiromitsu.* Then you tear the paper, fold it, place it in the red canister, seal it, and with the string from the mat, bandolier it to your body. Resume your pose.

Nighttime is a dark tunnel, starless and strange, the sound of water nibbling at the edges and in the distance the beating rotor blades of helicopters. You're being dragged, deeper to nowhere. You try your voice, just to keep yourself company. You sing to forget, pass time, stanch the fear. You sing to remind yourself that this is indeed you, in the wreckage of a debris field. It's an old song, your voice an imperfect husky tenor. On a raft drifting farther out to sea, you sing about high school.

Red evening sun is casting its shadow, . . .
Our voices bounce in the shadow of an elm tree.
Ah, we are third-year high school students.
Even if we get separated
We will be classmates forever.

Now the temperature drops—and as it does, your senses return. You sit, holding yourself in a tight ball, hands pulling knees to chest. The key is not to sleep. You remember this from a famous Japanese adventurer you once saw on television. *Do not sleep. Also: Do not think of Yuko tumbling beneath. Do not think of pigeons.* What's surprising is how strong your mind is, how well you forget, how childlike your wonder remains. You've maintained your optimism—an odd word given what's befallen you, but that's what it is, an openness to being bemused or astonished. You've tapped into some hidden spring of endurance. You're open to little miracles now, so let one come.

The blue light appears from the depths, shining up through the inky water. In your ball on the roof, you find yourself surrounded, inexplicably bathed by luminescence. You squint but can't identify the source. Might these be the spirits of the dead, meant to convey a message of hope or allegiance rather than surrender? That's how you take it, at least. And if a picture could be made of this moment, then the world would see you—the man named Hiromitsu—seated in serene meditation, staring in awe at the blue light that comes from the abyss, then laughing out loud.

At sunrise, the scene resolves itself: the black water, the blue sky, a thin band of land on the far horizon. Soon you will see an explosion, in the vicinity of the nuclear power plant, a loud blast and then a rust-colored cloud rising ominously, in atomic layers. *Do not look back.* You notice a fishing rod floating alongside you, one you glimpsed the night before, and realize that you're traveling in a slow-moving whirlpool of sorts, the same relics recurring, new ones entering the gyre and orbiting the roof as it gets sucked out farther and farther.

Yesterday seems long ago, and today, you tell yourself, must be the day of your rescue—you're willing it so. The helicopters come close, circling for survivors, and the dozen times you hear one, you climb to your feet, scream, and wave. There are boats in the distance, cutters and smaller lifeboats trolling, and for those, you holler even louder, though time after time they turn back before reaching your debris field, your minuscule ring of ocean. Is it that they don't believe anyone could be this far out?

In between, you fish more objects, including a futon and blankets, which you lay out in the sun to dry. You write in the margin of the comic book. *I just want to report that I am still alive on the twelfth and was with my wife, Yuko, yesterday. She was born January 12 of Showa 26.* You fold the page, place it in your empty can, and, ripping more string from the mat, tighten it across your chest, adding one more testimonial to your body.

So the hours linger, the sun beats, rust-colored smoke rises, and now you can feel your thirst clawing. Drink the second energy drink in slow, intermittent sips. When it's gone, you're gripped by an animal urge that nearly upends the disciplined regimen you've set for yourself. You fight the need to drink that third energy drink, hand fluttering for the holster—no, save it for tomorrow, if luck brings you that far. This is when you think to drink your pee. You collect it in your hands three times and drink—warm but not terrible.

There's another problem, too: The wood of the roof has become waterlogged, weak and rotten. And from time to time a low rumble comes up from the deep, aftershocks. At first the sound is startling but then you only worry about the waves. Has a swell begun to rise? What approaches from the east? You now have waking dreams, hallucinations: You're convinced you see a body coming near, and start screaming—*Help me!* But then it's a tree trunk. In another you see a huge wave hurtling toward the roof and imagine turning into a tree to save yourself. But just as you think to stand and hang your arms like branches, you stop yourself for fear the roof will tip.

One other thing: You're not uninjured after all. A nerve at the top of your palm has been cut—how you're not sure—but it radiates sharp pain. And your eyes have begun to swell shut. You opened them underwater, now some infection blurs your sight. Still you sit, knees drawn up, white hard hat in place for safety. Safety is important, you know that. You work in a lumberyard. You live in a village by the sea with your parents and wife, Yuko. You will be rescued soon, by concentrating on the sounds, engines and rotors and waves. On a scrap of wood, you write with the red marker—*SOS*—and if any machine approaches, even remotely, you stand and yell and wave at it. *Please.*

You muster the energy to sing again, same school song, second verse in your now hoarse tenor (*Help me!*):

> We had a day in tears.
> We had a day in jealousy.
> We will fondly remember those days.
> Ah, we are third-year high school students.
> Once you take her hand at folk dancing,
> Her black hair smells sweet.

A fat statuette of Daikoku, a god of fortune, bobs by, the round belly and happy demeanor, the rice barrels at his feet that signify plenty, plucked from someone's home and delivered here to you, a very good omen. His name translates as "the god of great darkness," and yet, as he wields a mallet, his broad smile conveys contentment. You think to bring him aboard, but you no longer trust the roof, nor your ability to balance on it. So you allow a small acknowledgment of the moment: one more laugh in diminishing light, the last of your good cheer.

Exhaustion, in its full flower, strikes on the second night as the ocean air drops to freezing. You can't keep from shaking, even wrapped in blankets. You crave sleep, a desire to be curled in bed. And in your mind, remembering stories from youth, you imagine yourself as the hero who survives the great calamity only to face, in a moment of cosmic irony, a different death. Dehydration, hypothermia, bodily dysfunction.

The second night is interminable. The stench of oil thickens as you shrivel. The water seems to rise. The grinding reverberates from the center of the earth. The roof is disintegrating beneath your feet. If there's a force trying to crush you, you realize now that it's neglect. Where nature brought the full bore of her attention on you, cleaving you from all that was precious, it has abandoned you here, in these black, oily fields. No singing now. At some point, the blue light returns—billowing pods, otherworldly ocean mushrooms, phosphorescent jellyfish, it turns out—but if someone could see you in that supernatural glow, they'd see a thin, hunched man, mouth in that grim line of your father's. You're too tired to be amused or feel optimism. The light can't feed or save you. Maybe it's not a sign after all. The tunnel narrows. You write another note, to your parents this time. *I am sorry for being unfilial,* it says.

Let it go, Hiromitsu, man of men. You had your reasons for staying—and you stayed. Two days before, there'd been another tsunami warning that came to naught. Some had rushed to high ground, and then . . . nothing. In a land of tremors and quakes, of errant waves and a history of coastal destruction, the people had grumbled a little. Too many false warnings—and with so much to get done. And when you came home and found the contents of your life strewn on the floor, willy-nilly, all the desire to flee left you. You decided to abdicate to nature—or stand up to it—because somewhere inside, you had a flash of invincibility; that is, you thought, *If my life is worthy and my house is well made, it will be strong enough to stand up to the wave—and the moon and stars* (none of which care for you, Hiromitsu, nor soothe nor feed nor augur). You realize now that once you arrived home, once shown the precious thing about to be taken away forever, once you saw the garden and barn, the koi pond and the pigeons, and Yuko arrived with the rice seed, you knew you wouldn't be able to leave—that you would be doomed by obligation and memory and sentimental attachment—which is how you've ended up here now, on the roof of your house, nine miles out to sea.

Let morning come. Let it come and with it all the helicopters and boats gathered around in some holy convocation, to rescue you from the rising sea and the goblin sharks, for you are pure, Hiromitsu. Or let morning come and suck you down in the last black hole, for you are not. After focusing so intently on survival, it almost doesn't matter now. You can't keep from shaking in the cold, and there may be advantages to slipping quietly under the cover of ocean (for one, to join your wife, whom you know to be both alive and dead, a mermaid and a body tumbling). But then you're imagining your parents again, both sitting around a low table, wordless, tea untouched. How could you ever explain to them that, after failing to heed the tsunami warning, after standing up to the wave in your concrete house and being smashed by your hubris in the form of tons of rushing water, after somersaulting and surfacing and clambering to safety, after being dragged out to sea and neglected there as you can see in the far

distance your ruined country in little fires on the coast, after
mustering your optimism and hope and fighting so hard to live
(three times you collected and drank your own pee), you came to
the third day and swaddled in last testaments roped to your body,
with visions of those who bore you in mind, how could you explain to them—your mother and, most especially, your father—
that you finally just gave up?

On that last morning, when the light leaks up from the water and
bleaches the sky, you fumble for the third energy drink, tip it to
cracked lips, and slurp greedily. You're too weak to stand now,
body swollen, hands frozen, your voice hoarse from yelling. You
sit on your roof, on the futon, cross-legged, unmoving like a
statue, wearing a white hard hat. You hold up your scrawled message, too—*SOS!*—so blurred by the water you can't even read it,
but still, you're not of logical mind. Perhaps someone else can.

At first you listen for the whirring sound of helicopter rotors or the gurgle of a boat engine. Even the faintest murmur
sparks an attempt to rise, shout, wave. But as the hours pass, you
descend into yourself, shutting the cupboards one by one. The
rice, the pigeons, the lumberyard, Yuko, your parents, your
daughter: It wasn't such a bad life, but for the ending. The debris
field has become so thick it looks like land, and the oil keeps
spreading. You're too tired to think or care. Head bowed, you
focus only on what's right before you, the fringe where the rot-
ted roof is being licked by salt water. Soon, you know, the dark
flank of sea will transform into rolling hills of water, and another
wave will come for you. Now black water bubbles up through the
planks and scraps of corrugated tin. A last note to your parents:
I'm in a lot of trouble. Sorry for dying before you. Please forgive me.

Just before you lie down on the futon and wait for death,

there comes a disturbance on the horizon again, the faraway shape of a boat, the whir of a propeller at the edge of your mind. The sound brings you shakily to your feet, where you shout and wave . . . until you watch the boat turn away, diminishing on the horizon.

A terrible lonesomeness fills this void now. It would be good to sleep, though that surely spells the end. But it's over now. In your beleaguered twilight, you either see or dream that the receding boat has changed course and is circling back. But who can trust these visions anymore? Before your eyes, it seems to grow into a gray lifeboat with one, two, three . . . *three times that,* nine rescue workers in green bodysuits and gray life vests. When the boat doesn't turn away, when you can feel a searchlight on your skin, you let loose your last primal yawp, "Help me!"

Out of the oblivion, a clear voice responds, "We're here," and the boat drifts alongside your roof-home, and the voice asks, "Which side is safest?" And you say, "The side toward land, please," as you strip the plastic container full of notes from your body and place it on the altar of your futon. Then one of the bundled figures steps out of the lifeboat onto the tippy roof and comes toward you with arms outstretched. The figure leads you across, five paces, and only when you lean forward into their boat and splay your body over its hard gunwale, like a glorious falling tree, do you know it's real. Immediately you're wrapped in blankets by the incredulous men. They want to know who you are, hand you yet another can of energy drink. Speechless, you take a long slurp, then burst into uncontrollable tears. *Who are you?* Your memory opens suddenly to a fire truck on the road before your house just before the wave, the loudspeaker announcement over and over again, "Please evacuate." And you remember directing your wife to move the rice seed into the barn while you went up to the terrace to stand lookout. Even a quarter mile to higher ground and she would otherwise be safe.

You're tested for radiation, transferred to a naval destroyer, and given porridge and *umeboshi,* pickled plum. You're placed in a hot bath, and the crew members are shocked by the amount of mud that comes off your body, even as you continue to shiver with such violence that they must remove your body from the warm water. Then you're on a helicopter, airlifted over the ravaged coastline—the ground below silt-blackened as if burned, the pornographic wreckage of houses and buildings, colorful entrails of bedsheets and curtains, people below digging with their bare hands for children, parents, spouses, mothers washing dead babies with spit—to a hospital outside the radiation zone. Meanwhile, the images of your rescue have been televised across the world, the man on his roof, dragged nine miles out to sea, found on the third day, a day almost devoid of survivors but you.

If you had supernatural powers, Hiromitsu, or thought yourself prophetic, now would be the moment to deliver your message to the world. Now would be your moment to make an example or speak uplifting words. To transubstantiate into a symbol. Of hope. Perseverance. Strength. For the news reports call you a miracle.

But you're more humble than that—and broken—fearful as well, for now you must tell your parents, your daughter, everyone, exactly what happened. You would rather make yourself invisible—almost rather have drowned—than reveal your disobedience, your stubborn selfishness, for that's what you think of it as: the sins of a child. You lie in your hospital bed with IVs, doctors who come and go. You're dehydrated and whittled down, face unrecognizable at first, bruised and cut but nonetheless in good recovery. You're out of the hospital that evening, and when you first see your father at your uncle's house, you're surprised by how spry he seems. In the days before the tsunami, he'd been struggling with his health, and slid downhill when you went missing, unable to sleep or eat. He wouldn't listen to the radio or watch the news. But your mother says that when friends arrived to say that you had floated onto the television screen that third day, he seemed to regenerate. In what is for him a great show of emotion, he says, "I'm glad you're alive. Many people made mistakes. You need to keep living." That's it—no encouragement or criticism, no questions, as if he doesn't want to know.

Of course, you tell your mother everything, because underneath, she's stronger than he—and then, shortly after, you go to Tokyo and you meet your daughter at the Kawasaki train station, standing anonymously among the hordes. You haven't seen your daughter cry since she was a teenager. And after a quick hug, describing how it was you who suggested that Yuko carry the rice seed to the barn while you went and stood on the terrace staring at the mountain, as your daughter reads between the lines (*You could have saved yourselves*), her expression even now is unchanging. She tells you she's glad that you're alive, and you believe her. When you've finished, she seems to absorb the truth—that her mother is gone, but that you've returned—and says, "Well, then, you must feel better, for you're talking a lot." Whatever else she thinks she holds inside and turns to go home, swallowed by the crowd. And you—you can't return to your razed house, to your neighborhood between the sea and the mountain, but relocate to a suburb of Tokyo, to a subsidized apartment big enough for you and your parents, in which you dream of the place you just left.

These are strange days, in this anonymous eight-story beige structure where, at first, you know nobody—and where the world carries on without reflection, the bustle of salarymen in the stations and streets, traffic rushing somewhere. You say nothing about who you are to the neighbors but spend your time trying to keep busy, all in order to forget, too. Unbidden, you begin a daily sweeping of the walkways at the complex. You and your broom, hoping to make yourselves useful. You also try to spend time with your grandson, who is now a short commute away, but of course mothering doesn't come as naturally to you as it did to Yuko. And so between your parents, who sit all day watching television in sad nostalgia for everything lost, and your daughter, whose life is busy and now motherless, your displacement is complete.

You're not a poet, in fact you've never read, let alone written, much of anything in your life—Yuko read feverishly, as if she were running out of time—and yet ever since you scribbled that first note on the roof at sea, words have become a conduit. They make the pain smaller, you say. Now you write poems and short fables, reflections and admonitions. All the scraps go in a black bag belted to your waist, the vault of your collected emotions and memories. You write one poem, "A Song of Five Lines," that goes as follows:

> Missing:
> How many days later
> Will you appear in my dream
> My beloved
> Wife?

This is how you speak to her, through the scraps in the bag, but also aloud sometimes. Before eating, you might murmur, "Thank you," as if she's prepared the food on your plate. You might do the same on a beautiful day, as if she's created it. And before bed each night, you tell her you love her. You say this to her presence or spirit, but you forgo mementos, little altars, or pictures on the wall. You can't bear the idea of seeing her again, as you knew her in all those endless days before the wave.

Here's how you think about it: Together you constructed

many things throughout your life. Then her body disappeared, but the constructions still remain. Human beings die: That's natural. But to accept her death is to lose all hope. And yet you know now in retrospect that there were so many small goodbyes, foretellings, and encouragements. There was a dream you had in the months before the tsunami: You were alone and couldn't find your wife—everywhere you looked, she wasn't there—and you woke up instantly, thinking, *I need to find an accountant,* because she did all the accounting. There was a trip Yuko made to see your grandson, one that lasted more than a week. She returned home and told you that since you'd survived ten days without her, cooking and cleaning, you were now ready for anything. And then, of course, she habitually ribbed you. If it came down to it, she'd ask, if the world came to an end and you could take only one thing with you, would it be the pigeons or me?

"The pigeons," you would say, just to see that look on her face, that instant of mock anger, admiration, and uncertainty.

Three months later, in June, you go back, traveling on the bullet train two hours north under hazy sun to the city of Fukushima, continuing to the coast by car. Unable to stay away, your parents have recently returned to the village, moved into temporary housing there, one-room modules in clusters off a main road, each with a television, a refrigerator, some rudimentary furniture, a latrine. The clothes are hung on hangers off nails in the wall. After driving through the mountains, through fluctuating radiation levels, a landscape steeped in cesium that will persist for decades, your first stop is the lumberyard where Mr. Mori, the boss, removes his white hard hat and greets you with bows that you return in double. "How is everything?" he asks after the formalities, placing a hand at the center of your back as he leads

you out into the yard, and you respond by saying, "She's still missing," and he shakes his head *what a shame*.

Mr. Komuro, Mr. Tomita, and all the other workers: They're
astounded and pleased to see you, so pleased that they keep asking, "When are you coming back?" You smile, for this is something you want more than anything—*to come back*—but have no
answer. Or do, but don't say: *I'm trying to fill the space left behind
by my wife*. They intuit some part of this anyway. Two here have
lost their homes; a colleague at a nearby yard died; Mr. Hamau-
chi, in the office, has lost his father, his body identified by DNA.
Most all of the men operated the heavy machinery—the back-
hoes and forklifts—used to try to dig out the tar-filled bodies
buried by the sea. Yours isn't the only survivor story they tell in
the yard. They tell of people swept off in cars who lived, of families carried inland who clung to trees, and when the wave sucked
back out to sea, it cleaved the wife, the husband, the child. "We
had a regular life until we felt how great the power of nature
could be," says Mr. Mori. "I went to the hills and watched the
waves coming. I could see people running, like it was a movie."

"I was too scared to look at the ocean," you say in return. "I
looked at the mountain."

And then you head toward the sea, to where the house once
stood. The landscape appears bulldozed, miles of decimation,
houses lopped from the earth as if they were rice stalks, chunks
of concrete set at unsettling angles. Your neighbors have lost six
of seven in their family; another family of four has disappeared.
Babies and grandparents alike, gone. Three hundred yards from
the ancient wood shrine is your driveway. Now down you go,
past the imaginary garden of corn and onion, potato, garlic, and
taro. The imaginary peonies are in full bloom, the invisible apricot tree bears small fruit, the imaginary koi pond teems. Here
was the greenhouse where the rice seeds were planted; the ware-

house that kept the machines, the combine, tractor, and rice-drying apparatus; the barn that kept your thirty pigeons. Perhaps, in the end, you did love them best, for they seemed unlovable to everyone else.

Your folly, the concrete house, is a pile of rubble. *(Here is the kitchen and here is the bathtub; here is the bedroom with the roof above.)* The foundation remains, a last footprint, but there's nothing else: no garden or outbuildings. Not even her ghost lingers. By the ruined koi pond, in a desolation of cinder block and metal rod, is a note intended for Yuko, left by one of her best friends, set beneath a rock near a guttering candle.

"I've come here for you," it reads. "How long are you going to play hide-and-seek? That's enough. Come out! . . . Yuko, can you hear me?"

Before the trip back to Tokyo, you visit your uncle, who has kept something for you. He reaches into the closet, wrestles with a heavy bag, and there on the floor at your feet are the clothes they found you in, nine miles out to sea.

Here is the flannel shirt and here are the pants. Here's the purple fleece—and the green down jacket. Here's the comic-book page scribbled with your note (*I'm in a lot of trouble . . .*) and the container in which you placed that note. And so you take them with you, the magical clothes that you wore on the last day of your former life.

You sleep that night in the makeshift home of your parents, on the floor beside them, listening to them breathe. You rise early so your father can cut your hair, the cold silver blade against your head while you sit under his hand, wordless, with gratitude. You ride the bullet train south, disembark at Kawasaki station to walk to your new home, the empty apartment, where you will sweep the sidewalks. You are here now, alive, adrift. The crowd—the salarymen and the schoolkids, everyone on their busy way—swells. It rises around you and bears you aloft and out into the light, where birds, too lovely and painful to gaze upon, swarm the sky.

THE HOUSE THAT THURMAN MUNSON BUILT

I GIVE YOU THURMAN MUNSON IN the eighth inning of a meaningless baseball game, in a half-empty stadium in a bad Yankee
year during a fourteen-season Yankee drought, and Thurman
Munson is running, arms pumping, busting his way from second
to third like he's taking Omaha Beach, sliding down in a cloud
of luminous, Saharan dust, then up on two feet, clapping his
hands, turtling his head once around, spitting diamonds of saliva:
safe.

I give you Thurman Munson getting beaned by a Nolan
Ryan fastball and then beaned by a Dick Drago fastball—and
then spiked for good measure at home plate by a 250-pound co-
lossus named George Scott, as he's been spiked before, blood
spurting everywhere, and the mustachioed catcher they call
Squatty Body/Jelly Belly/Bulldog/Pigpen refusing to leave the
game, hunching in the runway to the dugout at Yankee Stadium
in full battle gear, being stitched up and then hauling himself back
onto the field again.

I give you Thurman Munson in the hostile cities of

America—in Detroit and Oakland, Chicago and Kansas City, Boston and Baltimore—on the radio, on television, in the newspapers, in person, his body scarred and pale, bones broken and healed, arms and legs flickering with bruises that come and go like purple lights under his skin, a man crouched behind home plate or swinging on deck, jabbering incessantly, playing a game.

I give you a man and a boy, a father and a son, twenty years earlier, on the green expanse of a 1950s Canton, Ohio, lawn, in front of a stone house, playing ball. The father is a long-distance truck driver, disappears for weeks at a time, heading west over the plains, into the desert, to the Pacific Ocean, and then magically reappears with his hardfisted rules, his cold demand for perfection, and a photographic memory for the poetry he recites . . . *No fate, / can circumvent or hinder or control / the firm resolve of a determined soul.*

Now the father is slapping grounders at the son and the boy fields the balls. It is the end of the day and sunlight fizzes through the trees like sparklers. As the boy makes each play, the balls come harder. Again and again, until finally it's not a game anymore. Even when a ball takes a bad hop and catches the boy's nose and he's bleeding, the truck driver won't stop. It's already a thing between this father and son. To see who will break first. They go on until dusk, the bat smashing the ball, the ball crashing into the glove, the glove hiding the palm, which is red and raw, until the blood has dried in the boy's nose.

I give you the same bloody-nosed boy, Thurman Munson, in a batting cage now before his rookie year, taking his waggles, and a lithe future Hall of Famer named Roberto Clemente looking on. Clemente squints in the orange sun, analyzing the kid's swing, amazed by his hand speed, by the way he seems to beat each pitch into a line drive. If you ever bat .280 in the big leagues, he says to Thurman Munson by way of a compliment, consider it a bad year.

When the Yankees bring Thurman Munson to New York after only ninety-nine games in the minors—after playing in Binghamton and Syracuse—he just says to anyone who will listen: What took them so long? He's not mouthing off. He means it, is truly perplexed. What took them so goddamn long? Time is short, and the Yankees need a player, a real honest-to-God player who wants to win as much as blood needs oxygen or a wave needs water. It's that elemental.

And wham, Thurman Munson becomes that player. He wins the Rookie of the Year award in 1970. He takes the starting job from Jake Gibbs as if the guy's handing it to him and plays catcher for the next decade, the whole of the seventies. He's named the Yankees' first captain since Lou Gehrig forty years earlier and shows up at a press conference in a hunting vest. He wins the Most Valuable Player award in 1976, and he still wears bad clothes: big, pointy-collared shirts and dizzying plaid sport coats. Not even disco explains his wardrobe. He helps lead the Yankees from a season in which the team ends up twenty-one games out of first place to the 1976 World Series, where they fall in four straight to the Cincinnati Reds despite the fact that Thurman Munson bats over .500. Then he helps take the Yankees back to the Series in 1977 and 1978—two thrilling, heaven-hurled, city-rocking, ticker-tape-inducing wins!

And shoot if those seventies teams weren't a circus. The Bronx Zoo. Manager Billy Martin dogging superstar Reggie Jackson, superstar Reggie Jackson dogging pit bull Thurman Munson, pit bull Thurman Munson dogging everyone, and then George—you know, Steinbrenner—the ringmaster and demiurge, the agitator and Bismarckian force who wants to win as badly as Thurman Munson. Birds of a feather. And alongside, a hard-nosed gaggle of characters—Catfish Hunter, Graig Nettles, Ron Guidry, Lou Piniella, Sparky Lyle, Mickey Rivers, Goose Gossage, Bucky Dent, Willie Randolph—who are fourteen and a half games behind the Boston Red Sox in late July 1978 and come screaming back to beat them in a one-game playoff to win the division, then trounce the Royals to win the pennant and thump the Dodgers to win the World Series. One of the greatest comebacks of all time.

And since this is New York, the press has an opinion or two. They call Thurman Munson grouchy, brutish, stupid, petty, greedy, oversensitive. It becomes a soap opera: Thurman Munson pours a plate of spaghetti on one reporter's head and nearly kicks another's ass. But the fans—all they see is this walrus-looking guy who plays like he's a *possessed* walrus. During a game against Oakland, when he commits an error that scores Don Baylor and then he subsequently strikes out at the plate, they heap all kinds of abuse on him, and, heading back to the dugout, he just ups and gives them the finger. Hoists the finger to everyone at Yankee Stadium. That's not family entertainment! The next day when he comes to bat, when his name is announced and Thurman Munson steels himself for a rain of boos, the same fans begin to applaud, then give him a tremendous ovation.

See why? Bastard or not, the man cares. Thurman Munson cares. Never backed down from anyone in his life—not his father, not another man, not another team, let alone fifty thousand fans calling for his head. And they love him for it. To this day they hang photographs of him in barbershops and delis and restaurants all over the five boroughs—all over the country. A Thurman Munson cult. Tens of thousands of people who bawled the day he died.

Including me.

So, I give you a boy—me—and a pack of boys: Bobby Stanley and Jeff DeMaio, Chris Norton and Tommy Gatto, Keith Nelson and John D'Aquila. All kids from my neighborhood, playing ball in the 1970s. All of us—each of us—pretending to be someone else: Catfish Hunter pitching to George Brett or Ron Guidry pitching to Carl Yastrzemski or Reggie Jackson or Lou Piniella or Graig Nettles batting against Luis Tiant in the ninth inning of a hot summer eve in suburban Connecticut as blue shadows fall over the freshly mowed backyards.

In our town's baseball league, I play catcher. I suit up in oversized pads and move as if I'm carrying a pack of rocks on my back. When a pitcher starts out shaky—maybe walks the bases loaded and then walks in a couple of runs to boot—I call time and trot out to the mound, kick some dirt around, chew gum. Keep throwing like that, I say, but can you try to throw strikes?

And, naturally, my man is Thurman Munson. Or not so naturally. I mean, why would a skinny, hairless nine- or ten- or eleven-year-old twerp identify with a gruff, ungraceful grown man who's known to throw bats at cameramen? What shred of sameness could exist between a do-gooding altar boy and a foul-mouthed truck driver's son? But then, just playing Thurman Munson's position bestows some of his magic on me. Each wild pitch taken to the body, each bruise and jammed finger, is in honor of the ones taken by Thurman Munson. Each foul tip to the head becomes a migraine shared with Thurman Munson, and each hobbled knee brings a boy closer to the ecstatic revelations of a war-tested veteran, pain connecting two human beings on a level that goes beneath intellect and experience and age. Goes to a feeling. Writ on the body. We are the same dog.

At night during these muggy summers, my brothers and I watch the Yankees on television. When Munson takes the field and crouches behind home plate, or when he comes to bat, spitting into either glove and turtling his head once around, we watch. We watch him hoofing in the batter's box like an angry bull, excavating the earth, twinkle-toeing a pile of it in circles

like a ballerina, and then digging in. For some reason, his presence is mesmerizing. He bears a striking resemblance to the
butcher at our local supermarket: the same weak chin, the same
fleshy cheeks. He has a number of tics and twitches—cocks his
head, messes with his sleeves—as if being harassed by horseflies.
Yet somewhere deep in those brown eyes, he is as calm as a
northern pond waiting for ducks to land. In that place he is seeing things reflected before they actually happen, and then he
makes them happen.

And there is one magnificent night—October 6, 1978—
when Thurman Munson drives a Doug Bird fastball as deep as
you can take a pitcher to left-center field at Yankee Stadium for a
playoff home run that seals the deal: Yankees beat the Kansas City
Royals 6–5 despite George Brett's own three home runs and
then beat them once more for the pennant and it's nothing but
bedlam. At the stadium, the dam explodes; in this Connecticut
suburb where the leaves are turning in the fingers of an autumn
chill, four boys pump their fists, hooting and hollering and then
rioting themselves—pig-piling, whacking one another with pillows, hyperventilating with happiness. A free-for-all!

So I give you a boy and a neighborhood of boys and a town
of boys. I give you a suburbia of boys, and I give you five boroughs
of boys, a city following a team that is a circus. A stitched-together
bunch of brawlers and hustlers, cussers and bullies, led by their
captain, who, as Ron Guidry puts it, can make you laugh and then
just as soon turn around and put a bullet through your chest.

I'm not sure how the news about Thurman Munson gets
out—maybe someone's older brother hears it on the radio or
maybe someone's mother sees it on television. A friend dons a
Yankee uniform and disappears inside his house, watching the
news behind drawn curtains with his father and brother. Another
friend hears about it in the backseat on the way to football prac-

tice and puts on his helmet to blubber privately, behind his face mask. Another simply won't come out of his bedroom.

For me, August 2, 1979, has been like other summer days: swim-team practice, some baseball, lawn mowing, then down to the Sound with a friend to swim again. And that's where I hear that Thurman Munson is dead. I'm dripping salt water, and someone's brother says that Thurman Munson was burned alive.

When I get home, the downstairs is empty. Somewhere I can hear running water—my mom pouring a bath for my youngest brother. Something is cooking and I turn on the television. An anchorman and then the wrecked Cessna Citation, a charred carapace emblazoned with NY15, and strobe lights everywhere like some strange Mardi Gras.

It was an off day for the Yankees, and Thurman Munson was practicing takeoffs and landings, touch-and-gos. He'd had less than forty hours of experience with his new jet, and he accidentally put it into a stall. The Cessna dipped precipitously before the runway. It scraped trees, tumbled down toward a cornfield, hit the ground at about 108 miles per hour, spun, and had its wings shorn off. It crashed a thousand feet short of the runway and sailed to a stop some five hundred feet later, on Greensburg Road. The two other passengers—a friend and a flight instructor—survived, and they tried to drag Thurman Munson from the wreckage. He was conscious, probably paralyzed, calling for help. And all of a sudden jet fuel leaked, pooling near Thurman Munson, and the Cessna exploded.

Afterward, he was identified by dental records. Nearly 80 percent of his body was badly burned. The muscles of his left arm were wasted. He had a busted jaw and a broken rib, and the corneas of his eyes were made opaque by flame. He had a bruised heart and a bloody nose.

"The body is that of a well developed, well nourished, white

---

male," read the autopsy, "who has been subjected to considerable heat and fire, which has resulted in his body assuming the pugilistic attitude."

The truth is I've had only one hero in my life. And his death coincided with a hundred little deaths—of boyhood, the seventies, a great Yankee team, an era in baseball, some blind faith. I didn't go Goth after Thurman Munson's death, I just changed a little without knowing it, in full resistance to change. And to this day, I don't understand: What happens when your hero suddenly stands up from behind home plate, crosses some fold in time, and vanishes into thin air?

One answer: You go after him. You enter your own early thirties and, crossing the same fold, you try to bring him back, if only for a moment. You go to Canton, Ohio, on a hot day not unlike the day Thurman Munson died, to the house that Thurman Munson built, a fourteen-room colonial set on a knoll, a house with pillars out front like some smaller, white-brick, suburban version of Tara, and meet Thurman Munson's family—his wife, Diana, and the three kids: Tracy, who has three kids of her own now; Kelly, who just got married; and Michael, who was four when his father died and who himself played catcher in the Yankees' farm system.

Their father has been gone twenty years and they still don't exactly know who he is. Or he is something different for each of them, and then different in each moment. An ideal, an epiphany, a hero, a heartache. People didn't know Thurman, says Catfish Hunter today, they just loved the way he played. And sometimes his wife didn't know the real Thurman, either. He might visit some kids in a hospital, and later, when Diana learned about it, she'd get angry and say, Why didn't you tell me, your own wife?

'Cause you'd go tell the press, said Thurman Munson.

Maybe I would, she said. And why not? They think you're a spoiled ballplayer.

And Thurman Munson said, That's why. That's exactly why.

Show the world that he was a goofball? A sap? A romantic? The man was a koan even to himself—he couldn't be figured or unraveled. He'd help lead the Yankees to a World Series victory— one of the proudest, sweetest moments of his life, he told Diana—then, based on some perceived locker-room slight, re- fuse to go to the ticker-tape parade.

There were five, six, seven Thurman Munsons, not count- ing his soul, and the one who mattered most was the private one, the one who came walking down a long hall like the one at the beginning of *Get Smart,* with doors and walls closing behind him. When he walked over the threshold after a long road trip, he'd hug his wife and say "I love you" in German. *Ich liebe dich.* He wrote poetry to her. He scribbled philosophical aphorisms. He loved Neil Diamond—"Cracklin' Rosie," "I Am . . . I Said"— played the guy's music nonstop, incessantly, ad infinitum, ad nau- seam, carried it with him on a big boom box. Thurman Munson, the grim captain, identifying with picaresque songs about being on the road, lost and alone against the world, having something to prove, falling in love.

And the kids went bananas every time he came home, hang- ing off him like he was some kind of jungle gym. Two doe-eyed girls and a young, redheaded son who was afraid of the dark. Thurman Munson would sit at the kitchen table and eat an entire pack of marshmallow cookies with them. He'd take barrettes and elastic bands and disappear and do up his hair and then leap out of nowhere, Hi-yahing! from around a corner, wielding a baseball bat like a sword, doing his version of John Belushi's samurai. After the girls took a bath, Thurman Munson did the blow-drying. Then he combed out their hair. He never hurt us, remembers

Kelly, the second daughter. I mean, our mom would kill us with that stupid blow-dryer and brush, and he said, I don't want to hurt you. And he took so much time and our hair would be so smooth and he'd take the brush and make it go under and then comb it out.

When Michael, the youngest, couldn't sleep, his father went to him. As a kid, Thurman Munson was afraid of the dark, too, but in his father's world, Thurman Munson would lie there alone; you were humiliated for your fear, and you learned to be humiliated—often. On the day Yankee general manager Lee MacPhail came to Canton to sign Thurman Munson, the boy's father, Darrell, the truck driver, lay in his underwear on the couch, never once got up, never came into the kitchen to introduce himself. At one point, he just yelled, I sure do hope you know what you're doing! He ain't too good on the pop-ups!

But Thurman Munson would sit with his own boy in the wee hours—at two, three, four, five A.M. Often he couldn't sleep himself, lying heavily next to Diana, his body half black-and-blue, his swollen knees and inflamed shoulders and staph infections hounding him awake. So he'd just go down the hall and be with Michael a while. Just stretch out in the boy's bed. It's all right, he'd say. There's nothing to be afraid of.

And maybe, too, he was talking to himself, his body having aged three years for every one he played. So that at thirty-two, after a decade behind the plate, his body was old. In the very last game he played, he started at first but left after the third inning with an aggravated knee, just told the manager, Billy Martin, Nope, I don't have it. Went up the runway and was gone. But it was his body that was making money, realizing a life that far exceeded the life that had been given to him—or that he'd dreamed for himself. Including the perks: a Mercedes 450SL convertible, real estate, a $1.2 million Cessna Citation.

It's a life that Diana remembers wistfully when we go driving. We visit the cemetery. We talk about the current Yankees, and she confesses that she's just started following the team closely again, wonders if Thurman Munson means anything to today's players, is more than just some tragic name from the past. Like with her young grandkids, who know him as a photograph or an action figure.

Diana takes me to the crash site, too. Maybe takes me there to prove that she can do it, has done it, will do it again. Did it six months after the crash when the psychiatrist said that maybe Diana and the kids were always late for counseling because Diana was afraid to pass the airport. Maybe Diana is always late, thought Diana, because she has three little kids and no husband. And, right then and there, she put them in the car and drove to Greensburg Road, to the very place where Thurman Munson's plane left black char marks on the pavement. To prove to them—and herself—that Thurman Munson doesn't reside in this spot, five hundred feet away and forty feet below the embankment to runway 19 at Akron-Canton Regional Airport. The distance of one extremely long home run. No, she says to me now, he may live somewhere else, but he doesn't live here.

So I go to see Ron Guidry and Lou Piniella, Willie Randolph and Reggie Jackson, Bobby Murcer and Catfish Hunter. At Fenway, I talk to Bucky Dent. I talk to Goose Gossage and Graig Nettles. I go to Tampa and sit with the Force himself, George Steinbrenner. The old Bronx Zoo, minus a conspicuous few. There are stories about Thurman Munson, a thousand, it seems. Funny and sad and inspiring. And these men—they, too, are by turns funny and sad and inspiring.

When I visit Ron Guidry at his home in Lafayette, Louisiana, he's working alone in the barn, chewing tobacco. He's about to turn forty-nine, the same number he used to wear when he was pitching, when he was known as Gator and Louisiana Lightning. He looks as if he just stepped off the mound—all sinew and explosion. He works part-time as a pitching coach for the local minor league team, the Bayou Bullfrogs, and shows up for several weeks each year at the Yankees' spring-training facility in Tampa. Mostly, he hunts duck.

He remembers his first start as a Yankee. He came in from the bullpen, nervous and wired, and Thurman Munson walked up to him and said: Trust me. That's it. Trust me. Then walked away. As Guidry remembers it, everything after that was easy. Like playing catch with Thurman Munson. Thurman calls a fastball on the outside corner. Okay, fastball outside corner. He calls a slider. Okay, slider. Eighteen strikeouts in a game. A 25–3 record. The World Series. Just trusting Thurman Munson. Can't even remember the opposing teams, Guidry says, just remember looking for Thurman's mitt. Remembers that very first start: Thurman Munson came galumphing out to the mound, told him to throw a fastball right down the middle of the plate. Okay, no problem.

But I'm gonna tell the guy you're throwing a fastball right down the middle, says Thurman Munson.

Guidry says, Now, Thurman, why'n the hell would you do that?

Trust me, says Thurman Munson. Harrumphs back to the plate. Guidry can see him chatting to the batter, telling him the pitch, then he calls for a fastball right down the middle of the plate. Damn crazy fool. Guidry throws the fastball anyway, batter misses. Next pitch, Thurman Munson is talking to the batter again, calls a fastball on the outside corner, Guidry throws, batter swings and misses. Talking to the batter again, calls a slider, misses again. Strikeout. Thurman Munson telling most every batter just what Gator is going to throw and Gator throwing it right by them. After a while Thurman Munson doesn't say anything to the batters, and Gator, he's free and clear. Believes in himself. Which was the point, wasn't it?

I find Reggie Jackson at a Beanie Baby convention in Philadelphia, sitting at a booth. He's thicker around the waist and slighter of hair, but he's the same Reggie, by turns gives off an air of intimacy, then of distance. He's here to sign autographs and hawk his own version of a Beanie Baby, Mr. Octobear, after his nom de guerre, Mr. October—a name sarcastically coined by Thurman Munson after Reggie went two for sixteen against the Royals in the 1977 playoffs, before he redeemed himself with everyone, including Thurman Munson, when he hit three consecutive World Series dingers on three pitches to solidify his legend. Manufactured by a California company, the Octobear line includes a Mickey Mantle bear and a Lou Gehrig bear—and a Thurman Munson bear, too.

I don't like doing media, says Reggie. You can't win, and there's nothing for me to say. And then he starts. Says Thurman Munson was the one who told George Steinbrenner to sign Reggie Jackson. Says he never meant for there to be a rift between Reggie Jackson and Thurman Munson, that he mishandled it, and when that magazine article came out at the beginning of the 1977 season—when Reggie was quoted as saying that he was the straw that stirred the drink and Thurman Munson didn't enter into it at all, could only stir it bad—that's when Reggie Jackson was sunk.

I would take it back, says Reggie. I was having a piña colada at a place called the Banana Boat, and I was stirring it and I had a cherry in it, some pineapple, and I said it's kind of like everything's there and I'm the straw, the last little thing you need. That killed my relationship with Thurman, me apparently getting on a pedestal, saying I was the man and then disparaging him.

Near the end in 1979, says Reggie, we were getting along really well, and I was really happy about it, because feelings were rough there for a long time. You know, I wanted his friendship, and he wanted to make things easier.

The day of the crash, Reggie had business in Connecticut. I'll never forget that day, he says. I had on a white short-sleeve and a pair of jeans and penny shoes and I was driving a silver-and-blue Rolls-Royce with a blue top. Heard it over the radio: A great Yankee superstar was killed today. And at first, I thought it was me. I wanted to touch myself. I went like that . . . Reggie grabs his forearm, a forearm still the size of a ham hock, squeezes the muscle, tendon, and bone. He seems moved, or just spooked by the memory of how he imagined his own death being reported on the radio. He's driving his Rolls-Royce, and he's here at a Beanie Baby convention. He's hitting a home run at Yankee Stadium, and he's here, twenty years later, going down a line of autograph seekers, shaking with both hands, as if greeting his teammates one last time at the top of the dugout steps.

Of course, everyone else remembers that day, too. Bucky Dent was told by a parking lot attendant after a dinner at the World Trade Center and nearly fainted. Catfish got a call from George Steinbrenner and went across the street and told Graig Nettles, who was already talking to George himself, and both of them thought it was a joke at first, that someone was putting them on. Goose Gossage and his wife were in the bedroom, dressing to go see a Waylon Jennings concert. It was just, God damn, says Goose. We all felt bulletproof, and then you see such a strong man, a man's man, die. . . . Then it's like we're not shit on this earth, we're just little bitty matter.

Lou Piniella remembers arguing past midnight with Thurman Munson at Bobby Murcer's apartment in Chicago a couple of nights before the crash—the Yankees were in town playing the

White Sox; Murcer had just been traded from the Cubs back to the Yankees—arguing about hitting until Murcer couldn't stand it anymore, took himself to bed at about 2:00 A.M. Piniella was poolside at his house when George called. I was mad, says Piniella, now the manager of the Seattle Mariners, sitting before an ashtray of stubbed cigarettes in the visitors' clubhouse at Fenway before a game against the Red Sox. He doodles on a piece of paper, drawing staffs without notes. Over and over. I was mad, he repeats. I'm still mad.

Bobby Murcer, the last player to see Thurman Munson alive, remembers standing at the end of a runway with his wife and kids at a suburban airport north of Chicago where Thurman Munson was keeping his jet, declining his invitation to come to Canton, watching Thurman Munson barrel down the runway in this most powerful machine, then disappearing in the dark. Remembers him up there in all that night, afraid for the man.

And George Steinbrenner remembers it today in his Tampa office, surrounded by the curios of a sixty-nine-year life, some signed footballs, some framed photographs. He dyes his hair to hide the gray, but seems immortal. The living embodiment of the Yankees past and present. He has the longest desk I've ever seen.

He remembers clearly when Thurman came to his office at Yankee Stadium, flat-out refused to be captain, said he didn't want to be a flunky for George, and George finally talked him into it, said it was about mettle, not management. He remembers flying out to Canton at Thurman's request to see Thurman's real estate, eating breakfast with the family. And, of course, he remembers the day. He got a call from a friend at the Akron-Canton Airport and at first he didn't put two and two together, not until the man said, George, I've got some bad news. Then it hit him.

I just sat there, says George Steinbrenner now, folding his

hands on his lap. Sat paralyzed. Everything about Thurman came flooding back to me—his little mannerisms and the way he played. When George could move his arms again, he picked up the phone and started calling his players. I don't think the Yankees recovered for a long time afterward, he says. I'm not sure we have yet.

It's 1999 at Yankee Stadium. A papery light and the good sound of hard things hitting. And yet again, there are new faces, new names: Derek Jeter, Bernie Williams, David Cone, Paul O'Neill, Roger Clemens. Luis Sojo jabbering in Spanish, cracking up the Spanish-speaking contingent, Joe Girardi chewing someone out for slacking through warm-ups ("Keep smiling, rook," he says, "keep smiling all the way back to Tampa"), Hideki Irabu in mid-stretch, a big man from Japan, messing with a blade of grass, lost in some stunned reverie, contemplating his next move.

It's a team that last year came as near to perfection as any team in history, with a 125–50 record. If the 1977 Yankees, with their itinerant stars, were the first truly modern baseball club, then the 1998 Yankees were the first modern team to play like a ball club of yore, with no great standout, no uncontainable ego. A devouring organism, they just won.

The problem with a year like 1998 is a year like 1999: a great team playing great sometimes and looking anemic at other times. But always haunted: Paul O'Neill haunted by the 1998 Paul O'Neill; Jorge Posada haunted by the 1998 Jorge Posada. And then every Yankee haunted by every Yankee who's ever come before. Ruth, DiMaggio, Mantle. To this day, even though the clubhouse is a packed place—Bernie Williams is jammed in one corner with his Gibson guitar and crates of fan mail; big Roger Clemens is jammed next to O'Neill, no small man himself—

Thurman Munson's locker remains empty. It stands near Derek Jeter's, on the far left side of the blue-carpeted clubhouse, near the training room, a tiny number 15 stenciled above it.

When I ask Jeter if he remembers anything about Thurman Munson, he smiles, looks over his shoulder at the empty locker, and says, Not really. He was a bit before my time. Jeter is twenty-five, which would make him a Winfield-era Yankee fan. But when I ask Jeter if anyone ever uses it, even just to stow a pair of cleats or some extra bats or something, he looks at me quizzically and says, Uh, no, it's like his locker, man. It still belongs to him.

In Jorge Posada's locker, among knickknacks that include a crucifix and a San Miguel pendant, he's got a picture of Thurman Munson, in full armor, accompanied by a quote from a 1975 newspaper article: Look, I like hitting fourth and I like the good batting average, says Thurman Munson. But what I do every day behind the plate is a lot more important because it touches so many more people and so many more aspects of the game.

It's a sentiment that the twenty-seven-year-old Posada takes to heart. And it's not just Posada. Sandy Alomar, Jr., the catcher for the Cleveland Indians, wears number 15 on his uniform in memory of the man he calls his favorite player, a connection he was proud to acknowledge even when the Indians met the Yankees for the American League pennant last year. He says it brings him luck.

I try to imagine guys like Derek Jeter and Jorge Posada five, ten, fifteen years from now. Even as they've really just begun to play, they will stare down the ends of their careers, on their way to the Hall of Fame or whatever endorsement deal or restaurant ownership pops up. You play hard, hoard your memories, and then suddenly you can't see the ball or you get thrown out at second on what used to be a stand-up double, you separate a shoulder that won't heal or just miss your wife and children, and then you go home to Kalamazoo or Wichita or Canton, Ohio. And then who are you, anyway? Just another stiff who played ball.

Except you get the second half of your life. You get to try to resurrect yourself as the person you most want to be.

The house that Thurman Munson built first appears in a vision. One day Thurman Munson and his wife are driving around the suburbs of New Jersey when they turn a corner. Thurman Munson hits his brakes and says, Whoa, I have to live in that house! I'm serious, Diana, that's my dream house! It speaks to some ideal, something orderly, regal, and Germanic in him, a life beyond baseball, an afterlife, and he sheepishly rings the doorbell and does something he never does. I play catcher for the New York Yankees, he says, and I have to live in this house. I mean, not now. . . . I just want the plans. I promise you I won't build this house in New Jersey. This will be the only one of its kind in New Jersey. I'd build it in Canton, Ohio. This house. In Canton.

The woman eyes him suspiciously, takes his name and number, says her husband will call him. He figures that's the end of that. But the husband calls. Invites the Munsons for dinner. By then Thurman Munson has composed himself, and the man eventually gives him the plans. And then it really begins—years of Sisyphean work. First they have to find the perfect piece of land, which takes forever. Then, instead of hiring a contractor, Thurman Munson subs out the job, picks everything right down to the light fixtures himself. He gets stone for the fireplace from New Jersey; stone for the rec room from Alaska; stone for the living room from Arizona. He wants crown moldings in all the rooms. He wants a lot of oak and high-gloss and hand-carved cabinets. In the rec room, a big walk-down bar . . . then, no, wait a minute, not a big bar, a small bar, and more room to play with the kids. Pillows on the floor to listen to Neil Diamond on the headphones.

He flies home on off days during the season to check how things are going. But they're never going well enough. Thurman Munson rages and bellyaches. He throws tantrums. He has walls torn down and rebuilt. He chews out the workers like Billy Martin all over an ump. Like his own father all over him. The guys start to hide when they know he's coming. Sure, you want your house to look nice, but this guy's nuts. He's dangerous. He's Lear. He's Kurtz. He's a dick.

And the stone keeps coming. From Hawaii, Georgia, Colorado . . .

Then finally it's done. It's 1978. Thurman Munson's father, the truck driver, has abandoned his mother, moved to the desert, is working in a parking lot in Arizona, a dark shadow in a shack somewhere, and Thurman Munson moves his own family into the house that Thurman Munson built.

Something lifts off his shoulders then—after all the tumult, after the two World Series victories, after his body has begun to fail, after the constant rippings in the press. And yet, he's also become more inward and circumspect. He doesn't hang out with Goose and Nettles and Catfish for a few pops after games anymore. No, many nights, nights in the middle of a home stand, even, he goes straight to Teterboro Airport, where he keeps his plane, and flies back to Diana and the kids, follows the lights of the highway, the towns of Lancaster and Altoona and Clarion flashing below and the stars flashing above, until Canton appears like a bunch of candles. Sometimes he's home by midnight.

And here's the odd thing now: There's always someone in the house when he comes through the door. There's Thurman Munson and Thurman Munson's wife and Thurman Munson's kids, but there is someone else, too. A part of himself in this house. A presence, a feeling around the edge of who he is that waits for a moment to penetrate, to prick his consciousness, to change him once, forever.

Until it does: One summer evening on a day with no game when Thurman Munson has had three home-cooked meals and the family has finished dinner and the kids are playing. Diana is in the kitchen tidying, washing dishes. Thurman Munson is wearing a blue-and-white-checked shirt and gray slacks. He rolls up his sleeves, lights a cigar, goes out back, and lounges in a lawn chair, feet up on the brick wall. He's never one to relax, always has a yellow legal pad nearby, running numbers for some real estate deal. But it's that quiet time of evening, a few birds softly chirping in the maples, blue shadows falling over the backyard, the sweet scent of tobacco. Thurman Munson just gazes intently at the sparklers of lights in the trees, a wraith of smoke around him.

Diana glances out the kitchen window and sees his big, blue-and-white-checked back, sees Thurman Munson shaking his head. A little while later she looks out the window and again he's shaking his head. And then again, until she can't stand it any longer, and she barges out there and says, What are you looking at? Why are you shaking your head? Thurman Munson doesn't seem to know what to say, but when he looks at her, his eyes are all lit up and he's crying. It's one of the only times she's ever seen him cry.

I just never thought any of this would be possible, he says. And that's it. For one brief moment, the man he is and the man he wants to be meet on that back lawn, become one thing, and then it overwhelms him.

After the crash, the psychiatrist told Diana to get rid of her husband's clothes quickly or it would just get harder and harder. So that's what she did, she got rid of Thurman Munson's clothes, the hunting vest and bell-bottom pants, the bad hats and suits and coats. It took an afternoon, going through his entire wardrobe. Sometimes it made her laugh—to imagine him again. Sometimes it was harder than that. And she got rid of almost everything.

But that blue-and-white-checked shirt—she kept that.

I go to Catfish Hunter's farm in Hertford, North Carolina, not far from the Outer Banks, on a swampy summer night. He owns more than a thousand acres, grows cotton, peanuts, corn, and beans, and after retiring at the age of thirty-three, this is where he came. Always knew he was going to come back here after baseball, just thought his daddy would be here, too. But he died a week before Thurman Munson. The darkest days of Catfish's life. Out in the fields, living with the ghost of his father, sometimes something would pop into his mind and he would remember Thurman.

He could make a $500 suit look like $150, says Catfish now, then he smiles. In the past year, the fifty-three-year-old former pitcher has been diagnosed with amyotrophic lateral sclerosis, or Lou Gehrig's disease. Started as a tingle in his right hand when he was signing autographs down at Woodard's Pharmacy for the Lions Club in the spring, then he had to use two hands to turn the ignition on his pickup when he went dove hunting, by Halloween knew something was seriously wrong, and now his arms hang limply at his sides. Seems farcical and cruel. The same arm that won 224 games, that helped win five World Series rings, that put him in the Hall of Fame, lies dead next to him. Wife and kids and brothers and buddies help feed him, take him to the pee pot. And then no telling what the disease will do next.

If Thurman had played five more years, he'd own half the Yankees, says Catfish. Everybody liked the guy. The whites, the blacks, the Hispanics. We sit on a swing by the side of the house, the fields stretching behind us, family and friends out on the front lawn watching Taylor, the four-year-old grandchild, bash plastic baseballs with a plastic bat. A fly buzzes Catfish, but he can't lift his arms to wave it away. Even if he could, I'm not sure he would now. Remembering Thurman Munson keeps bringing Catfish back to his father, the proximity of their deaths, a double blow with which he still hasn't really come to terms. And his own condition—a thing suddenly hurtling him nearer to the end.

Every time I came home from playing ball, says Catfish, the first thing I always did was go over and see my dad. He lived seeing distance from here. My wife said, You think more of your daddy than you do of me. And every day that we went hunting, my wife would fix us bologna-and-cheese or ham-and-cheese sandwiches and every day I ate two and he ate one. When Thurman died, his uniform was still hanging in his locker. I just thought he was going to come back. Every time I walked in the clubhouse, I thought he was coming back.

His eyes well with tears, he seems to look out over the road, reaching for his daddy again or Thurman Munson, then shakes his head once. Remembers a story: Pitching to Dave Kingman in the All-Star Game, the same Dave Kingman who hit a Catfish change-up in a spring-training game for a home run the length of two fields, and here he is again, and here is Thurman Munson calling for a change-up again. Catfish shakes it off and Thurman Munson trundles to the mound, says, Gotta be shitting me, won't throw the change-up. Millions of people watching tonight that'd love to see him hit that long ball. Oh, let him hit it as long as he can! Munson goes back, shows the change-up, Catfish throws a fastball and pops him up. When he goes to the dugout, Thurman Munson shakes his head. Gotta be shitting me, he says, won't throw the change-up, then walks away.

Yes, Thurman Munson might put you on like that, but Catfish says he only saw him truly angry once. Saw the napalm Thurman Munson, the one who sought to undo the other Thurman Munsons. Some corporate sponsor gives Munson and Catfish a white Cadillac to drive around for the summer, and the two cruise everywhere in it. One night after a game, they walk out and see the front windshield is smashed, all these glass spiderwebs running helter-skelter. Catfish isn't happy, but Thurman Munson starts cussing and ranting and raving. He says, I'm gonna kill whatever sons of bitches did this! He goes berserk. Stalks toward the Caddy, opens the trunk, and suddenly pulls out a .44 Magnum revolver.

Catfish is standing in front of the Caddy, and when he sees Thurman Munson with that .44, his eyes nearly pop out of his head. He goes, Holy shit, Thurman, you got a gun!

I'm going to kill them, says Thurman Munson.

Kill who? says Catfish.

Kill whoever it is I see on the other side of that fence.

Don't load that gun, says Catfish.

Yes, I am, says Thurman Munson. And he does—then raises it, points it at shadows moving behind the fence, and fires. Crack!

Shit! yells Catfish.

Thurman Munson fires at the shadows again, and again—Crack! Crack! Without thinking, Catfish rushes him, gets his own powerful paws on the Magnum, and wrestles it away. Please, God, don't let someone be hit, prays Catfish out loud, because now my fingerprints are all over that damn thing.

I didn't hit anybody, says Thurman Munson. But I'm gonna run them over.

And that's what he tries to do. He gets in the car and barrels through the parking lot, people leaping out of the way.

Goddamn, you're crazy, says Catfish. Even today, Catfish can't figure it out. Could have ended up killing someone, thrown in prison. The man he says he loves actually shot at those shadows.

It's getting on toward evening now. When it's time for dinner, Catfish's wife comes and fetches us. Without my knowing it, I have been invited to stay. Because of Thurman Munson. And so I stand with Catfish Hunter and his family before a table full of food—lobster, a pan of warm corn bread, mashed potatoes, and slaw—on a June night in North Carolina, cicadas droning, heat releasing from the earth. Twenty of us gathered in a circle— fathers and sons, mothers and daughters—and everyone joins hands. Even Catfish, though he can't raise his at all. His wife takes his right hand and, following her lead, I take his left. A heavy, bearlike thing, warm and leathery and still calloused from farming. I bow my head with all of them. And we pray.

I give you a boy and a man, a son and a father—and then the father's father. Together for the first time, at Thurman Munson's funeral. The son wears a miniature version of the Yankee uniform that his father wore. The father lies in a coffin. And his father, the truck driver, has magically appeared from Arizona, sporting a straw sombrero. For a thin, hard man, he has a large nose.

It's the biggest funeral Canton has seen since the death of President McKinley, thousands gathering at the orange-brick civic center, hundreds more lining the route as the hearse drives to the cemetery. Thurman Munson's old golf buddy, a pro, waits on a knoll at the local course and doffs his cap when Thurman Munson passes. All the Yankees are there. Bobby Murcer and Lou Piniella deliver the eulogy. And that night Murcer, who's not penciled into the starting lineup, asks to play, knocks in five runs, including a two-run single to win the game, and limps from the field held up by Lou Piniella, then gives his bat to Diana Munson. A bat kept today somewhere in the house that Thurman Munson built.

When the hearse arrives, Thurman Munson is wheeled into

a mausoleum, followed by his family: Diana; the kids; Diana's mother, Pauline; and Diana's father, Tote, who over the years had become Thurman Munson's best friend. The old man, the truck driver, stands apart. When he's asked by a stranger how long it's been since he last saw his son, he says, Quite a while, quite a while. Thurman never found himself, he says.

Then he does something disturbing. The truck driver holds an impromptu press conference, not more than fifty feet from Thurman Munson's coffin, telling a group of reporters that his boy was never a great ballplayer, that it was really him, Darrell Munson, who was the talent, just didn't get the break. Later, he approaches the coffin and, according to Diana, addresses his son one last time, says something like: You always thought you were too big for this world. Well, look who's still standing, you son of a bitch.

That's when Tote can't stand it anymore. He rises from his seat, meaning to tear him limb from limb. The police jump in and the old man, Darrell, is escorted from the cemetery, vanishes again, back to the desert, a shadow in a shack somewhere.

And what happens to the son? Michael Munson is graced and doomed by his own name. He grows up and wants to play baseball, builds a batting cage in the backyard. As a sophomore in high school, he can't hit breaking balls or sliders, but he busts his ass until he can. He wills himself to hit. And then he does. He goes to Kent State, his father's alma mater, and stars as an out-fielder. In 1995, the Yankees sign him to their rookie league, switch him to catcher. Must think it's in the genes.

He goes over to the Giants and then winds up in Arizona, in the desert. He wakes at dawn, gets to the ballpark an hour and a half before everyone else. He's pale-skinned and freckled, has bright, clear eyes, the body of his father. He puts on his uniform and lifts, then runs and stretches. His arms bear bruises, his knees swell like grapefruits, the back of his neck is sun-scorched.

And every day he plays in the shadow of his father. He won't let himself be outhustled, outworked, outthought, if he can help it. Because now when he goes back and watches those old Yankee games, he can see what his dad was thinking, how he called a game, how his quick release came from throwing right where he caught the ball, how he had as many as ten different throwing motions depending on the ailment of the day, how he did a hundred little things to win. He can see his dad jabbering incessantly and smacking his mitt on Guidry's shoulder after a win. He can see how his teammates looked up to him. And it's something like love. He sits and watches his dad crouch behind the plate, in a tight situation, maybe bases loaded and the Yankees up by a run, maybe Goose on the mound, the season on the line, and Thurman Munson, the heart and soul of those seventies teams, doesn't even give a signal. Just waves, like, Bring it on, sucker. Trust me.

So I give you a boy—me—and a pack of boys and neighborhoods of boys who have grown into men. We are now stockbrokers and real estate agents, computer consultants and a steel guitarist for a country-western band. Some are buried in our hometown cemetery, and the others are fathers or fathers to be or have dreams of kids. My brothers are all lawyers, and I live in a house that I own with a woman who is going to be my wife.

I did cry the day Thurman Munson died. I'm glad to admit it. And I cried the night I left Catfish Hunter in North Carolina, driving straight into a huge orange moon. I hadn't cried like that in years, but I was thinking about them—and myself, too—and I just did.

What happens when your hero suddenly stands up from behind home plate, crosses some fold in time, and vanishes into thin air?

You go after him.

So I give you Thurman Munson, rounding third in the half-light of the ninth inning and gently combing out the hair of his daughters. I give you Thurman Munson, flying over America, looking down on the same roads his father drives, and returning home to his wife, speaking the words *Ich liebe dich*. I give you Thurman Munson shooting at shadows and leaping into the arms of his teammates. I give you Thurman Munson beaned in the head and sleeping next to his son again.

I give you the man on his own two feet.

THE LAST MEAL

THE NIGHT BEFORE THE LAST MEAL, I visit a stone church where Mass is being said. In the back row, a boy sits with his mother, his head tilting heavenward, tongue lolling, grunting, watching in an unfocused way the trapped birds that flutter and spin in the height of the church vault. About a hundred yards away, in the immense holy hangar, tulips bloom on the altar. It's the end of December— gray has fallen over Paris—and the tulips are lurid red, gathered in four vases, two to a side. A priest stands among them and raises his arms as if to fly.

Last I remember, I was on a plane, in a cab, in a hotel room—fluish, jet-lagged, snoozing. Then, by some Ouija force, some coincidence of foot on cobblestone, I came to a huge wrought-iron door. What brought me here to France in the first place was a story I'd heard about François Mitterrand, the former French president, who two years earlier had gorged himself on one last orgiastic feast before he'd died. For his last meal, he'd eaten oysters and foie gras and capon—all in copious quantities—

the succulent, tender, sweet tastes flooding his parched mouth. And then there was the meal's ultimate course: a small, yellow-throated songbird that was illegal to eat. Rare and seductive, the bird—ortolan—supposedly represented the French soul. And this old man, this ravenous president, had taken it whole—wings, feet, liver, heart. Swallowed it, bones and all. Consumed it beneath a white cloth so that God Himself couldn't witness the barbaric act.

I wondered then what a soul might taste like.

Now I find myself standing among clusters of sinners, all of them lined in pews, their repentant heads bent like serious hens. When the priest's quavery monotone comes from a staticky speaker, cutting the damp cold, it is full of tulips and birds.

Somewhere, a long time ago, religion let me down. And somehow, on this night before the last meal, before I don a white hood, I've ended up here, reliving the Last Meal, passing my hand unconsciously from my forehead to my heart and to either shoulder—no—yes, astonishingly pantomiming the pantomime of blessing myself.

Why?

When it comes time for Communion, why do I find myself floating up the aisle? Why, after more than a decade, do I offer my tongue with the joy of a boggled dog and accept His supposed body, the tasteless paper wafer, from the priest's notched, furry fingers? Why do I sip His supposed blood, the same blood that leaves a red stain on the white cloth that the priest uses to wipe my lip? Why am I suddenly this giddy Christ cannibal?

At the end of Mass, the priest raises his arms again—and the grunting boy suddenly raises his, too, and we are released.

Then I find the hotel again. I lie awake until dawn. Fighting down my hunger.

That's what I do the night before the last meal.

On his good days, the president imagined there was a lemon in his gut; on bad days, an overripe grapefruit, spilling its juices. He had reduced his affliction—cancer—to a problem of citrus. Big citrus and little citrus. The metaphor was comforting, for at least his body was a place where things still grew.

And yet each passing day subtracted more substance, brought up the points of his skeleton against the pale, bluish skin. He spent many of his waking hours remembering his life—the white river that ran through his hometown of Jarnac, the purple shadows of the womblike childhood attic where he had delivered speeches to a roomful of cornhusks. He sat, robed and blanketed now, studying how great men of ancient civilizations had left the earth, their final gestures in the space between life and death. Seneca and Hannibal went out as beautiful, swan-dive suicides; even the comical, licentious Nero fell gloriously on his own sword.

Yes, the gesture was everything. Important to go with dignity, to control your fate, not like the sad poet Aeschylus, who died when an eagle, looking to crack the shell of a tortoise in his beak, mistook his bald head for a rock. Or the Chinese poet Li Po, who drowned trying to embrace the full moon on the water's surface. Yes, the gesture was immortal. It would be insufferable to go out like a clown.

So what gesture would suit him? The president was a strange, contradictory man. Even at the height of his powers, he often seemed laconic and dreamy, more like a librarian than a world leader, with a strong, papal nose, glittering, beady eyes, and ears like the halved cap of a portobello mushroom. He valued loyalty, then wrathfully sacked his most devoted lieutenants. He railed against the corruptions of money, though his fourteen-year reign was shot through with financial scandals. A close friend, caught in the double-dealing, killed himself out of apparent disgust for the president's style of government. "Money and death," the friend angrily said shortly before the end. "That's all that interests him anymore."

And yet as others fell, the president survived—by tricks of agility and acumen, patrician charm and warthog ferocity. Now this last intruder hulked toward him. He shuffled with a cane, stooped and frosted silver like a gnarled tree in a wintry place. It took him an eternity to accomplish the most minor things: buttoning a shirt, bathing, walking the neighborhood, a simple crap.

And what would become of the universe he'd created? What would become of his citizens? And then his children and grandchildren, his wife and mistress? Was this the fate of all aged leaders when they were stripped of their magic: to sit like vegetables, surrounded by photographs and tokens of appreciation, by knickknacks and artifacts?

When he slept, he dreamed of living. When he ate, he ate the foods he would miss. But even then, somewhere in his mind, he began to prepare his *cérémonie des adieux*.

I'm going to tell you what happened next—the day of the last meal—for everything during this time in December shaped itself around the specter of eating the meal.

That morning, I pick up my girlfriend, Sara, at Orly airport. I've prevailed on her to come, as any meal shared around a table—the life lived inside each course—is only as good as the intimacies among people there. Through customs, she's alive with the first adrenaline rush of landing in a new country. But then, as we begin driving southwest toward the coast and Bordeaux, she falls fast asleep. It's gray and raining, and ocean wind sweeps inland and lashes the car. The trees have been scoured lifeless. Little men in little caps drive by our windows, undoubtedly hoarding wedges of cheese in their little cars. And then a huge nuclear power plant looms on the horizon, its cooling towers billowing thick, moiling clouds over a lone cow grazing in a fallow pasture.

There is something in the French countryside, with its flat, anytime light, that demands melancholy. And I wonder what it means to knowingly eat a last meal. It means knowing you're going to die, right? It means that you've been living under a long-held delusion that the world is infinite and you are immortal. So it means saying sayonara to everything, including the delusions that sustain you, at the same time that you've gained a deeper feeling about those delusions and how you might have lived with more passion and love and generosity.

And then the most difficult part: You must imagine yourself as a memory, laid out and naked and no longer yourself, no longer you, the remarkable Someone who chose a last meal. Rather, you're just a body full of that meal. So you have to imagine yourself gone—first as a pale figure in the basement of a funeral home, then as the lead in a eulogy about how remarkable you were, and then as a bunch of photographs and stories.

And that's when you must imagine one more time what you most need to eat, what last taste must rise to meet your hunger and thirst and linger a while on your tongue even as, before dessert, you're lowered into the grave.

It was just before Christmas 1995, the shortest days of the year. The president's doctor slept on the cold floor of the house in Latche while the president slept nearby in his bed, snoring lightly, looked down upon by a photograph of his deceased parents. He was seventy-nine, and the doctor could still feel the fight in him, even as he slept—the vain little man punching back. In conversation with the president's friends, the doctor had given him about a 30 percent chance of making it to December. And he had. "The only interesting thing is to live," said the president bluntly.

So there were lemon days and grapefruit days and this constant banter with the tumor: *How are you today? What can I get you? Another dose of free radicals? Enough radiation to kill the rats of Paris? Please go away now.* There was also a holy trinity of drugs—blessed Dilaudid, merciful Demerol, and beatific Elavil—that kept the pain at a blurry remove, convinced him in his soaring mind that perhaps this was happening to someone else and he was only bearing witness. Yes, could it be that his powers of empathy—for all his countrymen—were so strong that he'd taken on the burden of someone else's disease and then, at the last moment, would be gloriously released back into his own life again?

With the reprieve, he would walk the countryside near Latche, naming the birds and trees again, read his beloved Voltaire, compose, as he had hundreds of times before, love letters to his wife.

He planned his annual pilgrimage to Egypt—with his mistress and their daughter—to see the Pyramids, the monumental tombs of the pharaohs, and the eroded Sphinx. That's what his countrymen called him, the Sphinx, for no one really knew for sure who he was—aesthete or whoremonger, Catholic or atheist, fascist or socialist, anti-Semite or humanist, likable or despicable. And then there was his aloof imperial power. Later, his supporters simply called him *Dieu*—God.

He had come here for this final dialogue with the pharaohs, to mingle with their ghosts and look one last time upon their tombs. The cancer was moving to his head now, and each day that passed brought him closer to his own vanishing, a crystal point of pain that would subsume all the other pains. It would be so much easier . . . but then no. He made a phone call back to France. He asked that the rest of his family and friends be summoned to Latche and that a meal be prepared for New Year's Eve. He gave a precise account of what would be eaten at the table, a feast for thirty people, for he had decided that afterward, he would not eat again.

"I am fed up with myself," he told a friend.

And so we've come to a table set with a white cloth. An armada of floating wine goblets, the blinding weaponry of knives and forks and spoons. Two windows, shaded purple, stung by bullets of cold rain, lashed by the hurricane winds of an ocean storm.

The chef is a dark-haired man, fiftyish, with a bowling-ball belly. He stands in front of orange flames in his great stone chimney hung with stewpots, finely orchestrating each octave of taste, occasionally sipping his broths and various chorded concoctions with a miffed expression. In breaking the law to serve us ortolan, he gruffly claims that it is his duty, as a Frenchman, to serve the food of his region. He thinks the law against serving ortolan is stupid. And yet he had to call forty of his friends in search of the bird, for there were none to be found and almost everyone feared getting caught, risking fines and possible imprisonment.

But then another man, his forty-first friend, arrived an hour ago with three live ortolans in a small pouch—worth up to a hundred dollars each and each no bigger than a thumb. They're brown-backed, with pinkish bellies, classified as an Old World bunting. When they fly, they tend to keep low to the ground and, when the wind is high, swoop crazily for lack of weight. In all the world, they're really caught only in the pine forests of the southwestern Landes region of France, by about twenty families who lie in wait for the birds each fall as they fly from Europe to Africa. Once caught—they're literally snatched out of the air in traps called *matoles*—they're locked away in a dark room and fattened on millet; to achieve the same effect, French kings and Roman emperors once blinded the bird with a knife so, lost in the darkness, it would eat twenty-four hours a day.

A short time ago, these three ortolans—*our* three ortolans— were dunked and drowned in a glass of Armagnac and then plucked of their feathers. Now they lie delicately on their backs in three cassoulets, wings and legs tucked to their tiny, bloated bodies, skin the color of pale autumn corn, their eyes small, purple bruises and—here's the thing—wide open.

When we're invited back to the kitchen, that's what I notice, the open eyes on these already peppered, palsied birds and the gold glow of their skin. The kitchen staff crowds around, craning to see, and when we ask one of the dishwashers if he's ever tried ortolan, he looks scandalized, then looks back at the birds. "I'm too young, and now it's against the law," he says longingly. "But someday, when I can afford one . . ." Meanwhile, Sara has gone silent, looks pale looking at the birds.

Back at the chimney, the chef reiterates the menu for Mitterrand's last meal, including the last course, as he puts it, "the birdies." Perhaps he reads our uncertainty, a simultaneous flicker of doubt that passes over our respective faces. "It takes a culture of very good to appreciate the very good," the chef says, nosing the clear juices of the capon rotating in the fire. "And ortolan is beyond even the very good."

The guests had been told to hide their shock. They'd been warned that the president looked bad, but then there were such fine gradations. He already looked bad—could he look worse?

It seemed he could. On his return from Egypt, he'd kept

mostly to himself, out of sight of others; his doctor still attended him, but they had begun to quarrel. The president's stubbornness, his fits, and his silences—all of them seemed more acute now. When he entered the room, dressed in baggy pants and a peasant coat, he was colorless and stiff-legged. He was supported by two bodyguards, and a part of him seemed lost in dialogue with the thing sucking him from earth—with his own history, which was fast becoming the sum of his life. He was only half physical now and half spirit.

When the dying are present among the living, it creates an imbalance, for they randomly go through any number of dress rehearsals for death—nodding off at any time, slackening into a meaningful drool. They ebb and flow with each labored breath. Meanwhile, we hide our own panic by acting as if we were simply sitting in the company of a mannequin. It's a rule: In the vicinity of the dying, the inanity of conversation heightens while what's underneath—the thrumming of red tulips on the table and the lap of purple light on the windowpane, the oysters on crushed ice and the birds on the table, the wisp of errant hair drawn behind an ear and the shape of a lip—takes on a fantastic, last-time quality, slowly pulling everything under, to silence.

The president was carried to a reclining chair and table apart from the huge table where the guests sat. He was covered with blankets, seemed gone already. And yet when they brought the oysters—Marennes oysters, his favorite, harvested from the waters of this region—he summoned his energies, rose up in his chair, and began sucking them, the full flesh of them, from their half shells. He'd habitually eaten a hundred a week throughout his life and had been betrayed by bad oysters before, but oh no, not these! Hydrogen, nitrogen, phosphorus—a dozen, two dozen, and then, astonishingly, more. He couldn't help it, his ravenous attack. It was brain food, and he seemed to slurp them up against the cancer, let the saltwater juices flow to the back of his throat, change champagne-sweet, and then disappear in a flood before he started on the oyster itself. And that was another sublimity. The delicate tearing of a thing so full of ocean. Better than a paper wafer—heaven. When he was done, he lay back in his chair, oblivious to everyone else in the room, and fell fast asleep.

Now I have come to France, to the region of François Mitterrand's birth and his final resting place, and on this night, perhaps looking a bit wan myself, I begin by eating the Marennes oysters—round, fat, luscious oysters split open and peeled back to show their delicate green lungs. Shimmering pendulums of translucent meat, they weigh more than the heavy, carbuncled shells in which they lie. When you lift the shell to your mouth and suck, it's like the first time your tongue ever touched another tongue. The oysters are cool inside, then warm. Everything becomes heightened and alive. Nibbling turns to hormone-humming mastication. Your mouth swims with sensation: sugary, then salty, then again with Atlantic Ocean sweetness. And you try, as best you can, to prolong it. When they're gone, you taste the ghost of them.

These are the oysters.

And then the foie gras, smooth and surprisingly buttery, a light-brown pâté swirled with faint greens, pinks, and yellows, and glittering slightly, tasting not so much of animal but of earth. Accompanied by fresh, rough-crusted, homemade bread and the sweet Sauternes we drink (which itself is made from shriveled grapes of noble rot), the foie gras dissolves with the faint, rich sparkle of fresh-picked corn. It doesn't matter that it's fattened goose liver. It doesn't matter what it is. Time slows for it.

This is the foie gras.

The capon is superb—not too gamey or stringy—furiously basted to a high state of tenderness in which the meat falls cleanly from the bone with the help only of gravity. In its mildness, in its hint of olive oil and rosemary, it readies the tongue and its several thousand taste buds for the experience of what's coming next.

This is the capon.

And then the wines. Besides the Sauternes (a 1995 Les Remparts de Bastor, a 1995 Doisy Daëne), which we drink with the oysters and the foie gras, there are simple, full-bodied reds, for that's how Mitterrand liked them, simple and full-bodied: a Château Lestage Simon, a Château Poujeaux. They are long, old, and dark. Complicated potions of flower and fruit. Faint cherry on a tongue tip, the tingle of tannin along the gums. While one bottle is being imbibed, another is being decanted, and all the while there are certain chemical changes taking place between the wine and its new atmosphere and then finally between the changed wine and the atmosphere of your mouth.

This is the wine.

And so, on this evening in Bordeaux, in the region where Mitterrand was born and buried, the eating and drinking of these courses takes us four hours, but then time has spread out and dissipated, woodsmoke up the chimney. Mitterrand, who was famous for outwaiting his opponents, for always playing the long, patient game, once said, "You have to give time time."

And so we have, and time's time is nearing midnight, and there are three as-yet-unclaimed ortolans, back in the kitchen, that have just been placed in the oven. They will be cooked for seven minutes in their own fat—cooked, as it's gently put, until they sing.

With each course, the president had rallied from sleep, from his oyster dreams, from fever or arctic chill, not daring to miss the next to come: the foie gras slathered over homemade bread or the capon and then, of course, the wines. But what brought him to full attention was a commotion: Some of the guests were con-

fused when a man brought in a large platter of tiny, cooked ortolans laid out in rows. The president closely regarded his guests'
dismayed expressions, for it gave him quiet satisfaction—between
jabs of pain—to realize that he still had the power to surprise.

The ortolans were offered to the table, but not everyone
accepted. Those who did draped large, white cloth napkins over
their heads, took the ortolans in their fingertips, and disappeared.
The room shortly filled with wet noises and chewing. The bones
and intestines turned to paste, swallowed eventually in one gulp.
Some reveled in it; others spat it out. When they were through,
one by one they reappeared from beneath their hoods, slightly
dazed. The president himself took a long sip of wine, let it play in
his mouth. After nearly three dozen oysters and several courses,
he seemed insatiable, and there was one bird left. He took the
ortolan in his fingers, then dove again beneath the hood, the bony
impress of his skull against the white cloth—the guests in silence
and the self-pleasing, erotic slurps of the president filling the
room like a dirge.

At the table now, three ortolans, singing in their own fat. We'll
eat the birds because the ocean storm is at the purple windows;
because this man, our chef, has gone to great lengths to honor us
at his table; because we're finishers; because it's too late and too
far—the clock is literally striking midnight—to turn back.

We offer the third bird to the chef.

And so he's the first to go. An atheist, he doesn't take his
beneath the napkin. He just pops the bird in his mouth, bites off
the head with his incisors, and holds a thickly bundled napkin
over his lips, occasionally slipping it from side to side to sop up
the overflowing juices. Slowly, deliberately, he begins to chew. As
he does, he locks eyes with Sara. For long, painful minutes during

which we can hear the crunch and pop of bone and tendon, he stares deeply across the table at her, with the napkin to his mouth.

I believe the chef is trying to seduce my girlfriend, a scene mirrored by ortolan-eating lovers in Proust, Colette, and Fielding. But then I realize that he's not so much trying to take something from her as trying to find a still point from which he can focus on the chaos in his mouth. He's chewing, sucking, slobbering, savoring. And he's trying to manage all of the various, wild announcements of taste.

After he swallows and dabs his napkin daintily at the corners of his mouth, it's our turn. We raise our birds and place them in our mouths. I can't tell you what happens next in the outside world because, like Mitterrand, I go beneath the hood, which is meant to heighten the sensual experience by enveloping you in the aroma of ortolan. And the hood itself, with its intimation of Klan-like activity, might trouble me more if not for the sizzling bird on its back in my mouth, burning my tongue. The trick is to cool it by creating convections around it, by simply breathing. But even then, my mouth has gone on full alert. Some taste buds are scorched and half functioning, while others bloom for the first time and still others signal the sprinkler system of salivary glands.

And now, the hardest part: the first bite.

Like the chef, I sever the head and put it on the plate, where it lies in its own oil slick, then tentatively I try the body with bicuspids. The bird is surprisingly soft, gives completely, and then explodes with juices—liver, kidneys, lungs. Chestnut, corn, salt—all mix in an extraordinary current, the same warm, comforting flood as finely evolved consommé.

And so I begin chewing.

Here's what I taste: Yes, quidbits of meat and organs, the succulent, tiny strands of flesh between the ribs and tail. I put inside myself the last flowered bit of air and Armagnac in its lungs, the body of rainwater and berries. In there, too, is the ocean and Africa and the dip and plunge in a high wind. And the heart that bursts between my teeth.

It takes time. I'm forced to chew and chew again and again, for what seems like three days. And what happens after chewing for this long—as the mouth full of taste buds and glands does its work—is that I fall into a trance. I don't taste anything anymore, cease to exist as anything but taste itself.

And that's where I want to stay—but then can't because the sweetness of the bird is turning slightly bitter and the bones have announced themselves. When I think about forcing them down my throat, a wave of nausea passes through me. And that's when, with great difficulty, I swallow everything.

Afterward, I hold still for a moment, head bowed and hooded. I can feel my heart racing. Slowly, the sounds of the room filter back—the ting of wineglasses against plates, a shout back in the kitchen, laughter from another place. And then, underneath it, something soft and moving. Lungs filling and emptying. I can hear people breathing.

After the president's second ortolan—he had appeared from beneath the hood, wide-eyed, ecstatic, staring into a dark corner of the room—the guests approached him in groups of two and three and made brief small talk about the affairs of the country or Zola or the weather. They knew this was adieu, and yet they hid their sadness; they acted as if in a month's time he would still be among them.

And what about him? There was nothing left to subtract now. What of the white river that flowed through his childhood, the purple attic full of cornhusks? And then his beautiful books—Dostoyevsky, Voltaire, Camus? How would the world continue without him in it?

He tried to flail one last time against the proof of his death. But then he had no energy left. Just an unhappy body weighted with grapefruits, curving earthward. Everything moving toward the center and one final flash of pain. Soon after, he refused food and medicine; death took eight days.

"I'm eaten up inside," he said before he was carried from the room.

We wake late and senseless, hungover from food and wine, alone with our thoughts, feeling guilty and elated, sated and empty.

The day after Mitterrand's last meal seems to have no end. Huddled together, we wander the streets of Bordeaux, everyone on the sidewalks turning silver in the half-light. And then we drive out toward Jarnac, the village where Mitterrand is buried—through the winding miles of gnarled fruit trees in the gray gloom. We visit Mitterrand's tomb, a simple family sarcophagus in a thickly populated graveyard, and stand on the banks of his childhood river.

If I could, I would stay right here and describe the exact details of that next day. I would describe how we watched children riding a carousel until twilight, all of their heads tilting upward, hands fluttering and reaching for a brass ring that the ride master manipulated on a wire, how the stone village looked barbaric in the rain, with its demented buildings blackened by soot from the cognac distilleries.

We just seemed to be sleepwalking. Or vanishing. Until later. Until we were lost and the streets had emptied. Until night came and the wind carried with it the taste of salt water and the warm light in the *boulangerie* window shone on loaves of bread just drawn from the oven. And we were hungry again.

ACKNOWLEDGMENTS

To Sloan Harris, mudder/gentleman/warrior, there from the first word, my unswerving gratitude.

To Andy Ward, the twenty-minute Cortez solo of editors and friends—thank you for all . . . *again*.

To Jim Nelson, of polymathic mind and adventurous spirit, who has sent me far afield to find myself over and over again, thank you.

To David Granger, who has done the same, big gratitude.

To Peter Griffin, who edited seven of these pieces: Seven times thank you for showing me how.

To Colin Harrison, who took the first chance, my indebtedness.

For their generous support of these essays and stories, and for helping to improve them in their various moments of need, huge and humble appreciation goes to the great ones: Joel Lovell, Donovan Hohn, Ilena Silverman, Devin Friedman, Andrew Corsello, Gerry Marzorati, Lewis Lapham, Mark Warren, and Daniel Riley.

Among all the diligent fact-checkers, researchers, and others who helped bring these stories to life, outstanding debts are owed to Dan Torday, Raha Naddaf, Greg Veis, Luke Zaleski, Genevieve Roth, Kyla Jones, Nurit Zunger, Luke Mogelson, Bob Scheffler, Andrew Chaikivaky, John Kenney, Kevin McDonald, Alex French, Julie Greenberg, Angela Riechers, and Aida Edemariam.

Among those who read in a pinch, advised, encouraged, published and republished, and repeatedly stuck up for the efforts here as friends and professionals, heartfelt gratitude to Bill Lychack, Miles Harvey, Dan Coyle, Wil Hylton, Laura Hohnhold, Will Dana, Mark Bryant, Adam Moss, Dave Eggers, Robert Draper, Tom Junod, Tim Cahill, Patsy Sims, Norman Sims, Paige Williams, Michael Hainey, Tom Lake, Evan Ratliff, Doug Stanton, Justin Heckert, Liz Gilbert, Wright Thompson, Chris Jones, Sean Flynn, Jeanne Marie Laskas, Jenny Rosenstrach, Cammie McGovern, the Chautauqua Element, Ira Glass, Alix Spiegel, Kim Wasco, Charlie Baxter, Nicholas Delbanco, Anton Shammas, and Chris Heath.

To all the translators, fixers, and photographers with whom I've been privileged to collaborate—including Carlos Gomez in Spain and Tony Kieffer in China—my great luck has been to see these stories through your eyes, and art, too. And to those who indulged and sustained these efforts with food and drink, provocations and curiosity, including the Freaks and the Portland posse, thank you.

To the subjects of these stories who opened their worlds to me in a thousand unexpected ways, my appreciation and awe.

This book couldn't have happened without the beneficence and support of Susan Kamil, another guardian angel. And those at Random House who made it real, with thanks: Gina Centrello, Kaela Myers, Benjamin Dreyer, London King, Theresa Zoro, Leigh Marchant, Erika Seyfried, Giselle Roig, Evan Camfield,

Amelia Zalcman, and Chelsea Cardinal. And, as well, the ICMers who've done tireless work on my behalf: Ron Bernstein, Liz Farrell, Heather Karpas, Heather Bushong, John DeLaney, Kristyn Keene, Michael Griffo, Katharine Cluverius. Betsy Robbins, Gordon Wise, and Sophie Baker.

My most treasured readers are my parents—and my extended family—whose support has been invaluable. To my children, Leo, May, and Nicholas: I hope that in reading these someday, you'll realize there was a reason your dad sometimes looked a little cross-eyed in the morning. You made the hardest writing moments easy. This record was made for you, too, with love.